THE NEW PSYCHOLOGY
OF LANGUAGE

Cognitive and Functional
Approaches to Language Structure

THE NEW PSYCHOLOGY
OF LANGUAGE

Cognitive and Functional Approaches to Language Structure

Edited by

Michael Tomasello
Max Planck Institute for Evolutionary Anthropology
Leipzig, Germany

LEA LAWRENCE ERLBAUM ASSOCIATES, PUBLISHERS
1998   Mahwah, New Jersey   London

Lawrence Erlbaum Associates, Inc., Publishers
10 Industrial Avenue
Mahwah, New Jersey 07430

Cover design by Kathryn Houghtaling Lacey

Library of Congress Cataloging-in-Publication Data

The new psychology of language : cognitive and functional approaches
to language structure / edited by Michael Tomasello.
p.   cm.
Includes bibliographical references and index.
ISBN 0-8058-2576-2 (alk. paper). — ISBN 0-8058-2577-0 (pbk. :
alk. paper).
1. Psycholinguistics. I. Tomasello, Michael.
P37.N44 1998
401'.9—dc21   98-11415
                                                                   CIP

Contents

Introduction:
A Cognitive–Functional
Perspective on Language Structure

Michael Tomasello

Max Planck Institute for Evolutionary Anthropology
Leipzig, Germany

The attitude of psychologists toward linguistics has been problematic from the beginning. The titular founder of scientific psychology, Wilhelm Wundt, divided psychological phenomena into two types: those that could be measured and quantified in the laboratory (e.g., perceptual discriminations, behavioral reactions, etc.) and those that were culturally constituted and so best studied in their natural sociohistorical contexts. Wundt (1900–1909) called the study of these culturally constituted phenomena *Völkerpsychologie,* and he began his treatment of the subject with the most interesting of all cultural artifacts, language. Wundt's colleagues and immediate successors, however, were especially intrigued by the new laboratory methods, and so "The attitude favored by most of [psychology's] founding fathers was one of simple neglect. Other mental processes were given higher priority and language was left to the professional linguists" (Miller, 1990, p. 9). The situation did not improve in the 20th century as the behaviorists continued to ignore language—or else applied to it their special brand of nothing buttery (language is nothing but behavior; e.g., Skinner, 1957) to notoriously bad effect (Chomsky, 1959).

And so it was with Chomsky (1957, 1959) that the modern era began. As is well known, Chomskian linguistics was a central part of the Cognitive Revolution of the 1960s, and the fields of psycholinguistics, as first studied by George Miller and colleagues, and of developmental psycholinguistics, as first studied by Roger Brown and colleagues, were essentially founded on the Chomskian paradigm. But the honeymoon was over quickly as

Chomskian linguists distanced themselves from psychological experiments that attempted to translate the theory into performance models (perhaps because they yielded, to put it kindly, mixed results; Palermo, 1978). But the most vexing problem was that during the 1970s and 1980s, new linguistic theories that differed from Chomskian orthodoxy to varying degrees and in varying ways were being created almost weekly (e.g., Case Grammar, Generative Semantics, Lexical Functional Grammar, Relational Grammar, Generalized Phrase Structure Grammar, etc.), leaving many psychologists bewildered and wondering if perhaps Chomskian linguists had different explanatory goals than psychologists.

The effect was that for the past 20 years psychologists interested in language have, with a few notable exceptions, focused their attention on problems other than syntax. Psycholinguists have focused on such things as lexical access, discourse processing, and speech perception, whereas developmental psycholinguists have focused on such things as lexical development, pragmatics, and adult–child conversation. In both fields, virtually all of the empirical studies of syntactic structure have been concerned with narrow-range phenomena, or else they have relied on very generic descriptions that seemingly do not depend on any particular theory of syntax. But inevitably, due to the intertwined histories of the two disciplines since the cognitive revolution, the majority of these studies rest implicitly on a number of Chomskian assumptions and definitions—many of which fall under the general rubric of the *Autonomy of Syntax*. As just two examples, many psychologists implicitly believe that coherent, conceptually based definitions of the grammatical categories *noun* and *verb* are not possible (and so these syntactic categories are autonomous from the rest of cognition) and that structure dependencies such as subject–verb agreement depend exclusively on purely formal properties of sentences—both demonstrably false propositions (Langacker, 1987b, 1988).

Recently, there has emerged a new family of approaches to language structure that vary from one another in a number of ways but that are united in their rejection of the Autonomy of Syntax position. They are called either *Cognitive Linguistics* or *Functional Linguistics*. Historically, Cognitive Linguistics grew out of the Chomskian paradigm, as several of its practitioners, especially George Lakoff and Ronald Langacker, became more and more dissatisfied with its narrow scope and its neglect of the cognitive and social dimensions of linguistic communication. Functional Linguistics (or Functional-Typological Linguistics) arose somewhat independently based on the studies of linguists such as Joseph Greenberg and Talmy Givón, who were concerned with comparing different languages with one another typologically and historically and who found that Chomskian linguistics was of little or no help in this enterprise (also important were linguists of the Prague School who emphasized the importance of processes of communication in discourse and language). These two approaches have not yet congealed into one coherent scientific paradigm, but there is widespread agreement among both cognitive and functional linguists that language is not an autonomous "mental organ," but rather that it is a complex mosaic of cognitive and social communicative activities closely integrated with the rest of human psychology.

Given this explicitly psychological approach to language, it is curious that psycholinguists and developmental psycholinguists do not know more about these new theories. In my view, three main factors have contributed to the neglect:

1. The historical hegemony of the Chomskian paradigm in psychology.
2. The fact that linguistic descriptions and explanations require specialized linguistic terminology that discourages outsiders—and the cognitivists and functionalists have some of their own.
3. As is traditional in linguistics, some of the most important work is published in the proceedings of linguistics meetings (or dissertations or unpublished manuscripts) that are difficult for psychologists to access, or else in edited volumes whose price is prohibitive for all but the specialist.

The current volume is an attempt to address the second and third of these issues by having some of the leading proponents of Cognitive and Functional Linguistics explicate their views in a volume edited by a psychologist, who did his best to keep the specialized terminology to a minimum (with, I should admit, mixed success), and published by a publisher who will hopefully make it widely available to psychologists.

In the remainder of this introduction, I provide a small modicum of background and orientation for psychologists and other nonlinguists interested in this new way of thinking about language. Because all new ways of thinking about familiar phenomena require a certain amount of undoing of the old ways of thinking, I begin by contrasting the Cognitive–Functional view with the Generative Grammar view, which, in its broad outlines at least, is better known to psychologists. I do not summarize and provide very little direct commentary on the individual chapters that follow. They speak for themselves.

MATHEMATICS VERSUS PSYCHOLOGY

The most fundamental tenet of Generative Grammar is that there is a level of linguistic description, namely, syntax, that is independent of all other levels of linguistic description including semantics—and independent of all other aspects of cognition as well. This Autonomy of Syntax thesis is not an empirical discovery or even a hypothesis that is ever explicitly tested. It is a paradigm-defining definitional postulate that is a direct result of taking a mathematical approach to natural language. Indeed, in reality, Generative Grammar is nothing other than a form of mathematics, and thus it has been applied not just to language but also to music (Jackendoff, 1983), to genetics (Collado-Vides, 1991), and to dreaming (Foulkes, 1978). The nonempirical character of the Autonomy of Syntax thesis is also evident in the actual practice of generative grammarians. If there is an analysis of a specific linguistic phenomenon in which semantics appears to affect syntax, it is assumed that either: (a) there is something wrong with the analysis and so the structure is analyzed further until semantics is eliminated (Lakoff, 1990); or (b) the phenomenon is deemed to be outside of "core grammar" and placed into "the lexicon" or "the conceptual system" (Chomsky, 1980).

The goal of Generative Grammar is to provide the most mathematically elegant account of syntax possible, which is automatically assumed to be the one that underlies human linguistic competence. Thus, mathematical elegance was the justification for transformation rules in the first place (Chomsky, 1957, 1965), and new formalizations designed to increase elegance (e.g., the new minimalism; Chomsky, 1995) are immediately posited as constitutive of the human language capacity, with no empirical verification deemed necessary. The goal of mathematical elegance is difficult to discern in the several well-known versions of what might be called Generative Grammar Lite, including most prominently those of Jackendoff (1997) and Pinker (1994; Pinker & Bloom, 1990). But in these cases, the mathematics is simply hidden in several key features of language posited as universal by these theorists, for example, in X-bar phrase structure rules and long-range "movement rules" whose entire *raison d'être* is to make the hypothesized grammar more formally elegant.

This view of Generative Grammar as based on a pretheoretical commitment to a mathematical approach—which leads ineluctably to the Autonomy of Syntax thesis—is not widely recognized by psychologists. One reason for this is that a number of linguists and psychologists have attempted to amass empirical evidence in favor of the autonomy of syntax position—specifically, the thesis that autonomous syntax is an innate mental module—by invoking phenomena such as linguistic savants, brain-damaged individuals, children acquiring language in impoverished circumstances, and the nature of pidgins and creoles. This evidence is then combined with one or another version of Chomsky's theoretical arguments, such as the argument from the poverty of the stimulus (see Pinker, 1994, for a review). The rhetorical strategy most often used is to present the theoretical options as either: (a) those who believe in a biological basis for language (viz. generative grammarians), or (b) those who do not believe in a biological basis for language (viz. laypersons, humanists, and other linguists). But this dichotomy is false, because many linguists and psychologists believe that there is a biological basis for language, just not in the form of an autonomous Generative Grammar. Just as plausible for these linguists is the hypothesis that language rests on more general biological predispositions, such as the abilities to create and learn symbols, to form concepts and categories, to process vocal–auditory information rapidly, and to interact and communicate with other persons intersubjectively (Tomasello, 1995). Moreover, the argument from the poverty of the stimulus has recently been found to be inadequate in a number of ways when "the stimulus"—the language that learners actually hear—is examined empirically (Pullum, 1996).

As in all mathematics, Generative Grammar begins with an absolute distinction between syntax—abstract formulae that operate on meaningless category labels for variables—and semantics—interpretations of these formulae in the specific cases in which the values of the variables are insubstantiated. This works well for mathematicians—and the Generative Grammar literature is replete with all kinds of "proofs" of learnability and the like—but psychologists need not accept this initial slicing of the pie uncritically. Indeed, because they take a more psychological approach to human linguistic competence, cognitive and functional linguists do not accept the distinction between syntax and semantics as it is characterized by Generative Grammar. To these linguists, all language structures are symbolic instruments that serve to convey meaning, from the smallest morphemes to the most complex constructions. The major opposition in language is thus *not* between formal syntax and semantics, but between a linguistic symbol and its communicative significance; signifier and signified, form and function, symbol and meaning. Within the signifier/form/symbol pole, we may then distinguish among different types of linguistic signs, for example, lexical, morphological, and phrasal. Within the signified/function/meaning pole, we may distinguish between semantic and pragmatic functions. But there are no linguistic structures that operate independent of meaning in the cognitive-functional account.

The issue is perhaps made clearest by an example. In Generative Grammar, noun phrases (NPs) are category labels that are of central importance. Many syntactic rules (or the modern equivalent of rules) employ this category label. The Generative Grammar claim is that it has no meaning, nor do other labels of the same type, and so syntactic rules written with it are autonomous from semantics. But NP is a highly meaningful category. An NP is an element in an utterance that is used in discourse to isolate and identify for the listener some "thing"—where "thing" is simply a way of construing an aspect of experience, however abstract and intangible, as a bounded entity on analogy with a concrete object (Hopper & Thompson, 1984; Langacker, 1987b). Generative grammarians use this functional information implicitly, they just do not put it in their analyses. They must use it because it is the only way to identify and group together such structurally diverse linguistic forms as proper nouns (*John*), full NPs (*The boy*), complex NPs (*The boy wearing the hat*), and pronouns (*He*)—or else one must rely on the function the NP plays in the utterance as a whole (e.g., agent of an action). The category itself is thus meaningful, and so any complex linguistic expression that contains it incorporates both its form and its specific communicative function of identifying referents. To cite just the most obvious example, the subject or topic of an utterance is an NP rather than a VP (even if it depicts an event) simply because human communication requires that joint attention to some "entity" be established before new information is expressed.

This functional approach does not mean that all structures in language are determined by function in the sense that they are iconically related to their meanings, as many generative grammarians misconstrue the claim (e.g., Newmeyer, 1991). NPs and other linguistic structures are related to their communicative functions conventionally, just as lexical items are conventionally related to their communicative functions, with speakers of different languages adopting different conventions (see Bates & MacWhinney, 1982, 1989, for an enlightened discussion of different kinds of linguistic functionalism). The claim is simply that both cultural artifacts and biological structures are understood primarily in terms of their functions, and so to leave them out is to miss their point entirely. Thus, we could physically break open an artifact such as a traffic light and dissect its internal structure so as to determine the electrical wiring circuits that turn the lights on and off, the timing mechanism that determines when the lights change, and how the lights get their colors. But we can only understand a traffic light fully when we understand what it is meant to do. How else do we understand the fact that when the red is lit on one side, it is also lit on the opposite side, and the green is lit on the other two sides? We can only understand this pattern by relating it to the desired endstate of a particular pattern of automobile traffic flow in the world outside the traffic light itself. Of course, there might be other forms of traffic lights that control traffic flow in the same basic way (some of which exist), and some of the structures of traffic lights are only conventional and could easily be different (e.g., the specific colors of the lights). The point is simply that to understand traffic lights and how they work, we need to understand something about what they are designed to do, and much the same could be said of biological structures, such as the mammalian heart, that have evolved for specific biological functions as well (Givón, 1995, chap. 2, this volume).

A final word in this comparison of generative and cognitive–functional approaches concerns methodology. In the Generative Grammar view, only some phenomena are of interest, namely those that fall into *core grammar*.

Core grammar is autonomous syntax, of course, but it is less than that. It is only those aspects of syntax that are completely categorical and abstract; the peculiarities of complex idioms, irregularities, metaphors, and other noncanonical structures in a language are not of interest. Moreover, in Generative Grammar, all languages have the same underlying core or universal grammar (they only vary in the way some basic parameters are set), and so any language may be studied to discover the principles of universal grammar. The data that are actually used toward this end in Generative Grammar analyses are almost always disembodied sentences that analysts have made up ad hoc (typically derived implicitly from the genre of written language, which operates in some of its own unique ways, especially with respect to context (see Chafe, chap. 4, this volume; Hopper, chap. 6, this volume; Olson, 1994), rather than utterances produced by real people in real discourse situations.

In diametric opposition to these methodological assumptions and choices, cognitive–functional linguists take as their object of study all aspects of natural language understanding and use, including unruly idioms, metaphors, and irregularities. They (especially the more functionally oriented analysts) take as an important part of their data not disembodied sentences derived from introspection, but rather utterances or other longer sequences from naturally occurring discourse. Cognitive–functional linguists are committed to investigating empirically as many of the world's 4,000 to 8,000 languages as possible, with an eye toward establishing both universals and typological differences. They also have an explanatory commitment to provide descriptions and explanations of linguistic phenomena that are psychologically plausible, thus connecting linguistics to the other behavioral and cognitive sciences that study such things as cognition, communication, symbolization, categorization, schematization, imagery, metaphor, attention, automatization, and so forth and so on (Lakoff, 1990). The ultimate goal is not to create a mathematically coherent grammar that normatively parses the linguistic universe into grammatical and ungrammatical sentences, but rather to detail the "structured inventory of symbolic units" that make up particular natural languages (Langacker, 1987a, chap. 1, this volume).

Overall, then, we may say that the cognitive-functional approach to language takes a basically psychological approach to language—as opposed to the formal, mathematical approach of Generative Grammar—even if its practitioners do not do psychological experiments. This leads to the basic distinction between the things people want to communicate about (meanings, functions, communicative goals) and the social conventions by means of which they do so (linguistic symbols and structures). To explicate the cognitive–functional approach further, let us therefore look in a bit more detail first at some basic communicative functions, and then at the linguistic symbols and structures used in their service.

Functions

The overall function of language is communication in the sense that language evolved for purposes of communication phylogenetically, and it is learned for purposes of communication ontogenetically. Communicative function has two basic aspects, not totally separable from one another, that derive from the nature of the basic communicative situation; semantics and pragmatics. First, when two individuals communicate with one another linguistically, they are typically talking about something (the exceptions being "pure performatives" such as *Thank you* or *Goodbye*). We may call this the *referential event*, and its linguistic symbolization is the province of semantics. Second, and at the same time, however, these interlocutors are also adjusting their language for the particularities of the immediate communicative situation involving what their interlocutor knows and expects, what has been said in previous conversation, and what entities are perceptually available in the immediate context. We may call this the communicative event or speech event, and the speaker's efforts to adjust her language to take account of its particularities are the domain of pragmatics.

Again, an example will help to illustrate. Common nouns are category terms that are most often used in natural speech in conjunction with other linguistic material to specify an individual "thing" in the world. The term *dog* by itself may thus be said to have a semantics in the sense that English speakers know the class of items for which this word is typically used. But in real linguistic interaction, except in exceptional circumstances, speakers use a determiner such as *the* or *that* to indicate a particular dog, sometimes even resorting to more descriptive information such as *The dog we saw yesterday*. These determiners and other linguistic structures are used by speakers in an attempt to specify for their listeners which particular dog is being talked about; the speaker grounds the category label in the shared knowledge that characterizes this particular communicative event. Thus, in other circumstances, in which more is shared, the speaker may say *He* or *Rover* to refer to a specific dog, whereas in still other situations, she may make only rather vague specifications because they are all that are needed given a particular communicative goal (e.g., *A dog* or *Dogs in general*). The point is that the form of the NP is determined by its function both in the sense of *what* the speaker wants to talk about (the dog—its semantics) and in the sense of *how* the speaker chooses to talk about it, given the listener's background knowledge and expectations in the current context (with a pronoun, full NP, etc.—its pragmatics).

Nominal choice is not the only place where semantic and pragmatic functions intersect to determine the nature of the linguistic symbols produced. If we think about basic sentence constructions, we have many ways in English to talk about the same referential event in different communicative circumstances (Croft, 1991, chap. 3, this volume). As just one example:

Pete opened the door with the key.

The key opened the door.

The door opened.

The door was opened (by Pete).

It was Pete that opened the door.

It was the door that opened.

What happened was Pete opened the door.

What happened was the door opened.

Each of these options is used in some particular communicative (pragmatic) circumstance. For example, if the speaker assumes that the listener knows that something opened the door but does not know what she might emphasize, for example, "It was the key that . . ."; if she assumes that the listener knows that someone opened the door but not who she might emphasize, for example, "It was Pete that . . ."; or if she assumes that the listener knows that something happened but not what she might emphasize, for example, "What happened was . . ." In all cases, the semantics of the situation is the single event of Pete opening a door with a key, but the speaker's tailoring the utterances for the exigencies of the particular communicative situation pragmatically requires her to make choices among various types of syntactic constructions that have been "predesigned" historically for just these exigencies (Chafe, chap. 4, this volume; Hopper, chap. 6, this volume; Lambrecht, 1994). It should be noted that, at the level of full utterances, the speaker's "mood"—in terms of making a request, asking a question, and so forth—combines with the perspective needs of the listener to determine construction choice, leading to such things as *Was it Pete that opened the door?* and *Open the door, Pete!*

Understanding the semantics and pragmatics of communication is fundamental to understanding how particular languages evolved historically in the face of changing communicative needs and exigencies. For example, the future markers in many languages derive in one way or another from verbs meaning 'want', 'go', 'try', and the like—possibly because these all semantically depict forward motion or actions that have not yet happened. Thus, English has both a future marker from *will* as a lexical item (*I will it to break → I will break it*) and from *go* as a lexical item (*I'm going to the store in order to buy a shirt → I'm going to buy a shirt*). There are also interesting relations between various kinds of discourse sequencing for pragmatic purposes and syntactic structures, as in the historical relations among such things as left dislocated structures (e.g., *Jim's glass, I broke it*) and passive sentences (e.g., *Jim's glass got broken*). Diachronic (historical) processes thus shape languages in fundamental ways, sometimes at a systemic level, as in the transformation of English from a case-marking language to a word order language in the last several hundred years. The processes by which this happens are only now beginning to be investigated, but in general, they concern multiple "competing motivations," especially those between semantics and pragmatics and the different communicative needs of speakers and listeners (Bybee, 1985; DuBois, 1985; Givón, chap. 2, this volume; Slobin, in press).

Structures

Functions are embodied in structures. At the simplest level of analysis, all of the structures of a language are composed of some combination of four types of symbolic elements; words, markers on words (e.g., the English plural -*s*), word order, and intonation. This is a simple function of the vocal–auditory medium and how it works (Bates & MacWhinney, 1982, 1989). Each of the several thousand languages of the world uses these four elements, but in different ways. In English, for example, word order is most typically used for the basic function of indicating who-did-what-to-whom, intonation is used mainly to highlight or background certain information in the utterance pragmatically, and markers on words serve to indicate such things as tense and plurality. In Russian, on the other hand, who-did-what-to-whom is indicated by case markers on words, and word order is used mostly for highlighting and backgrounding information pragmatically. In some tone languages (e.g., Masai), who-did-what-to-whom is indicated via special intonational contours. In general, there is wide variability in how these four symbolic devices serve various semantic and pragmatic functions in different languages, and moreover, these structure-function relationships may change over time within a language (as in the English change from case marking to word order for indicating who-did-what-to-whom).

These four types of symbolic elements do not occur in isolation, but in each language, there are a variety of linguistic constructions composed of recurrent configurations of these elements (Fillmore, 1985, 1988; Goldberg, 1995, chap. 8, this volume; Taylor, 1996, chap. 7, this volume; Wierzbicka, chap. 5, this volume). Linguistic constructions are basically cognitive schemas of the same type that exist in other domains of cognition. These schemas or constructions may vary from simple and concrete to complex and abstract. For example, the one-word utterance *Fore!* is a very simple and concrete construction used for a specific function in the game of golf. *Thank You* and *Don't mention it* are more complex constructions used for relatively specific social functions. Some other constructions are composed of specific words along with "slots" into which whole classes of items may fit, for example, *Down with __!* and *Hurray for __!* Two other constructions of this type that have more general applications are:

the *way* construction:	She made her way through the crowd.
	I paid my way through college.
	He smiled his way into the meeting.
the *let alone* construction:	I wouldn't go to New York, let alone Boston.
	I'm too tired to get up, let alone go running around with you.
	I wouldn't read an article about, let alone a book written by, that swine.

Each of these constructions is defined by its use of certain specific words (*way, let alone*) and each thus conveys a certain relatively specific relational meaning, but each is also general in its application to different specific content (Fillmore, Kay, & O'Conner, 1988).

There are also constructions that are extremely general and abstract in the sense that they are not defined by any words in particular, but rather by categories of words and their relations. Thus, the ditransitive construction in English is represented by utterances such as *He gave the doctor money.* No particular words are a part of this construction; it is characterized totally schematically by means of certain categories of words in a particular order: NP + Verb + NP + NP. No construction is fully general, and so in the ditransitive construction the verb must involve at the very least some form of motion or transfer (as in *He threw Susan money,* but not *He stayed Susan money*). Other examples of very abstract English constructions are the various resultative constructions (e.g., *She knocked him silly, He wiped the table clean*), constituted by a particular ordering of particular categories of words, and the various passive constructions (e.g., *She was swindled by Harry, He got killed*), constituted by a particular order of word categories as well as by some specific words (e.g., *by*) and markers (e.g., *-ed*). All of these more abstract constructions are defined by general categories of words and their interrelations, and so each may be applied quite widely for many referential situations of a certain type. These abstract linguistic constructions may be thought of as cognitive schemas similar to those found in other cognitive domains, that is, as relatively automatized procedures that operate on a categorical level.

An important point is that each of these abstract linguistic schemas has a meaning of its own, in relative independence of the lexical items involved (Goldberg, 1995, chap. 8, this volume). Indeed, much of the creativity of language comes from fitting specific words into linguistic constructions that are nonprototypical for that word. Thus, in *Mary kicked John the football,* the verb *kick* is not typically used for transfer or motion, and so it is not prototypically used with the ditransitive construction; but in this context, it may be construed in that way (because kicking can impart directed motion). This process may extend even further to such things as *Mary sneezed John the football,* which requires an imaginative interpretation in which the verb *sneeze* is not used in its more typical intransitive sense (as in *Mary sneezed*), but rather as a verb in which the sneezing causes directed motion in the football. If the process is extended far enough, to verbs for which it is difficult to imagine directed motion, the process begins to break down—as in *Mary smiled John the football.* The important point is that in all of these examples, the transfer of possession meaning (that the football goes from Mary to John) comes from the construction itself, not from the specific words of which it is constituted. Linguistic constructions are thus an important part of the inventory of symbolic resources that language users control, and they create an important "top-down" component to the process of linguistic communication, in keeping with the role of abstract schemas in many other domains of human cognition.

All constructions, whether composed of one word, or of many words in specific orders with specific markers and intonations, and at whatever level of abstraction, derive from recurrent events or types of events, with respect to which the people of a culture have recurrent communicative goals. Because they are formed in this way historically, they exhibit prototypical structure just like other cognitive categories and schemas (Goldberg, chap. 8, this volume; Taylor, chap. 7, this volume). Thus, in English, the basic transitive construction has as its prototype utterances such as *He broke the vase* in which an animate actor does something to cause a change of state in an undergoer (Hopper & Thompson, 1980). But the construction over historical time has been extended to other, less prototypical situations in which the "force dynamics" are not so clear or are only metaphorical, as in, for example, *John entered the room* and *The car cost $400.* In German—one of the major source languages for English many hundreds of years ago, the transitive construction has stayed much closer to the prototype (Taylor, 1996, chap. 7, this volume).

And, of course, different languages are composed of different specific constructions and construction types. In some cases, these differences have become relatively conventionalized across different linguistic structures within a language so that we may speak of different *types* of languages with regard to how they symbolize certain recurrent events or states of affairs (Goldberg, 1995; Van Valin & LaPolla, 1998). For example, almost all people speaking almost all languages have general constructions for talking about someone causing something to happen, someone experiencing something, someone giving someone something, an object moving along a path, and an object changing state. As one instance, there are two very common ways that languages depict motion events, as characterized by Talmy (1988):

English: The bottle floated into the cave.

Spanish: La botella entró la cueva flotando (The bottle entered the cave floating).

In English, the path of the bottle is expressed in the preposition *into* and the manner of motion is expressed in the verb *float*, whereas in Spanish, the path is expressed in the verb *entró* and the manner of motion is expressed in the modifier *flotando*. Because this difference is pervasive and consistent in the two languages, we may say that in depicting motion events, Spanish is a verb-framed language (because the path of motion is typically expressed in the verb), whereas English is a satellite-framed language (because the path of motion is typically expressed in the preposition). There are other typological differences among languages as well.

Understanding how linguistic constructions arise and function is fundamental not only for an understanding of language diachrony/typology, but also for an understanding of language acquisition. Thus, children's first multiword constructions are based on specific lexical items, especially verbs, with categorical nominal slots (e.g., "Kiss ___"; Braine, 1976; Pine & Lieven, 1993; Tomasello, 1992). But soon, children begin to discern patterns that transcend individual verbs and so they begin to construct the kinds of abstract constructions (e.g., transitives, resultatives, passives) that characterize adult competence (Tomasello & Brooks, in press). Some of these constructions become more entrenched with repeated usage, and so they acquire a certain canonical structure, whereas other are less entrenched and so more malleable. It is this formation of abstract categories and schemas based on patterns of usage in adult language that leads children, on occasion, to overgeneralize these patterns with utterances such as "He giggled me" (Bowerman, 1982; Braine & Brooks, 1995). The most general point about acquisition is that the categories and schemas of a language are not given to children innately, as is demanded by the mathematical approach of Generative Grammar, but rather they are generalizations that children make on the basis of their own categorization skills working on the language they hear.

THIS VOLUME

The cognitive–functional view of language and the cognitive and communicative processes on which it depends is obviously very different from that of Generative Grammar and other formalistic approaches. But Cognitive–Functional Linguistics can nevertheless account for all of the major phenomena of Generative Grammar. For example, in the cognitive–functional view, natural language structures may be used creatively (generatively) by their speakers not because speakers possess a syntax divorced from semantics, as in Generative Grammar, but rather because they possess highly general linguistic constructions composed of word categories and abstract schemas that operate on the categorical level. Furthermore, for cognitive–functional linguists, the hierarchical structure on which so much of generative analysis depends is considered to be a straightforward result of the hierarchicalization process characteristic of skill formation in many other cognitive domains. Finally, the traditional syntactic function of the subject of a sentence receives a cognitive-functional treatment in Cognitive–Functional Linguistics in terms of the participant in an event or state of affairs on which the speaker is focused, or that the speaker chooses to make most prominent attentionally for the listener. For example, we say either that *The tree is next to the house* or *The house is next to the tree*, the only difference being which entity, the tree or the house, is taken as the attentional reference point (Langacker, 1991, chap. 1, this volume; Tomlin, 1995). Some of the more abstruse peculiarities of language, such as the so-called subjacency constraint, may be accounted for by basic functional–communicative principles as well (Van Valin, 1991, 1993, chap. 9, this volume; Van Valin & LaPolla, 1998).

A central point for psychologists, therefore, is that linguistic skills, including syntactic skills, may be explained in fundamentally the same terms as other complex cognitive skills (Fauconnier, 1997, chap. 10, this volume; Wierzbicka, chap. 5, this volume; Langacker, chap. 1, this volume). A language consists of nothing other than its inventory of symbols and constructions, and categorical generalizations of these, used for purposes of communication. There are quite concrete linguistic structures that speakers conventionally use to induce others to construe or attend to a situation in a particular way (specific words and combinations of words), and there are also more abstract and schematic constructions indicating more abstract meanings. Although the way cognition is manifest in language may have some of its own peculiarities because of the uses to which it is put (just as the way cognition as manifest in other activities displays its own peculiarities), in general it is accurate to say that the structures of language are taken directly from human cognition, and so linguistic communication, including its grammatical structure, should be studied in the same basic manner using the same basic theoretical constructs as all other cognitive skills.

Because of this basically psychological approach to language, I have chosen to call Cognitive–Functional Linguistics "the new psychology of language." But it is important to remember that the advocates of this new view are linguists, not psychologists, and this is most apparent in their choice of methods. Thus, cognitive–functional linguists are sometimes criticized by psychologists because they do not test their hypotheses with reaction time experiments or the like. But this is not their job. Their job is to establish regularities in human linguistic behavior, as when English speakers use the word *dog* to refer to a single mutt and *dogs* to refer to multiple mutts—and similarly for other objects. Such highly replicable observations are based in cognitive distinctions that speakers reliably make, and the naturally occurring behavior of language users is good evidence for this. If psychologists wish to do more controlled experiments that delve more deeply into how and why people behave linguistically in particular ways, that is their prerogative. But that does not gainsay the fact that cognitive–functional linguists are currently making systematic observations of human linguistic behavior that lead to a new view of language and how it works that is highly compatible with the way that psychologists and cognitive scientists view human behavior, perception, cognition, and communication in general.

Each of the authors in the current volume has her or his own take on Cognitive–Functional Linguistics, and I do not attempt to speak for them all. Indeed, at this point there is much diversity in Cognitive–Functional Linguistics, and this diversity is a part of the strength of the enterprise. But there is one thing on which they all would certainly agree: If we are ever to understand the many complexities of language, what we need are not more elegant mathematical formalizations, but rather more cooperation between psychologists and linguists in helping to determine how basic cognitive and social processes operate in the specialized domain of human linguistic communication.

REFERENCES

Bates, E., & MacWhinney, B. (1982). Functionalist approaches to grammar. In E. Wanner & L. Gleitman (Eds.), *Language acquisition: State of the art* (pp. 89–121). New York: Cambridge University Press.

Bates, E., & MacWhinney, B. (1989), (Eds.). *The cross-linguistic study of sentence processing.* New York: Cambridge University Press.

Bowerman, M. (1982). Reorganizational processes in lexical and syntactic development. In E. Wanner & L. R. Gleitman (Eds.), *Language acquisition: The state of the art* (pp. 319–346). New York: Cambridge University Press.

Braine, M. D. S. (1976). Children's first word combinations. *Monographs of the Society for Research in Child Development, 41* (Serial No. 164).

Braine, M. D. S., & Brooks, P. (1995). Verb-argument structure and the problem of avoiding an overgeneral grammar. In M. Tomasello & W. Merriman (Eds.), *Beyond names for things: Young children's acquisition of verbs.* Hillsdale, NJ: Lawrence Erlbaum Associates.

Bybee, J. (1985). *Morphology: A study of the relation between meaning and form.* Amsterdam: John Benjamins.

Chomsky, N. (1957). *Syntactic structures.* Mouton: The Hague.

Chomsky, N. (1959). A review of B. F. Skinner's "Verbal Behavior." *Language, 35,* 26–58.

Chomsky, N. (1965). *Aspects of the theory of syntax.* Cambridge, MA: MIT Press.

Chomsky, N. (1980). Rules and representations. *Behavioral and Brain Sciences, 3,* 1–61.

Chomsky, N. (1995). *Minimalism.* Cambridge, MA: MIT Press.

Collado-Vides, J. (1991). A syntactic representation of the units of genetic information. *Journal of Theoretical Biology, 148,* 401–429.

Croft, W. (1991). *Syntactic categories and grammatical relations: The cognitive organization of information.* Chicago: University of Chicago Press.

DuBois, J. (1985). Competing motivations. In J. Haiman (Ed.), *Iconicity in syntax* (pp. 1–30). Amsterdam: John Benjamins.

Fauconnier, G. (1997). *Mappings in thought and language.* New York: Cambridge University Press.

Fillmore, C. (1985). Syntactic intrusions and the notion of grammatical construction. *Berkeley Linguistic Society, 11,* 73–86.

Fillmore, C. (1988). The mechanisms of construction grammar. *Berkeley Linguistics Society, 14,* 35–55.

Fillmore, C. J., Kay, P., & O'Conner, M. C. (1988). Regularity and idiomaticity in grammatical constructions: The case of *let alone. Language, 64,* 501–538.

Foulkes, D. (1978). *A grammar of dreams.* New York: Basic Books.

Givón, T. (1995). *Functionalism and grammar.* Amsterdam: John Benjamins.

Goldberg, A. (1995). *Constructions: A construction grammar approach to argument structure.* Chicago: University of Chicago Press.

Hopper, P., & Thompson, S. (1980). Transitivity in grammar and discourse. *Language, 60,* 703–752.

Hopper, P., & Thompson, S. (1984). The discourse basis of lexical categories in universal grammar. *Language, 56,* 251–299.

Jackendoff, R. (1983). *A generative theory of tonal music.* Cambridge, MA: MIT Press.

Jackendoff, R. (1997). *The architecture of the language faculty.* Cambridge, MA: MIT Press.

Lakoff, G. (1990). The Invariance Hypothesis: Is abstract reason based on image schemas? *Cognitive Linguistics, 1,* 39–74.

Lambrecht, K. (1994). *Information structure and sentence form.* Cambridge, England: Cambridge University Press.

Langacker, R. (1987a). *Foundations of cognitive grammar* (Vol. 1). Stanford, CA: Stanford University Press.

Langacker, R. (1987b). Nouns and verbs. *Language, 63,* 53–94.

Langacker, R. (1988). Autonomy, agreement, and cognitive grammar. In D. Brentari (Eds.), *Agreement in grammatical theory* (pp. 25–49). Chicago: University of Chicago Press.

Langacker, R. (1991). *Foundations of cognitive grammar, Volume II.* Stanford, CA: Stanford University Press.

Miller, G. (1990). The place of language in a scientific psychology. *Psychological Science, 1,* 7–14.

Newmeyer, F. (1991). Functional explanation in linguistics and the origins of language. *Language and Communication, 11,* 3–28.

Olson, D. (1994). *The world on paper: The conceptual and cognitive implications of writing and reading.* New York: Cambridge University Press.

Palermo, D. (1978). *The psychology of language.* New York: Scott Foresman.

Pine, J. M., & Lieven, E. V. M. (1993). Reanalysing rote-learned phrases: Individual differences in the transition to multi-word speech. *Journal of Child Language, 20,* 551–571.

Pinker, S. (1994). *The language instinct: How the mind creates language.* New York: Morrow.

Pinker, S., & Bloom, P. (1990). Natural language and natural selection. *Behavioral and Brain Sciences, 13,* 707–784.

Pullum, G. (1996). Learnability, hyperlearning, and the poverty of the stimulus. *Proceedings of the Berkeley Linguistics Society, 22.*

Skinner, B. F. (1957). *Verbal behavior.* New York: Appleton-Century-Crofts.

Slobin, D. I. (in press). Why are grammaticizable notions special?—A reanalysis and a challenge to learning theory. In M. Bowerman & S. Levinson (Eds.), *Language acquisition and conceptual development*. Cambridge, MA: Cambridge University Press.

Talmy, L. (1988). The relation of grammar to cognition. In B. Rudzka-Ostyn (Ed.) *Topics in cognitive linguistics*. Amsterdam: John Benjamins.

Taylor, J. (1996). *Linguistic categorization* (2nd ed.). New York: Oxford University Press.

Tomasello, M. (1992). *First verbs: A case study of early grammatical development*. Cambridge, MA: Cambridge University Press.

Tomasello, M. (1995). Language is not an instinct. *Cognitive Development, 10,* 131–156.

Tomasello, M., & Brooks, P. (in press). Early syntactic development. In M. Barrett (Ed.), *The development of language*. London: UCL Press.

Tomlin, R. (1995). Focal attention, voice, and word order. In P. Downing & M. Noonan (Eds.), *Word order in discourse*. Amsterdam: John Benjamins.

Van Valin, R. D. (1991). Functionalist theory and language acquisition. *First Language, 31,* 7–40.

Van Valin, R. D. (1993). *Advances in role and reference grammar*. Amsterdam: John Benjamins.

Van Valin, R., & LaPolla, R. (1998). *Syntax: Structure, meaning, and function*. Cambridge, MA: Cambridge University Press.

Wundt, W. (1900–1909). *Völkerpsychologie: Eine Untersuchung der Entwicklungsgesetz von Sprache, Mythus und Sitte* [(Vols. 1–10). Leipzig: Engelmann].

Chapter 1

Conceptualization, Symbolization, and Grammar

Ronald W. Langacker
University of California, San Diego

1. INTRODUCTION

Language has two basic and closely related functions: a *semiological function*, allowing thoughts to be symbolized by means of sounds, gestures, or writing, as well as an *interactive function*, embracing communication, expressiveness, manipulation, and social communion. A pivotal issue in linguistic theory is whether the functions language serves should be taken as foundational or merely subsidiary to the problem of describing its form. The recognition of their foundational status is the primary feature distinguishing *functionalist* approaches to language from the *formalist* tradition (notably generative grammar).

The movement called *cognitive linguistics* belongs to the functionalist tradition. Although its concern with cognition hardly makes it unique, the label *cognitive* is not entirely arbitrary. Within functionalism, cognitive linguistics stands out by emphasizing the semiological function of language and the crucial role of conceptualization in social interaction. It contrasts with formalist approaches by viewing language as an integral facet of cognition (not as a separate "module" or "mental faculty"). Insofar as possible, linguistic structure is analyzed in terms of more basic systems and abilities (e.g., perception, attention, categorization) from which it cannot be dissociated.

The theory called *cognitive grammar* (Langacker, 1987a, 1990, 1991) represents one approach to cognitive linguistics. Its central claim is that grammar is per se a *symbolic* phenomenon, consisting of patterns for imposing and symbolizing particular schemes of conceptual structuring. It is held that lexicon, morphology, and syntax form a continuum fully describable as assemblies of *symbolic structures* (form–meaning pairings), and consequently, that all valid grammatical constructs have conceptual import. Although quite radical from the standpoint of orthodox linguistic theory, these positions are actually both natural and desirable. Reducing grammar to symbolic assemblies affords a major theoretical unification as well as great austerity in the kinds of entities analysts are allowed to posit. It is realistic from the psychological standpoint, for unlike semantics and phonology—grounded in the broader realms of conceptualization and sound—grammar is not connected to any independently accessible domain of experience. It is more naturally taken as residing in schematized representations of sound–meaning pairings, abstracted from (and immanent in) the specific symbolic configurations observable in complex expressions. Described in this manner, grammar (like lexicon) can be seen as directly reflecting the semiological function of language.

Although the analyses and theoretical claims of cognitive grammar are proposed and justified on the basis of linguistic evidence, some care is taken to stay within the bounds of psychological plausibility. A guiding principle is that language structure should be characterized relying only on mental abilities and phenomena that are either well known or easily demonstrated. This leads to a primary working strategy (described in Langacker, 1993a) based on the convergence of three kinds of considerations. The objective is to find descriptions of linguistic elements that simultaneously meet the conditions of being (a) reasonable from the psychological standpoint, (b) well motivated in purely semantic terms, and (c) optimal as a basis for analyzing grammar. In my view, this methodology has proved quite successful. It is argued in various works (e.g., Langacker, 1995b; van Hoek, 1995) that conceptually grounded descriptions satisfying conditions (a) and (b) support revealing accounts of classic grammatical problems. The advantages of reducing grammar to symbolic assemblies are not purchased at the expense of descriptive adequacy, but quite the contrary.

The presentation begins by sketching a conceptualist approach to semantics. We next consider symbolic assemblies and the gradation between lexicon and grammar. Following this is a discussion of how cognitive grammar handles some basic problems of grammatical description. Finally, as a case study, an attempt is made to justify (or at least render plausible) a conceptual characterization of the grammatical notions *subject* and *object*. The supposed impossibility of such a characterization is of course a central argument for the autonomy of syntax.

2. SEMANTICS

Views of grammar are critically dependent on assumptions made about semantics. In particular, the autonomy of grammar appears self-evident given the prevalent assumption that meanings consist of truth conditions. The meaningfulness of grammatical elements becomes apparent only by adopting a conceptualist semantics that properly accommodates our ability to conceive and portray the same objective situation in alternate ways. The term *conceptualization* is interpreted broadly as embracing any kind of mental experience. It subsumes (a) both established and novel conceptions; (b) not only abstract or intellectual "concepts" but also sensory, motor, and emotive experience; (c) conceptions that are not instantaneous but change or unfold through processing time; and (d) full apprehension of the physical, social, cultural, and linguistic context. Thus, far from being either static or solipsistic, conceptualization is viewed as the dynamic activity of embodied minds interacting with their environment.

Linguistic semantics has traditionally posited a definite boundary between "semantics" and "pragmatics." It is further assumed that lexical items have fixed, well-delimited meanings (far less inclusive than speakers' general knowledge of the entities they denote), and that sentence meanings are fully derivable from lexical meanings by rules of semantic composition. Attractive though it is, a semantics of this sort is actually quite problematic. It reflects the dubious metaphorical supposition that linguistic elements are containers from which discrete components of meaning need only be extracted and assembled in building-block fashion (cf. Reddy, 1979). In practice, motivated boundaries between "linguistic" and "extralinguistic" facets of meaning have proved notoriously hard to establish.

The basic vision of *cognitive semantics* is radically different. Rather than imposing artificial boundaries, it posits a gradation between semantics and pragmatics, and also between linguistic and general knowledge. It views expressions as evoking (rather than containing) meanings, which emerge via an elaborate process of *meaning construction* drawing on all available resources—linguistic, psychological, and contextual. Even at the lexical level, meanings are variable and malleable. The *encyclopedic* approach (Haiman, 1980; Langacker, 1987a; cf. Wierzbicka, 1995) treats lexical items as points of entry into vast conceptual networks. Although the access they afford to these networks is to some degree conventionally established, it is nonetheless flexible, open-ended, and highly subject to priming. To the extent that distinct paths of access become entrenched and conventionalized, the result is the common situation of *polysemy*, where a lexical item has a number of related senses, any one of which might be activated on a given occasion. These senses form a *complex category* describable as a network, usually centered on a *prototype* (Lakoff, 1987; Langacker, 1987a; Taylor, 1995).

At higher levels of organization, the essential role of meaning construction is even more evident. Multifaceted research in cognitive semantics has demonstrated that the meanings of complex expressions are not in general algorithmically derivable from their parts—at least given a representative range of data (not selected just to avoid the problem) and a realistic definition of "meaning" (not so impoverished as to be trivial in relation to natural language understanding). Patterns of semantic composition do of course exist (they are considered an inherent aspect of grammar) and their importance is undeniable. Still, because language is neither autonomous nor encapsulated, semantically it exhibits only *partial compositionality*. The meanings contributed by lexical and grammatical elements evoke and constrain—but do not fully constitute—the overall conceptualization evoked by a complex expression, its *composite* semantic structure. This is an entity in its own right with many possible sources of extracompositionality. It may, for instance, be crucially dependent for its coherence on discourse or contextual clues to supplement the fragmentary information explicitly encoded. It may invoke domains of knowledge not accessed by any component element taken individually. It is likely to require the construction and manipulation of an elaborate set of connected *mental spaces* (Fauconnier, 1985; Fauconnier & Sweetser, 1996). Almost certain to be involved are basic and ubiquitous phenomena such as *metaphor* (Lakoff & Johnson, 1980; Lakoff & Turner, 1989), *metonymy* (Langacker, 1995b; Nunberg, 1995), and *conceptual blending* (Fauconnier & Turner, 1994, 1996; Turner & Fauconnier, 1995). It might then seem attractive to distinguish between *evoked* and *encoded* meaning, equating semantic structure with just the latter (Harder, 1996). The feasibility of such a move is anything but obvious, however. There is no clear boundary between evoked and encoded meaning, nor is the latter necessarily either independently coherent or separately apprehended.

Fundamental to cognitive semantics is *construal*, our manifest capacity for conceptualizing the same situation in alternate ways. At least for mortals, construal is inescapable—there is no completely neutral way of apprehending a situation (although there are of course defaults). Meaning is thus a function of both conceptual "content" and how that content is construed. As an inherent aspect of their conventional semantic value, linguistic elements impose a particular construal on the content they evoke, and speakers adopt it for purposes of linguistic expression. Differences in conventional patterns of construal are largely responsible for the impression that languages embody contrasting "worldviews." A strong claim of linguistic relativity, that language drastically and unavoidably shapes thought, is not however warranted. The effect of linguistically imposed construal may be fairly superficial (Slobin, 1987). The content evoked by expressions can be largely the same (affording the basis for understanding and rough translation) even when construed very differently. Moreover, the symbolic resources of a single language provide an enormous range of options for construing any given situation, and speakers show great dexterity in shifting from one to another.

One dimension of construal is "granularity," i.e. the degree of precision and detail with which a situation is characterized. The lexicon of a language allows an entity to be described at varying levels of *specificity* (conversely, *schematicity*), the choice depending on circumstances and communicative objectives. For instance, the same feline might be described specifically as a *Siamese*, more abstractly (in coarser grained detail) as a *cat*, and still more schematically with terms like *animal, creature,* or even *thing.* Complex expressions obviously allow indefinite variation along this parameter, as illustrated by the progressively more schematic descriptions in (1):

1. *Your wretched Siamese just gobbled up my crème brûlée. > Your cat just ate my dessert. > An animal did something. > Something happened.*

The meanings of grammatical elements are usually quite schematic (cf. Talmy, 1988). This does not distinguish them sharply from lexical items, because the latter vary widely along the dimension of specificity. There is rather a gradation, such that the more schematic an element is semantically, the more likely it is to be regarded by linguists as grammatical rather than lexical.

Numerous aspects of construal reflect a very general ability to conceive of one structure against the *background* provided by another. One kind of background consists of assumptions, expectations, and presuppositions, which expressions evoke with varying degrees of explicitness and specificity. Consider the sentences in (2), which might be used to describe the same objective situation:

2. a. *He has published few articles in refereed journals.*
   b. *He has published a few articles in refereed journals.*

In (2a), *few* indicates that the quantity of articles is less than anticipated. By contrast, *a few* in (2b) assumes a baseline of zero and specifies a small departure from it in a positive direction. The difference between a negative vs. a positive displacement from a presupposed value is not without grammatical consequences. Observe that *any* cooccurs with *few,* but not with *a few*:

3. a. *He has published few articles which make any sense.*
   b. **He has published a few articles which make any sense.*

It is well known that *any* requires a negative context (e.g., *He doesn't have any money*, but **He has any money*). Its distribution in cases like (3) is thus sensitive to how the objective situation is construed in terms of background expectations.

The previous discourse constitutes an essential background for the current expression. Most obviously, previous specification in the discourse allows entities to be referred to more schematically than when they are first introduced:

4. *My psychiatrist would prefer to interview patients in her own study. However, she never actually does it there.*

Less often noted is the fact that expressions judged ungrammatical and semantically anomalous when considered in isolation often appear coherent, natural, and grammatically well formed when situated in the appropriate discourse context. For instance, whereas linguists would normally append an asterisk (for ungrammaticality) to a sentence like (5a), it seems perfectly appropriate when uttered in response to (5b):

5. a. *(*)I think diced slightly tipsy.*
   b. *Is there any way of preparing them so that Cedric might be willing to eat carrots while in any conceivable mental state?*

It is a basic principle of cognitive linguistics that well-formedness judgments always presuppose some context, if only an implicit one based on default assumptions.

Another background phenomenon is metaphor, in which a *target domain* is construed in relation to a *source domain*. A theory, for example, can be viewed metaphorically as a building, an airplane, or even as a bucket (Lakoff & Johnson, 1980):

6. a. *His theory rested on such poor foundations that, despite all his attempts to buttress it, it finally just collapsed.*
   b. *Your theory just won't fly; in any case, it could be shot down by any halfway competent linguist.*
   c. *That theory is full of holes; it won't hold water.*

Categorization can also be considered a background phenomenon, in that the target is interpreted as instantiating a particular preexisting conceptual frame. Even if the objective behavior is just the same, it makes a difference whether contributions to a political candidate are construed as *gaining access* or *buying influence.*

Numerous dimensions of construal can be grouped under the rubric of *perspective*. The most obvious is the *vantage point* from which a situation is conceptualized. Thus (7a), with *come*, implies that the speaker is in the attic, whereas *go* in (7b) implicates the opposite:

7. a. *Why don't you come up into the attic?*
   b. *Why don't you go up into the attic?*

Of course, speakers display great agility in recognizing other vantage points and mentally adopting them for expressive purposes. In (8a), for instance, the use of *come* conveys empathy and solidarity by indicating that the speaker is adopting the vantage point of the addressee:

8. a. *I'll come to your place Tuesday morning.*
   b. *Ellen was writing furiously. Tomorrow was the deadline for the manuscript.*

In (8b), the second sentence is readily interpreted as reflecting Ellen's vantage point rather than the speaker's. The incongruity of using *tomorrow* with a past-tense verb signals this transfer to the mental space representing Ellen's consciousness at the time of writing.

Another aspect of perspective is the overall *viewing arrangement* an expression presupposes. This is best illustrated by a classic example due to Len Talmy (1988):

9. *There's a cottage every now and then through the valley.*

A cottage is not the sort of thing that goes in and out of existence, as suggested by the adverbial phrase *every now and then*. Nor is anything explicitly described as moving, as suggested by the path phrase *through the valley*. On the face of it, then, the sentence ought to be semantically and grammatically incoherent. Yet, we immediately and easily understand it as making perfect sense. In contrast to the default of a static viewer reporting on a series of events, it presupposes the special arrangement in which a moving viewer describes what appears in the "viewing frame" (e.g., the window of a vehicle) during a journey. *Every now and then* pertains to the frequency of a cottage being observed in that frame. Likewise, *through the valley* describes the path followed by the moving observer. Note, however, that the sentence makes no explicit reference to the mover, the journey, or the viewing activity. These notions have to be supplied by the conceptualizers (i.e., the speaker and the addressee), who create the basis for semantic and grammatical coherence by engaging in an active process of meaning construction.

A distinct but related phenomenon involves the conceptualizer traversing a static situation by means of "fictive" or "subjective" motion (Langacker, 1986; Matsumoto, 1996a, 1996b; Talmy, 1996). The contrast in (10), for example, depends solely on the direction of *mental scanning*, as indicated by the prepositional phrases:

10. a. *An ugly scar runs all the way from his knee to his ankle.*
    b. *An ugly scar runs all the way from his ankle to his knee.*

Mental scanning of this sort is by no means limited to spatial configurations but can be manifested in any conceptual domain:

11. a. *The prices on this model run from about $18,000 all the way to $27,000 depending on optional equipment.*
    b. *As average body size increases, the typical gestation period gets progressively longer.*

The sentences in (10) and (11) all describe situations that are locally stable with respect to the actual passage of time. The sense of movement and directionality reflect the order in which a range of options (spatial or otherwise) are mentally accessed by the conceptualizer in the process of building up to the full apprehension of a complex structure.

Lastly, our capacity for construal comprises various ways of rendering certain entities more *prominent* than others. Numerous types of prominence need to be distinguished for linguistic purposes. One kind of prominence attaches to elements that are *new* in relation to what has already been established in the discourse. Collectively called the *focus*, these elements stand out against the background of information said to be *old* or *given*. In English, focus is generally marked by unreduced stress (indicated here by small caps):

12. *He said she was wearing a white blouse with black polka dots, but actually she was wearing a white SWEATER with black STRIPES.*

Rather different is the inherent cognitive salience of certain kinds of entities and experiential domains. Examples include the salience of a whole relative to its parts, the special status of animate entities (especially humans) in relation to inanimate objects, that of physical entities as opposed to abstractions, and the psychological primacy of visual and spatial experience. Among the linguistic manifestations of these salience asymmetries are the usual directions of metaphor and metonymy. It is well known, for instance, that abstract notions tend to be structured metaphorically in terms of source domains pertaining to physical experience, as in (6). Some cases of metonymy are given in (13). In (13a), *a whole turkey* refers metonymically to the turkey's edible flesh; presumably the bones, feathers, and other sundry parts were not consumed.

13. a. *For Thanksgiving we ate a whole turkey.*
    b. *I'm in the phone book.*

The metonymic use of the pronoun *I* in (13b) illustrates the inherent salience of humans as well as physical entities. Under normal circumstances, it would actually only be a graphic representation of the speaker's name, address, and telephone number that appears in the phone book.

Especially important for grammar are two kinds of prominence intuitively describable as involving the focusing of attention. The first, called *profiling*, characterizes expressions of any size or type. Within the full conceptualization it evokes, an expression directs attention to some particular substructure—its *profile*—as being the entity that it designates or refers to. An expression's profile is thus its "referent," in a psychological (as opposed to a logical or philosophical) sense of that term. The noun *lid*, for example, evokes the conception of a container together with a cover serving to close an opening in its top, as sketched in Fig. 1.1(a). This entire conception is necessary, because a lid can be identified as such only in relation to a container and its covering/closing function. Yet, the full conception is not per se the meaning of *lid*, because a lid is not equivalent to a container-cover assembly. A crucial semantic property of *lid* is that, within this assembly, it specifies the cover in particular as being its referent. The cover is thus its profile, as shown in Fig. 1.1(b). In the diagrammatic representations of cognitive grammar (which are heuristic rather than formal), profiling is indicated by heavy lines.

An expression can profile either a *thing* or a *relationship* (assuming abstract and broadly inclusive definitions of those terms; see Langacker, 1987b). Consider the words *advise*, *advisor*, and *advisee*. As shown in Fig.

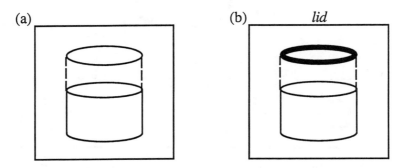

FIG. 1.1. The effect of profiling.

1.2, they evoke the conception of two individuals engaging in a particular kind of verbally mediated social and psychological interaction. A dashed arrow represents this experiential relationship, its alignment indicating the primary direction of influence. Note that this entire conception figures in the meaning of all three expressions: A person does not qualify as an advisor or advisee except by virtue of participating in an interaction of this sort, nor can one conceive of the advising process without conceptualizing its participants. Because *advise*, *advisor*, and *advisee* have the same conceptual content, the semantic contrast among them resides in profiling, an aspect of construal. The verb *advise* profiles the relationship, including the participants essential to its conception. On the other hand, the nouns *advisor* and *advisee* profile only the respective participants, identified and distinguished by their role in the process.

Such examples clearly demonstrate that an expression's meaning depends on both content and profiling. Yet, these alone are not sufficient. We can see this from semantic oppositions like *above* vs. *below*, diagrammed in Fig. 1.3. Both expressions designate a spatial relationship between two things (shown as circles) occupying different positions along the vertical axis. They thus evoke the same conceptual content. Moreover, they have the same profile (represented by the heavy dashed lines)—referentially, an *above* relationship is also a *below* relationship. Some other factor must therefore be responsible for the contrast in meaning. This factor, a final dimension of construal, is the relative prominence accorded the participants in a profiled relationship.

In a relational expression, there is usually a participant that stands out either as the one being located or characterized, or as the one whose activity is being followed. Called the *trajector* (tr), this entity can be described as the primary figure in the scene. Often, a second participant, called the

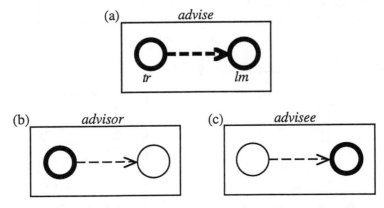

FIG. 1.2. The profiling of a relationship versus the profiling of its participants.

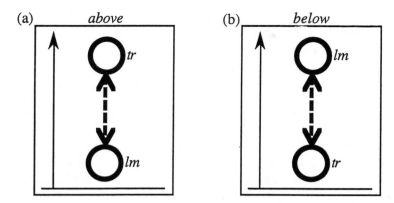

FIG. 1.3. Expressions that differ in trajector/landmark alignment.

landmark (lm), stands out as a secondary figure. The semantic contrast between *above* and *below* resides in whether the upper participant is focused as trajector and the lower one as landmark, or conversely. If I say, for example, that *The knob is above the keyhole,* I am using the keyhole as a spatial landmark to specify the location of the knob. I do the opposite in saying that *The keyhole is below the knob.* Observe, however, that the notions trajector and landmark are not defined spatially, but as a matter of focal prominence, hence, they are applicable to any kind of relationship. In Fig. 1.2(a), for instance, the source and the target of advice are respectively identified as the trajector and landmark of *advise.*

3. LEXICON AND GRAMMAR

Both lexicon and grammar are claimed to be fully and properly describable as assemblies of symbolic structures. The term "symbolic" does not imply operations on strings of empty markers (as when "symbolic processing" is contrasted with connectionist approaches). On the contrary, it refers to the semiological function of language and the symbolization of meanings by phonological sequences. In cognitive grammar, a *symbolic structure* is defined as consisting in the association between a *semantic structure* and a *phonological structure*—its semantic and phonological *poles.* Every lexical and grammatical element is thus attributed some kind of semantic and phonological value, whether specific or schematic.

   Lexicon is defined in cognitive grammar as the set of fixed expressions in a language, regardless of their size or type. Each lexical item is an assembly of symbolic structures. A *morpheme* can be regarded as a minimal symbolic assembly, degenerate by virtue of having no symbolic substructures. The morpheme *door,* for example, can be given as [DOOR/door], where upper- and lower-case orthographic sequences respectively stand for semantic and phonological structures. The lexical unit *garage door* is more typical in being symbolically complex. As shown in Fig. 1.4 (where dashed-line boxes delimit complex assemblies), it comprises two component symbolic structures, [GARAGE/garage] and [DOOR/door], together with the symbolic structure defined by the composite form and meaning of the overall expression: [GARAGE DOOR/garage door]. At a higher level of organization, this entire assembly combines with *opener*, itself complex, to form the lexical unit *garage door opener*. There is clearly no inherent upper limit on the symbolic complexity expressions can exhibit.

A lexical item is "fixed" in the sense of being both learned by individual speakers and conventional within a certain speech community. Because both are matters of degree, there is no strict boundary between lexical items and "novel" expressions. The latter, of course, are usually novel only in limited respects. How much is actually novel in the sentence *The garage door opener is broken*, for example? *Garage door opener* comes prepackaged as a lexical unit, and for those who have such a device, the full noun phrase *the garage door opener* is probably a familiar expression. Moreover, although the phrase *is broken* is not traditionally considered a lexical item, a typical speaker has used it on many occasions and may very well store it as a prefabricated unit. The truly novel aspect of the sentence may in fact be limited to combining *the garage door opener* and *is broken* as subject and predicate. More generally, the fluency of real-time speech may only be possible owing to the substantial proportion of boilerplate language and standard expressive schemes it employs.

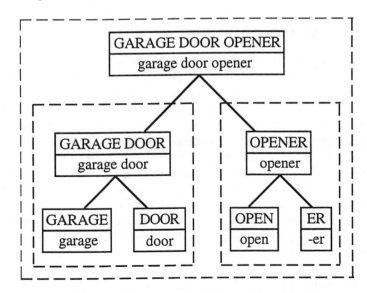

FIG. 1.4. A lexical item with levels of symbolic complexity.

Both fixed and novel expressions consist of symbolic assemblies of any potential size, at least partially constructed in accordance with regular grammatical patterns. Either are capable of diverging from such patterns, especially at the semantic pole, where an elaborate process of meaning construction may intervene between the meanings of component elements and the composite semantic value. In the case of a lexical item, deviations from regularity and strict compositionality are accepted as part of its linguistic characterization, because the entire assembly is familiar and conventional (by definition). With novel expressions, where this is not so (at least not yet), comparable deviations are normally regarded by linguists as involving ungrammaticality or facets of meaning that are extralinguistic (hence beyond the scope of semantics). But the difference is more apparent than real, hinging only on the degree of entrenchment and conventionality. The standard doctrine that lexical items are idiosyncratic and semantically unpredictable, whereas novel expressions are regular and semantically compositional, does not stem from any empirical finding but rather from a tacit decision to consider only those facets of the latter that are already sanctioned by established convention.

Be it fixed or novel, a linguistic *expression* is a symbolic assembly whose composite structure is specified in enough detail—particularly at the phonological pole—that it can actually be uttered and understood. Linguists, however, are less interested in expressions per se than in the patterns and regularities they instantiate. In cognitive grammar, linguistic generalizations (the functional equivalent of "rules") are simply *schemas* abstracted from occurring expressions. A schema is a template representing the coarse-grained commonality exhibited by a set of expressions with respect to some facet of their structure. It is reasonably supposed that schemas are *immanent* in their instantiating expressions, and emerge as cognitive entities by reinforcement of the structural properties they share at a certain level of abstraction. We have already noted degrees of schematization for semantic structures (e.g., in example 1). Moreover, because linguists are concerned with phonological structures as mental representations (not just as actual sounds), these too are susceptible to schematization. Schematized symbolic structures constitute grammar.

Cognitive grammar is highly restrictive and very down-to-earth in regard to the kinds of structures it allows in linguistic descriptions. On the one hand, it specifies that only semantic, phonological, and symbolic structures are permitted. Thus, every linguistic element contributes directly to the semiological function of language by virtue of having some kind of semantic and/or phonological value. On the other hand, cognitive grammar imposes strong restrictions on the relation between linguistic structures and the primary data of occurring expressions. It specifies that the only structures validly posited are those that figure directly in the data (i.e., actual expressions and their parts), or that emerge from the data via the basic cognitive processes of abstraction (schematization) and categorization. To take a phonological example, particular segments such as [m], [n], and [ŋ] can be posited because they occur as parts of actual expressions. Permitted as an abstraction from these elements is the schematic segment [N], i.e. a nasal consonant unspecified as to place of articulation. It represents the generalization that nasal consonants occur in the language, and embodies the commonality that makes them a natural phonological class. Also permitted are the categorizing relationships identifying each nasal segment as an instance of that class: [[N] → [m]], [[N] → [n]], and [[N] → [ŋ]]. Similarly, we can posit the semantic structures [LID], [DOOR], and [CAP], permitted because they occur as the respective meanings of *lid, door,* and *cap.* Also allowed is the schematized conception they all instantiate, [COVER FOR OPENING], as well as categorizations such as [[COVER FOR OPENING] → [LID]].

The most striking and controversial claim of cognitive grammar is that these same few possibilities—applied to symbolic structures—are sufficient for a full and optimal account of lexicon, morphology, and syntax. Note first that lexical items are permitted in a linguistic description by virtue of being actual, recurring expressions. As shown in Fig. 1.4, these include symbolic assemblies of any size, some of which function as components of others. Also permitted are schematizations of occurring expressions (not limited to lexical items). These schematic symbolic assemblies, potentially having any degree of complexity, embody the coarse-grained commonality inherent in sets of expressions. Such assemblies constitute grammatical structure, and their categorization of specific expressions (both fixed and novel) constitutes the structural characterization of those expressions.

Consider expressions like *jar lid, pot lid, box lid,* and *coffin lid.* Each is an assembly comprised of two component symbolic structures (e.g. [JAR/jar] and [LID/lid]) together with the composite symbolic structure giving the meaning and form of the expression as a whole (e.g. [JAR LID/jar lid]). Although they vary in both frequency of occurrence and lexical status, they exhibit a structural parallelism that provides a basis for schematization. The resulting schema, which we can abbreviate as *CONTAINER lid,* represents a particular low-level pattern of forming nominal compounds. Higher level abstractions are of course possible, such as the general schema for noun–noun compounds like *pencil eraser, desk clerk, tomato juice, broom handle, luggage strap, movie star, tooth filling, cab driver, fire alarm, dust rag, computer virus,* and so forth. This highly schematic assembly—call it *THING THING*—is instantiated by *CONTAINER lid* and numerous other subschemas describing special cases of the general pattern. We can therefore posit schematic hierarchies, for example, *THING THING → CONTAINER lid → jar lid.*

We must further recognize *extensions* from a basic pattern. Thus, *eyelid* is an instance of *THING THING* but an extension vis-à-vis *CONTAINER lid*, for an eye is not a container; *CONTAINER lid* ---> *eyelid*. It is quite typical for the full description of a grammatical construction to involve a substantial number of constructional variants. These are characterized at different levels of specificity and linked by categorizing relationships to form a network, often centered on a prototype (Goldberg, 1995; Janda, 1990; Lakoff, 1987). The same may be said for the alternate senses of a polysemous lexical item, and indeed, for linguistic categories in general (Langacker, 1987a, 1988).

4. GRAMMATICAL STRUCTURE

Why should there be such a thing as grammar? It would not exist were lexical units available to symbolize every conception one would want to express. However, lexical items form a limited set, whereas the conceptions we wish to encode linguistically are open ended and indefinitely varied. We overcome this by resorting to complex expressions comprising multiple lexical elements. Each component element evokes some facet of the overall conception, a facet singled out precisely because it is susceptible to individual lexical encoding. Collectively, these individually symbolized conceptual "chunks" provide enough clues about the composite conception intended by the speaker that the addressee (especially in context) is able to reconstruct some approximation to it. But this reconstruction cannot proceed effectively without some kind of systematic indication of how the conceptual chunks are supposed to fit together. The role of grammar is to provide this information.

We can start by examining a specific symbolic assembly, namely *jar lid*, sketched in Fig. 1.5. The composite structure is shown at the top, the two component structures below. At the semantic pole, *lid* profiles the cover to a schematic container, *jar* profiles a specific container, and *jar lid* profiles the cover to a container of that type. (The pictorial representations are only mnemonic; they have to be understood as abbreviating multifaceted conceptualizations.) Phonologically, the components *jar* and *lid* are single words (W), the composite expression being a two-word sequence with accent on the first. The component and composite structures form an assembly by virtue of *correspondences*, represented diagrammatically by dotted lines. In particular, a semantic correspondence equates the profile of *jar* with the schematic container evoked by *lid*, whereas at the phonological pole, *jar* is identified with the word directly preceding *lid*. When elements of the component structures correspond, they project to the same composite structure element. Correspondences can thus be regarded as instructions for "integrating" components to form the composite structure.

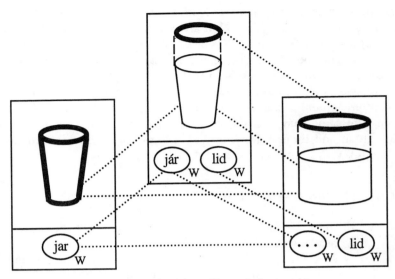

FIG. 1.5. Details of a specific symbolic assembly.

The specific symbolic assembly in Fig. 1.5 instantiates schematized assemblies such as *CONTAINER lid* and *THING THING*, describing conventional compounding patterns at different levels of abstraction. The schema describing the general pattern is depicted in Fig. 1.6. Phonologically, it indicates word order and the characteristic stress pattern of compounds without specifying any particular segmental content. At the semantic pole,

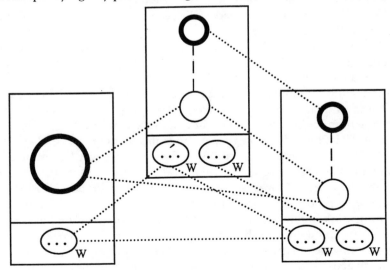

FIG. 1.6. Details of a schematic symbolic assembly.

the component and composite structures are characterized abstractly as profiling things (represented by circles). The profile of the first component corresponds to a thing associated in some unspecified fashion with the profile of the second, which also prevails as the composite structure profile.

The correspondences inherited from the sanctioning schema indicate how the conceptual "chunks" provided by the component structures are supposed to be combined in forming the composite semantic structure. Typically, however, the composite structure incorporates extracompositional properties and therefore has to be recognized as an entity in its own right. For instance, compounds like *lipstick* and *apple polisher* evoke conceptual "frames" not associated with either of their component elements taken individually (cf. Downing, 1977; Ryder, 1994). Neither *lip* nor *stick* by itself reliably evokes the cultural practice of females coloring their lips with a paintlike substance packaged in a sticklike shape. Although this cultural frame is necessary for the conceptual coherence of *lipstick*, it is neither mechanically determined nor fully constituted by the individual meanings of *lip* and *stick*, which explicitly encode only selected aspects of it. Semantics is only partially compositional; conventional patterns of composition (the semantic poles of schematic symbolic assemblies) are only one of the factors in the process of meaning construction that intervenes between component and composite conceptions in complex expressions. Compositional rules do not function in isolation, nor does their fully compositional "output" necessarily exist or have any independent cognitive status.

If the basic idea of symbolic assemblies is clear, it must next be asked whether they are able in principle to provide a full account of grammatical structure. Can they actually accommodate the various phenomena generally interpreted as demanding that grammar be treated autonomously? By way of partial demonstration that they can, let us briefly consider some fundamental problems: grammatical classes, grammatical markers, constituency, and distributional restrictions. An additional problem, how to characterize the grammatical relations subject and object, is the topic of section 5.

To this very day, standard linguistic doctrine holds that basic grammatical classes (noun, verb, adjective, etc.) are not semantically definable. The arguments are anything but conclusive, however, for they consider only the most simplistic semantic characterizations and completely ignore our ability to impose alternate construals on the same conceptual content (see, e.g., Jackendoff, 1994, pp. 68–69). It is argued, for example, that because not every noun names a physical object, and not every verb names an action, these classes cannot be defined on the basis of any meaning shared by all of their members. The impossibility of a semantic definition is also argued on the grounds that expressions with the same meaning sometimes belong to different grammatical classes, for example, *explode* (a verb) and *explosion* (a noun). But, it should be evident that if all nouns or all verbs have something in common semantically, it must be more abstract than notions like 'physical object' and 'action' (which do however describe the category prototypes), and it must be independent of any specific conceptual content. A viable conceptual characterization should instead be sought at the level of general cognitive abilities, in particular our capacity to conceive of the same situation in alternate ways. Category membership does not reflect conceptual content so much as it does the construal imposed on it.

What sort of cognitive abilities might be invoked in a conceptual characterization of the noun class? One is profiling. As we saw in Fig. 1.2, the words *advise, advisor,* and *advisee* have basically the same conceptual content, the semantic contrast residing in their choice of profile. It is in fact the nature of an expression's profile—not its overall content—that determines its grammatical class. *Advise* is thus a verb because it profiles a certain kind of relationship, whereas *advisor* and *advisee* are nouns because they profile "things" (identified by their role as participants in that relationship). The claim, then, is that a noun profiles a *thing*, in an abstract and broadly inclusive sense of that term. This is the conceptual property that all nouns have in common, and they are nouns precisely because they have this property.

But what is a "thing"? My working hypothesis is that a thing is the product of two fundamental and ubiquitous cognitive phenomena. The first is *grouping*, whereby entities are singled out and conceived in relation to one another to the exclusion of others. Most familiar are the gestaltist principles of grouping by contiguity and similarity. In viewing (14a), we can hardly avoid forming groups of two and three x's on the basis of contiguity, whereas in (14b), similarity affords a basis for singling out certain entities (the x's) that can then be grouped by proximity.

14. a. x x   x x x
    b. --- x-x-x-x----------x-x-x-x----------x-x-x-x---

We can also recognize more abstract bases for grouping. For instance, the members of an orchestra are mentally grouped because they are conceived as interacting to collectively fulfill a certain function. A number of stars are grouped to form a constellation because they are conceived as points in the outline of a schematic image. The second relevant phenomenon, call it *reification*, is the manipulation of a group as a unitary entity for higher level cognitive purposes. In (14b), for example, I reify the groups of x's when I count them, observe that all three are the same, note that they form a straight line, and so forth. I reify an orchestra when I compare it to another in size or quality, or when I think of it as joining with others to form an orchestra association (a higher level group).

A "thing" is thus defined as any product of grouping and reification, and a noun is characterized as an expression that profiles a thing. Large numbers of nouns are straightforwardly describable in this manner; *group, team, club, stack, pile, alphabet, archipelago, swarm, herd, jigsaw puzzle, chess set, lexicon, bouquet, collection, orchard, chord, squad, galaxy,* and so on indefinitely. Each such noun designates a set of constitutive entities that obviously are grouped and conceptually wielded as a single unit for linguistic and other purposes. I suggest that the same description applies to physical objects, even those whose constitutive entities are nothing more than arbitrarily delimited "splotches" of material substance continuously distributed throughout a certain expanse of space. The splotches constituting a rock, for example, are neither individuated nor consciously recognized, yet the very apprehension of their continuous extensionality effects their grouping to yield the conception of a unitary object. The reason physical objects are prototypical for nouns is that the grouping and reification of their constitutive entities is so basic and automatic that any awareness of them requires subsequent, higher level analysis. I have argued elsewhere (Langacker 1987b, 1991) that mass nouns, abstract nouns, and others also conform to this general description.

I have no definite proof for this conceptual characterization of nouns. If basically correct, it will nonetheless have to be refined, properly formulated, and empirically tested from the psychological standpoint by those with proper expertise. It is merely offered as a coherent proposal with some claim to linguistic adequacy and cognitive plausibility. Even so, by indicating what a viable conceptual description of nouns might look like, it underscores the simplistic nature of standard arguments for the impossibility of a semantic definition. I personally find it hard to imagine that fundamental and universal categories like noun and verb would not have a conceptual basis (cf. Gentner, 1981, 1982; Kellogg, 1994, 1996). As a general matter, I believe that such categories reflect inborn cognitive abilities that are initially manifested in the category prototype and that become more apparent when extended to other kinds of circumstances. (This is not in principle incompatible with an account based on metaphor, e.g., the notion that nominal referents are metaphorically construed as physical objects.)

The prototype for verbs is an action, i.e. an event producing observable change carried out by a volitional agent. The more schematic conception that all verbs share, I suggest, is that of a relationship mentally scanned sequentially—instant by instant—in its evolution through time. I refer to this as a *process*. Every verb is thus said to profile a process, just as every noun profiles a thing. Other basic classes, such as prepositions and adjectives, are characterized as profiling different sorts of relationships viewed "holistically," in the sense that their evolution through time is not in focus. A preposition like *above*, for instance, profiles a nonprocessual relationship with a thing as its landmark (Fig. 1.3); although this relationship is likely to endure through time, its temporal evolution is not essential to its description or identification (it can be identified in a configuration viewed only instantaneously). An adjective profiles a relationship with a thing as trajector but no salient landmark. The adjective *square*, for example, profiles a complex relationship—involving length of sides, parallelism, perpendicularity, etc.—holding among various facets of its trajector. (As a noun, *square* profiles a thing consisting of connected line segments whose configuration instantiates the relationship profiled by the adjective.) Participles and infinitives derive from verbs, hence they evoke the conception of a process, but in one way or another, they construe it holistically to form a higher level conception that is nonprocessual. For instance, one kind of past participle restricts the profile of a change-of-state verb to the final state resulting from the change. Thus, whereas the verb *melt* profiles the process of a solid (its trajector) gradually becoming liquid, the participle *melted* profiles just the latter situation. By virtue of profiling a single-participant, nonprocessual relationship, such participles actually qualify as adjectives and behave that way grammatically (e.g., *melted ice cube*; *The ice cube is finally melted*).

Standard linguistic doctrine notwithstanding, I see nothing problematic or inherently implausible about the notion that the members of a basic grammatical class all share an abstract commonality. It is thus proposed that every noun instantiates the symbolic schema [THING/. . .] (i.e., it profiles a thing, but need not have any particular phonological properties). Likewise, every verb instantiates the schema [PROCESS/. . .]. Although class membership is usually taken as demonstrating the need for irreducible grammatical primitives, it is coherently and more naturally seen as residing in categorizing relationships between specific and schematic symbolic structures: [[THING/. . .] → [EXPLOSION/explosion]]; [[PROCESS/. . .] → [EXPLODE/explode]]. It needs to be emphasized that these characterizations do not invoke any specific conceptual content. The schematic conception immanent in all nouns, or in all verbs, is primarily a matter of construal: A noun profiles a product of grouping and reification, whereas a verb profiles a relationship whose temporal evolution is scanned sequentially. These alternate modes of construal can perfectly well be applied to the same conceptual content, resulting in a difference in grammatical class. If *explode* and *explosion* evoke the same basic conception, they nonetheless impose distinct construals on it. As a verb, *explode* construes the event as a dynamic process and simply tracks its occurrence through time. On the other hand, the noun *explosion* profiles an abstract "thing" created by the reification of such a process. Its constitutive entities are the successive phases of the process (i.e., the situations obtaining at each successive point in time), and the very act of scanning through them sequentially provides the basis for their grouping. Hence, *explosion* designates a reified event consisting of one instance of the process *explode.*

As this example indicates, the semantic import of grammar is largely a matter of the construal it imposes on the content supplied by lexical elements (cf. Talmy, 1988). The reason why the meaningfulness of grammar is not generally recognized is that semantics has not generally acknowledged the critical role of construal. Especially in the formalist tradition, linguists have consequently analyzed many elements as "purely grammatical" markers whose meaning is ignored and often explicitly denied. I have argued, to the contrary, that all grammatical markers have at least schematic conceptual import, and have proposed and justified particular meanings for a substantial number of representative instances (e.g., Langacker, 1990, 1991, 1992). Semantically, such markers are comparable to the schemas describing grammatical classes. As overtly realized grammatical markers, however, they differ from class schemas by virtue of being phonologically specific.

Consider the auxiliary verb *do,* which occurs with negation (*I do not see them*), in questions (*Did you wash it?*), and for emphasis in statements (*I DO love you!*). It is often viewed as meaningless, being inserted just for grammatical purposes (e.g., Chomsky, 1957). However, the fact that *do* serves a grammatical function does not mean that it has no meaning (cf. Reid, 1991). It is cogently analyzed as a maximally schematic verb, i.e. one whose semantic pole is equivalent to the verb-class schema despite its phonological specificity: [PROCESS/do]. This accounts for its taking verbal inflection, and also for its use as a kind of verbal anaphor: *Can you fix it? I already did.* One reason *do* appears to have no meaning is that it refers schematically to the same process that the lexical verb it combines with describes in more specific terms, hence it contributes no additional content. Yet, semantic overlap is characteristic of all grammatical constructions (see Fig. 1.6), and full inclusion is just an expected limiting case.

Most derivational and inflectional morphemes are reasonably described as being schematic for the class they derive, their semantic contribution residing in the construal they impose on the stems they combine with, especially in regard to profiling. For example, the derivational morphemes *-er* and *-ee* profile things characterized only by their agent or patientlike role in a schematically specified process; they impose this nominal profile on the specific process designated by the verb stem they attach to. I would thus describe *-er* and *-ee* as schematic agentive and patientive nouns, which forms like *advisor* and *advisee* respectively instantiate. By the same token, the nominalizing morpheme *-ion* (as in *explosion*) profiles a thing characterized as the reification of a schematic process, and the past participial morpheme *-ed* (as in *melted*) profiles the state resulting from a schematic change-of-state process. Of course, these same elements have alternate semantic values—just like other lexical items, grammatical markers are often polysemous. (For the polysemy of *-er*, see Ryder, 1991.)

We have so far discussed how certain basic grammatical phenomena—namely rules, classes, and markers—are in principle describable in terms of symbolic assemblies. Other phenomena commonly taken as supporting the autonomy of grammar include constituency as well as the problem of "distribution" or "structure dependency," i.e. arbitrary restrictions on the structural contexts in which elements are allowed to occur. In fact, however, the symbolic view of grammar readily handles them both.

To represent constituency, generative grammar posits syntactic phrase trees in which lexical items are "inserted" and function as terminal nodes. These tree structures are thought of as purely grammatical entities essential to syntactic description. Although they may play a role in semantic and phonological interpretation, the trees themselves draw on syntactic primitives and have no intrinsic semantic or phonological value. Three kinds of information are represented in these phrase trees: constituency, grammatical category (given by node labels), and linear order. All of these are clearly important for grammar. Only the status of phrase trees as autonomous syntactic objects is being called into question.

Constituency per se is hardly unique to grammar. It is just a matter of component elements being incorporated as facets of more complex structures at successively higher levels of organization. As such, it is evident in virtually every domain of experience: in motor experience, where component routines are coordinated into higher level routines (as in learning to type); in perception, as in (14b), where x's cluster into groups of four, which can then be perceived as forming a cluster of three such groups; and so on. Constituency emerges in symbolic assemblies when a composite symbolic structure at a given level of organization functions in turn as a component structure at a higher level. For example, we see in Fig. 1.4 that [GARAGE DOOR/garage door] and [OPENER/opener], each a composite structure with respect to its morphemic components, are themselves component structures with respect to the overall composite structure [GARAGE DOOR OPENER/garage door opener]. To the extent that they have this kind of hierarchical arrangement, symbolic assemblies are reasonably depicted as trees in the manner of Fig. 1.4. These trees are quite different from the phrase trees of generative grammar, however. Most importantly, every "node" is symbolic, having both a semantic and a phonological value, whereas the nodes of a generative phrase tree have neither.

Another difference is that the components of a symbolic assembly are not linearly ordered with respect to one another (hence assemblies like Fig. 1.4 are more like mobiles than trees). Linear ordering is actually the temporal ordering of speech. Although temporal ordering is exploited for the symbolization of grammatical relationships, it is properly regarded as a dimension of phonological structure. Temporal sequencing is therefore specified internally to every component and composite symbolic structure as an inherent aspect of its phonological characterization (e.g., the phonological pole of [GARAGE DOOR/garage door] specifies that *garage* directly precedes *door* in the temporal sequence). In similar fashion, grammatical category—which phrase trees indicate by means of node labels—is properly regarded as an inherent aspect of a symbolic structure's semantic characterization. In Fig. 1.5, for instance, the component and composite structures of *jar lid* are all classed as nouns because each profiles a thing (the noun-class schema is immanent in each of them).

We see, then, that the kinds of information represented in phrase trees are all available in symbolic assemblies as different aspects of their intrinsic organization. Interpreted as distinct and autonomous syntactic objects, phrase trees are therefore held to be unnecessary theoretical artifacts, a product of linguistic gerrymandering. Moreover, cognitive grammar views constituency as being less essential than does generative theory, and also as more fluid and variable (Langacker, 1995a, 1997b). Phenomena for which syntactic phrase trees per se have been considered indispensable (e.g., the definition of subject and object, discussed in section 5) are claimed to be better analyzed in other ways.

Turning now to distributional problems, I must first offer a point of clarification concerning grammatical classes. The claim that such classes are susceptible to schematic semantic descriptions valid for all members is specifically intended for basic and universal classes like noun and verb, for their major subclasses (e.g., count vs. mass noun), and for certain other "part-of-speech" type classes (such as adjectives, adpositions, and particular kinds of participles). It is definitely not asserted that every class a linguist might validly posit is definable in this manner. Such a claim would obviously be untenable for many distributional classes consisting of the lexical items conventionally allowed to participate in a given syntactic, morphological, or even phonological pattern. Even when a construction has a semantic basis, and the lexical items entering into it exhibit some degree of semantic coherence (as in the English passive), the exact inventory is often conventionally determined and less than fully predictable. The membership of some classes (e.g., the class of verbs taking a particular irregular past tense form) may be totally arbitrary.

Because the membership of certain classes cannot be predicted, it has to be specifically learned by speakers and explicitly described by linguists. This does not by itself establish the autonomy of grammar, except in the weakest sense (acknowledged by every linguist) that functional considerations fail to fully and uniquely determine every detail of language structure—the specific patterns and distributions of a language are shaped by convention and acquired through social interaction. Whether distributional restrictions support any stronger form of autonomy depends on what kind of apparatus is needed to describe them. There is in fact every reason to believe that only symbolic assemblies are necessary.

Complex expressions consist of symbolic assemblies, and the conventional patterns they instantiate consist of schematizations of such assemblies (recall Figs. 1.5 and 1.6). Depending on the supporting data, the process of schematization can be carried to any degree, and to different degrees for different facets of a construction. This produces hierarchies of schematized assemblies, illustrated by our previous example *THING THING* → *CONTAINER lid* → *jar lid* (where *THING THING* represents a very general pattern for nominal compounds, and *CONTAINER lid* is the low-level pattern abstracted from forms like *jar lid, pot lid, box lid,* and *coffin lid*). In view of the many possible levels and dimensions of schematization, as well as the many kinds of similarity exhibited by overlapping sets of complex expressions, we can reasonably envisage the emergence of vast, intersecting networks of schemas representing patterns with varying degrees of generality and salience. The full characterization of what linguists might consider to be a unified construction—e.g. nominal compounding, passive voice, or past tense formation—requires a substantial network in which certain schemas are categorized as instantiations or as extensions vis-à-vis others that are more abstract or more prototypical. Despite its complexity (which I believe to be both linguistically necessary and cognitively realistic), such a characterization does not imply a loss of generality: Any valid generalization is captured by a schema at the appropriate level of abstraction.

These networks are the locus of distributional knowledge. Even in cases where a high-level schema presumably emerges (e.g., *THING THING*), a network of instantiating structures specifies which regions within the large space of possibilities it defines are in fact conventionally exploited. Among these structures, capturing local generalizations, are low-level schemas pertaining to narrowly defined classes of elements. The lowest level structures in such a network are schemas incorporating specific lexical items as components (e.g., *CONTAINER lid*) and even actual expressions learned as units (*jar lid*). Symbolic assemblies that incorporate specific lexical items embody a speaker's knowledge of their distributional idiosyncrasies. Consider the English ditransitive construction, where a verb takes two postverbal nominal complements:

15. *She {gave/lent/bequeathed/*transferred} him a substantial amount of money.*

Not every verb potentially occurring in this construction actually does so, and although various partial regularities are captured by a network of low-level schemas (Goldberg, 1992, 1995), a certain amount of lexical specification is also necessary. It is provided by subschemas that mention particular verb stems. For example, the information that *bequeath* occurs in this construction resides in a subschema that incorporates this specific verb but that is schematic with regard to the nominal complements (there is no such schema for *transfer*). Similarly, the information that *break* follows a certain minor pattern in forming its past tense resides in the knowledge of the specific form *broke*, which instantiates that pattern.

Because language is learned through usage, it ought not be surprising that the preponderance of linguistic knowledge consists of specific expressions and low-level patterns, many of which incorporate particular lexical items. This is not to deny the existence and importance of general, productive patterns represented by high-level schemas. I would however suggest that fully general patterns constitute a distinct minority, that lower level structures provide critical information and do much if not most of the work in speaking and understanding. Attempts to impose a strict boundary between structural regularity and idiosyncrasy—attributing them to distinct modules or processing systems (Chomsky, 1965; Pinker & Prince, 1991)—are, I believe, both linguistically untenable and psychologically dubious. Instead, I envision a dynamic, interactive process whereby structures at all levels of abstraction compete for activation and for the privilege of being invoked in producing and understanding utterances (cf. Elman & McClelland, 1984; Langacker, 1988). Particular high-level schemas may be so entrenched and accessible (relative to alternative patterns or to subschemas) that they normally win the competition and prevail as general or default-case patterns. But even in such circumstances, specific instantiating expressions can be learned and accessed as units if they occur with sufficient frequency (Stemberger & MacWhinney, 1988). And in general, lower level structures have a built-in competitive advantage because their greater specificity enables them to match a potential target in many more respects, each contributing to their activation.

5. SUBJECT AND OBJECT

Although radical in relation to current dogma, cognitive grammar is not at all fanciful. It is highly conservative in what it assumes about cognition and what it allows the analyst to posit in describing a language. It has been successfully applied to a myriad of problems in diverse languages (see, for example, Achard, 1993; Casad, 1982; Cook, 1988; Janda, 1993; Maldonado, 1992; Manney, 1993; Rice, 1987; Rubba, 1993; Smith, 1993; Tuggy, 1988). Moreover, detailed accounts have been given of representative phenomena that have figured prominently in the theoretical literature and have often been cited in support of autonomous syntax. In particular, I would argue that the cognitive linguistic descriptions of English passives, "raising" constructions, and pronoun–antecedent relationships are more adequate and more revelatory than generative analyses (Langacker, 1982, 1995b; van Hoek, 1995, 1997).

One basic problem for a symbolic account of grammar is to characterize the notions of *subject* and *object*. There are few topics on which linguistic theorists exhibit such a striking lack of consensus. About the only thing virtually all of them agree on is that a conceptual definition valid for all subjects or all objects is just not feasible. I believe that such a characterization is indeed possible. It must however be suitably abstract, as well as psychologically plausible. As in the case of grammatical classes, we must seek a broadly applicable description at the level of general cognitive abilities initially manifested in the prototype. I propose that subject and object status ultimately reduces to a kind of *focal prominence* conferred on participants in a profiled relationship.

In particular, subject and object nominals are identified as respectively specifying the *trajector* and the *landmark* of a profiled relationship. These latter notions have in turn been described in various ways (Langacker, 1990, 1991, 1997a). I characterized a trajector as (a) the *primary figure* in a profiled relationship, (b) the element one is *primarily* concerned with describing or locating (a clause-internal "topic"), and (c) the *initial focus of attention* ("starting point") in a chain representing the order in which elements are *accessed* in building up to a full conception of the profiled relation. The characterization of a landmark is obtained by replacing the words *primary*, *primarily*, and *initial* with *secondary*, *secondarily*, and *second* (i.e., changing "1" to "2"). I conceive of points (a) to (c) as being complementary and mutually compatible. In referring to trajector and landmark as *primary* and *secondary focal participants*, I intend to subsume all three.

Stated more precisely, the proposal is as follows: A *subject* (or *object*), at a given level of organization, is a nominal element that elaborates the trajector (or landmark) of the relationship profiled at that level. A nominal element is one that profiles a thing, and it elaborates a trajector or landmark by virtue of its profile corresponding to it. Consider the sentence *Alice admires Bill*, whose semantic pole (ignoring tense) is sketched in Fig. 1.7. *Admire(s)* profiles a relationship of mental experience (indicated by a dashed arrow). Its trajector is the experiencer, and its landmark is the target of experience. *Alice* and *Bill* are nominal expressions, for they profile "things," whose semantic specifications are abbreviated as "A" and "B." Following usual assumptions regarding constituency, *admires* and *Bill* combine, at one level of organization, to form the composite structure *admires Bill*. At a higher level of organization, *admires Bill* combines with *Alice* to give the overall composite structure *Alice admires Bill*. Observe that the same experiential process is profiled at three levels: by the verb *admire(s)*, by the "verb phrase" *admires Bill*, and by the full clause *Alice admires Bill*. Tracing along correspondence lines (both vertical and horizontal) reveals

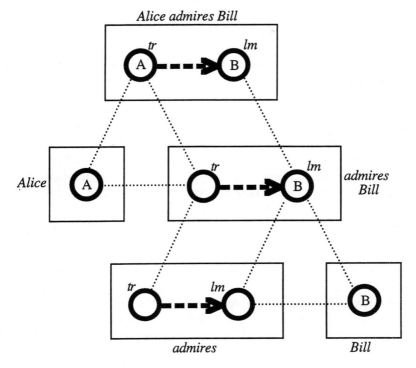

FIG. 1.7. A symbolic assembly illustrating the definition of subject and object.

that *Alice* elaborates the trajector of this process at all three levels, and *Bill* the landmark. Thus, *Alice* is identified as the subject, and *Bill* the object, with respect to the verb, the verb phrase, and the clause.

This proposal exemplifies the working strategy noted at the outset, namely to seek characterizations that are simultaneously reasonable from the psychological standpoint, well motivated in purely semantic terms, and optimal as a basis for analyzing grammar. Let us first consider semantic motivation. I have already indicated that the trajector/landmark distinction is necessary just to describe the meanings of relational expressions. An adequate description has to capture the semantic contrast between pairs like *above* and *below* (also *before* vs. *after*, *in front of* vs. *in back of*, *precede* vs. *follow*, etc.), which have the same conceptual content and which profile the same relationship (Fig. 1.3). Constructs like trajector and landmark, pertaining to the salience and accessibility of the relational participants, would seem to offer the only possible basis for distinguishing them. The claim, then, is that a sentence like (16a) is primarily concerned with locating the alarm button, and evokes the light switch as a landmark for doing so, whereas (16b) shows the opposite alignment:

16. a. *The alarm button is just above the light switch.*
    b. *The light switch is just below the alarm button.*

Discourse considerations provide supporting evidence. Observe that only (16a) is natural in response to the question *Where is the alarm button?*, whereas (16b) responds to *Where is the light switch?* This illustrates Chafe's discourse-based characterization of a subject as "a starting point to which other information is added" (1994, p. 92). The question *Where is X?* establishes *X* in the discourse as the obvious point of departure for the answer.

What about cognitive plausibility? We can start by noting that figure/ground organization is a well established perceptual phenomenon and that the figure in a scene is the first element to catch our attention. Moreover, I presume there is nothing inherently implausible about supposing that figure/ground organization (or something directly analogous to it) is also prevalent at higher levels of conceptualization. The trajector/landmark asymmetry in relational expressions does in fact exhibit certain tendencies suggesting a strong affinity to figure/ground organization. Talmy (1978) pointed out that factors contributing to the choice of perceptual figure—notably compactness and mobility—also tend to be associated with the elements I would identify as relational trajectors. For instance, (17a) is far more natural than (17b), given usual assumptions about the relative size and mobility of the participants:

17. a. *The bicycle is next to the church.*
    b. *?*The church is next to the bicycle.*

There are, of course, many cases where opposite trajector/landmark alignments are both permitted, e.g. the active/passive alternation, as in (18), or lexical alternations like *above/below, in front of/in back of, before/after,* and so forth:

18. a. *Iraq invaded Kuwait.*
    b. *Kuwait was invaded by Iraq.*

Intuitively I regard these alternations as being quite comparable to the phenomenon of figure/ground reversal. Partial support for this comparison derives from the fact that in both cases, there is usually a preference for one of the alternate alignments. In (14b), for example, it is easier to perceive groups of x's standing out as figure against a background of dashes than to do the opposite. Likewise, an active is unmarked relative to its corresponding passive, and forms like *above, in front of,* and *before* are the default members of their respective pairs. Furthermore, the neutral member of these oppositions is usually the one that confers trajector status on the entity that is most easily chosen as the perceptual figure. As the terms themselves indicate, an "active" clause subject tends to be more mobile and energetic than its "passive" clause counterpart. Also, if X is *above* or *in front of* Y, it is X that we are more likely to see, and if X comes *before* Y, it is X that we will first encounter.

A variety of experimental findings are interpretable as lending plausibility to the proposed characterization of grammatical subjects. I hasten to add that the interpretation is in each case my own, and that the investigators were not specifically concerned with subjects per se. To show the relevance of this work, I need to say just a word about the broader theoretical context in which my proposal is situated (Langacker, 1993b, 1997a). Myriad linguistic phenomena call out for description in terms of conceptualizations that are *dynamic* in the sense that the temporal axis—how they unfold through processing time—is critical to their value. They involve successive foci of attention, each occurring in a context evoked by its predecessor. In a *focus chain* of this sort, directing attention to a given element results in the conceptualizer orienting to a new context within which the next focus can be detected. Equivalently, I speak of a *reference point* providing mental *access* to a set of potential *targets*, which collectively constitute its *dominion*. The initial focus (or reference point) in such a chain can be called a *starting point*. We find clear examples of reference point chains in certain possessive and locative constructions:

19. a. *Tom's mother's cousin's friend's lover's psychiatrist*
    b. *Your keys are downstairs, in the study, on the desk, under some papers.*

In (19a), a focus chain leads from Tom, the starting point, to a particular psychiatrist, the ultimate target. Each possessor serves in turn as a reference point, in which capacity it evokes a dominion containing the possessed, which can then be put in focus as the next reference point. Similarly, the successive locatives in (19b) direct attention to smaller and smaller spatial areas, each of which contains the next, and thus affords mental access to it.

It needs to be emphasized that the conceptualizations associated with most expressions are complex and multifaceted, so that no single ordering accounts for all their properties. There are numerous kinds of focus chains, which can coexist without necessarily being coaligned, each pertaining to a different level or dimension of linguistic organization. Besides possession and location, exemplified in (19), natural orderings are given by such factors as the temporal sequence of events, the transmission of force from participant to participant along a causal chain, and successive access to a series of minds, each conceiving of the next (e.g., *Fred believes Sally suspects*

Bob knows Martha likes him). Along the axis of speech time, the words in a sentence constitute a focus chain that can correlate with any of the others and thereby heighten its salience. With respect to the tracking of referents in a discourse, salient nominals emerge as reference points, establishing structural dominions within which compatible pronouns are freely interpretable as being coreferential to them. A "topic" (at a given level of organization) is a reference point anchoring a realm of knowledge or experience (its dominion) into which one or a series of propositions is to be integrated.

In the context of this general scheme, it is reasonable to view the trajector/landmark asymmetry as a special kind of focus chain. Trajector and landmark would then be characterized as initial and second focus in a natural ordering pertaining to relational participants. Specifically, because the conception of a relationship presupposes the conception of its participants, we can describe a trajector (and landmark) as the first (and optionally the second) participant saliently evoked in building up to the full conceptualization of a profiled relation. If I conceive of a person, for example, I can use this as a starting point to anchor the more elaborate conception of a person engaging in some activity—such as motion, perception, or the exertion of force—that may well involve its interaction with a second focused participant. Verbs impose this kind of asymmetry as an inherent aspect of their lexical semantic value. At the lexical level (where events are categorized into conventionally recognized types), the more active participant is usually chosen as a starting point. At higher levels of grammatical organization, where discourse considerations come into play, other options are available. For instance, the passive construction allows us to evoke a nonactive participant as a starting point, using it to anchor the more elaborate conception of an event in which it has a patientlike role.

Turning now to the experimental findings, MacWhinney (1977) presented a variety of evidence (from experimental tasks involving rating, elicited production, problem solving, verification, production, and recall) that "the speaker uses the first element in the English sentence as a starting point for the organization of the sentence as a whole," where a starting point serves as basis for "the ACTIVE CONSTRUCTION OF AN ACTIVE PERSPECTIVE" (p. 152). Similarly, Gernsbacher and Hargreaves (1992) explained numerous experimental results, notably pertaining to the "privilege" of initial elements, in terms of the "structure building framework." They suggest that building coherent mental representations first involves "laying a foundation," and that subsequent information that "coheres or relates to previous information is mapped onto the developing structure" (p. 87). Moreover, recent experimental work by Verfaillie and Daems (1996) pointed to agents being accessed more rapidly than patients:

> . . . [W]hen a prototypical causal relation can be perceived directly and when the participants in the event maintain their role for an extended time interval, agent information is accessed more rapidly than patient information. The prominence of the agent over the patient in grammatical phenomena is parallelled by a privileged status of the agent at the level of perceptual processing. It is tempting to speculate that the observation that the agent is a prototypical subject and that the subject in canonical sentences surfaces before the object, can be traced back to the fact that, during visual event perception, agent information is available earlier for further processing than patient information. (p. 144)

Although these formulations do not refer specifically to grammatical subjects, they help render plausible the general type of characterization proposed. In most of the cases cited by MacWhinney and by Gernsbacher and Hargreaves, the initial element was in fact the subject. We can further note the cross-linguistic tendency for agents to be chosen as subjects, and for subjects to precede objects in basic word order. These studies strongly suggest that order of access is important in language processing, and that the conception evoked by a clause is actively constructed on the foundation provided by a starting point. In the overall scheme outlined earlier, a complex expression comprises numerous natural orderings pertaining to different levels and dimensions of organization. Hence, there ought to be some proclivity for their starting points to coincide, which we do in fact observe in canonical clauses like *He broke it*, where the initial word is also the subject, the agent, and the topic. By the same token, experimental findings indicating that agents are accessed quickly and that initial elements provide the starting point for structure building lend some credence to the characterization of subjects in such terms.

If the studies just described offer circumstantial evidence for the proposed characterization of subjects, some experimental results reported by Tomlin (1995) are perhaps the equivalent of a smoking gun (see also Forrest, 1996). Tomlin's basic hypothesis—fully compatible with my proposal—was that, at the time of utterance formulation, the speaker codes the referent currently in focal attention as the syntactic subject of the sentence. He tested it by controlling the attention of experimental subjects as they observed a two-participant event, which they then encoded verbally with either an active or a passive sentence. The event consisted of one fish swallowing another, and attention was directed to one of the fish (by means of an arrow flashed on the screen) just 150 ms prior to the swallowing—too brief an interval for attention to wander in between. Tomlin thus predicted that attention focused on the swallowing fish would lead to the production of an active sentence (e.g., *The red fish swallowed the blue fish*), whereas attention focused on the swallowee would lead to production of a passive (*The blue fish was swallowed by the red fish*). This proved to be the case nearly 100% of the time.

Tomlin's results are of course insufficient to conclusively establish the proposed characterization of subjects. They do not, for example, clearly distinguish between grammatical subject and initial clausal element. They do, however, enhance the plausibility of claiming that subjecthood is ultimately a matter of focal prominence, interpretable as order of access to relational participants. Pointing in the same direction are numerous grammatical considerations, some of which are now briefly summarized.

An initial point is that the characterization is sufficiently abstract, hence flexible enough in application, to handle the full range of subjects and objects. Depending on what relationship is profiled, for example, the subject can occupy any position in a causal chain (cf. Fillmore, 1968):

20. a. *She opened the door with this key.* [subject = agent]
    b. *This key opened the door.* [subject = instrument]
    c. *The door opened.* [subject = patient]

The characterization accommodates the subject in passives and various other "special" constructions, without requiring derivation from hypothetical underlying structures. It also accounts directly for a striking asymmetry: A landmark implies a trajector, but not conversely. In (20c), for example, the single participant has an objectlike semantic role but is nonetheless realized as the grammatical subject. This is a consequence of the trajector and landmark being the *initial* and *second* focal elements: Something can be second only if something else comes first. Note that this asymmetry pertains specifically to trajector/landmark alignment—"argument structure"—irrespective of whether the focal elements are actually spelled out by overt nominal expressions. For instance, an imperative like *Shut the door!* has both a trajector (understood as the addressee) and a landmark, even though only the latter is overtly realized.

The proposed characterization of subject and object makes no reference to grammatical constituency, but rather to correspondences, profiling, and focal prominence: A nominal expression qualifies as a subject by virtue of its profile corresponding to the trajector of a profiled relationship, and as an object when its profile corresponds to the landmark. Although Fig. 1.7 assumes the familiar S[VO] constituency for *Alice saw Bill*, the same grammatical relations are assigned with [SV]O constituency (where *Alice* first combines with *saw*, and *Bill* then elaborates the landmark of *Alice saw*), or even with a "flat" SVO structure. There are indeed constructions that manifest [SV] constituents:

21. a. *The lawyer [we hired] was incompetent.*
    b. *[Jack sort of liked] but [Jill really detested] that movie we plan to see.*

In cognitive grammar, these can simply be assembled as [SV] constituents—there is no need to posit derivations from underlying structures with the canonical S[VO] arrangement. And of course, the well-known problem posed by languages with VSO word order does not even arise, because the characterization of objects does not depend on a [VO] constituent.

The characterization of subject and object in terms of primary and secondary focal prominence is fully consonant with, if not responsible for, their high levels of grammatical activity. Although every construction has its own rationale, and other factors (including other sorts of prominence) come into play, it stands to reason that focal participants tend to be recruited for purposes of agreement, clause linkage, antecedence, etc. Keenan and Comrie (1977) posited a universal hierarchy for access to relative clause formation that we can abbreviate as Subject > Object > Other, and most frameworks adopt this hierarchy for various reasons. In my view, the high accessibility of subjects and objects directly reflects their intrinsic nature.

Particularly strong support comes from van Hoek's analysis of pronoun-antecedent relationships (van Hoek, 1995, 1997). She achieved an impressively comprehensive and unified account in terms of reference-point organization, such that a nominal with sufficient salience establishes a dominion within which a suitable pronoun is freely interpretable as being coreferential to it. The hierarchy Subject > Object > Other proves quite important in this regard. As shown in (22), a subject can function as the antecedent of any other nominal element, but not conversely, and an object can serve as antecedent for any element other than the subject (elements in bold are to be construed as coreferential):

22. a. **Tom** likes **his** mother.
    b. *__He__ likes **Tom's** mother.
    c. Jenny put **the kitten** in **its** box.
    d. *Jenny put **it** in **the kitten's** box.

The special, ranked ability of subject and object to serve as reference points in pronominal anaphora nicely corroborates their characterization as first and second foci on the reference-point chain defined in terms of access to relational participants.

It needs to be emphasized that the focal prominence of subject and object is not *inherited from* the entities chosen for this status, but rather is *imposed on* them by the very fact of their being singled out in this way. Trajector/landmark alignment is an aspect of construal, inherent in how a situation is conceptualized, as opposed to being objectively given. Although trajector status will naturally tend to be conferred on an entity that is salient for other reasons, such as an agent or a discourse topic, it is not fully predictable from such factors, nor reducible to them. From this perspective, examples with so-called "dummy" subjects, as in (23), are not necessarily problematic:

23. a. *There are alligators in the moat.*
    b. *It was obvious that the house had not been cleaned.*

I do regard items like *there* and *it* as meaningful. They can be thought of as abstract "settings" or "presentational frames," subjective counterparts of the deictic *there* and referential *it*. Instead of referring to a specific place or thing, they announce the subsequent introduction of a local or global circumstance. Now, certainly an abstract presentational frame has no objective basis or intrinsic salience—it is not there beforehand to *attract* focal prominence, and its abstract nature ensures that it will not seem terribly salient even when invoked to bear it. I suggest, then, that such elements are coherently subsumed in the proposed analysis as a limiting case. Recall that primary focal prominence is being explicated in terms of *initial access* in conceptualizing a relationship. This is quite compatible with the description of *there* and *it* as referring to presentational frames announcing the subsequent introduction of a situation.

Observe next the privileged status of subjects in equational sentences, which specify the identity of nominal referents. Now, identity per se would seem to be a symmetrical relationship. Objectively, the sentences in (24) describe the same situation:

24. a. *My father is the mayor.*
    b. *The mayor is my father.*

Yet, they contrast linguistically in just the way predicted by the characterization of subject as starting point, as the element one is primarily concerned with describing or locating. Hence, (24a) would be the more natural response if I asked you to tell me about your father, and (24b) if I asked you to tell me about the mayor. The linguistic asymmetry is especially striking with plural generics:

25. a. *Wombats are marsupials.*
    b. **Marsupials are wombats.*

I would analyze these as equational sentences that establish identity between sets of indefinite size comprising "arbitrary instances" of the wombat and marsupial categories (Langacker, 1991). Because the extension of wombats is included in the extension of marsupials, a set of wombats (even the maximal set) can always be equated with a set of marsupials, but not conversely. Thus (25a) will always be valid, for it initially focuses on a set of wombats and describes it as coinciding with a set of marsupials. But if we start with a set of marsupials, as in (25b), its coincidence with a set of wombats cannot be assumed.

Finally, I mention that numerous grammatical phenomena point to a special affinity between subjects (and secondarily, objects) on the one hand, and possessors on the other. To take just one example, it is very common across languages for possessive constructions to be used in specifying the trajector, and often the landmark, of a nominalized verb. English makes liberal use of both options, e.g. *Booth's assassination (of Lincoln), Lincoln's assassination (by Booth)*. This affinity is quite expected given my description of possessors as reference points affording mental access to the entities possessed (Langacker, 1993b). A possessive relationship holds between two things, one accessible via the other, whereas a verbal trajector and landmark are points of access to the conception of a process. When a verb is nominalized (e.g., *assassinate* ---> *assassination*), the process it designates undergoes a conceptual reification and is thereby construed as an abstract thing. As a consequence, the reference-point relationship between a processual participant and the reified process becomes a relation between two things, which makes it susceptible to possessive encoding.

6. CONCLUSION

Cognitive grammar identifies meaning with conceptualization and emphasizes our capacity for construing the same situation in alternate ways. Once construal is properly recognized and accommodated, the meaningfulness of grammatical structure becomes apparent. Grammar is symbolic in nature, wholly reducible to assemblies of symbolic structures (form-meaning pairings). It consists of patterns for imposing and symbolizing particular ways of construing the more specific conceptual content provided by lexical items. But specificity is a matter of degree, and lexical items also impose construals. Despite the traditional dichotomy, lexicon and grammar form a continuous spectrum of symbolic assemblies distinguished primarily by their level of abstraction, hence the generality of the patterns they embody. Cognitive grammar treats them all in a unified manner and acknowledges the critical role of low-level schemas (often incorporating particular lexical items) representing generalizations of limited scope. By reducing lexicon, morphology, and syntax to a continuum of symbolic assemblies, the framework achieves a major conceptual unification. It is also highly restrictive, in that all structures ascribed to a linguistic system must either be directly encountered as parts of occurring expressions, or else capable of emerging from them through the basic processes of abstraction and categorization.

The descriptive and theoretical notions of cognitive grammar were formulated primarily on the basis of linguistic considerations and justified by their efficacy in handling the subtle complexities of representative language data. Although certain assumptions are indeed made about cognitive processing, and various psychological phenomena are invoked (e.g., fig-ure/ground alignment, prototype categorization, grouping, focusing of attention), for the most part these are either well established or virtually self-evident. Less straightforward (and certainly controversial) is the issue of whether the specific use made of them for the description of language structure is optimal and appropriate. I believe the internal coherence and descriptive achievements of the framework suggest a positive answer. At some point, however, other kinds of evidence have to be sought more systematically and on a larger scale than they have to date. To be sure, particular claims and ideas of cognitive grammar have been employed or tested in a number of acquisitional, clinical, computational, and experi-mental studies (e.g., Barsalou et al., 1993; Holmqvist, 1993; Jurafsky, 1996; Kellogg, 1993, 1994, 1996; Ryder, 1994; Sandra & Rice, 1995; Tomasello, 1992; Verfaillie & Daems, 1996). Such research is steadily gaining preva-lence and influence in all facets of linguistics. It is especially welcome in cognitive linguistics and cognitive grammar.

REFERENCES

Achard, M. (1993). *Complementation in French: A cognitive perspective.* Unpublished doctoral dissertation, University of California, San Diego.

Barsalou, L. W., Yeh, W., Luka, B. J., Olseth, K. L., Mix, K. S., & Wu, L.-L. (1993). Concepts and meaning. *Papers from the Regional Meeting of the Chicago Linguistic Society, 29*(2), 23–61.

Casad, E. H. (1982). *Cora locationals and structured imagery.* Unpublished doctoral dissertation, University of California, San Diego.

Chafe, W. (1994). *Discourse, consciousness, and time: The flow and displacement of conscious experience in speaking and writing.* Chicago and London: University of Chicago Press.

Chomsky, N. (1957). *Syntactic structures.* The Hague: Mouton.

Chomsky, N. (1965). *Aspects of the theory of syntax.* Cambridge, MA: MIT Press.

Cook, K. W. (1988). *A cognitive analysis of grammatical relations, case, and transitivity in Samoan.* Unpublished doctoral dissertation, University of California, San Diego.

Downing, P. (1977). On the creation and use of English compound nouns. *Language, 53,* 810–842.

Elman, J. L., & McClelland, J. L. (1984). Speech perception as a cognitive process: The interactive activation model. In N. Lass (Ed.), *Speech and language* (pp. 337–374). New York: Academic Press.

Fauconnier, G. (1985). *Mental spaces: Aspects of meaning construction in natural language.* Cambridge, MA and London: MIT Press/Bradford.

Fauconnier, G., & Sweetser, E. (Eds.). (1996). *Spaces, worlds, and grammar.* Chicago and London: University of Chicago Press.

Fauconnier, G., & Turner, M. (1994). *Conceptual projection and middle spaces* (Report No. 9401). San Diego: Department of Cognitive Science, University of California.

Fauconnier, G., & Turner, M. (1996). Blending as a central process of grammar. In A. E. Goldberg (Ed.), *Conceptual structure, discourse and language* (pp. 113–130). Stanford: CSLI Publications.

Fillmore, C. J. (1968). The case for case. In E. Bach & R. T. Harms (Eds.), *Universals in linguistic theory* (pp. 1–88). New York: Holt, Rinehart & Winston.

Forrest, L. B. (1996). Discourse goals and attentional processes in sentence production: The dynamic construal of events. In A. E. Goldberg (Ed.), *Conceptual structure, discourse and language* (pp. 149–161). Stanford: CSLI Publications.

Gentner, D. (1981). Some interesting differences between verbs and nouns. *Cognition and Brain Theory, 4,* 161–178.

Gentner, D. (1982). Why nouns are learned before verbs: Linguistic relativity versus natural patterning. In S. Kuczaj (Ed.), *Language development I: Syntax and semantics* (pp. 301–334). Hillsdale, NJ: Lawrence Erlbaum Associates.

Gernsbacher, M. A., & Hargreaves, D. (1992). The privilege of primacy: Experimental data and cognitive explanations. In D. L. Payne (Ed.), *Pragmatics of word order flexibility* (pp. 83–116). Amsterdam and Philadelphia: John Benjamins.

Goldberg, A. E. (1992). The inherent semantics of argument structure: The case of the English ditransitive construction. *Cognitive Linguistics, 3,* 37–74.

Goldberg, A. E. (1995). *Constructions: A construction grammar approach to argument structure.* Chicago and London: University of Chicago Press.

Haiman, J. (1980). Dictionaries and encyclopedias. *Lingua, 50,* 329–357.

Harder, P. (1996). *Functional semantics: A theory of meaning, structure and tense in English.* Berlin and New York: Mouton.

Holmqvist, K. (1993). *Implementing cognitive semantics.* Lund, Sweden: Lund University, Department of Cognitive Science.

Jackendoff, R. (1994). *Patterns in the mind: Language and human nature.* New York: Basic Books.

Janda, L. A. (1990). The radial network of a grammatical category—its genesis and dynamic structure. *Cognitive Linguistics, 1,* 269–288.

Janda, L. A. (1993). *A geography of case semantics: The Czech dative and the Russian instrumental.* Berlin and New York: Mouton.

Jurafsky, D. (1996). A probabilistic model of lexical and syntactic access and disambiguation. *Cognitive Science, 20,* 137–194.

Keenan, E. L., & Comrie, B. (1977). Noun phrase accessibility and universal grammar. *Linguistic Inquiry, 8,* 63–99.

Kellogg, M. K. (1993). When a "cat" is a "cow" and "hearing" is "understanding"; paraphasia and the conceptualization of nouns and verbs. *Papers from the Regional Meeting of the Chicago Linguistic Society, 29*(2), 201–215.

Kellogg, M. K. (1994). Conceptual mechanisms underlying noun and verb categorization: Evidence from paraphasia. *Proceedings of the Annual Meeting of the Berkeley Linguistics Society, 20,* 300–309.

Kellogg, M. K. (1996). *Neurolinguistic evidence of some conceptual properties of nouns and verbs.* Unpublished doctoral dissertation, University of California, San Diego.

Lakoff, G. (1987). *Women, fire, and dangerous things: What categories reveal about the mind.* Chicago and London: University of Chicago Press.

Lakoff, G., & Johnson, M. (1980). *Metaphors we live by.* Chicago: University of Chicago Press.

Lakoff, G., & Turner, M. (1989). *More than cool reason: A field guide to poetic metaphor.* Chicago and London: University of Chicago Press.

Langacker, R. W. (1982). Space grammar, analysability, and the English passive. *Language, 58,* 22–80.

Langacker, R. W. (1986). Abstract motion. *Proceedings of the Annual Meeting of the Berkeley Linguistics Society, 12,* 455–471.

Langacker, R. W. (1987a). *Foundations of cognitive grammar* (Vol. 1). Stanford: Stanford University Press.

Langacker, R. W. (1987b). Nouns and verbs. *Language, 63,* 53–94.

Langacker, R. W. (1988). A usage-based model. In B. Rudzka-Ostyn (Ed.), *Topics in cognitive linguistics* (pp. 127–161). Amsterdam and Philadelphia: John Benjamins.

Langacker, R. W. (1990). *Concept, image, and symbol: The cognitive basis of grammar.* Berlin and New York: Mouton.

Langacker, R. W. (1991). *Foundations of cognitive grammar* (Vol. 2). Stanford: Stanford University Press.

Langacker, R. W. (1992). The symbolic nature of cognitive grammar: The meaning of *of* and of *of*-periphrasis. In M. Pütz (Ed.), *Thirty years of linguistic evolution: Studies in honour of René Dirven on the occasion of his sixtieth birthday* (pp. 483–502). Philadelphia and Amsterdam: John Benjamins.

Langacker, R. W. (1993a). Grammatical traces of some "invisible" semantic constructs. *Language Sciences, 15,* 323–355.

Langacker, R. W. (1993b). Reference-point constructions. *Cognitive Linguistics, 4,* 1–38.

Langacker, R. W. (1995a). Conceptual grouping and constituency in cognitive grammar. In Linguistic Society of Korea (Ed.), *Linguistics in the morning calm 3* (pp. 149–172). Seoul: Hanshin.

Langacker, R. W. (1995b). Raising and transparency. *Language, 71,* 1–62.

Langacker, R. W. (1997a). A dynamic account of grammatical function. In J. Bybee, J. Haiman, & S. A. Thompson (Eds.), *Essays on language function and language type dedicated to T. Givón* (pp. 249–273). Amsterdam and Philadelphia: John Benjamins.

Langacker, R. W. (1997b). Constituency, dependency, and conceptual grouping. *Cognitive Linguistics, 8,* 1–32.

MacWhinney, B. (1977). Starting points. *Language, 53,* 152–168.

Maldonado, R. (1992). *Middle voice: The case of Spanish "se".* Unpublished doctoral dissertation, University of California, San Diego.

Manney, L. (1993). *Middle voice in Modern Greek.* Unpublished doctoral dissertation, University of California, San Diego.

Matsumoto, Y. (1996a). Subject motion and English and Japanese verbs. *Cognitive Linguistics, 7,* 183–226.

Matsumoto, Y. (1996b). Subjective-change expressions in Japanese and their cognitive and linguistic bases. In G. Fauconnier & E. Sweetser (Eds.), *Spaces, worlds, and grammar* (pp. 124–156). Chicago and London: University of Chicago Press.

Nunberg, G. (1995). Transfers of meaning. *Journal of Semantics, 12,* 109–132.

Pinker, S., & Prince, A. (1991). Regular and irregular morphology and the psychological status of rules of grammar. *Proceedings of the Annual Meeting of the Berkeley Linguistics Society, 17,* 230–251.

Reddy, M. J. (1979). The conduit metaphor—a case of frame conflict in our language about language. In A. Ortony (Ed.), *Metaphor and thought* (pp. 284–324). Cambridge, England: Cambridge University Press.

Reid, W. (1991). *Verb and noun number in English: A functional explanation.* London and New York: Longman.

Rice, S. (1987). *Towards a cognitive model of transitivity.* Unpublished doctoral dissertation, University of California, San Diego.

Rubba, J. E. (1993). *Discontinuous morphology in Modern Aramaic.* Unpublished doctoral dissertation, University of California, San Diego.

Ryder, M. E. (1991). Mixers, mufflers and mousers: The extending of the -er suffix as a case of prototype reanalysis. *Proceedings of the Annual Meeting of the Berkeley Linguistics Society, 17,* 299–311.

Ryder, M. E. (1994). *Ordered chaos: The interpretation of English noun–noun compounds.* Berkeley: University of California Press.

Sandra, D., & Rice, S. (1995). Network analyses of prepositional meaning: Mirroring whose mind—the linguist's or the language user's? *Cognitive Linguistics, 6,* 89–130.

Slobin, D. I. (1987). Thinking for speaking. *Proceedings of the Annual Meeting of the Berkeley Linguistics Society, 13,* 435–445.

Smith, M. B. (1993). Aspects of German clause structure from a cognitive grammar perspective. *Studi Italiani di Linguistica Teorica e Applicata, 22,* 601–638.

Stemberger, J. P., & MacWhinney, B. (1988). Are inflected forms stored in the lexicon? In M. Hammond & M. Noonan (Eds.), *Theoretical morphology: Approaches in modern linguistics* (pp. 101–116). San Diego: Academic Press.

Talmy, L. (1978). Figure and ground in complex sentences. In J. H. Greenberg (Ed.), *Universals of human language* (Vol. 4, pp. 625–649). Stanford: Stanford University Press.

Talmy, L. (1988). The relation of grammar to cognition. In B. Rudzka-Ostyn (Ed.), *Topics in cognitive linguistics* (pp. 165–205). Amsterdam and Philadelphia: John Benjamins.

Talmy, L. (1996). Fictive motion in language and "ception." In P. Bloom, M. A. Peterson, L. Nadel, & M. F. Garrett (Eds.), *Language and space.* Cambridge, MA: MIT Press.

Taylor, J. R. (1995). *Linguistic categorization: Prototypes in linguistic theory* (2nd ed.). Oxford, England: Clarendon.

Tomasello, M. (1992). *First verbs: A case study of early grammatical development.* Cambridge, England: Cambridge University Press.

Tomlin, R. S. (1995). Focal attention, voice, and word order. In P. Downing & M. Noonan (Eds.), *Word order in discourse* (pp. 517–554). Amsterdam and Philadelphia: John Benjamins.

Tuggy, D. (1988). Náhuatl causative/applicatives in cognitive grammar. In B. Rudzka-Ostyn (Ed.), *Topics in cognitive linguistics* (pp. 587–618). Amsterdam and Philadelphia: John Benjamins.

Turner, M., & Fauconnier, G. (1995). Conceptual integration and formal expression. *Metaphor and Symbolic Activity, 10,* 183–204.

van Hoek, K. (1995). Conceptual reference points: A cognitive grammar account of pronominal anaphora constraints. *Language, 71,* 310–340.

van Hoek, K. (1997). *Anaphora and conceptual structure.* Chicago: University of Chicago Press.

Verfaillie, K., & Daems, A. (1996). The priority of the agent in visual event perception: On the cognitive basis of grammatical agent–patient asymmetries. *Cognitive Linguistics, 7,* 131–147.

Wierzbicka, A. (1995). Dictionaries vs. encyclopaedias: How to draw the line. In P. W. Davis (Ed.), *Alternative linguistics: Descriptive and theoretical modes* (pp. 289–315). Amsterdam and Philadelphia: John Benjamins.

Chapter 2

The Functional Approach to Grammar

T. Givón
University of Oregon

1. INTRODUCTION

It is hardly controversial to assert that human language as we know it combines two major mega-functions:

- representation of knowledge
- communication of represented knowledge

The best point of departure for a functional approach to human language should be the evolutionary-adaptive approach to Biology, a discipline that has been profoundly functionalist for over 2,000 years.

Functionalism in Biology harkens back to Aristotle, who more or less single-handedly dislodged the two structuralist schools that had dominated Greek biological thought up to his time. Both schools sought to understand live organisms it terms of, purely, their structure, the way they understood inorganic matter. The Empedoclean school proposed to explain living organisms by their component elements, i.e. their chemistry. The Democritan school opted for understanding organisms through their component parts, i.e. their structure.

In his *De Partibus Animalium*, Aristotle concludes his refutation of these structuralist approaches as follows:

> . . . if a piece of wood is to be split with an axe, the axe must of necessity be hard; and, if hard, it must of necessity be made of bronze or iron. Now

exactly in the same way the body, which like the axe is an *instrument*—for both the body as a whole and its several parts individually have definite operations for which they are made; just in the same way, I say, the body if it is to do its work [i.e. function; TG], must of necessity be of such and such character . . . (*De Partibus Animalium*, McKeon (Ed.), 1941, p. 650; italics added)

Ever since Aristotle, structuralism—the idea that biological structure is arbitrary and thus requires no explanation, or worse, somehow explains itself—has been a dead horse in biology, a discipline where common-sense functionalism is taken for granted like mother's milk. As one contemporary introductory textbook puts it:

. . . anatomy is the science that deals with the structure of the body . . . physiology is defined as the science of function. Anatomy and physiology have more meaning when studied together . . . (Crouch, 1978, pp. 9–10)

Unfortunately, it was also Aristotle in his discussion of the relation between external reality, mind and language who inaugurated the structuralist approach to language. In his *De Interpretatione*, Aristotle presents one of the earliest discussions about the relation between reality, mind and language:

. . . Now spoken sounds ['words'] are symbols of affections of the soul ['thoughts'], and written marks are symbols of spoken sounds. And just as written marks are not the same for all men ['are language specific'], neither are spoken sounds. But what these are in the first place signs of—affections of the soul—are the same for all ['are universal']; and what are these affections are likenesses of—actual things—are also the same for all men . . . (*De Interpretatione*, Tr. & Ed. by J. L. Ackrill, 1963)

From Aristotle's empiricist perspective, thoughts ('affections of the soul') reflect external reality ('actual things') faithfully, indeed iconically ('are likenesses of'). And this reflective relation is universal ('the same for all men'). In contrast, linguistic expressions ('words') bear an arbitrary relation ('are symbols of') to thoughts. And this relation is not universal ('not the same for all men').

It is true, of course, that Aristotle's doctrine of the arbitrariness of the linguistic sign, i.e. the arbitrariness of cross-language differences, referred only to the phonological coding of concepts (words). But the structuralist linguists of early 20th Century, from Saussure to Bloomfield and ultimately to Chomsky, unreflectively extended the arbitrariness doctrine to grammar.

In this chapter, I would like to outline the main tenets of a functionalist approach to grammar. In particular, I would like to show how extremely compatible this approach is with cognitive neuropsychology. I will begin with surveying the place of grammar within the human knowledge-representation and communication system.

2. GRAMMAR AND HUMAN INFORMATION PROCESSING

2.1. The Components of Human Communication

Well-coded human communicative system combines a number of distinct modules that can be divided, broadly, into two sub-systems:

- The cognitive representation system
- The communicative code system

The human cognitive representation system comprises of three concentrically linked levels:

- The conceptual lexicon
- Propositional information
- Multi-propositional discourse

The communicative coding system comprises of two distinct coding instruments:

- The peripheral sensory-motor code
- The grammatical code

2.2. The Cognitive Representation System

2.2.1. The Conceptual Lexicon

The human lexicon is a repository of relatively time-stable, socially-shared, well-coded knowledge about our external-physical, social-cultural and internal-mental universe. By 'relatively time-stable' one means knowledge that is not in rapid flux. By 'socially shared' one means that when launching into communication, speakers take it for granted that words have roughly the same meaning for all members of the same speech community. By 'well-coded' one means that each chunk of lexically-stored knowledge is more-or-less uniquely—or at least strongly—associated with its own perceptual code-label.

The conceptual lexicon is most likely organized as a network of nodes and connections. Given a certain level of homophony ('ambiguity'), the uniqueness of the code-meaning relations is not absolute, but is rather a strong tendency. A word-node automatically activates a prototypical cluster of other, closely-related, word-nodes (Swinney, 1979), in a pattern that used to be referred to as *spreading activation* (Neeley, 1990). But the degree ('distance') to which the activation a single node on a single occasion spreads within the network is the subject of considerable contextual variation, not to mention debate.

Within the lexical-semantic network, nodes stand for individual concepts or words, each with its own distinct meaning and code-label. By 'concepts' one means types of conventionalized experience (rather than individual token subsumed under those types). Such conventionalization presumably involves the development of a prototypical activation pattern of a cluster of connected nodes. The conceptual lexicon is thus repository of conventional, generic types of experience. 'Generic' and 'conventional' go hand in hand: The process of conventionalization subsumes abstraction and generalization.

A lexical concept may represent a relatively time-stable entity—physical object, landmark, location, plant, animal, person, cultural institution or abstract concept—thus typically a *noun*. It may be represent an action, event, processes or relations, thus typically a *verb*. It may represent a quality, property or temporary state, thus typically an *adjective*. Or it may convey some adverbial meaning, thus typically am *adverb*.

Cognitive psychologists have long recognized the conceptual lexicon under the label of *permanent semantic memory* (Atkinson & Shiffrin, 1968). Both brain location and processing mode of this cognitive capacity are distinct from those of the *episodic memory* (Atkinson & Shiffrin, 1968; Squire, 1987; Petri & Mishkin, 1994), in which input about uniquely experienced events or uniquely encountered entities is processed. But a somewhat reciprocal relation holds between the two types of mental representation, so that:

- Developmentally, memory traces of unique but similar individual experiences presumably give rise, after sufficient repetition, to time-stable concepts, habits or skills. And:
- In processing unique experiences, one recognizes the entities, states, events or relations involved in them as tokens of well-known lexical types.

2.2.2. Propositional Information

Clauses ('simple sentences') combine concepts (words) to convey propositional information about *relations*, *qualities*, *states* or *events* in which entities partake. Such relations, qualities, states or events may pertain either to the external world, to the internal (mental) world, to the culturally mediated world, or to various combinations thereof.

Propositional information about specific states and events is processed, at least initially, by the hippocampus-based episodic memory (Squire, 1987; Squire & Zola-Morgan, 1991; Petri & Mishkin, 1994).

2.2.3. Multi-Propositional Discourse

Individual event/state clauses (propositions) are combined together into coherent discourse. Human discourse is predominantly multi-propositional, and its coherence thus transcends the bounds of its component clauses. Multi-propositional information is also processed in the hippocampus-based episodic memory system.

2.2.4. The Interaction Between Lexicon, Propositions and Discourse

As an illustration of the combinatorial relation of conceptual meaning, propositional information and discourse coherence, consider the simple-minded examples in (1), (2) and (3) below.

1. **Concepts = words:**
   a. drive   b. insane
   c. constant   d. abuse
   e. maid   f. kill
   g. butler   h. knife
   i. hide   j. fridge

2. **Clauses = propositions:**
   a. The maid was driven insane.
   b. The butler constantly abused the maid.
   c. The maid killed the butler with a knife.
   d. The maid hid the knife in the fridge last night.

3. **Multi-propositional discourse:**
   Having been driven insane
   by constant abuse,
   the maid killed the butler with the knife
   that she had hidden in the fridge the night before.

Taken by themselves, outside any propositional context, the words in (1a–j) convey only conceptual *meaning*. That is, you may only ask about them questions such as:

4. a. What does "drive" mean?

    b. Does "drive" mean the same as "abuse"?

    c. If someone is a "maid", can she also a "butler", or a "woman"?

    d. Is "kill" related in meaning to "murder", and if so how?

Combined into clauses, as in (2a–d), the very same words now partake in the coding of propositional *information*. In addition to questions of meaning as in (4), the individual clauses in (2) may now prompt many questions of information, such as:

5. a. Was the maid driven insane?
    b. Who abused the maid?
    c. Who killed the butler?
    d. Who did the maid kill?
    e. What did the maid kill the butler with?
    f. Did the maid kill the butler?
    g. Where did the maid hide the knife?
    h. When did the maid hide the knife in the fridge?

Finally, the multi-propositional text in (3), in which the very same propositions of (2) are now combined, has discourse *coherence*. In addition to questions of meaning such as (4), and of information such as (5), one may now ask questions that pertain to that coherence; such as:

6. a. Why did she kill him?
    b. How come she had a knife?
    c. Why had the maid hidden the knife in the fridge?
    d. Could she perhaps have talked to him first before taking such a drastic step?
    e. Was her action reasonable? Was it defensible in a court of law?

Questions (6) may appear deceptively like those in (5). However, each questions in (5) can be answered on the basis of knowing only one of the atomic proposition in (2). In contrast, none of the questions in (6) can be answered on the basis of such atomic propositional knowledge. Rather, the knowledge of several propositions in the connected discourse (3), or even of the entire coherent text, is required in order to answer such questions.

The partial dissociation between conceptual meaning and propositional information is easy to demonstrate by constructing grammatically well-formed sentences that make no sense; that is, sentences whose words are perfectly meaningful each taken by itself, but still do not combine into a cogent proposition, as in Chomsky's ubiquitous example (7):

7. Colorless green ideas sleep furiously

The meaning clashes that make proposition (7) bizarre—'colorless green', 'green ideas', 'ideas sleep', 'sleep furiously'—are all due to the considerable semantic specificity of individual words. The relation between lexical meaning and propositional information is thus an inclusion relation or a one-way conditional. That is:

> One can understand the meaning of words independent of the proposition in which they are embedded; but one cannot understand a proposition without understanding the meaning of the words that make it up.

The partial dissociation between propositional information and discourse coherence can be just as easily demonstrated, by stringing together perfectly informative but incoherently combined propositions. For example, re-scrambling the coherent discourse in (3) yields the incoherent (8) below.

8. a. Having killed the butler with the knife
    b. by constant abuse,
    c. the maid had been driven insane
    d. and had hidden it in the fridge the night before.

No propositional-semantic anomaly is discernible in any of the individual clauses (8a–d). The bizarreness of (8) as connected discourse is only due to lack of cross-clausal—combinatorial—coherence. The relation between propositional information and discourse coherence is thus also an inclusion relation or a one-way conditional. That is:

> One can understand the meaning of clauses independent of the discourse they are embedded in; but one cannot understand the discourse without understanding the propositions that make it up.

2.3. The Human Communicative Codes

2.3.1. Peripheral Sensory-Motor Code

The peripheral sensory-motor coding system of human communication involves two components:

a. **The decoder:** This component translate perceived incoming code ('input') into information. The perceptual modality of the incoming code may be auditory, visual (ASL, reading), or tactile (Braille reading). For at two of these perceptual modalities—auditory and visual—language-specific decoding modules have been identified in the relevant sensory areas in the cortex.

b. **The encoder**: This component translates outgoing information ('output') into motor instructions. Likewise, the motor modality of the output may vary: It may be oral-vocal, manual (typing, writing), or gestural (ASL). The motor programs associated with these coding modalities are probably language specific and governed by various sub-areas of the primary motor cortex.

2.3.2. The Grammar Code

The grammatical code is probably the latest evolutionary addition to the arsenal of human communication (Givón, 1979; Lieberman, 1984; Bickerton, 1990). While the evolutionary argument remains conjectural, it is supported by a coherent body of suggestive evidence.

Ontogenetically, both hearing and signing children acquire the lexicon, and then pre-grammatical ('pidgin') communication using the lexicon, much earlier than grammar. Natural second language acquisition follows the very same course. In the natural communication of pre-human species, the existence of lexical-semantic concepts of both entities (nouns) and events (verbs) must be taken for granted, if one is to make sense of behavior, communicative as well as secular. Such lexical concepts are already well-coded in natural communication (e.g. Cheney & Seyfarth, 1990; Marler, Karakashian, & Gyger, 1991; *inter alia*).

Further, birds, dogs, horses, primates and other pre-human species are easily taught auditory or visual lexical code-labels for nouns, verbs and adjectives (see e.g. Premak, 1971; Gardner & Gardner, 1971; Fouts, 1973; Terrace, 1985; Greenfield & Savage-Rambaugh, 1991; Pepperberg, 1991; *inter alia*). And the seeming ease with which such lexical learning takes place strongly suggests that the underlying cognitive structure and its supporting neurology are already in place.

In pre-human primates, the supporting neurology for both semantic and episodic memory is essentially the same one as in humans (Petri & Mishkin, 1994). In contrast, observing the natural use of anything remotely resembling human grammar—morphology and syntax—in communicating animals, or teaching it to them, has been almost a uniform failure.

The grammar of human language is a much more abstract and complex device than the sensory–motor codes of the lexicon. At its most concrete level, the primary grammatical signal involves four major devices:

9. **Coding devices of the primary grammatical signal:**
   a. Morphology
   b. Intonation:
      (i)   clause-level melodic contours
      (ii) word-level stress or tone

c. Rhythmics:
  (i) pace or length
  (ii) pauses
d. Sequential order of words or morphemes

Some coding devices—morphology (9a), intonation and stress (9b)—are more concrete. They involve the very same physical coding-devices (sounds, letters, or gestures) that code lexical meaning. But these concrete devices are integrated into a complex whole with the more abstract elements of the code—rhythmics (9c) and sequential order (9d). These more abstract elements of the grammatical code are probably second-order constructions, inferred from the more concrete signals.

From the primary grammatical signals (9), hearers must extract information concerning *both* the propositional (clausal) and multi-propositional levels of communication. With respect to the individual clause, the extracted information involves, at the very least, the following elements of internal organization:

10. **Information extracted from the primary grammatical signal:**
    - Hierarchic constituency organization of the various components of the clauses (morphemes into words, words into phrases, phrases into clauses)
    - The grammatical category-labels of the components (noun, verb, adjective; noun phrase, verb phrase)
    - Scope and relevance relations among components (operator-operand relations, noun-modifier relations, subject and object relations)
    - Government or control relations among components (agreement, coreference, modality, finiteness)

The elements of clausal organization in (10) are the more abstract components of grammar. How they extracted from the primary signals of grammar, i.e. from (9), is a central question for those who study language processing.

2.3.3. Pre-Grammatical vs. Grammaticalized Communication

As noted above, humans can—under a variety of developmental or neurological conditions—communicate readily without grammar, using a well-coded lexicon with some rudimentary combinatorial rules. The difference—structural, functional and cognitive—between pre-grammatical and grammaticalized communication are summarized in (11) below.

11. **Pre-grammatical vs. grammatical discourse processing**
    (after Givón, 1979, chap. 5; 1995, chap. 9)

properties	grammatical mode	pre-grammatical mode
STRUCTURAL:		
a. **Grammatical morphology**	abundant	absent
b. **Syntactic constructions**	complex/ embedded	simple/ conjoined
c. **Use of word-order:**	grammatical (subj/obj)	pragmatic (topic/comment)
d. **Pauses:**	fluent	halting
FUNCTIONAL:		
e. **processing speed:**	fast	slow
f. **Mental effort:**	effortless	laborious
g. **Error rate:**	lower	higher
h. **Context dependence:**	lower	higher
COGNITIVE:		
i. **Processing mode:**	automated	attended
j. **acquisition:**	late	early
k. **evolution:**	late	early

Slow and analytic, pre-grammatical communication is heavily vocabulary-dependent and knowledge-driven (Kintsch 1992). This tallies with the fact that vocabulary is acquired before grammar in both first and second language acquisition. Pre-grammatical children, adult pidgin speaker and agrammatical aphasics all comprehend and produce coherent, connected discourse, albeit at slower speeds and high error rates than is characteristic of grammaticalized communication. The identification of grammar as an automated, streamlined, conventionalized, speeded-up language processing system has long been recognized (Givón, 1979, chap. 5; 1989, chap. 7; 1993; Blumstein & Milberg, 1983; Lieberman, 1984; Schnitzer, 1989).

As an example of coherent pre-grammatical child narrative text, consider the following, from a 2-year-old boy:[1]

12. [Context: anticipating a trip]
    In atnga. Sit dawn. tan ki.
    in airplane sit down turn key
      '(We'll go) in the airplane, sit down, turn the key,

> Vruum vruum! Tan tu da rayt. Atnga!
> vr.   vr.   turn to the right airplane
> And vroom vroom! (We'll) turn to the right.
> Airplane (flies)!'

As an example of coherent adult second-language pidgin, consider:[2]

13. ". . . oh me? . . . oh me over there . . .
    nineteen-twenty over there say come . . .
    store me stop begin open . . . me sixty year . . .
    little more sixty year . . . now me ninety . . .
    nah ehm . . . little more . . . this man ninety-two . . .
    yeah, this month over . . . me Hawaii come-*desu* . . .
    nineteen seven come . . . me number first here . . .
    me-*wa* tell . . . you sabe gurumeru? . . .
    you no sabe gurumeru? . . .
    yeah this place come . . .
    this place been two-four-five year . . .
    stop, ey . . . then me go home . . . Japan . . .
    by-n-by . . . little boy . . . come . . .
    by-n-by he been come here . . . ey . . .
    by-n-by come . . .
    by-n-by me before Hui-Hui stop . . .
    Hui-Hui this . . . eh . . . he . . . this a . . .
    Manuel . . . you sabe-*ka* . . ."

As an example of coherent narrative produced by an agrammatic aphasia
patient, consider (Menn, 1990, p. 165):

15. ". . . I had stroke . . . blood pressure . . . low pressure . . .
    period . . . Ah . . . pass out . . . Uh . . . Rosa and I, and . . .
    friends . . . of mine . . . uh . . . uh . . . shore . . . uh drink,
    talk, pass out . . ."
    ". . . Hahnemann Hospital . . . uh, uh I . . . uh uh wife, Rosa . . .
    uh . . . take . . . uh . . . love . . . ladies . . . uh Ocean uh Hospital
    and transfer Hahnemann Hospital ambulance . . . uh . . .
    half'n hour . . . uh . . . uh it's . . . uh . . . motion, motion . . .
    uh . . . bad . . . patient . . . I uh . . . flat on the back . . .
    um . . . it's . . . uh . . . shaved, shaved . . . nurse, shaved me . . .
    uh . . . shaved me, nurse . . . [sigh] . . . wheel chair . . . uh . . .
    Hahnemann Hospital . . . a week, a week . . . uh . . . then uh . . .
    strength . . . uh . . . mood . . . uh . . . up . . . uh . . . legs and

> arms, left side uh . . . weak . . . and . . . Moss Hospital . . .
> two week . . . no, two months . . ."

In the absence of morpho-syntax, the bulk of the well-coded clues for establishing text coherence in pre-grammatical discourse are furnished by the lexical vocabulary. Still, a small beach-head of what one may wish to call *proto-grammar* is already evident in pre-grammatical communication (see Givón, 1995, chap. 9). Further, non-coded clues derived from the situational and generic-cultural contexts remain ever-present. Neither reliance on lexical information nor reliance on situational and cultural contexts disappear in grammaticalized communication. They remains parallel processing channels alongside the more automated grammar channel (Kintsch, 1992; Givón, 1993). In the transition from pidgin to grammaticalized communication, the relative functional load of vocabulary and contextual clues for discourse coherence is diminished, with the slack picked up by grammar.

2.4. Summary of Mapping Between Codes and Functions

The peripheral sensory-motor codes are responsible primarily for signalling lexical-semantic meaning, but are also exploited in the grammatical code—in morphology and intonation. Of these two, the use of intonation in grammar is, in all likelihood, a carryover from its use in pre-grammatical communication.

The use of the sound-code for morphology is derived diachronically from its primary use to code lexical meaning: All grammatical morphemes ultimately arise from erstwhile lexical words (Givón, 1971, 1979 chap. 5; Heine & Traugott (Eds.), 1991; Heine, Claudi, & Hu"nnemeyer, 1991; *inter alia*). But a similar lexical origin of grammatical morphology ('inflection') may not be the case in gesturally visually coded language. For example, in American Sign Language (ASL), the bulk of grammatical inflections have most likely evolved directly from non-lexical gestural sources, thus bypassing the lexicon altogether (Petitto, 1992).

As noted above, grammar is the joint coding instrument for both propositional-semantic information (clauses) and discourse-pragmatic coherence (discourse). But the part of grammar responsible for propositional semantics is relatively small:

- semantic roles of participant
- semantic transitivity (state vs. event vs. action)

The bulk of the grammatical code is deployed in the realm of discourse pragmatics, signalling the coherence of information within its wider—cross-clausal, situational, cultural—context.

The semiotic relation between the three main cognitive-functional components of human communication and the two main coding systems may be given schematically as:

16. **Mapping relation between cognitive-communicative functions and well-coded signals in grammaticalized language:**

function		code
lexical meaning	<===>	sensory-motor
propositional semantics	<===>	
discourse pragmatics	<===>	grammar

In pre-grammatical (Pidgin, Broca's aphasia) communication, the grammatical code is missing. To compensate, speakers–hearers must rely much more on scanning and analyzing the various shades and gradations of context. That is, they must indulge in slower, analytic, attended processing. One may thus view the evolutionary rise of the two human communicative codes, vocabulary and grammar, as two successive steps toward the partial—though never complete—liberation of human communication from heavy dependence on slow, laborious contextual analysis.

3. WHAT GRAMMAR DOES: THE PARADOX
OF CLAUSAL GRAMMAR

Both linguists and psychologists often ignore the fact that grammar is the coding instrument for *both* cognitive components that feed into episodic memory: propositional semantics and discourse coherence. This is indeed one of the most baffling facts about grammar as a code: Although it is located largely in the clause itself, its functional scope is not only—not even primarily—about the propositional information in the clause in which grammar resides. Grammar is not, primarily, about extracting the information of 'who did what to whom when and where and how'. Rather, the functional scope of grammar is, predominantly though not absolutely, about the *coherence relations* of the information in the clause to its surrounding discourse.

The traditional structuralist methodology, of examining (or experimenting on) isolated clauses (sentences) has tended to obscure this overwhelming fact about what grammar does. And this has been unfortunately true in both linguistics and psycho-linguistics.

It is of course not the case that all grammatically coded distinctions have only discourse-pragmatic scope. But the overwhelming majority of grammatical sub-systems clearly do. Among those, the most obvious ones are:

17. **The most discourse-pragmatically oriented grammatical systems:**
    a. Grammatical roles of subject and direct object
    b. definiteness and reference
    c. anaphora, pronouns and agreement
    d. tense-aspect-modality and negation
    e. de-transitive voice
    f. topicalization
    g. focus and contrast
    h. relativization
    i. speech acts
    j. clausal conjunction and subordination

Predominance or distinctness, however, does not mean lack of overlap or interaction between clause-level propositional semantics and discourse-level pragmatics.

Consider for example, *case-marking* types, which are a major arena where boundaries between propositional semantics and discourse pragmatics can overlap. One major case-marking type, active-stative, is oriented primarily toward semantic roles, marking event participants morphologically as either:

18. • agent = initiator of event, actor
    • patient = being in state or changing state
    • dative = conscious experiencer

Another type, nominative-accusative, is oriented predominantly toward the pragmatics of topicality, marking event participants regardless of their semantic roles as:

19. • subject = main-topic
    • object = secondary-topic
    • indirect object = non-topical

Another type, ergative-absolutive, straddles the fence between the first two, displaying aspects of both in the complex arena of transitivity:

20. • ergative = subject/agent of transitive event
    • absolutive = subject of intransitive event or object of transitive
                event)
    • oblique = none of the above

Likewise, in the domain of voice and de-transitivity, one can easily identify more semantically-oriented processes, such as middle-voice, reflexive,
reciprocal, as in:

21. a. **active-transitive:**
       The goat broke the fence
       The goat bit the cow
    b. **middle:**
       The fence is breakable
       The fence is broken
       The fence broke
    c. **Reflexive:**
       The goat bit itself
    d. **Reciprocal:**
       The goat and the cow bit each other

But one can also identify more pragmatic processes, such as the passive,
impersonal, inverse, L-dislocation or antipassive, as in:

22. a. **Passive:**
       The fence was broken by the goat
    b. **Impersonal:**
       One breaks fences around here
    c. **Inverse:**
       The fence the goat broke, the cow it only bit
    d. **L-dislocation:**
       As for the fence, the goat broke it
    e. **Antipassive:**
       (watch out), this goat bites (cows)
       This goat is a fence-breaker

The erroneous traditional assumption that grammar functions primarily
in the domain of propositional semantics, combined with the undeniable
overlap between the largely pragmatic but marginally semantic functional
correlates of grammar, have led to much unnecessary mischief in work on
grammar by both linguists and psychologists. Since the problem has a vast
methodological underpinning, it would be useful to survey how it intersects
with problems of methodology in the study of human language.

4. THE LIMITS OF CONSCIOUS REFLECTION

The traditional descriptive method, however intuitive, has always rested on unimpeachable empirical foundations. To determine the semantic correlates of a form, you hold all variables constant—but one. You then manipulate that one variable, and record the semantic effect of the manipulation. As a quick illustration of this method, consider the elicitation of Swahili verbal paradigms:

23. a. **Manipulating variable a (subject pronoun):**
      ni-limuona = '**I** saw him/her'
      ku-limuona = '**You** saw him/her'
      a-limuona = '**S/he** saw him/her'
    b. **Manipulating variable b (tense-aspect):**
      ni-**li**-muona = 'I **saw** him/her'
      ni-**na**-muona = 'I **see** him/her'
      ni-**ta**-muona = 'I **will see** him/her'
      ni-**me**-muona = 'I **have seen** him/her'
    c. **Manipulating variable c (object pronoun):**
      a-li-**ni**-ona = 'S/he saw **me**'
      a-li-**ku**-ona = 'S/he saw **you**'
      a-li-**mu**-ona = 'S/he saw **him/her**'
      a-li-**ki**-ona = 'S/he saw **it**'
    d. **Manipulating variable d (verb stem):**
      a-li-ki-**ona** = 'S/he **saw** it'
      a-li-ki-**piga** = 'S/he **hit** it'
      a-li-ki-**amba** = 'S/he **said** it'
    e. **Manipulating variable e (transitivity):**
      a-li-ki-on-**a** = 'S/he saw it'
      a-li-mu-on-**ea** = 'S/he saw it for him/her'
      ki-li-on-**ewa** = 'It was seen'
      ki-li-on-**eka** = 'It was visible'
      a-li-mu-on-**esha** = 'S/he showed him/her'
      wa-li-on-**ana** = 'They saw each other'

Our manipulations have yielded rich data concerning the various form-meaning associations along the verb-inflectional paradigm. But the validity of our results rests upon the two related assumptions:

a. The meaning of the manipulated forms is accessible to conscious reflection.
b. All speakers will respond uniformly.

The grammar-in-text methodology is designed to take over precisely where assumption (a) is weak and assumption (b) thus becomes untenable. But under certain conditions—and given another set of goals—the grammar-in-text method too is likely to reach its natural limits. Whereby one must let go and reach for other methods.

One of the most striking facts that all grammarians—be they Aristotle, Bopp, Jespersen, Bloomfield, Tesnière, Harris or Chomsky—could not but notice is that roughly-the-same informational contents can be packaged into a wide array of different syntactic clausal structures. That is:

24. a. Marla saw Henry
    b. **Marla** didn't **see Henry**
    c. Go **see Henry**!
    d. Who **saw Henry**?
    e. Did **Marla see Henry**?

25. a. Marla saw Henry
    b. She **saw Henry**
    c. **Marla saw** him
    d. **Henry** was **seen** (by **Marla**)
    e. The woman who **saw Henry** was **Marla**
    f. The man **Marla saw** (was **Henry**)
    g. We told **Marla** to **see Henry**
    h. We suspected that **Marla saw Henry**
    i. We suspected **Marla** of **seeing Henry**
    j. As for **Henry**, **Marla saw** him
    k. Having **seen Henry**, (**Marla** left)
    l. After **Marla saw Henry** . . .

Harris' (1956) early transformational observations hinged on noting these *co-occurrences* of meaningful units. That is, all the clauses in (24) and (25) seem to more or less involve the same agent/subject, patient/object and verb, and thus in a sense "refer to the same event." The variation in syntactic structure in (24)/(25)—with all lexical variables held constant—must surely map onto a parallel variation in meaning.

So far, the analytic task seems to parallel the verb-paradigm manipulations in (23). And indeed, in the case of negation (24b) and non-declarative speech-acts (24c,d,e), the functional correlates of structural variation seem obvious and accessible. In contrast, both the speakers' and the linguist's intuitions about the functional correlates of syntactic structure are much harder to nail down with any degree of cross-subject reliability in the case of manipulations (25)—pronouns (25b,c), passives (25d), relative clauses (25e,f), verb complements (25g,h), raising to object (25i), L-dislocation (25j), adverbial clauses (25k,l).

Our propositional semantic intuition about agents, patients and verbs seems both accessible and replicable. But our discourse-pragmatic intuition about the communicative function of grammar turns out to be rather fickle. This is where linguist must give up the traditional method of conscious reflection about what grammar is and what grammar does, and search for non-intuitionist empirical methods, ones capable of teasing out the correlation between grammatical form and communicative (or cognitive) function.

5. MENTAL MODELS AND LANGUAGE PROCESSING

5.1. Preamble

As noted earlier above (section 2), two cognitive representation systems are crucially involved in supporting the representational functions of human language:

- permanent semantic memory (lexicon)
- episodic memory (propositions, discourse)

It is time now to consider the third one:

- working memory (current attention focus)

Working memory is a small capacity, short span storage-cum-activation component that involves both modality specific and general components, both conscious and subconscious ones (Baddeley, 1986, 1992; Gathercole & Baddeley, 1993; Carpenter & Just, 1998; Just & Carpenter, 1990). Some activation in working memory, whether conscious or not, is a pre-condition for reaching longer-term episodic memory (Ericsson & Kintsch, 1995). And that is true of non-verbal (sensory) modalities as well (Treisman, 1995).

In this section, I would like to illustrate how three core components of human communication depend systematically on these three systems of knowledge representation. In all three cases, the examples I will cite relate to the central communicative task of establishing the commonality of relevant mental representation (background knowledge) between the two communicating minds.

While most of the examples cited below involve the task of ascertaining *referential accessibility,* or rather, with the conditions under which a speaker is entitled to assume that a referent is known ('accessible') to the hearer, referent tracking in discourse is only one communicative task out of many that depend on the three major memory systems.

5.2. Accessibility Due to Shared Cultural Frames
(Permanent Semantic Memory)

Culturally shared, generic-lexical knowledge is represented mentally in the permanent semantic memory. Referents may be grounded to this mental structure in two distinct ways. First, some referents are *globally accessible* because they are uniquely identifiable to all members of the relevant speech community ('culture', 'sub-culture', 'village', 'family') at all times. Some examples of such referents are:

26. **Globally-accessible ('generic') definite referents:**

referent	relevant social unit
a. **The sun** came out.	all humans
b. **The president** has resigned.	a nation-state
c. They went to **the cemetery**.	a community
d. **The river** is frozen over.	a community
e. Call **the sheriff**!	a county
f. **The Gods** are angry.	a religion
g. **Daddy** is home!	a family

Generic access to definite referents is often intermixed with episodic text-based access, yielding a hybrid system of double grounding. A double-grounded referent is accessible partly through an anaphoric connection to its episodic trace in the episodic representation of the current text, and partly through connection(s) to generic-lexical knowledge. This hybrid type of grounding is often referred to as *framed-based* or *script-based* reference (Anderson, Garrod & Sanford, 1983; Yekovich & Walker, 1986; Walker & Yekovich, 1987). Typical examples are:

27. **Double-grounded frame-based reference:**
    a. My boy missed **school** today,
       he was late for **the bus**.
    b. He showed us this gorgeous **house**,
       but **the living room** was too small.
    c. She went into a **restaurant**
       and asked **the waiter** for **the menu**.

The definite referent 'the bus' in (27a) receives its anaphoric grounding from two separate sources—the antecedent referent 'school' in the preceding text, plus generic-lexical knowledge of the frame 'school' and its sub-component 'bus'. Similarly in (27b), the definite referent 'the living room' receives its anaphoric grounding in part from the antecedent referent 'this gorgeous house' in the preceding text, and in part from generic-lexical knowledge of the frame 'house' and its sub-component 'living room'.

Likewise in (27c), both definite referents 'the waiter' and 'the menu' receive their grounding in part from the antecedent referent 'a restaurant' in the preceding text, and in part from generic-lexical knowledge of the frame 'restaurant' and its sub-components 'waiter' and 'menu'.

Frame-based referential access is often accomplished through conventional knowledge of whole-part, possessor-possessed relations:

28. **Whole-part, possessor-possessed frame-based access:**
    a. She grabbed **the fish** and chopped off **its head**.
    b. **John** just got a job working for **his father**.
    c. **The house** was a mess, **the roof** leaked.
    d. **She**'s upset. **Her kids** keep flunking high-school.
    e. **The table** is missing **one of its legs**.
    f. **My wife** called and said . . .
    g. **Your house** is on fire.

In (28f,g), the anaphoric antecedent is not accessible from the current text itself, but rather from the *speech situation* (see below) i.e. the identity of the speaker and hearer. But the use of frame-based knowledge to affect full grounding of the definite referent is of the same type.

5.3. Accessibility Due to Shared Current Discourse (Episodic Memory)

Referents may be deemed by the speaker as accessible to the hearer due to the presumption of either currentvactivation in working memory (attention), or the presence of a mental trace in episodic-memory representation of the current text. A large array of grammatical devices are used to indicate the various contexts of such accessibility—or lack of.[3]

29. a. **Zero anaphor:**
       (Mary looked at the food) and **[0]** didn't like it.
    b. **Anaphoric pronoun:**
       (Mary looked at the food.) **She** didn't like it.
       (After Mary talked to Bill,) **she** left.
    c. **Stressed pronoun:**
       (After Mary talked to Bill,) **HE** left but **SHE** didn't.
       (I decide to reward both of them.) So I gave the book to **HIM**.
       To **HER** I gave the photograph.
    d. **Indefinite noun:**
       Mary met **a man** at **a bar** last night and . . .

e. **Definite noun:**
(Mary met **a man** at the bar, had a few drinks with him and then excused herself and went home.) The following Sunday **the man** called and . . .

f. **Definite noun with restrictive REL-clause:**
(Mary met **two men** at a bar, and had a few drinks with them before going home alone. One of them talked all the time, the other said nothing). The following Sunday **the** man **who said nothing** called and . . .

Zero anaphors (29a) are used typically when the referent is currently activated in working memory (focus of attention) and thus the activation simply continues (default condition).

Anaphoric (unstressed) pronouns (29b) are used in very similar contexts as zero anaphors—as far as referential continuity goes. But the high degree of *thematic* continuity that prompts their use is a bit lower. Such a difference in thematic continuity is expressed, in written English, as the contrast between zero/comma punctuation (29a) vs. period punctuation (29b), respectively.

Stressed pronouns (29c) are used, typically, when two referents have activated in short order, and the focus of attention then shifts from one to the other. The shift may also involve changing the role of the *same* referent from object to subject. Subject continuity is considered the default case in discourse, and is typically coded by either zero anaphors (29a) or unstressed anaphoric pronouns (29b).

Full nouns (NPs) are used when a referent is not currently activated. Several options are then available. First, if the speaker assumes the hearer does not have an accessible episodic trace of the referent, indefinite grammatical marking is used (34d). The referent is being introduced for the first time into the discourse. If attention focus it to falls on the new referent, the currently-active referent must be de-activated.[4]

Second, the speaker may assumes that a referent that is not currently activated is nevertheless accessible to the hearer as a mental trace in the episodic memory of the current text. Under such conditions, a definite noun (29e) is used. Such usage presumably signals to the hearer to search for the mental episodic trace of the referent and retrieve it. As with indefinite nouns, if the retrieved referent is then to be re-activated, the currently active referent must be extinguished.

Finally, restrictive REL-clauses on definite nouns (29f) are used under rather similar activation-and-search conditions as definite nouns. But the search for the episodic mental trace of the referent is more problematic here, for a variety of possible reasons. On top of definite marking, the speaker also supplies the relative clause as a *search guide*. The REL-clause

codes a salient state or event in which the referent took part in the preceding discourse. The hearer then presumably identify the referent more
precisely by matching the event in the REL-clause with its episodic memory
trace, perhaps in a similar fashion as matching referents.

5.4. Accessibility Due to Shared Speech Situation
      (Working Memory, Current Attention Focus)

The most well-known cases of relying on the currently-activated mental
model of the speech situation for referential access involve *deictic* expressions such as:

30. a. **Interlocutors:**
        'I', 'you', 'we', 'y'all'
    b. **Other referents:**
        'this one', that one', 'that one over there'
    c. **Location:**
        'here', 'there', 'way over there'
    d. **Time:**
        'now', 'then', 'long ago', 'in the future'
        'today', 'yesterday', 'tomorrow'
        'this week', 'last week', 'next week'

The constantly shifting nature of working-memory representation of the
current speech situation is best illustrated by the shift in the reference of
'I', 'you', 'here' and 'there' in (31) below. Whenever the speaker (and/or
hearer) changes, the reference of these deictic expressions also change.

31. So Mary said:
        "I told you I wasn't going to be here".
    To which Marvin replied:
        "But I knew you were there".

In addition to reference, the constantly shifting working-memory representation of the current speech situation also involves the propositional
attitudes (beliefs) and speech-acts (intentions). That is, the constantly shifting *belief and intention states* of the interlocutor. These are, broadly, the
Gricean conversational postulates (Grice, 1968/1975; see also Dickinson
& Givón, 1997). As an illustration of this, consider the following dialogue
between speakers A and B:

32. A.i: So she got up and left.
    B.i: You didn't stop her?

    A.ii: Would you?
    B.ii: I don't know. Where was she sitting?
    A.iii: Why?
    B.iii: Never mind, just tell me.

In the first conversational turn (32A.i), speaker A executes a declarative speech acts, which involves, roughly, the following presuppositions about hearer B's current mental states:

33. a. The hearer doesn't know proposition (32A.i)   [belief]
    b. The hearer is disposed to assume the speaker
       knows that proposition   [belief]
    c. The hearer would like to know that information   [intention]

By the next turn (32B.i), speaker B executes the yes/no question speech-act, which involves, roughly, the following presuppositions about hearer A's current mental states:

34. a. The hearer knows the proposition (37B.i)
    b. The hearer is disposed to assume the speaker   [belief]
       doesn't know the proposition   [belief]
    c. The hearer is willing to supply the speaker
       with the information   [intention]

As one can see, at every turn the speakers mental model of the hearer's belief and intention states changes. A corresponding change presumably also occurs in the hearer's mental model of the speaker's belief and intention states. The most natural cognitive module to take care of such temporary representations is working memory (Dickinson & Givón, 1997).

6. CLOSURE

It is only natural that disciplines that develop in isolation from each other, isolation of theory but especially of methodology, should find it hard to communicate even about matters of common concerns. The most disheartening thing about the relation between the functionally oriented linguist and the empirically oriented psycholinguist is how little each knows or appreciates what the other does.

    Because of such isolation, psycholinguists have spent decades on studying how subjects in the narrow confines of laboratory cubby-holes parse and interpret isolated sentences that bear little relation to either the type of clauses used in natural communication, the communicative context in which such clauses are used, or the linguistic context in which clauses in natural communication are produced and interpreted.

Likewise, linguists of various ideological stripes have spent decades in splendid disciplinary isolation, constructing ever-more-elaborate theories of language whose cognitive, neurological and evolutionary plausibility approaches *nihil*.

Most puzzling perhaps, psycholinguists by and large have tended to adopt their perspective on language from the formal, modularity-obsessed, innatist school of linguistics, the one that ignores the evolution of human language as an *adaptive tool*, one intimately constrained by the two major facets of its adaptive environment—cognition and communication.

I have attempted to point out how empirical psycholinguistics and functionally and cognitively oriented linguistics can, rather naturally, constrain and illuminate each other. Human language, once viewed in its natural adaptive context, can be studied most fruitfully through a combined meta-discipline that is yet to be born—cognitive neuro-linguistics.

NOTES

1. From my own field notes ca. Dec. 1980.
2. A Japanese-born old man in conversation with Derek Bickerton in Hawaii, ca. 1975.
3. For an extensive discussion, see Givón (1993; 1995 chap. 8).
4. Activation (attention) is a limiting capacity. This is underscored by the facts of grammar, which seem to suggest that only one clausal referent at a time is activated.

REFERENCES

Ackrill, J. L. (Tr. & Ed.) (1963). *Aristotle's Categories and De Interpretatione*. Oxford: Clarendon Press.

Anderson, A. S., Garrod, C., & Sanford, A. J. (1983) The accessibility of pronominal antecedents as a function of episodic shift in narrative text. *Quarterly Journal of Experimental Psychology*, 35A.

Atkinson, R. C., & Shiffrin, R. M. (1968). Human memory: A proposed system and its control processes. In K. W. Spence & T. Spence (Eds.), *The Psychology of Learning and Motivation* (Vol. 2). New York: Academic Press.

Baddeley, A. D. (1986). *Working Memory*. Oxford, England: Oxford University Press.

Baddeley, A. D. (1992). Working memory: The interface between memory and cognition. *Journal of Cognitive Neuroscience*, 4(3), 281–288.

Bickerton, D. (1990). *Language and Species*. Chicago: University of Chicago Press.

Blumstein, S., & Milberg, W. (1983). Automated and controlled deficits in speech/language deficits in aphasia. *Symposium on Automatic Speech*. Minneapolis: Academy of Aphasia.

Carpenter, P. A., & Just, M. A. (1988). The role of working memory in language comprehension. In D. Klar & K. Kotovsky (Eds.), *Complex Information Processing: The Impact of Herbert Simon*. Hillsdale, NJ: Lawrence Erlbaum Associates.

Cheney, D. L., & Seyfarth, R. M. (1990). *How monkeys see the world*. Chicago: University of Chicago Press.

Crouch, J. E. (1978). *Functional human anatomy* (3rd ed.). Philadelphia: Lea & Fabiger.

Dickinson, C., & Givón, T. (1997). Memory and conversation. In T. Givón (Ed.), *Conversation: Cognitive, communicative and social perspectives*. Amsterdam: John Benjamins.

Ericsson, K. A., & Kintsch, W. (1995). Long-term working memory. *Psychological Review, 102*(2).

Fouts, R. S. (1973). Acquisition and testing of gestural signs in four young chimpanzees. *Science*, 180.

Gardner, B. T., & Gardner, R. A. (1971). Two-way communication with an infant chimpanzee. In A. Schrier & F. Stollnitz (Eds.), *Behavior of non-human primates*. New York: Academic Press.

Gathercole, S. E., & Baddeley, A. D. (1993). *Working memory and language*. Hillsdale, NJ: Lawrence Erlbaum Associates.

Givón, T. (1971). Historical syntax and synchronic morphology: An archaeologist's field trip (CLS #7). University of Chicago, Chicago Linguistics Society.

Givón, T. (1979). *On understanding grammar*. New York: Academic Press.

Givón, T. (1989). *Mind, code and context: Essays in pragmatics*. Hillsdale, NJ: Lawrence Erlbaum Associates.

Givón, T. (1993). Coherence in text, coherence in mind. *Pragmatics and Cognition, 1*(2).

Givón, T. (1995). *Functionalism and grammar*. Amsterdam: John Benjamins.

Greenfield, P. M., & Savage-Rambaugh, E. S. (1991). Imitation, grammatical development and the invention of proto-grammar by an ape. In N. Krasnegor, M. Studdert-Kennedy, & R. Schiefelbuch (Eds), *Biobehavioral foundations of Language Development*. Hillsdale, NJ: Lawrence Erlbaum Associates.

Grice, H. P. (1975). Logic and conversation. In P. Cole & J. Morgan (Eds), *Speech acts, syntax and semantics 3*. New York: Academic Press. (Original work published 1968)

Harris, Z. (1956). Co-occurrence and transformation in linguistic structure. *Language, 33*(3).

Heine, B., Claudi, U., & Hu"nnemeyer, F. (1991). *Grammaticalization: A conceptual framework*. Chicago: University of Chicago Press.

Heine, B. & Traugott, E. (Eds). (1991). *Approaches to grammaticalization* (TSL #19, 2 vols). Amsterdam: John Benjamins.

Just, M. A., & Carpenter, P. A. (1992). A capacity theory of comprehension: Individual differences in working memory. *Psychological Review, 99*(1).

Kintsch, W. (1992). How readers construct situation models for stories: The role of syntactic cues and causal inference. In A. F. Healy, S. Kosslyn, & R. M. Shiffrin (Eds.), *Essays in honor of William K. Estes*. Hillsdale, NJ: Lawrence Erlbaum Associates.

Lieberman, P. (1984). *The biology and evolution of language*. Cambridge: Harvard University Press.

Marler, P., Karakashian, S., & Gyger, M. (1991). Do animals have the option of withholding signals when communication is inappropriate? The audience effect. In C. A. Ristau (Ed.), *Cognitive ethology*. Hillsdale, NJ: Lawrence Erlbaum Associates.

McKeon, R. (Ed.). (1941). *The basic works of Aristotle* (22nd ed.). New York: Random House.

Menn, L. (1990). Agrammatism in English: Two case studies. In L. Menn & E. Obler (Eds), *Agrammatic aphasia: A cross-language narrative source-book*. John Benjamins.

Neeley, J. H. (1990). Semantic priming effects in visual word recognition: A selective review of current findings and theories. In D. Besner & G. Humphreys (Eds.), *Basic processes in reading: Visual word recognition*. Hillsdale, NJ: Lawrence Erlbaum Associates.

Pepperberg, I. M. (1991). A communicative approach to animal cognition: A study of conceptual abilities of an African grey parrot. In C. A. Ristau (Ed.), *Cognitive ethology.* Hillsdale, NJ: Lawrence Erlbaum Associates.

Petitto, L. A. (1991). From gesture to symbol: The relation between form and meaning in the acquisition of personal pronouns. *Papers and reports from child language development.* Unpublished manuscript.

Petri, H. L., & Mishkin, M. (1994). Behaviorism, cognitivism and the neuropsychology of memory. *American Scientist, 82.*

Premak, D. (1971). Language in chimpanzee. *Science,* 172.

Ristau, C. A. (Ed.). (1991). *Cognitive ethology.* Hillsdale, NJ: Lawrence Erlbaum Associates.

Schnitzer, M. (1989). *The pragmatic basis of aphasia.* Hillsdale, NJ: Lawrence Erlbaum Associates.

Squire, L. R. (1987). *Memory and brain.* Oxford, England: Oxford University Press.

Squire, L. R., & Zola-Morgan, S. (1991). The medial temporal lobe memory system. *Science, 253,* 1380–1386.

Swinney, D. A. (1979). Lexical access during sentence comprehension: (Re)consideration of context effects. *J.V.L.V.B., 18.*

Terrace, H. S. (1985). In the beginning there was the "name." *American Psychologist, 40.*

Treisman, A. (1995, April). *Object tokens, attention and visual memory.* Attneave Memorial Lecture, University of Oregon, Eugene.

Walker, C. H., & Yekovich, F. R. (1987). Activation and use of script-based antecedents in anaphoric reference. *Journal of Memory and Language, 26.*

Yekovich, F. R., & Walker, C. H. (1986). The activation and use of scripted knowledge in reading about routine activities. In B. K. Britton (Ed.), *Executive control processes in reading.* Hillsdale, NJ: Lawrence Erlbaum Associates.

Chapter 3

The Structure of Events and the Structure of Language

William Croft
University of Manchester

INTRODUCTION

Perhaps the two most basic syntactic structures of human languages are the clause and the phrase (noun phrase or prepositional/postpositional phrase; it generally functions as a subject, object, or oblique element related to the main verb of the clause). The clause and the phrase are centered around the communication of *events* and *objects*, respectively. Events include both *actions* (processes involving change) and *states* (where no change is involved). Objects include persons and things that function as participants in those events. Obviously this description is an oversimplification of the semantics of clauses and phrases, but it is a useful starting point for delving into their true cognitive complexity.

Objects, particularly physical objects, look deceptively easy to handle from a cognitive point of view. They generally (although not always) come neatly individuated. Objects can be spatially isolated in our physical environment, are also physically manipulable, and persist through time. All three of these properties suggest that the identification and categorization of objects is an easy cognitive ability to model. In fact, it is not so easy as that, as is evidenced by the well-known psychological research of Rosch (e.g., Rosch, 1978) into prototypes and basic-level categories and the linguistic research by Fillmore (1982, 1985) into how lexical categories can frame our experience in different ways.

Events, on the other hand, have never deceived. In terms of categorization and cognition, they are hard to handle from the beginning. Events are largely transitory (although some are less transitory than others), and are not physically manipulable; hence, there is less we can learn and more we need to remember in order to identify them. Worse, events, even physical events, are not causally or temporally isolated in our environment. The world appears to be made up of an extremely complex causal network constantly unfolding through time of which we encounter just fragments. Deciding which segment of a fragment of experience counts as an event is obviously a complex cognitive process.

It is the purpose of this chapter to describe both some of the complexities involved in events, and an approach based on cognitive linguistics for analyzing the complexity. As in most other work in cognitive linguistics, the analyses here are based on the semantic interpretation by the analysts of invented or (less often) naturally occurring sentences, using a family of theoretical constructs whose lineage can be traced back to cognitive psychology or philosophy. The presentation here will, I hope, suggest how relevant the cognitive linguistic research is to psychological theories, and how cognitive linguistic analyses can be tested in experimental psychological paradigms.

ASPECT: THE TEMPORAL STRUCTURE OF EVENTS

Although every clause illustrates the full complexity of the conceptualization of events, we cannot deal with all of this complexity at once. I begin by looking at the relation of events to time and leave the discussion of causality in events until the next section.

As was noted in the introduction, events are essentially temporal. This is in itself a matter of *conceptualization*. If I use the phrase *my pickup truck* as in *My pickup truck broke down last week*, then I am treating the pickup truck as an object, namely, without reference to its temporal duration in this world. If, on the other hand, I use the predicate *be my pickup truck*, as in *That is my pickup truck*, I am construing this fact—the identification of *That*—as a state of affairs with a temporal duration (for as long as I own the truck, or for as long as the truck exists before being junked). In the clause and in the phrase, I am talking about the same thing, namely my pickup truck, whose lifetime is therefore also the same. But in the clause, temporal duration is an essential part of the meaning, whereas in the phrase, temporal duration is irrelevant.

Because events exist in time, they can also be situated in time. The grammatical category of *tense* situates events in time with respect to the time of the speech act. English has a basic, apparently simple system;

present (event holds at the time of the speech act), past (event occurs prior to the time of the speech act), and future (event occurs subsequent to the time of the speech act). Tense does not refer to the internal temporal structure of events, and so is set aside here. But it is worth noting that even with a simple system like tense, conceptualization plays a role: The present tense can be used for past events in the "historical present" (*This guy comes up to me and asks me for a light...*), which transfers the immediacy of the present to the narrative, and for "scheduled" future events (e.g., *The train leaves in ten minutes*), where the present tense conveys the virtual certainty of the future event.

What interests us here is that because events exist in time, they have temporal structure. That is, events have an internal temporal contour. For instance, the aforementioned distinction between actions (processes) and states represents a difference in the temporal contour of the two event types: Processes involve change of some sort over time, whereas states do not. Of course, the interest in this intuitive model of events for us is the fact that grammatical distinctions are sensitive to the temporal contour of events. Those grammatical distinctions are called *aspectual* distinctions.

The most salient grammatical distinction that is sensitive to aspect is the choice between the *simple present* verb form (verb plus present tense inflection) and the *present progressive* verb form (*be VERBing*) to describe a state of affairs that is true at this moment. To convey that a state is true at this moment, an English speaker must use the simple present, not the present progressive, which is unacceptable.

1. a. *She is tall.*
   b. **She is being tall.*

To convey that a process is true at this moment, on the other hand, one must use the present progressive:

2. a. *Tess is playing the flute.*
   b. *Tess plays the flute.*

The simple present is not ungrammatical with processes (2b), but it does not convey that the process is true at this moment. Instead, it conveys that this is an habitual activity or generic ability of the subject; the process need not actually be taking place at this moment.

There is one subclass of processes that disallows both the simple present and the present progressive for conveying what is true at this very moment:

3. a. **He is shattering the windowpane.*
   b. **He shatters the windowpane.*

The relevant temporal feature of these events, called *achievements* following Vendler (1957/1967), is that they are conceived as taking place instantaneously, that is, as if they have no temporal duration. I say "as if" because it is obviously true that they do have a temporal duration, albeit extremely short, at or beyond the boundary of perceptual discrimination. With achievements, the event is conceptualized or *construed* as being instantaneous, and this fact is reflected in the inability of expressing the event in the present tense, whether in the simple present or in the present progressive. Linguists interpret the absence of present tense forms as reflecting the inability to align the point in time of the achievement and the point in time of the present. Instead, one must say something like *He just shattered the windowpane*, with a past tense form and an adverb (*just*) indicating immediate past.

At this point, there is a three-way distinction between event types based on their temporal contour:

(i)   States, which do not involve change and are extended in time;
(ii) Processes, which do involve change and are extended in time;
(iii) Achievements, which involve change but are points (not extended) in time.

There are two semantic dimensions here; whether or not the event involves change and whether or not the event is extended in time. There is a fourth logical possibility that is also found:

(iv) *Point states*, which do not involve change and are points in time. For example:

4. *It is eight o'clock.*

5. *The train is on time.*

Hence, it is clear that the temporal structure of events, named by verbs, in part determines the grammatical patterns of English. But there is a rather odd mismatch between grammatical form and temporal meaning. For the temporal meaning of "true at this moment," one must use the simple present for states but the present progressive for processes. Conversely, the grammatical form of the simple present has a true-at-this-moment meaning with states and an habitual/generic meaning with processes. Why does the grammar of English have this semantically unnatural complication? In fact, we will see it is not unnatural at all, but represents a deeper fact about English grammar: The aspectual grammatical constructions in part determine the temporal structure of the event it describes via conceptualization.

Let us begin with a simpler example, though. Some states that appear to be unacceptable with the present progressive, in fact do allow it under the right circumstances:

6. a. *Sylvia is resembling her mother.
   b. Sylvia is resembling her mother more and more every year.
7. a. *I am understanding the semantics of aspect.
   b. I am understanding the semantics of aspect better and better every day.
8. a. *I am loving her.
   b. I am loving her more and more, the better I get to know her.

These "states" are interpretable in the present progressive if the time scale is enlarged beyond just the present moment and if there is an assumption of a (gradual) change in degree in the relation between the subject and the object of the verb. If one takes a broader or more "coarse-grained" temporal perspective, then the state turns out to involve some change after all, in these circumstances, and so the progressive can be used. If, however, one uses a smaller, more normal, time scale, of the sort assumed in the (a) examples without any context, then no change is perceptible and the progressive is unacceptable. Thus, a shift in temporal scale leads to a shift in the acceptability of the present progressive for this class of events, which I call *gradable relations*.

This is not the only way in which a state can be interpreted in the present progressive, however:

9. a. Jeff is a jerk.
   b. Jeff is being a jerk (again).
10. a. She is nice to him.
    b. She is being nice to him (for once).

The (a) sentences in (9) and (10) indicate a property of the person taken as a whole, which is true at this moment. The (b) sentences cannot be interpreted as a property of the person, but instead are descriptions of a particular action that is manifesting the property. The (b) sentences could be paraphrased with the process verb *act (like a jerk, nice*, etc.), but this is not necessary in order to produce an acceptable English sentence.

This class of events, which I call *dispositions*, can be construed either as involving no change, in which case it is taken to be an inherent property of the person, or as involving change, in which case it is taken to be a property of a transitory action. Why is this so? We conceptualize being nice or being a jerk as a (possible) character trait of a person. But this trait is only manifested to us in particular actions of the person at particular times. When we encounter such actions, we can construe them as representing an inherent character trait of the person, or alternatively construe them as "one-off" properties of the action. The choice of simple present or present progressive determines the construal of the dispositional property to be conveyed by the speaker as belonging to either the person or the action.

Again, we can represent this in terms of the scalar perspective of the temporal contour of the event. If we are focusing on a single incident of niceness, we are taking a "fine-grained" view on the temporal scale, and correspondingly the process—the presence of change in the action—is salient. If we construe niceness as a character trait, we are assuming that the person is nice on many occasions, that is, we are enlarging the time scale to a very coarse-grained view. When we do so, we simultaneously abstract away from the specifics of the individual actions that are nice, and construe it as an unchanging state of the person.

A similar phenomenon is found with another class of events, which I call *inactive actions*, such as verbs of posture:

11. a. *Bill is standing in the doorway.*
    b. *The Pennines lie to the east of Manchester.*

Examples (11a) and (11b) show that either the present progressive or the simple present can be used to convey that the event is true at this moment. However, the two aspectual constructions are not interchangeable in these contexts:

12. a. *Bill stands in the doorway.*
    b. *The Pennines are lying to the east of Manchester.*

Example (12a) suggests that Bill is a permanent fixture in the doorway, whereas (12b) suggests that the Pennines are pausing briefly on a march across the British countryside. Intuition suggests a difference in interpretation that Goldsmith and Woisetschlaeger (1982) described as "structural" (simple present) versus "phenomenal" (present progressive). A structural state of affairs is one that is construed to represent the inherent way of the world, whereas a phenomenal state of affairs is a passing fancy, so to speak. Goldsmith and Woisetschlaeger demonstrated that the structural-phenomenal distinction cannot be simply equated with the length of "actual" time by giving the following examples:

13. a. *The statue of Tom Paine stands at the corner of Kirkland and College (but everybody expects the new Administration to move it).*
    b. *The statue of Tom Paine is standing at the corner of Kirkland and College (and nobody thinks the deadlocked City Council will ever find a proper place for it).* (p. 84)

It could be the case that the "actual" time that statue of Tom Paine has been standing at the corner of Kirkland and College in (13b) is longer than the time in (13a). But what matters is whether the speaker construes the position of the statue as permanent (the structural interpretation) or transitory (the phenomenal interpretation).

If the simple present represents a construal of an event as permanent (and so unchanging), and the present progressive a construal of the event as transitory (and thus changing as it occurs), then one can interpret the "mismatch" of use of the simple present and present progressive described earlier. Processes, that is, individual occurrences of processes, are transitory, and so, call for the present progressive to convey that they are occurring at this moment. States are normally inherent, lasting events and therefore normally employ the simple present to convey that they are true at this moment.

For a process to occur in the simple present, it must be construed as a lasting state of affairs. This can be achieved by casting the process as either an habitual or a generic activity, not unlike construing an act of being nice as an inherent property of a person. If I say Tess plays the flute, then I am describing the process of playing the flute as an inherent characteristic or ability of Tess that is true over time, and I am abstracting away from the specific processes and construing playing the flute as a lasting state.

Conversely, for a state to occur in the present progressive, it must be construed as a transitory process. There is no single general way in which this can be done, and the examples given previously show how it can be done for a variety of event types; enlarging the time scale for gradually changing relations, such as *understand*, or focusing on a single manifestation of the property in an action for dispositions, such as *be nice*. These construals are generally interpretable with a minimum of context provided. But even an apparently uninterpretable sentence such as (1b) can be given a construal: It could, for instance, describe a situation where she gets up on a box to be taller than the others (suggested by Anna Mawhinney, personal communication, 1997). In this case, the present progressive is used to construe the event as a temporary, passing action.[1]

There are several lessons to be drawn from these observations. Words such as verbs cannot be strictly divided into semantic classes on the basis of the grammatical constructions in which they occur. The grammatical constructions themselves convey a conceptualization of the event denoted by the verb. What matters in understanding the semantics of aspect is the semantic interpretation (if any) of a particular semantic class of verbs when used with either the simple present or the present progressive. In principle, any verb can be combined with any aspectual construction, although in practice, some construals are impossible to imagine. Lastly, the semantic features required for a hearer to interpret a verb plus grammatical construction include quite detailed and even context-specific information (as in *She is being tall*), which suggests that there is no sharp dividing line between "linguistic meaning," general knowledge about a concept, and specific knowledge about the context.

If we turn to achievements, there is a similar story to tell. Achievements supposedly cannot occur in the present progressive to describe the point-like event as happening at this very moment. This is due to the fact that although the present progressive construes an event as transitory and as involving change, it also construes the event as being extended in time. But some pointlike processes do allow the progressive:

14. a. *She just died.*
    b. *Help! She's dying!*

15. a. *The light just flashed.*
    b. *The light is flashing.*

Example (14a) describes the point of time when her life ended, that is, a pointlike transition from life to death. Example (14b) is interpretable, but instead of referring to the pointlike transition, it describes a process leading up to that point. It must be some specific process: I cannot say *I'm dying* this very moment just because I am mortal; I have to be terminally ill, or mortally wounded, that is, in the middle of a process that normally leads to the pointlike transition. I call these *run-up achievements* (where the present progressive describes the run-up process to the achievement normally denoted in the past tense).

The examples in (15) demonstrate a different way in which an achievement can be construed with the present progressive. Example (15a) can be interpreted as a single flash, a pointlike event. Example (15b) is interpretable as describing not a single flash, but a series of flashes. Putting the series of flashes together over a larger time scale than a single flash, the sequence can be construed as a change (on-off-on-off-etc.) over time, which can then be conveyed by the present progressive. I call these *cyclic achievements*.

In fact, (15b) has another easily obtainable interpretation. Imagine watching a distant lighthouse whose light turns around relatively slowly; I could utter (15b) just as the light is coming around to our view. In other words, an achievement is an achievement only to the extent that a speaker construes it to be a single, pointlike event. Even a verb like *shatter* can be construed in the progressive, by allowing it to refer to iterated events: If you asked someone who was brazenly engaged in a major act of vandalism what he was doing, he might reply, *Oh, I'm shattering windowpanes*. Moreover, there is no single interpretation assignable to a combination of a verb denoting an event and an aspectual grammatical construction. The interpretation of such a combination depends largely on both the speaker's and the hearer's real-world knowledge about how such events take place, and/or their imagination in figuring out a plausible scenario for which that combination of verb (event) and aspectual conceptualization is appropriate.

The shifts in interpretation are not merely quirks of the simple pres-ent–present progressive distinction. To illustrate this, I introduce another aspectual semantic distinction, *telicity* (also known as *boundedness* or the *perfective/imperfective* distinction). A telic event (called an *accomplishment*) is one that has a "natural" endpoint or resulting state, whereas an atelic event (an *activity*) does not:

16. a. *I wrote the letter/three letters (in an hour).*
    b. *I slept (for three hours).*
    c. *I wrote letters (for three hours).*

Example (16a) is an example of a telic event. Writing a single letter has a natural endpoint, namely, when you have completed the letter. There is a special adverbial phrase in English using *in*, called the *container adverbial,* which specifies the amount of time from beginning to completion of the telic event. Example (16b) is an atelic event. There is no "natural," specified endpoint to sleeping. One can sleep for any length of time; there is no measurement to show that you have "finished" sleeping, as opposed to simply having stopped sleeping. English uses a different adverbial phrase with *for*, the *durative adverbial,* to indicate how long an atelic event goes on. Example (16c) shows that the process described by *write* (and many other verbs) is telic only if the direct object is a definite or measured quantity. If the direct object of *write* is an indefinite amount or quantity, then the action is atelic: One can go on writing letters; without specifying the number of letters, there is no natural endpoint to the process.

Now, both container and durative adverbials require an interval of time, and so are incompatible with achievements when the latter are construed as pointlike events. Achievements are instead compatible with pointlike temporal adverbs, such as *suddenly:*

17. a. *The window suddenly shattered.*
    b. *The cockroach suddenly died.*
    c. *The light suddenly flashed.*

However, one can combine achievements with container and durative adverbials, with exactly the same sorts of interpretations as are found in the counterpart progressive sentences:

18. a. *He fell ill and died in two weeks.*
    b. *They reached the summit in five hours.*
    c. *The light flashed for five minutes.*
    d. *He shattered windowpanes for half an hour, and then moved on to smashing doors.*

For run-up achievements as in (18a–b), the container adverbial describes the length of time of the run-up process; and the container adverbial is used because the actual pointlike transition is a natural endpoint of the run-up process. For cyclic achievements as in (18c), and the iterative interpretation of typical achievements as in (18d), the durative adverbial describes the length of time of the iterated achievement; and the durative adverbial is used because there is no natural endpoint (iteration of the event is open ended).

Run-up achievements illustrate the problem of individuating events: In simple past tense uses, the event denoted is the pointlike transition, but in the progressive, the event denoted is the run-up process. Another example of variation in what part of the event is denoted by a verb-plus-aspectual-construction is found with verbs of perception and cognition, which I call *inceptive states*:

19. a. *I went around the bend and suddenly saw the mountain lion.*
    b. *Yes, I see the warbler near the top of the tree.*
    c. **I am seeing the warbler near the top of the tree.*

20. a. *I suddenly understood what was happening.*
    b. *I understand how to fill out this form.*
    c. **I am understanding how to fill out this form.*

The (a) sentences in (19–20) describe the inception of the perceptual/cognitive state (as indicated by the acceptability of *suddenly*), while the (b) sentences describe the perceptual/cognitive state itself. The (c) sentences are unacceptable because the construal of the present progressive is not compatible with the construal of the event as either the pointlike inception or the resulting state (of course, [20c] would be acceptable with a coarse-grained, gradual change interpretation). Nevertheless, it is clear that both the inceptive and state interpretations are about equally natural in the appropriate grammatical constructions (simple past for the former, simple present for the latter).

A proper description of the semantic combination of inceptive state verb and construction for (19–20) must include a representation of the inception (the transition from not seeing/understanding/etc. to seeing/understanding/etc.) as well as of the resulting state. But it is more complicated than that. Either the container or the durative adverbial can be used with inceptive state verbs, but they describe different parts of the event:

21. a. *I remembered the answer for five minutes.*
    b. *I remembered the answer in five minutes.*

Example (21a) follows the expected pattern in which the (atelic) state is described as lasting for five minutes. But (21b) describes the period of time up to the inception of the state, not unlike a run-up achievement. Moreover, the pattern in (21b)—describing a run-up process before the inception of the event—is found with ordinary atelic processes, states, and achievements as in (22a–c):

22. a. *In two years, she was president of the company.*
    b. *The horse was galloping in two minutes.*
    c. *The light flashed in a few seconds.*

The observations in this section lead us to two conclusions. The first is that the semantic representation of an event denoted by a verb must be complex, involving not only what we normally think of as "what the verb means" but also the event leading up to it (the run-up process or preceding state) and the event leading out of it (resulting state or, in the case of cyclic achievements, the return to the original state). Hence, we must be able to specify what part of the event is actually described in the sentence and what part is the "background." The part actually described is called the *profile* (following Langacker, 1987) and the "background" part is called the *base* (Langacker, 1987) or *frame* (Fillmore, 1982, 1985).

The second conclusion is that some adverbs and adverbial phrases (e.g., *suddenly, for a week, in two hours, almost*), like the simple present and progressive constructions, also involve a construal of the event, specifically, some particular time interval; but which time interval is profiled depends on the temporal structure of the event. The container adverbial profiles a process leading up to the last natural transition point in the event frame—the endpoint for telic events and the inception for atelic events (including states, inceptive states, and achievements). The durative adverbial profiles an event continuing beyond the first transition point in the event frame—that is, the inception for all event types, including telic events (23):

23. *I read* War and Peace *for two hours (and then fell asleep).*

A *punctual adverbial* like *suddenly* profiles the pointlike transition (24a–c):

24. a. *Suddenly I saw Jack.*
    b. *Suddenly he was in a large cavern.*
    c. *Suddenly the horse galloped.*

If the event is telic, the interval from inception to completion is construed as the transition point (25a), and if that interval cannot be construed as a point in time, the sentence is unacceptable (25b):

25. a. *She suddenly shut the door.* (cf. *She was shutting the door*)
    b. **I suddenly read* War and Peace.

The transition points, or boundaries, are relevant to other aspectual constructions as well. The adverb, *almost,* the *prospective be about to,* and the *conative try* all appear to profile a process leading up to the first transition point:

26. a. *She almost ran/was about to run/tried to run.*
    b. *The mouse almost squeaked/was about to squeak/tried to squeak.*
    c. *She almost was chair/was about to be chair/tried to be chair.*

However, when applied to a telic event, instead of profiling only the run-up to the inception of the event, or construing the event as a pointlike transition, these aspectual constructions are ambiguous as to whether they profile the run-up to the inception (in [27], before entering the river) or the process which would lead to completion of the event (here, reaching the other side of the river):

27. a. *She almost crossed the river.*
    b. *She was about to cross the river.*
    c. *She tried to cross the river.*

That is to say, the adverb, *almost,* the prospective and the conative profile a process leading up to any transition point in the event frame, either the first transition point (the beginning of the event) or the last one (the natural completion point of the event, if there is any). Other aspectual constructions can also be defined in terms of what part of the event frame is profiled by the combination of verb and construction; *begin to* VERB/*begin* VERB*ing* (first transition point), *finish* VERB*ing* (natural endpoint of a telic event), *stop VERBing* (termination point other than the natural endpoint of a telic event), and so forth.

In this section, we have seen why the semantic category of aspect has been one of the more difficult areas of grammatical semantics to analyze. On the one hand, we have a complex representation of an event and its temporal structure. On the other hand, we have aspectual grammatical constructions whose meaning does not simply match (or fail to match) the temporal structure of the event. Instead, the aspectual grammatical construction provides a conceptualization of the temporal structure of an event, and speakers have considerable flexibility in adjusting the temporal structure of the event frame denoted by the verb so that an appropriate part of the structure is profiled by the sentence. The conceptualization processes include the invocation of general real-world knowledge of the event; innovative exploitation of specific aspects of the context; selectively attending to a relevant part of the event in the event frame; and "scalar adjustments" of the scale of the temporal dimension and the dimension of change over time (also presumably an attentional phenomenon).

Having seen how the interaction between lexicon and grammar is mediated by conceptualization processes in the temporal structure of events, we now turn to the conceptualization processes underlying the grammar of the causal structure of events.

GRAMMATICAL RELATIONS AND VOICE: THE CAUSAL STRUCTURE OF EVENTS

In several examples in the preceding section, the event structure was complex, and what part of the event structure was actually profiled by the verb varied with the aspectual grammatical construction with which the verb was used. In the most complex cases, there was some sort of run-up activity that brought about a (usually pointlike) transition that resulted in a new state of the object in question. These examples all suggest that the basic structure of events is causal: Event structure is part of the causal network that unfolds over time.

How, then, are events "cut out" of the causal network and expressed in language? That is, what general cognitive and semantic principles are involved? There are basically two salient features of events that have major grammatical consequences on the organization of clauses. The first is the temporal contour, that is, the states, processes, and transitions described in the preceding section, which are linked together causally. The second are the participants in the events and their causal interactions. In the examples of temporal contours in the preceding section, either just one participant was involved, or we quietly ignored the existence of multiple participants. In this section, I examine the grammatical status of participants in events in greater detail.

Before doing so, however, I must point out that the structure of the fragment of the causal network expressed in a clause is itself dependent on the speaker's point of view. Consider the following two sentences (Croft, 1991, p. 163):

28. a. *John was sick.*
    b. *The virus attacked John's throat, which became inflamed, resulting in laryngitis, until the immune system succeeded in destroying the infection.*

Examples (28a) and (28b) could be used to describe the same segment of the causal network. But, (28a) conceptualizes it as a single, simple, transitory state, whereas (28b) conceptualizes it as a complex set of processes that causally interact. Either conceptualization is possible and is available to the English speaker; it only matters what "grain size" (level of attention) the speaker wishes to use for describing the phenomenon. Nevertheless, there is a significant commitment that the speaker makes: The choice of grain size determines the choice of what objects count as participants in the event. This is further evidence that the participants help to determine the causal structure of events for encoding in language.

Examples (28a–b) also illustrate another important difference in conceptualization. Example (28b) is a complex sentence, that is, it contains multiple clauses. Because clauses denote events, causation is construed here as events causing other events. This is generally the case for the formulation of causal relations in complex sentences. Example (28a), however, is a simple clause; it contains one participant, but clauses can contain two, three, or even more participants, expressed as the *subject, object,* or an *oblique* expressed by a prepositional phrase (e.g., *for, with, to,* etc.). When a segment of the causal chain is expressed in a single clause, the causal relations are encoded in terms of participants acting on other participants. This insight was first explicitly described by Talmy (1972, 1976), but is now used widely by a variety of cognitively oriented linguists. I do not discuss complex sentences any further, and therefore, focus my attention on single clauses in order to see how the causal interaction of participants determines choice of subject, object, and oblique for a variety of clauses in English.

The value of causal structure for understanding how participants in an event are assigned to subject or object is best demonstrated by briefly outlining the difficulties of one of the most popular approaches to the semantics of grammatical relations, namely the semantic classification of participants according to semantic roles (also called *thematic roles* or *case roles*). The following examples illustrate some of the more common semantic roles, with rough definitions and how they are expressed in English (roles and many of the examples are from Frawley, 1992):

Agent: a volitional being that brings about a change

29. a. *TOMMY drove the car.*
    b. *The food was eaten BY RACCOONS.*

Author: a nonvolitional object (typically a natural force) that brings about a change

30. a. *LIGHTNING struck the tree.*
    b. *The tree was struck BY LIGHTNING.*

Instrument: an object under the control of an agent that brings about a change

31. a. *Ellen cut the salami WITH A KNIFE.*
    b. *THE KEY opened the door.*
    c. *THIS KNIFE can really cut through cardboard.*

Patient: an object that undergoes a change of state of some sort

32. a. *The man cleaned THE CAR.*
    b. *The authorities burned THE BOOK.*
    c. *THE BOOK was banned by the authorities.*
    d. *THIS MEAT cuts easily.*

Experiencer: a being whose mental state is altered by some external stimulus

33. a. *BUDDY smelled the flowers.*
    b. *The dog scared ME.*

Stimulus: an object that brings about a change in mental state in an experiencer

34. a. *Buddy smelled THE FLOWERS.*
    b. *THE DOG scared me.*

Benefactive: a person who benefits from an action being carried out, sometimes by receiving something as a result of the action

35. a. *I sang the song FOR FRED.*
    b. *Mary bought BOB lunch.* (actually recipient)

Theme/Figure: an object whose location/motion is described by the verb; figure contrasts with ground as in Gestalt psychology (the terminology was borrowed by Talmy, 1974, 1983)

36. a. *Bill rolled THE BALL across the floor.*
    b. *THE BALL rolled across the floor.*
    c. *The bus spattered the sidewalk WITH MUD.*

Spatial goal: the ground (reference point) for motion of a theme to or toward the ground object

37. a. *They went TO NORMANDY.*
    b. *The bus spattered THE SIDEWALK with mud.*

Metaphorical goal: the endpoint of a nonspatial process that is metaphorically construed as motion

38. a. *Wine can turn INTO VINEGAR.*
    b. *We made VINEGAR out of the wine.*

Spatial source: the ground for motion of a theme away from the ground object

39. a. *The cat leaped FROM THE KITCHEN COUNTER.*
    b. *The porcupines stripped THE SPRUCE of its bark.*

Metaphorical source: the starting point of a nonspatial process that is metaphorically construed as motion

40. a. *WINE can turn into vinegar.*
    b. *We turned THE BENCH into a coffee table.*
    c. *The publisher bought the rights FROM THE AUTHOR.*

The examples of semantic roles given in (29–40) demonstrate that they are simply not helpful for predicting the semantics of grammatical relations: Almost any semantic role can occur in almost any grammatical relation. Yet, intuitively, the choice of subject, object, and oblique in English (and in other languages) is not chaotic. Moreover, semantic roles are not independent semantic constructs. Semantic roles are defined with respect to other semantic roles. All semantic roles are defined with respect to the sorts of events with which they are found. This apparent problem is in fact the pointer to a solution to the puzzle of the semantics of grammatical relations.

Choice of subject and object (and as we see shortly, also obliques), is largely relative: The subject must act on the object in some way (physical or otherwise). Agents, authors, and instruments act on patients and themes. Hence, if one of the former and one of the latter appear in an active transitive sentence, the agent/etc. will be subject and the patient or theme will be object (the passive, and alternation between object and oblique, is discussed later). This prototypical event type is called the "transmission-of-force" model by Talmy (1976) and the "billiard-ball" model by Langacker (1991): One participant interacts with another participant and transmits its force to the other participant, which then undergoes a change. In later work, Talmy recognized that there were other kinds of *force-dynamic* relations (as he now calls them; Talmy, 1988) than the basic billiard-ball model:

41. a. *I kicked the ball.*
    b. *I pushed the ball.*
    c. *I held the ball.*
    d. *I stopped the ball.*
    e. *I dropped/let go of the ball.*
    f. *I left the ball (in the house).*

Example (41a) conforms to the billiard-ball model: I make contact with the ball and it goes off. Example (41b) is the most similar to (41a) but the *initiator* of the action continually applies force to the *endpoint*[2] (*extended* causation vs. the *onset* causation of [41a]). Example (41c) is quite a bit different. Unlike (41a–b), the endpoint (the ball) has a natural tendency to motion (due to gravity) rather than to rest; the initiator must apply continuous force to keep the endpoint at rest; Talmy described this as extended causation of rest ([41a–b] are causation of motion or more generally, change of state). Extended causation of rest events, incidentally, are inactive actions: Even though no change takes place, the dynamic character of the action as manifested in the progressive is due to the application of force by the initiator. Example (41d) illustrates onset causation of rest: The moving ball makes contact with my foot and stops moving; I could remove my foot and the ball won't move (in some uses of this sentence). Examples (41e–f) illustrate *letting* rather than *causing* (in Talmy's terminology); the initiator "acts on" the endpoint by refraining to exercise its force-dynamic potential, thus allowing the endpoint either to undergo change (letting of motion; [41e]), or not (letting of rest; [41f]). Talmy also recognized *helping* and *hindering* force-dynamic relations in addition to causing and letting.

The examples in (41) are ranked in rough order of frequency of expression as simple transitive verbs. In fact, many of the less prototypical sorts of force-dynamic relations are typically expressed through verbs that take complements (*let X* VERB, *keep* VERBing, *keep X from* VERBing, *leave X to* VERB, *help X* VERB, etc.). But when any force-dynamic relationship is expressed by a simple active transitive verb, the assignment of participants as subject and object is clear: The initiator is the subject and the endpoint is the object.

The force-dynamic relations between participants analyzed in the preceding paragraphs are all examples of causation of physical events, typically by volitional agents but also by physical objects. Talmy (1976) recognized that there are other kinds of causal relations in which the endpoint of the force-dynamic relation undergoes a change of mental state rather than of physical state; he called these *affective* causation or *inducive* causation (depending on whether the initiator was physical or volitional, respectively). These are the verbs whose participants are experiencer and stimulus. Unlike physical events, however, some mental verbs make the experiencer the object (42a–c) and others make the experiencer the subject (43a–d):

42. a. *The dog frightened me.*
    b. *The performance pleased her.*
    c. *Her behavior puzzled him.*

43. a. *I looked at the elk.*
    b. *I listened to the sonata.*
    c. *I thought about my presentation.*
    d. *I grieved over her death.*

The reason that mental verbs fall into two separate types (a third is discussed later) is that mental processes are fundamentally ambivalent force dynamically. The experiencer directs her or his attention to the stimulus (an inactive action) and the stimulus simultaneously alters the mental state of the experiencer. The sentences in (42) and (43) selectively attend to different aspects of the causal relationship between experiencer and stimulus. The sentences in (42) describe the change in mental state of experiencer caused by the stimulus, and so the experiencer is object. The sentences in (43), on the other hand, describe the experiencer directing her or his attention to the stimulus; in this case, it is the experiencer that carries out a change of state (the experiencer's own state), whereas the stimulus isn't doing anything. (In fact, the stimulus in such sentences is typically an oblique, not a direct object, because of its lack of affectedness by the event; this is discussed further.)

Cross-linguistically, this pattern is largely maintained: Verbs highlighting how the stimulus causes a change in the experiencer's mental state make the stimulus the subject and the experiencer the object (sometimes the indirect object); whereas verbs highlighting the experiencer, directing their attention to the stimulus, make the experiencer the subject and the stimulus an object (or an oblique, because it is not directly affected by the experiencer's action).

There is a third type of mental verb for which there is significant cross-linguistic variation in how the experiencer and the stimulus are expressed.

These are stative mental relations, where the verb simply indicates that a mental state of an experiencer holds with respect to the stimulus, as in *I like cats.* In mental states, there is no force-dynamic relationship: The competing force-dynamic directions are balanced. Hence, in some languages (such as English), the experiencer is normally made subject; in other languages (such as Russian and languages of south-central Asia), the experiencer is normally made (indirect) object; in still other languages, the experiencer and stimulus are both encoded either as subjects (Japanese "double-*ga*" constructions) or as objects (Eastern Pomo; for details, see Croft, 1993).

In general, a noncausal stative relation can be expressed in different ways; the force-dynamic model of subject–object assignment makes no a priori prediction, and across languages, one finds variation. The two most common relations are the spatial relation between figure and ground, and the possessive relation between possessor and possessed. Despite the cross-linguistic variation, however, there appear to be systematic patterns as to how noncausal relations are incorporated into the causal structure of events. Essentially, it appears that noncausal relations are construed as force-dynamic relations in experientially plausible ways.

Beginning with spatial relations, we find the following systematic pattern in English and in other languages:

44. a. *Bobby loaded rutabagas on the wagon.*
    b. *Bobby loaded the wagon with rutabagas.*

45. a. *The beaver stripped bark from the trees.*
    b. *The beaver stripped the trees of bark.*

In the (a) sentences, the figure is the direct object and the ground is an oblique phrase governed by a spatial preposition, which varies depending on the spatial relation. In the (b) sentences, the ground is the direct object and the figure is an oblique phrase governed by *with* (if the figure ends up in contact with the ground) or *of* (if not). This pattern persists with possession and other relations:

46. a. *They supplied arms to the Azeris.*
    b. *They supplied the Azeris with arms.*

47. a. *They robbed/stole $50 from him.*
    b. *They robbed him of $50.*

48. a. *I substituted a set of readings for the textbook.*
    b. *I replaced the textbook with a set of readings.*

These patterns, which are systematic and which are found across languages, can be explained by the following account. First, there is a systematic construal of noncausal relations as indicated in (49):

49. Causal: *Initiator*   *Endpoint*
    Spatial: *Figure*   *Ground*
    Possessive: *Possessed*   *Possessor*
    Substitutive: *New*   *Former*

The construal is natural, in that generally, an agent acts on the figure to alter its spatial relationship with the ground, acts on a possessed item in order to transfer it to the possessor, and introduces a new object to take the place of the former object.

Second, although subjects must always be antecedent to objects in the causal chain, oblique referents may be either antecedent or subsequent to the object in the causal chain. However, oblique prepositions divide themselves into two types, those that indicate *antecedent* oblique phrases and those that indicate *subsequent* oblique phrases, as listed in (50):

50. Antecedent Oblique: *with, by, of,* metaphorical *from, out of*
    Subsequent Oblique: *to, for,* all spatial prepositions (*in, out, on, off, from,* etc.)

These two hypotheses account for (46–48), as well as for many other sentences. For instance, in (46a), the figure is a direct object and the ground is an oblique. Because the ground is construed as subsequent to the figure in the causal chain, it must be governed by a normal spatial preposition. In (46b), on the other hand, the ground is the direct object and the figure is an oblique. Because the figure is construed as antecedent to the ground, it must be governed by an antecedent preposition, namely *with.*

Similar arguments apply to (47–48). Moreover, these examples fit in with the standard pattern with purely causal chains:

51. a. *He stirred the soup with a spoon.*
    b. *He made the soup for Sandra.*

52. *This house was designed by Frank Lloyd Wright.*

In (51a), the agent acts on the spoon, which acts on the soup. Hence, the spoon is antecedent to the direct object *soup* in the causal chain, and so requires an antecedent oblique preposition, *with.* In (51b), on the other hand, Sandra receives a positive benefit from the making of the soup. Hence, Sandra is subsequent to the direct object *soup* in the causal chain, and so requires a subsequent oblique preposition, for. Finally, in the passive sentence in (52), the house is the subject; because the agent is antecedent in the causal chain to the subject (let alone a direct object, which is absent here), it must be governed by an antecedent oblique preposition, namely by (the passive voice is discussed further).

The distinction between antecedent and subsequent obliques is such a basic one that it appears to be acquired by young children and used innovatively. English has several antecedent oblique prepositions, and children tend to substitute one for another, but not to substitute a subsequent preposition for an antecedent one. For example, children sometimes substitute by for the instrumental with ([53a], from Bowerman, 1983, pp. 463–465; and [53b] from Tomasello, 1992, p. 176); or the antecedent prepositions from, of, or with for the passive agent by ([53c] from Bowerman, 1989, p. 29; cf. Clark & Carpenter, 1989); or the subsequent preposition for for to ([53d] from Tomasello, 1992, p. 175):

53. a. 'I just eat it BY my spoon' [C 4;4].
    b. 'Can I pick it up BY my hands' [T 1;10–2;0].
    c. 'Sometimes Eva needs to be feeded WITH you because she doesn't eat' [C 4;4].
    d. 'Santa Claus gave it FOR me' [T 1;10–2;0].

More strikingly, children take a verb that occurs with only one direct object option in adult English—ground only as in (54a) or figure only as in (54b)—and use it in the other direct object option, with an antecedent or subsequent oblique preposition as appropriate (Bowerman, 1982, pp. 338–339):

54. a. '. . . 'cause I'm going to touch it [hand] ON your pants' [E 3;0]. (figure is incorrectly made direct object, but appropriate subsequent oblique preposition governing ground is chosen)
    b. 'I don't want it because I spilled it [toast] OF orange juice' [E 4;11]. (ground is incorrectly made direct object, but appropriate antecedent oblique preposition governing figure is chosen)

These examples demonstrate that English children come to understand the force-dynamic model underlying the choice of subject, object, and (antecedent or subsequent) oblique in adult English, and sometimes to use it productively.

The variation in assigning participants in events to subject, object, and oblique grammatical relations is thus based on a systematic understanding by the speaker of the force-dynamic interactions of those participants in the events in question. As with the temporal contour of events, the force-dynamic relationships constitute the event frame, and only part of the event in the event frame is profiled by the verb, combined with a particular assignment of subject, object, and oblique. Specifically, I hypothesize that the part of the causal chain that is profiled is the part of the chain that goes from the subject to the object (if there is one). Of course, this hypothesis would be more convincing if there was a semantic correlate to the "beginning" and "end" of the verbal profile, that is, to subject and object status where a choice is possible. In fact, there is such a correlation, namely control for subjects and affectedness for objects. Moreover, these semantic properties suggest an answer to a major question posed at the beginning of this chapter: How do speakers individuate events out of the causal chain and encode them with verbs and their grammatical dependents?

It has long been observed that the choice of figure or ground as the direct object in (46a–46b) involves a subtle difference in meaning. If (46a) is chosen, then it is inferrable that all of the rutabagas have been loaded onto the wagon, but it is not necessarily inferrable that the wagon is full. If (46b) is chosen, the opposite is true: It is inferrable that the wagon is full but it is not necessarily inferrable that all the rutabagas have been put on the wagon. In other words, the participant assigned to direct object position can be inferred to be fully affected by the action, whereas one cannot make the same inference for the participant assigned to the oblique position.

The association of direct object status with a higher degree of affectedness can be found in other types of examples. I noted previously that in mental verbs that describe the experiencer, directing their attention to the stimulus, the stimulus is not physically altered and is usually found as an oblique rather than as a direct object (43a–43d). Other verbs allow a participant to be either the direct object or an oblique, with a corresponding difference in affectedness:

55. a. *I shot the sheriff.*
    b. *I shot at the sheriff.*

56. a. *Johnny chewed on the bone.*
    b. *Johnny chewed the bone.*

Example (55a) entails that the sheriff was struck by a bullet (in some contexts, it even implies the sheriff was killed); (55b) does not. Example (56a) implies that Johnny did not break the bone, whereas (56b) implies that he did (and in fact probably put the entire bone in his mouth).

Whereas full affectedness appears to be the salient semantic feature for assignment as object, full control appears to be the salient semantic feature for assignment to the subject position. Normally, an agent is the subject in an active sentence. Authors, i.e. natural forces, can also function as the subject, largely because they appear to act without a further external force acting on them. Instruments do not normally appear as subjects, precisely because they are under the external control of an agent. Yet, they can appear as subjects, as in (31b–31c). In (31b), the key is the subject because its shape determines that the door can be opened; in this context, *open* can be paraphrased as *unlock*. In (31c), ability to cut cardboard well is attributed to properties of the knife (rather than to properties of the agent wielding the knife); the knife is construed as the ultimate cause of the event and is assigned to subject position. Even a patient can be construed as responsible for the outcome of an active voice verb, as in (32d), where it is the tenderness of the meat that renders it easily cuttable.

Why are control and affectedness associated with subject and object assignment, that is, the two "edges" of the verbal profile in an event frame? Consider what is almost universally taken to be the prototypical causal event type: A volitional agent acting on her or his own brings about a complete change of state to a patient, so that the patient cannot change any further in the relevant semantic dimension. An event of this type is the easiest to isolate from the causal network. The agent is construed as acting entirely under her or his volition, and so there is no obvious antecedent participant causing the agent to act. The patient undergoes a full change of state, which means no further process can lead to another event in the causal chain (this is the natural endpoint of a telic event). Moreover, states generally do not have causal consequences, hence no further participants are usually involved in the causal chain.

In other words, a segment of the causal chain whose initiator is in full control and whose endpoint is fully affected is the most completely individuated from the causal network (Croft, 1994). It is thus not surprising that this is the prototypical event type encoded by verbs. Of course, many events (perhaps most events) are not really like this. Agents act under duress or out of some emotional response. Or the initiator isn't even an agent, but a natural force or an instrument with some salient relevant properties (a sharp knife). Patients are not completely affected, so further consequences may follow; or the event is atelic; or the change of state affects the mental state of another participant, leading to another causal chain. To some degree, the assignment of grammatical relations to participants is determined by the way the world is, that is, our real-world knowledge of particular kinds of causal relations and our knowledge of specific circumstances. But to a considerable degree, it is up to the speaker's construal of the event. Was it I, or my knife, or the meat itself that led to an easy cutting event? Was I the agent in control of the action, or did someone make me do it? And so on.

Lastly, I consider the phenomenon of passive voice in the context of the individuation of events for communication. The analysis of the passive voice is straightforward in this model: The event frame is the same as the active voice counterpart, but the passive verb form profiles only the segment of the causal chain including the patient's change to a resulting state. The passive verbal profile accounts for the assignment of patient as subject in (32c) and (52), and the use of an antecedent oblique for the passive agent when it is expressed, as in (29b), (30b), and (52). The choice of passive vs. active voice is generally considered to be governed by discourse factors, e.g. focus of attention on the patient vs. the agent. The discourse analysis of the passive is not incompatible with the cognitive account given here: The verbal profile is "shortened," excluding the agent's causal role, precisely for the purpose of communicating to the hearer that the portion of the causal network involving the patient only is the most relevant for the purposes at hand. (In fact, Langacker, 1987, suggested that profiling is an attentional phenomenon.) In general, it should not be forgotten that the cognitive construal of experience in language is ultimately done for the purpose of communication in discourse, and cannot be separated from that function (Croft, 1994).

CONCLUSION: SEMANTICS AND GRAMMAR

In this chapter, I outlined a cognitive linguistic approach to the grammar of event structure in English aspectual constructions and grammatical relations. The emphasis was how the event structure underlying verb meanings interacts with the conceptualization of events provided by the semantics of grammatical constructions. I wish to conclude with some remarks on the relationship of this approach to traditional issues in grammatical analysis.

The central starting point for the analysis of grammatical structure in linguistics is what is called *distributional analysis*; the distribution of words (in this case, verbs and the phrases dependent on them) across grammatical constructions (such as the simple present vs. the present progressive, container vs. durative adverbials, and subject, object, and oblique grammatical relations). The assumptions behind distributional analysis are: (a) words have a fixed distribution across constructions—they are either acceptable or not in those constructions; (b) their distribution can be used to define grammatical categories; and (c) grammatical categories and constructions can be defined distributionally without reference to their meaning or use.

Cognitive linguistics employs distributional analysis as well, but the facts require us to abandon all three assumptions about the nature of distributional analysis. Words do not have a fixed distribution across constructions. To some degree, any word can be used in principle in any construction.

Hence, distributional patterns do not establish grammatical categories in the strict sense. What matters is the semantic interpretation of a word in a particular grammatical construction. By examining the meanings of verbs in constructions, we can establish semantic classes of events and conceptual meanings of constructions, as we have done in this chapter. The interaction between verbs and the event frames they evoke on the one hand, and grammatical constructions and the temporal and causal structures they construe events as having on the other hand, is dynamic and flexible. In fact, this interplay between grammatical constructions and the words that speakers fit into them is the source of the richness and flexibility of language as a means of communicating experience.

The flexibility of grammar is limited to some extent by our expectations of what the world is like and how different types of events can be plausibly construed. It is also limited by conventionalized construals of events that have historically become fixed in languages and that also tend to vary across languages. It is a fact of English, for example, that the experiencers in mental states are subjects and not objects. The underlying conceptual processes are subordinated to grammatical convention here (that is, how often speakers of English in the past have chosen to encode the relevant relations). But those underlying processes do manifest themselves, not only in the latent motivation of conventional patterns, but also in the creative learning of language by children, and in the creative, innovative use of language by adults.

NOTES

1. In fact, it appears that the expression of transitory states in English is a fuzzy boundary case. The conventional grammatical way to describe some transitory states is by use of the simple present: *Gary is sick/Rhonda is the winner*. This usage does not fit the general pattern of the simple present conceptualizing the event as an inherent unchanging property. On the other hand, the novel interpretation of *She is being tall* exploits the present progressive to indicate a transitory state, in contrast to the inherent state described by the simple present *She is tall*.
2. Talmy calls the initiator the Antagonist and the endpoint the Agonist; I am retaining the terminology of Croft, 1991, and subsequent papers that elaborate Talmy's model for the mapping of participants into grammatical relations.

REFERENCES

Bowerman, M. (1982). Reorganizational processes in lexical and syntactic development. In E. Wanner & L. R. Gleitman (Eds.), *Language acquisition: The state of the art* (pp. 319–345). Cambridge, England: Cambridge University Press.

Bowerman, M. (1983). Hidden meanings: The role of covert conceptual structures in children's development of language. In D. R. Rogers & J. A. Sloboda (Eds.), *The acquisition of symbolic skills* (pp. 445–470). New York: Plenum.

Bowerman, M. (1989). *When a patient is the subject: Sorting out passives, anticausatives, and middles in the acquisition of English.* Unpublished manuscript.

Clark, E. V., & Carpenter, K. L. (1989). The notion of source in language acquisition. *Language, 65*, 1–30.

Croft, W. (1991). *Syntactic categories and grammatical relations: The cognitive organization of information.* Chicago: University of Chicago Press.

Croft, W. (1993). Case marking and the semantics of mental verbs. In J. Pustejovsky (Ed.), *Semantics and the lexicon* (pp. 55–72). Dordrecht: Kluwer Academic.

Croft, W. (1994). Voice: Beyond control and affectedness. In P. J. Hopper & B. A. Fox (Eds.), *Voice: Form and function* (pp. 89–117). Amsterdam: John Benjamins.

Fillmore, C. J. (1982). Frame semantics. In The Linguistic Society of Korea (Ed.), *Linguistics in the morning calm* (pp. 111–137). Seoul: Hanshin.

Fillmore, C. J. (1985). Frames and the semantics of understanding. *Quaderni di semantica, 6,* 222–254.

Frawley, W. (1992). *Linguistic semantics.* Hillsdale, NJ: Lawrence Erlbaum Associates.

Goldsmith, J., & Woisetschlaeger, E. (1982). The logic of the English progressive. *Linguistic Inquiry, 13,* 79–89.

Langacker, R. W. (1987). *Foundations of cognitive grammar: Vol. 1. Theoretical prerequisites.* Stanford, CA: Stanford University Press.

Langacker, R. W. (1991). *Foundations of cognitive grammar: Vol. 2. Descriptive application.* Stanford, CA: Stanford University Press.

Rosch, E. (1978). Principles of categorization. In E. Rosch & B. Lloyd (Eds.), *Cognition and categorization* (pp. 27–48). Hillsdale, NJ: Lawrence Erlbaum Associates.

Talmy, L. (1972). *Semantic structures in English and Atsugewi.* Unpublished doctoral dissertation, Department of Linguistics, University of California, Berkeley.

Talmy, L. (1974). Semantics and syntax of motion. In J. Kimball (Ed.), *Syntax and semantics* (Vol. 4, pp. 181–238). New York: Academic Press.

Talmy, L. (1976). Semantic causative types. In M. Shibatani (Ed.), *The grammar of causative constructions* (pp. 43–116). New York: Academic Press.

Talmy, L. (1983). How language structures space. In H. L. Pick, Jr. & L. P. Acredolo (Eds.), *Spatial orientation: Theory, research and application* (pp. 225–282). New York: Plenum.

Talmy, L. (1988). Force dynamics in language and cognition. *Cognitive Science, 12,* 49–100.

Tomasello, M. (1992). *First verbs.* Cambridge, England: Cambridge University Press.

Vendler, Z. (1967). Verbs and times. In Z. Vendler (Ed.), *Linguistics in philosophy* (pp. 97–121). Ithaca, NY: Cornell University Press. (Original work published 1957)

Chapter 4

Language and the Flow of Thought

Wallace Chafe
University of California, Santa Barbara

It is a curious fact that efforts to understand the human mind have never taken very much account of how people actually talk. It is not that there has been a neglect of language—far from it—but that studies relating language and the mind have largely ignored insights that can be derived from a close and systematic examination of ordinary speech, the kind of talk that all of us produce and hear around us constantly in our daily lives. There is still no widespread appreciation of what ordinary talk can tell us about the mind, or even of how one can go about exploiting it as a valuable source of understanding. The study of natural conversation has been left largely to sociologists, whose interests have led them more in the direction of studying social interaction (e.g., Atkinson & Heritage, 1984; Goodwin, 1981; Gumperz, 1982).

There are various reasons for this neglect. For one thing, speech is evanescent. The sounds people make as they talk, and even many of the thoughts expressed by those sounds, quickly fade away. The methods of Western science depend fundamentally on an ability to pin down what one observes, usually in visual form, and to return to it again and again. Speech itself does not allow that kind of storage and manipulation. It is true that the invention of writing provided a way to convert sounds and ideas into something visible. It is thus easy to understand why most systematic studies of language through the ages have been based on written language. But visual representations of language always leave out much that is present in actual speech; when we speak of "reducing" language to writing, the implications of the word "reducing" are cogent.

By the early years of the 20th century, there were some linguistic scholars who had begun to recognize the special importance of spoken language, and some went to great trouble to reproduce the sounds of language in writing as faithfully as possible. Particularly in studies of exotic languages, linguists would sit with "native speakers" and carefully transcribe what was dictated. Much was learned in that way, but not only was transcription limited as a way of capturing the total richness of the language, the language itself had to be less than completely natural, its normal flow impeded by the slow pace of the transcription process. The transcriptions, furthermore, were usually limited to folktales and other types of "oral literature" that are remembered and repeated in ways that ordinary conversational language is not.

By the middle of the 20th century, the commercial availability of tape recorders made it possible, for the first time in human history, to preserve ordinary speech in a form that allowed repeated listening and manipulation, to enrich thereby the detail of transcriptions, and to perform electronic analyses whose sophistication continues to develop. Although language itself remains evanescent, its sounds at least can be preserved and studied in ways that were never before possible.

Every language provides ways not only of organizing sounds, but also thoughts, along with ways of relating these two disparate phenomena. There are two great benefits. Most obviously, associating thoughts with sounds makes it possible for thoughts to be communicated. Sounds can be produced by one individual and received by another, and through this process, the first person can give the second some idea of what he or she is thinking. The reproduction of one person's thoughts in another person's mind can obviously never be complete; one can never fully know what another is thinking. Nevertheless, the sounds of language allow exchanges of thoughts among humans in ways that far surpass the abilities of other creatures.

The other benefit of language lies in the organization of the thoughts themselves. In order for them to be communicated, they must first be associated somehow with configurations of sounds that are already familiar to the listener. Otherwise the sounds would "make no sense." But because the number of possible thoughts is infinite in the sense that every individual's ongoing experiences are unique, it would be impossible for every particular thought to be associated with a particular configuration of sounds that was already known to a listener. As Franz Boas (1911) commented in the early years of the 20th century:

> Since the total range of personal experience which language serves to express is infinitely varied, and its whole scope must be expressed by a limited number of phonetic groups, it is obvious that an extended classification of experiences must underlie all articulate speech. (p. 22)

This "extended classification of experiences" amounts to the interpretation of particular, unique events and objects as instances of already familiar categories (Lakoff, 1987). Each such category has two benefits, a communicative one and a conceptual one. Communicatively, a category provides language users with what Boas called a "phonetic group," a familiar configuration of sounds. The category thus serves to communicate, however partially and imperfectly, the speaker's unique mental experience. If, for example, I am thinking of a particular object I interpret as an instance of the light bulb category, I can make the sound written "light bulb" and thereby give my listener at least a rough idea of what I have in mind. At the same time, my assignment of the object to that category enables me to think about the object in a familiar way and to have certain expectations concerning it; that it can be screwed into a light socket, that it will produce light when the current is turned on, that it will shatter and make a noise if dropped on a cement floor, and so on. In short, this ability to interpret unique experiences as instances of familiar categories makes it possible to communicate them with familiar sound combinations, and at the same time, makes it possible to think of them in familiar ways, and thus to behave toward them in ways that are familiar too.

Modern technology has enhanced the study of language by making its sounds observable in greater detail and with greater accuracy than ever before, but the thoughts associated with those sounds remain problematic. Currently developing techniques of brain imaging are allowing us to observe for the first time which parts of the brain are active in different circumstances. They do not, however, show experiences themselves, which may always remain hidden from public observation. There is a sense in which each of us knows what we are thinking, although we may not always have a good way of verbalizing it. But the only way we can know what someone else is thinking is through what that person says, or through some other overt action—a facial expression or gesture, perhaps—from which that person's thoughts may be inferred, or from imagining what we ourselves would be thinking in similar circumstances. The only direct access we have to thoughts is through introspection, as William James recognized 100 years ago, pointing out that "*introspection is difficult and fallible . . .* The only safeguard is in the final *consensus* of our farther knowledge about the thing in question, later views correcting earlier ones, until at last the harmony of a consistent system is reached" (James, 1890/1950, pp. 191–192). But James emphasized, in a chapter called "The Methods and Snares of Psychology," that "introspective observation is what we have to rely on first and foremost and always" (James, 1890/1950, p. 185).

Not long after he wrote those words, most of psychology set off in quite a different direction, forcefully rejecting introspection altogether as a method of observation, and putting all its money on overt behavior. That limitation still constrains much work on the nature of the mind, and introspection still fails to be taken very seriously. Much research on the mind thus follows the pattern of the drunk who lost his keys in a dark corner, but was looking for them by a lamppost because the light was better there. The potential for understanding the mind has thus been limited to searches under the bright light of overt behavior. What James called "looking into our own minds and reporting what we there discover" has been dismissed as unusable (James, 1890/1950, p. 185).

Linguistics has been less constrained in this regard. Perhaps because of an ancestry in both anthropology and the humanities, and perhaps also because its 19th-century successes in unraveling some of the mysteries of language change and language relationships gave it less of a need to mimic the physical sciences, linguistics has been more willing to confront introspective evidence. To be sure, American linguistics in the 1920s came under the influence of behaviorist psychology, and in the 1930s of logical positivism, and for a while there were linguists who hoped they could avoid the observation of meanings, to which only introspection provided direct access, by examining the distributions of sound configurations in huge samples of language, ignoring what those configurations meant. Today, however, most linguists are willing to consult their knowledge of the English language to observe, say, that "the boy" conveys the idea of one individual and "the boys" of more than one, or that "he's here" involves a present time and place and "he was there" a location more distant in time and space. In the end, it is important to recognize that language serves both to organize and to communicate thoughts, that when we speak or listen it is in fact the thoughts of which we are ordinarily the most conscious, and that we cannot expect to use linguistic evidence to understand the mind unless we are willing to confront the nature of those thoughts.

Language is used in a variety of ways, each of which affects the shape that language takes. Since the 1970s, ever-increasing attention has been paid to differences between spoken language and written language, and it has become clear that each of these two broad categories allows for diverse uses and forms. Written language, for example, is used in novels and short stories, news reports, encyclopedias, shopping lists, and so forth. Spoken language has its many uses too; speeches, debates, interviews, and so forth. Each use shapes language in ways that are adapted to it (Biber, 1988; Chafe & Tannen, 1987). Ordinary conversational talk, however, occupies a special place as the kind of language that is most natural in both form and function, the kind of language humans must be designed by evolution to produce and comprehend. It requires no special training or skill to be able to talk casually with others, and every normal person acquires this ability as a natural part of maturation. Because conversation is the form of language least influenced by acquired skills, it provides us with the most direct and uncontaminated access to natural mental processes. Every other use people make of language is a skill that has to be deliberately learned.

Why, in the course of human evolution, might this ability to converse have developed as it did? What adaptive value might it have? Although sometimes it may have an obvious and immediate benefit, much of the time conversation serves no clear instrumental purpose. When people get together for a meal, or talk on a bus or plane, there is usually no practical result beyond the satisfaction that comes from interpersonal contact. But people do it all the time, naturally and effectively. It helps to think of casual conversation as a way separate minds are connected into networks of other minds. Individual experiences can be shared and passed on so that they become the second, third, or fourthhand experiences of others. Each experience may be trivial in itself, but the gradual accumulation of experiences within each individual and within a social network builds a fund of shared knowledge that far surpasses what any one person could have acquired if limited to what he or she experienced directly.

AN EXAMPLE

The presentation of linguistic findings usually relies on the citation of examples, samples of language that illustrate the points being made. So long as the findings are restricted to phonology, morphology, or syntax, it is relatively easy to cite enough examples to substantiate whatever general findings are being discussed. Studies of discourse—or longer stretches of talk—are more problematic in this regard. It is impractical to include an example of an entire conversation, but even selected excerpts can be too long to allow more than one or two of them, at best, to be cited in an academic paper. Furthermore, the findings themselves are likely to be many and multifaceted, requiring numerous and lengthy illustrations for adequate confirmation. Although it may be a poor compromise to provide no more than a single sample for discussion, there is some compensation in the fact that every sample of natural speech provides a rich, and in some respects, unique combination of observations. If the discussion has the appearance of an "explication of the text," the fact is that any sample of natural speech illustrates a host of general findings, findings that can be observed in other samples in other combinations. The limitations of discourse presentation, however, mean that their generality has to be taken on faith.

Within these limitations, the discussion to follow is based on a brief excerpt from a conversation between a sister and brother in their retirement years who were reminiscing about things that happened while they were growing up. The sister was the main speaker here, and the brother's remarks are given in italics. Three dots indicate a measured pause, with the measurement (in seconds) given in parentheses. Two dots show a brief break in timing. The acute accent mark indicates a relatively high pitch and amplitude, the grave accent mark a relatively high pitch without a corresponding amplitude increase. A period at the end of a line shows a falling pitch, a question mark a high-rising pitch, a hyphen a level pitch, and a comma any other phrase-final pitch contour. The down arrows bracket a segment of speech pronounced with lower pitch and amplitude, the up arrows the reverse. Finally, the square brackets in (16) and (17) show a segment of speech that overlapped:

1. ...(2.6) Í can't belíeve,
2. ...(0.5) Yòu knòw Móm was prétty bráve.
3. .. ↓ When you come-
4. .. when it comes right dówn tó it. ↓
5. ...(0.3) ↑ **Did Í téll you what** ↑ **Vérna tóld me òne tìme-**
6. ...(0.5) that when she líved thère alòne she kept-
7. ...(0.4) òld líght bùlbs-
8. .. up in her béd róom?
9. ...(0.4) and if shé héard a nóise at níght,
10. ...(0.6) she would táke a líght bùlb-
11. .. and thrów it on the cemènt wálk and it'd póp,
12. .. just líke a pìstol gòin' òff.
13. ...(0.2) *Whó.*
14. *Móm díd?*
15. ...(0.2) ↑ **Yéah.** ↑
16. ...(0.6) Shè ùsed to tell Vèrna to sàve [all the líght] bùlbs.
17. [*Óh I knów it.*]
18. ...(0.2) *Yéah I remémber they màde a lòt of nóise,*
19. *.. cause they have-*
20. *.. it's a vácuum in em.*
21. ...(0.3) And the-
22. .. whèn she would thrów them dówn,
23. ...(0.5) théy would póp;
24. .. like a pístol.
25. ...(0.2) Shé was prètty-
26. Hów lòng did she líve thère alòne.
27. ...(2.7) *Wéll,*

The first thing to notice about this sample is its division into separate lines, each of which can be viewed from either a phonetic or a semantic point of view. (From now on, I use the term "phonetic" to refer to the organization of sounds, and "semantic" to refer to the organization of meanings, the components of thoughts.) One thing that can be observed in any sample of spoken language is that its sounds are produced, not in a continuous stream but in segments that are often bounded by pauses, and that terminate in pitch contours perceived as indicating the ends of larger or smaller chunks of content. The separate lines in this transcription reflect such a segmentation, and I refer to the phonetic material in each line as an "intonation unit." Most such units are separated by pauses, although in some cases there is only a break in timing, and between (13) and (14), as well as between (25) and (26), there was no break at all. The coherence of intonation units is sometimes manifested phonetically in other ways—for example, with an accelerated tempo at the beginning and retardation at the end, or a change in voice quality (see Du Bois, Schuetze-Coburn, Cumming, & Paolino, 1993, for a fuller discussion).

Figure 4.1 shows some of the acoustic features of (2), a prototypical intonation unit. It was preceded by a half second of silence, but was separated from what followed by only a break in timing. It ended in a falling pitch, perceived as closure. Also observable is an overall decline in both pitch and amplitude from beginning to end. Many intonation units follow such a pattern, beginning with a vigorous pronunciation that slackens toward the end.

I assume that as a speaker (and reader) of the English language, when you read this entire example you were not primarily conscious of its sounds (or letters), but rather with the thoughts expressed by them. You were probably conscious, for example, of the idea of a woman throwing old light bulbs onto a cement walk and the noise they made, perhaps forming

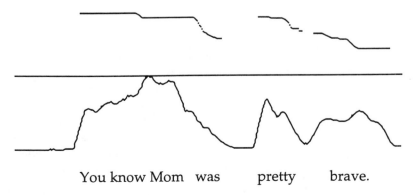

You know Mom was   pretty   brave.

FIG. 4.1. Fundamental frequency (above) and intensity (below) of Intonation Unit (2).

a visual or auditory image of such an event, and perhaps forming an opinion of it, finding it bizarre or interesting. The thoughts that are communicated by language involve experiences with both perceptual and affective components, as I hope are illustrated here.

If we combine the phonetic notion of intonation units with the semantic content of such units, each intonation unit can be viewed as the expression of what may be called a single "focus of consciousness"; a segment of thought on which the speaker's consciousness was focused at the time the intonation unit was uttered (or perhaps just preceding that time), and on which the speaker intended the listener's consciousness to be focused as a result of hearing the sound (Chafe, 1994, pp. 53–70). The flow of language can thus be seen as consisting in part of a sequence of foci of consciousness, each verbalized in an intonation unit. Language shows that each focus is replaced by another at approximately 1- to 2-second intervals. It would be interesting to know whether silent thought or daydreaming, lacking the constraints of overt language production, follows a similar time course.

A focus of consciousness is very limited in the amount of information it can contain, and in fact, language provides good evidence of this limited capacity of active consciousness, the same phenomenon that psychologists have discussed in terms of short-term memory. There are two different ways of viewing what is evidently the same mental phenomenon. The short-term memory view suggests a fixed workspace into which ideas enter and from which they leave. The active consciousness view suggests a restless spotlight that illuminates first one idea and then another. Some ideas may be newly acquired by the speaker at almost the very moment that they are activated and verbalized, but more often they are already stored in the speaker's mind, having been active at some previous time, and are then reactivated in sequence by the spotlight of consciousness as talk proceeds. That is the view on which the following depends.

TOPICS

Up to a point, then, language can be seen as a succession of foci of consciousness, each expressed in an intonation unit. But, of course, the foci are not unrelated thoughts that arise briefly in the speaker's mind in some random fashion, quickly to be replaced by others equally randomly. Each focus is part of some larger thought conglomerate, within which it follows from preceding thoughts and anticipates thoughts to come. A special role in this process is played by a larger thought unit to which it is appropriate to give the label "topic." The excerpt above was chosen to illustrate such a topic.

If each intonation unit expresses what is in the speaker's fully active consciousness during a 1- to 2-second interval, a topic is a unified thought complex that occupies, for a longer period of time, the speaker's *semiactive* consciousness. The capacity of active consciousness is too limited to permit it to focus on a topic all at once, and so a speaker must navigate through it, bringing first one focus and then another under the spotlight of active consciousness. Once a topic has been introduced, it exerts a force that drives thoughts forward until the speaker decides it has been adequately verbalized. Opening a topic is like creating an open parenthesis that calls for eventual closure before the next topic can be opened. William James (1890/1950) recognized the power of this force of topics when he wrote:

> In all our voluntary thinking there is some topic or subject about which all the members of the thought revolve. Half the time this topic is a problem, a gap we cannot yet fill with a definite picture, word, or phrase, but which ... influences us in an intensely active and determinate psychic way. Whatever may be the images and phrases that pass before us, we feel their relation to this aching gap. To fill it up is our thought's destiny. Some bring us nearer to that consummation. Some the gap negates as quite irrelevant. Each swims in a felt fringe of relations of which the aforesaid gap is the term. (p. 259)

How, then, are topics chosen? A great deal of individual experience is trivial and mundane and not likely to be of value to others. It is from this fact that one of the special properties of conversational language takes its relevance. People, it can be observed, make an effort to talk about things that are *interesting*. The property of being interesting has a strong effect on mental life, and conversations provide a wealth of data on what it entails. Roughly put, a topic of conversation is judged to be interesting when it includes events or situations that are in some way unexpected, that deviate in some way from the mundane knowledge already well established in people's minds. What is interesting depends, of course, on who is talking with whom about what. Topics that are interesting in one group may well be mundane in another. People differ, too, in their ability to judge what is interesting to others. Presumably "good conversationalists" are people who are especially good at judging what will be interesting to their listeners. But the drive to say something interesting appears to be the strongest factor influencing the choice of a conversational topic, and it can be seen as contributing to the value of conversation. From conversations, people are continually acquiring knowledge that, because it is not wholly mundane, changes in some small way their interpretation of the world. This accumulation and integration of new knowledge in tiny increments is a gradual, random, but generally pleasurable process.

The topic illustrated here has the special property of focusing entirely on "generic" knowledge, not on particular, unique events. The speaker did not tell about a single instance of Mom's bravery, but implied that there were various occasions on which she performed the action described. Memory of a particular event would have been verbalized, perhaps, as "one night she heard a noise, and she took a light bulb and threw it on the cement walk, and it popped." The generic quality of the excerpt given is not a quirk of this example, but something highly characteristic of long-term memories. In examining accounts of things that happened long ago, one finds again and again that memory blurs particulars and leaves behind this generic sort of recall.

Navigation through a topic always follows some sort of path, although the path may not always be well laid out at the beginning and may change as the speaker proceeds, or as interlocutors deflect the topic in other directions. In Chafe (1994, pp. 120–136), I illustrated two patterns of topic development, one involving interaction between several interlocutors, the other following a familiar narrative schema. It is characteristic of many topics that they progress toward a climax, an experience whose departure from mundane reality justifies the introduction of the topic in the first place. In the example here, the climax set forth Mom's unusual practice of frightening intruders by throwing used light bulbs on a cement walk, thus mimicking the sound of a pistol. But speakers lead up to a climax with preparatory information. It will thus be instructive to follow this speaker's progress through the light bulb topic to examine the contribution of each focus of consciousness, considering the manner in which each contributed to building up the totality that was present in her semiactive consciousness.

Speakers frequently open a topic by providing an orientation in time and space, saying things like "Last week, when I was in San Francisco . . ." Language gives evidence that the mind finds it essential to possess such a spatiotemporal orientation, no matter how vague, in order to assimilate properly the events to follow (Chafe, 1994, pp. 128–129). In this particular case, however, a spatiotemporal orientation was unnecessary because the conversation had already established that the participants were talking about their childhood and the place where they grew up, that general orientation forming a kind of "supertopic." Important here instead was a placement of the topic in "epistemological space": the evaluation that what she was about to say was incredible. It was this incredibility that established the interestingness of the topic to come:

1. ...(2.6) Í can't belíeve,

This topic opening was truncated, and the speaker quickly rephrased her thought.

Speakers sometimes provide a summary of a topic before navigating through its details. There may be an encapsulated statement of the events about to be presented, but here there was a statement of what might be called the topic's point:

2. ...(0.5) Yòu knòw Móm was prétty bráve.

This idea remained accessible in the speaker's semiactive consciousness until it she judged it appropriate to verbalize again. The idea of Mom's bravery came to function as a frame for the entire topic—an opening and closing parenthesis. Activated first in (2), it was reactivated at the end in (25) after the topic had been explored in detail:

25. ...(0.2) Shé was prètty-

This was a truncated statement like that in (1).

The idea of Mom's bravery expressed in (2) and repeated in (25) was immediately followed by an evaluation in a sotto voce aside:

3. .. ↓ When you come-
4. .. when it comes right dówn tó it. ↓

The expression "comes (right) down to it" had an idiomatic meaning roughly paraphrasable as "at the essence of the matter." The speaker decided to make the evaluation as impersonal as possible by reformulating it from the "you" in (3) to the "it" in (4). A special affective quality had been conveyed by the pitch contour of (2), as can be seen in Fig. 4.1. The fact that the pitch of "brave" was lower than that of "pretty" gave her statement an attitude of definitiveness—of something that couldn't be argued with. The aside in (3) and (4) then served to reinforce that attitude.

Next came a further orienting statement expressed as a question to the interlocutor, but one that did not expect an answer:

5. ...(0.3) ↑ Did Í téll you what ↑ Vérna tóld me òne tìme-

The question format can be viewed as a way of heightening her brother's involvement in the topic, thus again ensuring that it would be interesting. The up arrows bracket a portion pronounced on a higher pitch and with greater volume than the surrounding talk, thus capturing the extra vigor that often accompanies the beginning of a topic proper. The function of (5), like that of (1), was epistemic, this time specifying that what was to follow had not been observed directly by the speaker, but had been acquired through earlier language produced by Verna. Then came (6), which provided a more specific spatiotemporal orientation than was available from the general context—the period when Mom lived there alone:

6. ...(0.5) that when she líved thère alòne she kept-

Looking back on the entire beginning of this topic, one can identify a nesting of four levels of orientation, from the epistemology of incredibility in (1), to the establishment of a point in (2), to the source of the information in (5), to the spatio-temporal orientation in (6):

1. ...(2.6) Í can't belíeve,
2. ...(0.5) You know Móm was prétty bráve.
5. ...(0.3) ↑ Did Í téll you what ↑ Vérna tóld me òne tìme:
6. ...(0.5) that when she líved thère alòne she kept-

Having thus placed what would follow in epistemic and temporal space, and having thereby satisfied the orientational needs of her listener's consciousness, the speaker now proceeded to the proper content of her topic, already begun at the end of (6), by describing the background situation:

6. she kept-
7. ...(0.4) òld líght bùlbs-
8. .. up in her béd róom?

This was all the preparation she judged necessary, and she was now ready to move ahead to the topic's climax, the event toward which the orientation and background situation had been aimed:

9. ...(0.4) and if shé héard a nóise at níght,
10. ...(0.6) she would táke a líght bùlb-
11. .. and thrów it on the cemènt wálk and it'd póp,
12. .. just líke a pìstol gòin' òff.

Climaxes are typically followed by responses, validating the speaker's judgment that the topic was worth telling. In this case, the initial response was, on the surface, nothing more than a request for clarification, but its insertion at just this point showed the brother's recognition that this was the proper time to say something:

13. ...(0.2) *Whó.*
14. *Móm díd?*

The answer came with a significantly heightened pitch, reflecting the increase in affect usually associated with a climax:

15. ...(0.2) ↑ Yéah. ↑

To drive home a climax, speakers often repeat it, hoping thereby to reinforce its effectiveness. In this case, the speaker began her repetition with a reprise in (16) of what she had said in (5) through (8):

16. ...(0.6) Shè ùsed to tell Vèrna to sàve [àll the líght] bùlbs.

But her brother chimed in again to demonstrate his understanding and appreciation:

17. [*Óh I knów it.*]
18. ...(0.2) *Yéah I remémber they màde a lòt of nóise,*
19. .. *cause they have-*
20. .. *it's a vácuum in em.*

His sister ignored this intervention, and went on with her repetition:

21. ...(0.3) And the-
22. .. whèn she would thrów them dówn,
23. ...(0.5) théy would póp;
24. .. like a pístol.

Finally came the truncated reprise of (2), providing the topic with its closing frame:

25. ...(0.2) Shé was pretty-

The topic had now been fully scanned and verbalized, but the speaker's mind jumped ahead to information that she realized she had lacked as she navigated through the topic, and that she thought her brother could supply:

26. Hów lòng did she líve thère alòne.

Her question functioned as an invitation to her brother to open a new topic. It succeeded, but only after a 2.7-second pause during which he must have been searching for an appropriate answer. He then initiated the next topic with a common topic introducer:

27. ...(2.7) *Wéll,*

As shown by (26), speakers may feel a need to keep a conversation going after they judge a topic to have been concluded. People don't like conversations to die.

INSIDE FOCI OF CONSCIOUSNESS

So far we have looked at the flow of thought as expressed in the sequencing of intonation units within a topic. But other things can be learned from looking inside foci of consciousness and by examining the cognitive functions of what they contain. We can start by returning once again to (2):

2. ...(0.5) Yòu knòw Móm was prétty bráve.

To understand the several roles of the meanings included here, it is important to recognize a fundamental distinction between two types of meanings. On the one hand, there are meanings derived above all from perceptual experiences, or from emotions that are focused on. I refer to them as "ideas," in a technical sense. On the other hand, there are meanings that support and regulate those ideas, forming the "infrastructure" of thought. Ideas can be subdivided into ideas of events and states—of things that happen and the way things are—and ideas of the participants in those events and states. For the latter, I use the term "referents." In (2) there were two ideas. The more encompassing was the idea of a state, of being brave. The other was a referent, the idea of the person who was in that state, the person called Mom.

Belonging to the infrastructure of (2) was the meaning expressed by the words "you know." This "discourse marker" (Schiffrin, 1987) was an attempt to ensure that the speaker was getting through to her listener. In general, *you know* "enlists the hearer's participation as an audience to the storytelling by drawing the hearer's attention to material which is important for his/her understanding of why the story is being told" (Schiffrin, 1987, p. 284), in this case an understanding that the story was an illustration of Mom's bravery. Also contributing to the infrastructure of (2) was the word "pretty," which functioned to intensify the idea of being brave.

Language suggests that ideas, but not elements of the infrastructure, exact what may be called an activation cost. A particular idea may, at any one time, be in any one of three states in a person's mind; fully active, semiactive, or fully inactive. An analogy with vision can be helpful. Active ideas are in the forefront of consciousness, analogous to foveal vision, whereas semiactive ideas are analogous to material in peripheral vision. Inactive ideas are like phenomena that lie outside of the visual field altogether. Some inactive ideas are in long-term memory, having been active at some earlier time, whereas others are activated at this moment for the first time.

In the flow of thought, there is a greater cognitive cost associated with activating and verbalizing an idea that was previously inactive. Such an idea is often called "new information." At the other end of the continuum, an already active idea that is verbalized while it is still active is called "given information." Intermediate between these two is the activation and verbalization of an idea that was previously semiactive, where it is useful to speak of "accessible information." Ideas of these three types—given, accessible, and new—affect differently the shape that language takes and, conversely, by examining language, we are able to make inferences concerning these three cognitive states (Chafe, 1994, pp. 71–81).

Of the two ideas activated in (2), the idea of being brave and of Mom, only the idea of being brave was new. The idea of bravery had not been explicitly talked about before, and the chief purpose of this intonation unit was to activate it, after it had become active in the speaker's mind, in the mind of the listener. The idea of Mom, the person who was in that state, was not fully active just before this point in the conversation, but it had been activated repeatedly before this, and in fact, the preceding topic had dealt with the way Mom used to kill snakes on the farm. The idea of Mom, therefore, was accessible in the minds of both the speaker and the listener prior to the utterance of (2).

Does activation cost, in the sense just described, have to do with the processing of information in the mind of the speaker or in the mind of the listener? Because it is the speaker who produces the language itself, one might conclude that it is the speaker's mind that is involved. However, language works best if the speaker constantly assesses the state of information in the mind of the listener. Language that does not take the listener's mind into account can lead to misunderstandings. When language performs its proper function, a given idea is one already fully active for the speaker, but also one the speaker assumes is already fully active in the listener's mind as well. Similarly, an accessible idea is one previously semiactive for the speaker, but also one the speaker assumes is semiactive for the listener, as with the idea of Mom in (2). Finally, a new idea is one the speaker has activated from a previously inactive state, exacting the greatest cognitive cost, but the speaker assumes that the same process is necessary in the listener's mind too.

Two other factors affected the flow of thought as the present topic was being verbalized. One involved a discourse property of referents that has traditionally been called "definiteness," but that is more accurately called "identifiability." An identifiable referent is one already shared between the speaker and (the speaker assumes) the listener, although the sharing is sometimes indirect and based on inference (Chafe, 1994, pp. 93–107; 1996). But for a referent to be identifiable, it must also be verbalized in such a way that the listener will know which, among the many shared referents, this one is. Obviously, knowledge of Mom was already shared between these two siblings, and its identifiability was assured with the use of the word "Mom." Quite differently, in the following sequence, the idea of a particular light bulb was not previously shared, as was made explicit with the use of the indefinite article in the phrase "a light bulb":

10. ...(0.6) she would táke a líght bùlb-
11. .. and thrów it on the cemènt wálk and it'd póp,

Once a referent has been made identifiable, as in (10), it may subsequently be expressed with a pronoun like the "it" that occurs twice in (11), so long as it remains given or, if it later recedes in semiactive consciousness and thus becomes accessible rather than given, with the definite article. This speaker might later have reactivated the same idea with the words "the light bulb."

The other factor affecting the flow of thought that is illustrated in (2) was the occurrence of "Mom" as a grammatical "subject," the subject of the phrase "was pretty brave." The verb "was," for example, "agrees with" the third person singular property of this referent: "I am," "you were," "she was." Grammatical subjects function as the "starting points" for the clauses in which they occur. The new information in (2) was "attached to" the idea of Mom as a point of departure. The idea of Mom continued to be verbalized as a subject in intonation units (6) (where it occurred twice in that role), (9), (10), (11) (where it was understood to be the subject of "throw"), (16), (22), (25), and (26). It is typical, in the development of a topic, for one such referent to occur repeatedly as a starting point. A referent in this function has been characterized as "highly topical" (Givón, 1983). It makes sense to say that this topic is "about Mom."

Activation cost (ideas that are given, accessible, or new), identifiability, and status as a starting point are partially independent properties a referent may have, but there is some interaction between them. For example, it is almost always the case that a nonidentifiable referent is new, as with "a light bulb" in (10). It is also usually the case that starting points are given, although in a minority of cases they are accessible, as we saw to be the case with the idea of Mom in (2). Starting points are only rarely new, and when they are, they always perform some specialized function (Chafe, 1994, pp. 90–91). A good example here is the idea of Verna, introduced as a new referent in (5):

5. ...(0.3) ↑ Did Í téll you what ↑ Vérna tóld me òne tìme-

This topic was not at all "about" Verna, who was introduced in (5) simply as the source of the knowledge about to be verbalized; Verna was the one who had told the speaker about it. The phrase "what Verna told me" established the information source for that knowledge, and thus functioned as a kind of "evidential" (Chafe & Nichols, 1986). An information source plays quite a different role in the flow of thought from a "topical" referent like Mom.

It has proved fruitful to hypothesize that a single focus of consciousness can process no more than one new idea—only one event, state, or referent that is activated from a previously inactive state (Chafe, 1994, pp. 108–119). This "one-new-idea" hypothesis helps clarify what it means to be a single idea. It also helps explain how ideas are so frequently apportioned among separate intonation units, as in the case of (6–8):

6. ...(0.5) that when she líved thère alòne she kept-
7. ...(0.4) òld líght bùlbs-
8. .. up in her béd róom?

The speaker must at first have intended to incorporate the new idea expressed by "old light bulbs" in the same intonation unit as the new idea of her mother living alone, but because she could not combine these two ideas without, as it were, taking a cognitive breath, she necessarily broke off (6) and introduced the light bulbs in a separate intonation unit in (7), proceeding to create still another such unit in (8) to introduce the idea of where the light bulbs had been stored.

When the one-new-idea constraint appears to have been violated, it can be rewarding to examine the circumstances under which that can occur. In the present example, there seems to be a violation in (11):

11. .. and thrów it on the cemènt wálk and it'd póp,

Even if the idea of the cement walk may have been accessible to the two interlocutors, it would seem that the ideas of throwing and popping were both new. One might have expected a distribution among two separate intonation units, as in fact happened in the reprise of this material:

22. .. whèn she would thrów them dówn,
23. ...(0.5) théy would póp;

The best explanation of the apparently overloaded (11) may be that the speaker conceptualized the throwing and popping as a single event, one that was for her at this point cognitively inseparable. English provides no resource that would combine both these events in a single verb, and the speaker could only concatenate the two verbs in (11) despite the conceptual unity of the idea.

CONCLUSION

I have tried to show a few ways in which examining ordinary talk can shed light on people's thought processes. Any sample of actual speech can provide a rich mine of information on mental functioning, and here I could only suggest some of the ways one speaker's illustration of her mother's bravery can help toward an understanding of the workings of the mind. The reader must for the moment take it on faith that what was discussed so briefly here can be reproduced and expanded when one examines further materials of this kind. The only way to confirm provisional understandings is to confront them with further data, in this case with data from larger samples of ordinary talk, but supplemented ultimately with experimental and observational data of other kinds.

Among the findings discussed here is the segmentation of speech and thought into foci of active consciousness that are constantly replaced at 1- to 2-second intervals. Larger segments constitute semiactive topics within which those foci are deployed in accordance with familiar, although labile, patterns of topic development. The elements within each active focus may be, on the one hand, "ideas" of events, states, and the referents that participate in them or, on the other hand, "infrastructural" elements that regulate and support those ideas. Prior to the activation of a focus of consciousness, the ideas within it may have already been active, semiactive, or inactive, and varying amounts of cognitive cost are associated with activation from those three states. Each focus may be constrained in such a way that it can activate no more than one new idea, a hypothesis that helps shed light on what it means for an idea to be unitary.

The exploitation of natural speech as evidence for the nature of the human mind has hardly begun, and it can offer exciting discoveries to those who are willing to explore it with their own minds open.

REFERENCES

Atkinson, J. M., & Heritage, J. (Eds.). (1984). *Structures of social action: Studies in conversation analysis.* Cambridge, England: Cambridge University Press.

Biber, D. (1988). *Variation across speech and writing.* Cambridge, England: Cambridge University Press.

Boas, F. (1911). Introduction. In F. Boas (Ed.), *Handbook of American Indian languages* (Vol. 1, pp. 1–83). Washington, DC: U.S. Government Printing Office.

Chafe, W. (1994). *Discourse, consciousness, and time: The flow and displacement of conscious experience in speaking and writing.* Chicago: University of Chicago Press.

Chafe, W., & Nichols, J. (Eds.). (1986). *Evidentiality: The linguistic coding of epistemology.* Norwood, NJ: Ablex.

Chafe, W., & Tannen, D. (1987). The relation between written and spoken language. *Annual Review of Anthropology, 16,* 383–407.

Du Bois, J. W., Schuetze-Coburn, S., Cumming, S., & Paolino, D. (1993). Outline of discourse transcription. In J. A. Edwards & M. D. Lampert (Eds.), *Talking data: Transcription and coding in discourse research.* Hillsdale, NJ: Lawrence Erlbaum Associates.

Givón, T. (1983). *Topic continuity in discourse: Quantified cross-language studies.* Amsterdam and Philadelphia: John Benjamins.

Goodwin, C. (1981). *Conversational organization: Interaction between speakers and hearers.* New York: Academic Press.

Gumperz, J. J. (1982). *Discourse strategies.* Cambridge, England: Cambridge University Press.

James, W. (1950). *The principles of psychology* (Vol. 1). New York: Dover. (Original work published 1890)

Lakoff, G. (1987). *Women, fire, and dangerous things: What categories reveal about the mind.* Chicago: University of Chicago Press.

Schiffrin, D. (1987). *Discourse markers.* Cambridge, England: Cambridge University Press.

Chapter 5

The Semantics of English Causative Constructions in a Universal-Typological Perspective

Anna Wierzbicka
Australian National University

1. INTRODUCTION[1]

The approach to linguistic description illustrated in this chapter—the so-called "NSM" (from "Natural Semantic Metalanguage")—approach is based on two fundamental assumptions: that every language has an irreducible core in terms of which the speakers can understand all complex thoughts and utterances, and that the irreducible cores of all natural languages match, so that we can speak, effectively, of the irreducible core of all languages, reflecting the irreducible core of human thought.

To someone unfamiliar with the work carried out within this framework over the last 30 years, both of these assumptions, but especially the second one, may seem unconvincing. For even if it can be shown that any language investigated in depth can be "reduced" to an irreducible core in terms of which everything else in this language can be explained and made sense of, why should the cores of all languages coincide—given the tremendous diversity of human languages revealed by modern linguistics?

The empirical and conceptual work done within the NSM approach seeks to demonstrate the validity of the two assumptions stated earlier, and their fruitfulness in the practical work of describing and comparing languages in their lexicons, grammars, and pragmatics. The justification for the approach used in this chapter lies, therefore, in the large body of work of which this chapter is only one example. (See references listed in Goddard, 1997a, 1997b, 1998; Goddard & Wierzbicka, 1994; Wierzbicka, 1991,

1992, 1996, 1997.) A few basic ideas, however, need to be explained here, too.

One such basic idea is that (as Leibniz, 1704/1961, eloquently argued) not everything can be explained: at some point, all explanations must come to an end, for a regressus ad infinitum explains nothing. Some things must be self-explanatory (intuitively clear), or we could never understand anything. The explanatory power of any explanation depends therefore on the intuitive clarity of the indefinable conceptual primitives that constitute its ultimate foundation.

A natural language is a powerful system in which very complex and diverse meanings can be formulated and conveyed to other people. But the intelligibility of all such meanings depends on the existence of a basic set of conceptual primitives that do not require any explanations for they are innate and intuitively clear to us.

In the NSM theory of language, it is assumed that such a set of conceptual primitives does indeed exist and that it can be found through in-depth analysis of any natural language. This is, then, the irreducible core of any language, on which all complex meanings are founded. If this core is innate (as my colleagues and I think it must be), it is hardly surprising that it is essentially the same in all languages. Words differ of course from language to language, but the fundamental innate elementary meanings are the same. For example, all languages have a word (or bound morpheme) that means NO (negation), as in "I did not do it"—in Russian, *ne*, in German, *nicht*, in Mangap-Mbula, *som* (cf. Bugenhagen, 1994, p. 96), and so on.

Cross-linguistic empirical work undertaken within the NSM framework suggests that there are close to 60 universal conceptual primitives such as NO. Using their English exponents, we can present them as follows (cf. Goddard & Wierzbicka, 1994; Wierzbicka, 1996):

Proposed universal semantic primes (1996)

Substantives	I, YOU, SOMEONE(PERSON), SOMETHING(THING), PEOPLE, BODY
Determiners	THIS, THE SAME, OTHER
Quantifiers	ONE, TWO, SOME, MANY/MUCH, ALL
Attributes	GOOD, BAD, BIG, SMALL
Mental predicates	THINK, KNOW, WANT, FEEL, SEE, HEAR
Speech	SAY, WORD, TRUE
Actions, events, movements	DO, HAPPEN, MOVE
Existence and possession	THERE IS, HAVE
Life and death	LIVE, DIE

Logical concepts	NOT, MAYBE, CAN, BECAUSE, IF
Time	WHEN(TIME), NOW, AFTER, BEFORE, A LONG TIME, A SHORT TIME, FOR SOME TIME
Space	WHERE(PLACE), HERE, ABOVE, BELOW, FAR, NEAR; SIDE, INSIDE
Intensifier, Augmentor	VERY, MORE
Taxonomy, partonomy	KIND OF, PART OF
Similarity	LIKE

The first hypothesis is, then, that in all languages, lexical exponents for each of the 60 or so elements (conceptual primitives) can be found. The second, concomitant, hypothesis is that in all languages, conceptual primitives can enter into the same combinations. For example, it can be expected not only that in any language, lexical exponents for the basic notions PEOPLE, THING, THIS, TWO, ALL, BIG, BAD, DO, SEE, MOVE, HAPPEN, and CAN, can be found, but also that in any language, these elements can be put together to create meaningful combinations such as the following:

ALL PEOPLE DO THIS

I SEE TWO BIG THINGS

IF YOU DO THIS, SOMETHING BAD CAN HAPPEN TO YOU

Of course, the word order and the morphological "trappings" may differ from language to language, but the hypothesis is that the elements, their combinations, and their meaning will be the same. This means that just as we can have a rudimentary universal lexicon of indefinable concepts, we can also have a rudimentary universal grammar of such concepts, and if we have a mini-lexicon and a mini-grammar, then we can have a mini-language—a mini-language that is carved out of natural languages and that can be used for the description and comparisons of languages, both in their lexicon and in their grammar.

The great majority of words in any language are language specific in their meaning and cannot be matched exactly across languages. For example, the English word *fate* doesn't mean the same as the Russian word *sud'ba*, and the English word *freedom* doesn't mean the same as the Russian word *svoboda* (cf. Wierzbicka, 1992, 1997). But evidence suggests that the 60 or so words listed as conceptual primitives do match in meaning across languages. Similarly, the great majority of grammatical constructions are

language specific, but evidence suggests that there are also some constructions that do match in meaning. For example, if we compare the English
sentence *all these people do this* with its Russian counterpart *vse èti ljudi èto
delajut,* we can say that these sentences have exactly the same meaning
because not only the individual words but also their combinations can be
matched in meaning (e.g., "all these people" = "vse èti ljudi").

Thus, what applies to the lexicon applies to grammar, too: not everything
can be explained, all explanations must come to an end. There is no point
in trying to "explain" the meaning of simple and intuitively clear words such
as THIS in terms of complex and obscure words like "referentiality," "deictic-
ity," or "ostensiveness." Similarly, there is no point in trying to explain the
meaning of a combination of primitives like GOOD PEOPLE or BIG THINGS in
terms of complex and obscure words or phrases such as "attributive relation."
On the contrary, a complex notion like "attributive relation" should be
explained with reference to simple and universal exemplars such as GOOD
PEOPLE and BIG THINGS (cf. Wierzbicka, 1998).

Most words and most grammatical constructions in any language have
a complex meaning that can be explained—but it can only be explained
in terms of something else: some other words and some other constructions. All analysis comes to an end when the indefinable concepts (like
GOOD or BIG, THING or PEOPLE) and indefinable combinations of concepts
(like GOOD PEOPLE, BIG THINGS) are reached. To try to go further than
that would mean trying to "explain" something simple with something
complex, something clear with something obscure, and—last but not
least—something universal with something language specific. The natural
semantic metalanguage (NSM) employed in this chapter and in other NSM
works mentioned earlier leads in the opposite direction: from complex to
simple, from obscure to clear, and from language specific to universal.[2]

Because this metalanguage is carved out of natural language (any natural
language), the semantic explications constructed in it are intuitively meaningful and have psychological reality. Consequently, unlike semantic formulae based on various artificial formalisms, NSM formulae are open to
verification (they can be tested against native speakers intuitions).

2. THE MEANING OF CAUSATIVES
    IN A CROSS-LINGUISTIC PERSPECTIVE

The literature on the syntax of causative constructions in different languages is huge; the literature on their semantics is relatively modest. But
the use of such constructions is largely determined by their meaning.
Because little is known about their meaning, a language learner looking
for some guidelines to the actual use of such constructions can seldom

find any statements anywhere that are clear, precise, and reliable. But it is not just the language learner who would be disappointed by the literature on causatives. The area of causation has an enormous inherent interest from the point of view of the "philosophy of grammar" and the psychology of language: after all, the causative constructions a language has show how the speakers of this language draw distinctions between different kinds of causal relations, how they perceive and interpret causal links between events and human actions. And yet our knowledge and understanding of "ethnocausology" is incomparably far behind that of ethnozoology, ethnobotany, or ethnogeology.

Of course the folk interpretations of causal links are less accessible to direct observation than those of more tangible, concrete phenomena, but they are not inaccessible to empirical study. The syntax of a language provides a wealth of evidence in this regard—if we can find ways of analyzing this evidence in an illuminating and nonarbitrary way.

I believe that here as elsewhere—and perhaps even more in this case— the key to such analysis lies in the choice of a suitable semantic metalanguage. In the existing literature on causatives, the semantics of different constructions is usually discussed in terms of ready-made labels such as *direct* vs. *indirect causation, contactive* vs. *distant causation, strong coercion* vs. *weak coercion, authority* vs. *absence of authority, factitive* vs. *permissive causation,* or *manipulative* vs. *directive causation* (cf., for example, Comrie, 1974, 1985; Givón, 1975; Kachru, 1976; Ruwet, 1973/1976; Shibatani, 1973, 1976; Song, 1996; Talmy, 1976; Xolodovič, 1969). But labels of this kind are often more misleading than helpful and they don't have much explanatory or predictive power, for the meaning of the constructions to which they are applied differs from language to language.

Generally speaking, the common use of ready-made labels such as *direct/indirect causation, contactive/distant causation,* or *strongly coercive/weakly coercive causatives* is based on the mistaken (in my view) assumption that there are certain types of causation that can first be described a priori, and then identified in individual languages. But detailed semantic analysis shows that the actual causative constructions are usually rather unique in the meaning they encapsulate. What is called direct causation or strongly coercive causation in one language is usually different from what is called direct causation or strongly coercive causation in another. This is not to say that there are no recurring motives, no cross-linguistic similarities in the area of causation. Far from it. The point is that usually causative constructions encapsulate a unique combination of components. The individual components—such as, for example, "Y wanted it" or "Y didn't want it"—frequently recur in the world's languages. But the configurations of such components tend to be unique, and cannot be adequately captured in global labels such as *indirect, manipulative, distant,* and the like.

From the point of view advocated here, finding out the configuration of universal concepts encoded in a given causative construction is not seen as a final touch that can be added to the presentation of the results once the main analysis has already been completed. Rather, finding out (by trial and error) what this hidden configuration of universal concepts is is the essence of the analysis. Assigning to a construction a label such as *coercion, authority,* or *contact* does not bring us any closer to the understanding of its meaning; it only creates an illusion that progress has been made.

As another example, consider the German periphrastic causative construction with the auxiliary verb *lassen* (combined with an action verb). In different contexts, this construction is best translated into English with different constructions, based on the verbs *make, have, get, cause,* or *let,* but as this very fact shows, it cannot be semantically equated with any one of these constructions. Yet, the meaning of this German construction can be represented in English quite accurately by means of a set of components phrased in universal human concepts. An example from Speer, 1975:

Ich habe mir   Bleistift und neues Papier geben lassen. (p. 19)
I   have to-me pencil   and new   paper   to-give let/have
I have asked for a pencil and new paper [and got it].

The verb *lassen* does not mean "ask for," but how else can one render in English the meaning of the phrase *geben lassen* when it refers (as in this case) to a request from a prisoner to the prison authorities? Clearly, the prisoner can neither "make" the guards give him new writing paper nor "have" them give it to him. He could perhaps "get" them to do it, but by translating *lassen* as *get,* we would significantly distort the meaning of the original sentence, for "getting someone to do something" implies something like overcoming some actual or potential unwillingness on the part of the causee, and there is no trace of this in the German sentence.

In this example, then, and also in the following one, the best translation might be one relying on speech act verbs such as *ask for* or *request* rather than on any general causatives:

Vom Doktor eine Schlaftablette   geben lassen. (Speer, 1975, p. 44)
from doctor one sleeping tablet to give let/have/make/get
[to ask] the doctor for a sleeping tablet (and get one). [A note in a
    diary.]

But a translation based on the verb *ask for* or *request* is not accurate either, for it doesn't convey the idea that the request was effective. Furthermore, consider the following sentence from Speer (1975):

> Im Anschluß an seinen Monolog drückte Hitler auf den
> Klingelknopf und ließ Borman kommen. (p. 101)

> Having completed his monologue Hitler pressed the bell and [thus]
> summoned Borman.

In this case, the speech act verbs *ask for* and *request* are clearly inappropriate, and *summon* is much more suitable; but clearly *summon* brings with it presuppositions that are absent from the earlier two examples.

In the following example from Speer (1975), where the causee is the causer's personal assistant, the English *have* construction seems to fit the context best:

> Im Jahre 1938 hatte er [Streicher] ihm durch seinen
> persönlichen Adjutanten zum Geburtstag demonstrativ
> einen großen Distelstrauß überreichen lassen. (p. 173)

> In 1938, Streicher [a Gauleiter of Nuremberg] had his
> personal assistant deliver to him (Leibel, mayor of
> Nuremberg) on his birthday, demonstratively, a large
> bunch of thistles.

As we have seen, the range of the *lassen* causative (of the type discussed here) is so broad that it can accommodate requests from a prisoner to the prison authorities, instructions from a district chief to his assistant, and orders from a dictator to his underlings. There is no causative verb or construction in English that would fit a range of relations as broad as that. Yet the meaning of the *lassen* causative can be accurately portrayed in the following formula:

Person X ließ (let/made/had/asked etc.) person Y to do Z =
a. X wanted Y to do Z
b. because of this X did something
c. because of this Y knew that X wanted this
d. because of this Y did Z

What applies to the cross-linguistic comparison of causative constructions applies also to the comparison of different causative constructions within one language. For example, in English, "interpersonal causation" can be described by means of several different causative constructions:

1. Mary had John return the money.
2. Mary made John return the money.
3. Mary got John to return the money.

4. Mary forced John to return the money.

5. Mary talked John into returning the money.

Each of the sentences above means something different, and no labels such as direct, indirect, strong, weak, coercive, manipulative, or contactive can clarify the nature of these differences (as they could not clarify the differences between any of these constructions and the German *lassen* construction).

In what follows, I will first discuss fairly briefly three of the English constructions listed earlier (1, 3, and 5), and then I will examine more extensively a whole family of English causative constructions based on the verb *make*, including the one illustrated in (2). In the course of this extensive discussion of *make* causatives, I will also compare the meaning of the *make* causative illustrated in (2) with that of the *force* causative illustrated in (4).

3. THREE ENGLISH CAUSATIVES: "HAVE," "GET," AND "INTO"

3.1. Having Someone Do Something

The following sentence from a novel nicely illustrates the contrast between *make* and *have* causatives:

She had the girls clean his bicycle and made Anand pump the tyres every morning. (Naipaul, 1969, p. 481)

In the story, the wife, Shama, is trying to please and appease her husband in various ways, and in particular, by getting the children to do things for him. The girls are expected to be compliant and willing to do what their mother wants them to do, whereas the boy, Anand, has to be "made" to pump the tyres every morning.

Person X had Person Y do Z =
a. X wanted Z to happen (to W)
b. because of this X wanted Y to do Z (to W)
c. because of this, X said something to someone
d. because of this Y did Z
e. X could think that when X says something like this (about something like this) Y can't say: "I don't want to do this"

The *have* construction does not imply that the causee didn't want to perform the action. Nor does it imply that the causee HAD TO perform the action. It does imply, however, something like a hierarchical relationship, within which the causer can say that he or she wants the causee to do something, and the causee can't say in response "I don't want to do it."

This does not mean that the causer has power over the causee and that the causee has to do whatever the causer wants. The compliance may well be limited to some particular sphere (such as the professional duties of a secretary to whom her boss can give directions). Within this sphere, however, the causer does not have to exert any special pressure to achieve the desired effect: simply saying what he or she wants is enough. In fact, the causer's will does not even have to be expressed directly to the causee; it can be conveyed through another person. Because the causee does not really have to do what the causer wants, it might seem that it would be better to phrase component (e) as ". . . Y wouldn't say: 'I don't want to do it' " rather than ". . . Y can't say: 'I don't want to do it.' " This alternative formulation, however, could apply also to situations where the causer is counting on the causee's good heart ("when I ask her to do something she will not say no"); it is therefore inappropriate in the case of the *have* construction. In a hierarchical relationship, a person CAN think that someone in a subordinate position "can't" refuse to take directions.

Thus, in the *have* causative, the causer assumes the causee's "readiness to take directions"; the causee is treated here as a cooperative performer of the causer's will, as someone to whom the causer's will can be communicated (either directly or by an intermediary) and who will be neither unable to understand it nor unwilling to perform it. This explains why, as pointed out by Talmy (1976, p. 107) the causee of the *have* causative normally has to be human:

*I had the squirrel leave its tree.[3]

The trainer made/?had the lion dance.

One could say, vaguely, that both the *make* causative and the *have* causative imply some sort of "power" relation between the causer and the causee. But clearly, the nature of this relation is in each case perceived differently. The *make* causative implies that the causee is acting unwillingly (what exactly this means will be discussed later). The *have* causative doesn't imply that; here, the causee is expected to comply with the causer's will, and there is no assumption, or expectation, of unwillingness on his or her part. Nonetheless, the expected compliance of the causee is not seen as due entirely to good will: there is also an assumption of dependence reflected in the component "Y can't say: 'I don't want to do this.'"

Finally, the *have* construction does not imply that the causer is seeking to control the causee's actions and it is not compatible with a situation when someone is seeking to impose their will on another person just to enjoy arbitrary power. Rather, the *have* construction implies a goal that transcends the causee's actions: from the causer's point of view, the causee is like an instrument in achieving some objective (as signaled in the component "X wanted something to happen") rather than as the target of the causee's will. Presumably, this is the reason why the *have* causatives normally occur with transitive rather than intransitive verbs:

> X made Y wait (sit still).
> ?X had Y wait (sit still).

Furthermore, the transitive verbs in the *have* construction usually take definite rather than indefinite objects:

> A. X made Y eat fish.
> B. ?X had Y eat fish.
> C. X had Y return the fish to the shop.

The *have* construction implies that the causer wants something to happen to some object (in this case, the fish), rather than to the causee as such. The *make* construction, however, is quite compatible with exercises in arbitrary power, deliberate cruelty, malice, punishment, and so on:

> [She] used to make us kneel on graters for a thing like that. (Naipaul, 1969, p. 236)
> ?She used to have us kneel on graters for a thing like that.

It is also interesting to note that in contrast to the *make* construction, the *have* construction does not allow the passive:

> A. He was made to pump the tyres every morning.
> B. *He was had to pump the tyres every morning.

The causee of a *make* construction can be topicalized (by means of a passive) because the causee is the target of the causer's action, and so is potentially worthy of interest; but the causee of the *have* construction is not the target of the causer's action but a mere "instrument."

This is also consistent with the fact that in one of its variants, the *have* construction readily takes subjectless complements, as in the following sentences:

> I had my shoes mended.
> I had my calculations checked by my assistant.

Again, this is in stark contrast to the *make* construction:

*She made her shoes mended (calculations checked).

Of course, the *have* construction used in sentences like "I had my shoes mended" is not exactly the same as the one with a named causee and an active form of the verb in the complement, and the meaning is not the same either, but it is very close:

X had Z done [to W]. =
a. X wanted Z to happen to W
b. because of this X wanted someone to do Z to W
c. because of this, X said something
d. because of this someone did Z
e. X could think that when X says something like this (about something like this) this person can't say: "I don't want to do this"

In both cases, X wants something to happen (component a), and because of this, X wants someone to do something (component b), but in the variant with a subjectless and passive complement, the identity of the causee is not relevant (no "Y" is specified) and the "affected object" (W) has to be identified.

3.2. Getting Someone to Do Something

The interpersonal causative construction based on the auxiliary verb *get* can be illustrated with the following sentence:

. . . Anand got Shama to bring a coloured print of the goddess Lakshmi from Hanuman House. (Naipaul, 1969, p. 383)

The boy Anand has no authority over his mother and he cannot "have" or "make" her do anything. Nevertheless, he can "get" her to do something for him.

The *get* construction illustrated by this sentence is not the only *get* causative available in English. Causative *get* sentences with an inanimate causee are also possible (for example, "she got the sauce to thicken"), but as we shall see later, the semantic conditions on such sentences are different from those on the interpersonal sentences presently under discussion, with both key noun phrases human and a verb of action, that is of the type

NP^1_{Human} got $NP^2_{Human\ (or\ human-like)}$ to $VERB_{Do}$

The *get* causative of the type discussed here implies that the causee does something not because he or she wants to do it, but because somebody else wants them to do it. At the same time, the action is not imposed on the causee by virtue of the causer's power or authority. The causer realizes that the causee may not want to comply, and unlike in the case of *have*, the causer has no power or authority over the addressee to overcome his or her possible reluctance or unwillingness to do what the causer wants. Because of this, the causer does (typically, says) something to the causee in the expectation that this might influence the causee's will and that as a result, the causee will do the desired action willingly, and indeed, this happens: the causee does what is wanted by the causer and does it willingly. And what does the causer get out of it? Often—but not always—what the causee does can be seen as good for the causer. In all cases, however, the causer can think that what he or she wanted to happen, happened (component f).

How does one get another person to do something that we want them to do? Usually, by SAYING something, as in the case of the *have* construction, but not necessarily so. For example, one can get a dog to do something (say, swallow a pill) by putting it in a piece of meat, or by smearing it with jam. One can also use the *get* construction when speaking of machines that appear to have "a will of their own," for example,

How did you get the washing machine to go? I couldn't.

The *have* construction, which relies on a speech act, and on conscious acceptance of somebody else's authority, cannot be used like that.

?She had the dog swallow the pill.
?She had the washing machine go.

Thus, the overall semantic conditions on the *get* construction (with a human or human-like causee) can be summarized as follows:

Person X got person Y to do Z. =
a. X wanted Y to do Z
b. X knew that if Y didn't want to do it Y would not do it
c. X thought that if Y wanted to do it Y would do it
d. because of this X did (said) something to Y
e. because of this after this Y wanted to do Z
f. because of this Y did Z
g. because of this X could think:
  "I wanted something to happen
  it happened"

Although the action is done willingly (component (e)), the strategy used by the causer smacks a little of manipulation, for the causee's action is brought about by the causer's, rather than the causee's, own will. Nonetheless, getting someone to do something cannot be seen as real manipulation, for the causer does not conceal his or her goal and the causee is not acting AGAINST his or her will (there is no assumption that the causee doesn't want to do what the causer wants, although it is assumed that if the causee didn't want to do it, he or she would not do it). In both these respects, "getting" people to do something differs from the truly "manipulative" scenario discussed in the next section and linked with yet another—semantically more complex—causative construction.

3.3. Manipulating Someone "Into Doing Something"

The construction discussed in this section is identified not in terms of an auxiliary verb (such as *make*, *have*, or *get*), but rather in terms of a preposition: *into*. But the set of main verbs that can be used in this construction is quite limited and gives a clear clue to this construction's meaning. Thus, one can not only "talk" someone "into" doing something, but also "trick" them, "manoeuver" them, or "push" them. On the other hand, one cannot "encourage" or "induce" someone "into" doing anything. Roughly speaking, the generalization seems to be as follows: the *into* construction takes verbs that either imply or at least are compatible with, the idea of manipulation (tricking, manoeuvring, and the like). More precisely, the meaning of the *into* construction can be portrayed as follows:

Person X "Verbed" person Y into doing Z. =
a. X wanted Y to do Z
b. Y didn't want to do Z
c. X didn't say to Y: "I want you to do Z"
d. X thought that if X said this Y wouldn't do Z
e. because of this X did something else
f. because of this after this Y did Z
g. Y didn't do it because Y wanted to do it
h. Y did it because X wanted Y to do it
i. Y wouldn't have done it if X had not done this

There are some clear similarities, as well as some clear differences, between the *into* construction and the *get* construction. The main differences are: first, in the case of the *into* construction, the causee originally didn't want to do what he or she did, whereas in the case of the *get* construction, there is no such assumption; second, in the *into* construction, the causee's action is "triggered" by the causer's will, not by the causee's own will, whereas in the *get* construction, the causee is acting in accordance with both his or her own will and the causer's will; third, in the *into* construction, the causee is unaware of what is happening (namely, that his or her action is "triggered" by the causer's will), whereas in the *get* construction, there is no such assumption.

Given these differences, it is not surprising that one can use the *get* causative, but not an *into* causative, performatively (as a request), for example:

I'll get you to sign this.
*I'll talk you into signing this.

The speaker of a *get* sentence does not seek to conceal his or her wish for the causee to do something, although he or she does not regard the mere expression of their wish as a sufficient "trigger" for the causee's action. For this reason, a performative *get* sentence may even be used in the service of politeness, for it sounds less presumptuous than would a bare expression of the causer's will: "I want you to sign this." Using a sentence like "I'll get you to sign this" rather than simply "I want you to sign this," the speaker signals that he or she does not regard their want as a sufficient reason for the causee to act, and also that he or she expects the causee to act willingly (in accordance with the speaker's wishes, but "freely").

4. MAKING SOMETHING HAPPEN OR SOMEONE DO SOMETHING

4.1. Introduction

English has many different *make* constructions. The meaning of each of these constructions constitutes a unique configuration of components. It appears, however, that two components may be shared: one causal component and one counterfactual. Roughly, the overall semantic "theme" of *make* constructions can be represented as follows:

A happened
because of this B happened
B wouldn't have happened if A had not happened

I do not claim, however, that this overall theme can be seen as either a full meaning or even a shared semantic core, in the strict sense, for, as we shall see, there may be other necessary components depending on the nature of the events labeled here as A and B, and also because the causal and counterfactual links may hold between predicates other than those specified in the formula above. The precise meaning of a *make* construction depends, I suggest, on the following factors:

1. is the causer different from the causee?
2. is the causer a person? a thing? an event?
3. is the causee a person? a thing? an event?
4. does the causer DO something?
5. does the causee DO something?
6. if the causee does something, is this something that can only be done intentionally (e.g., *write, read*) or is it something that doesn't have to be done intentionally (e.g., *cry, laugh*)?
7. does something HAPPEN to the causee?
8. does the causee THINK something?

The simplest variant of the *make* construction can be illustrated with sentences of the following type: "it made me think that X," that is, sentences meeting the following formula:

$$NP^1_{Abstract} \text{ made } NP^2_{Human} \text{ VERB}_{Think} \text{ [+ complement]}$$

For example:

It made me realize how lucky I was.
This made me think of Mary.
What you said made me think of something my sister said (. . .)

The meaning conveyed in such sentences can be represented as follows:

It (X) made Y think W. =
a. X happened
b. because of this person Y thought something (W)
c. Y wouldn't have thought this (W) if X had not happened

This type of *make* sentence is particularly simple, because the outcome referred to is not presented as *bad, unwanted, involuntary, unexpected,* or *(seen as) necessary:* No restrictions on what the causee thinks are implied. As we will see, in most other types of *make* sentences this is not the case.

In the survey of *make* constructions that follows, I first discuss sentences of the "interpersonal" type, that is, sentences where both the causer and the causee are human and where they are different persons. Sentence types where either the causer or the causee is not human (or where neither of them is human) are discussed later (except of course for the "it made me think" type, with which we have started).

There appear to be six interpersonal (causative) *make* constructions in English. They can be illustrated with the following sentences:

1. Person X made person Y fall.
2. Person X made person Y feel guilty.
3. Person X made person Y think about Z.
4. Person X made person Y want something.
5. Person X made person Y cry (laugh).
6. Person X made person Y apologize.

In type 1, something *happens* to the causee and the causee does not have to feel anything or do anything. In type 2, nothing happens to the causee (apart from what the causer does or says), and the causee does not do anything but he or she *feels* something. In type 3, nothing happens to the causee, and the causee neither does nor feels anything, but he or she has to *think* something. In type 4, nothing happens to the causee and the causee does not have to do, feel, or think anything, but he or she has to *want* something. In type 5, the causee *feels* something and because of this, *does* something, but something that he or she *does not want* to do, that is to say something that is done involuntarily (and that, presumably, is triggered by something happening in the person's body). Finally, in type 6, the causee *does* something that can only be done *intentionally* (even if it is done unwillingly—a distinction that is discussed in some detail later). Let us examine the semantic conditions on each of these types.

4.2. Making Something Happen to Someone

Make sentences can be used for accusations, as in the sentence "You made me fall over!" What the speaker appears to be implying by his or her choice of this construction type can be spelled out as follows:

person X did something
because of this something bad (Z) happened to person Y
Z wouldn't have happened to person Y if X had not done this

In order to see that the event referred to has to be really perceived as "bad" it is useful to compare sentences A and B in the following pairs:

1. A. You bastard, you made me lose my job!
   B. ?I'm so grateful to you, you made me get a job!
2. A. He made her lose her temper.
   B. ?He made her recover her composure.
3. A. You made me get worse.
   B. ?You made me get better.

In each pair, sentence B sounds worse than sentence A and in fact, is often perceived as unacceptable. The difference seems clear: in A, something bad happens to the causee, and in B, something good. This is not to say that a sentence such as "He made her get a job" must always imply that getting a job is seen as something bad. Far from it. It can be seen as something good, but only on the condition that the causer acted intentionally—a condition that does not apply if the event is seen as "bad." To account for these facts, we need to postulate separate interpersonal *make happen* constructions: (1) causer's action not (necessarily) intentional, the effect on the causee "bad"; (2) causer's action intentional, the effect on the causee not (necessarily) "bad." Because the conditions on the two types of sentences (those when the causer is acting intentionally and those where this is not the case) are different, these two types cannot be accommodated by one semantic formula (not without a loss of predictive power).

It could be suggested that the event referred to in the *make something happen* construction should be seen as "unwanted" rather than as "bad." The question of which of the two hypotheses ("bad" or "unwanted") is a better one is difficult to test, for in the world of human affairs, "unwanted" usually tends to be interpreted as "bad." On balance, however, in this case, facts seem to be better explained by the "bad" rather than the "unwanted" version. Let us consider a sentence such as "You made me fall!" against the following hypothetical formula:

a. you did something
b. because of this something happened to me
c. I did not want it to happen
d. it wouldn't have happened if you had not done this

What seems unsatisfactory about this formula is that it fails to account for the impression of blame and accusation; and in any case, what would be the point in denying that I wanted to fall? Of course I did not want to fall, people normally don't, and it is hardly necessary to say so. The hypothesis that what happened to the causee is seen as something "bad" (rather than as something "not wanted" or "unwanted") does not run into any such difficulties.

What is particularly telling is the contrast between the *make happen (to)* constructions and various other *make* constructions that have no negative implications whatsoever. For example, one can say "She made it happen" with reference to something good and desirable: "happen," but not "happen TO someone." One can also say "She made him happy," and of course this is fine too—but *happy* is an adjective, not a verb, and it is *make+Verb* constructions that we are now looking at. Furthermore, one can say "She made me see (realize) . . . ," again, without any negative implications, but here, we are dealing with a verb of thinking (a category to be discussed below), not with a verb of happening. Finally, let us compare the following two sentences:

A. Eat your spinach—spinach will make you grow big and strong!
B. ?She made him grow big and strong by giving him spinach every day.

The *make* construction used in sentence A (with an inanimate causer and a human causee) is perfectly consistent with a positive result, but the interpersonal *make* construction used in sentence B (with a human causer as well as a human causee) is not consistent with a positive outcome, and as a result, sentence B sounds odd.

I conclude, then, (though only tentatively) that the *make* construction under discussion (person X made something happen to person Y) does imply that what happened to the causer is seen as "bad" (for the causee), and I propose the following explication for this type:

Person X made Z happen to person Y. =
a. X did something
b. because of this something bad (Z) happened to Y
c. Z wouldn't have happened to Y if X had not done this

4.3. Making Someone Feel Something

Sentences about feelings may seem to contradict the formula proposed in the proceeding section. For example, one can say to someone, "You made me feel a lot better," and surely, "feeling better" is not seen as something bad that happens to the causee.

In fact, however, "feeling" does not have to be seen as something that "happens" to a person at all. There are indeed different conditions on "making something HAPPEN to someone" and "making someone FEEL something." To account for this fact, we need to posit two separate semantic formulae for the two types of sentences rather than trying to accommodate them in one formula. If we were to posit a single formula for both of these types, we might seem to gain in economy of description but we would lose in predictive power, for a unitary formula could not preserve the link between "happen" and "bad."

In the case of *feel* (*make feel*), the feeling brought about by the causer can be either good or bad:

She made him feel needed.

He made her feel guilty.

He made her feel proud of her background.

He made her feel ashamed of her background.

To account for these facts, we could posit (as a first approximation) the following formula (to be revised later):

person X did something

because of this person Y felt something (Z)

Y wouldn't have felt this (Z) if X had not done this

One reason why this formula may need revision is that it allows for physical feelings (sensations) as well as for mental feelings (emotions), whereas in fact *make feel* (with a human causer) is only compatible with the latter kind:

A. He made me feel miserable/happy.

B. ?He made me feel cold/hot.

The mental feelings in question do not have to be emotions such as "happy" or "miserable." For example, one can also say:

You make me feel special.

He makes me feel stupid.

You make me feel sick (i.e., disgusted).

The feeling cannot be purely physical, it has to imply some thought. Even if the causer is placing pieces of ice, or hot compresses, on the causee's body, sentence B would still sound odd. This suggests that in the semantic structure, the causative *make* combines with the element FEEL not directly but rather via the element THINK: apparently *making* someone *feel* something presupposes making them think something.

On the other hand, in impersonal *make feel* sentences, such as "The whisky made me feel sick," a physical feeling is quite possible. The condi-

tions on the two types are therefore different. The explication that follows
refers only to the interpersonal *make feel* type:

NP¹$_{Human}$ made NP²$_{Human}$ VERB$_{Feel}$ [Complement]

Person X made person Y feel something (Z). =
a. X did something
b. because of this Y thought something
c. because of this Y felt something (Z)
d. Y wouldn't have felt this (Z) if X had not done this

Rather than multiply various *make* constructions beyond necessity, I will
say here that the *make feel* construction has some extensions that seem to
fit the same basic explication. These extensions can be illustrated with the
following two sentences from *Alice in Wonderland*:

> . . . she pictured to herself . . . how she would gather about her other
> little children, and make *their* eyes bright and eager with many a
> strange tale . . .

> The Queen's argument was that if something wasn't done about it in
> less than no time, she'd have everybody executed, all round. (It was
> this last remark that had made the whole party look so grave and
> anxious).

In the first of these sentences, a person is said to make someone else's
eyes bright and eager; what is meant, however, is that the causer is making
the causee "feel interested" (with a further implication that the interest
will be reflected in the causee's eyes). In the second sentence, one person's
remark is said to make other people look grave and anxious; what is meant,
however, is that one person said something and that other people felt
anxious because of this (again, with a further implication that the feeling
of anxiety is reflected in these people's faces).

4.4. Making Someone Think Something

Closely related to the *make feel* type is the *make think* type, which can be
illustrated with common sentences such as the following ones:

> You made me realize that Z.
> He made her forget her troubles.
> She made him think of other matters (other people).
> He made me see that I was on the wrong path.

Here, too, there is no implication that what happened as a result of the causer's action is seen as "bad." Nor are there any other implications about the nature of Z: It may be good or not good, wanted or not wanted, wise or foolish, and so on. In this case, too, therefore, a neutral formula is in order:

Person X made person Y think something (Z). =
a. X did something
b. because of this Y thought something (Z)
c. Y wouldn't have thought this (Z) if X had not done this

It is worth noting that the interpersonal *make think* construction discussed here, too, corresponds closely to its counterpart with an impersonal causer discussed earlier (e.g., "it made me think of other matters" vs. "she made me think of other matters"). The differences between the two types consist only in the contrast between "someone" and "something" and "do" and "happen."

4.5. Making Someone Want Something

As one can "make someone feel something" and "make someone think something," one can also "make someone want something." For example, one can say "You made me want to try again!" This further application of the *make feel* and *make think* pattern may seem trivial and hardly worth mentioning, for it parallels exactly the other two patterns. Yet, each pattern needs to be listed, if only to exclude the nonexistent ones, such as for example "make know"; for one cannot say in English "he made me know this," although the closest equivalents of *make* in, say, Italian, can be used in the corresponding phrase:

Maria mi ha fatto sapere questo.
'Mary "made" me know this.'

(One can of course say in English "let know," but not "make know.")

For the sake of completeness, then, I will also write an explication for the *make want* type (note that Z stands here for a complement clause, cf. Wierzbicka, 1996):

Person X made person Y want something (Z). =
a. X did something
b. because of this Y thought something
c. because of this Y wanted Z

d. Y wouldn't have wanted this (Z) if X had not done this

One point worth noting is that in this case, as in the case of *make feel*, the causal link holds between the causee's wanting something and the causee's thinking something, whereas the counterfactual link holds between the causee's wanting something and the causer's doing something. Another point worth noting is that wanting does not have to refer in this case to wanting to do something, for one can also say, for example, "You made me want to be good." For this reason, the relevant component is formulated simply as "Y wanted Z."

Finally, it should be noted that the interpersonal *make want* type, too, has its counterpart with an impersonal causer, e.g. "it made me want to try again."

4.6. Making Someone Cry (an Involuntary Emotional Response)

A person can make another person cry or laugh.

A. John made Mary cry.
B. Mary made John laugh.

To account for such sentences, I propose another *make* construction, which can be called "*make* of involuntary emotional response." The conditions of this construction can be spelled out as follows:

Person X made person Y cry/laugh. =
a. X did something
b. because of this Y thought something
c. because of this Y felt something
d. because of this Y did something (Z)
e. Y didn't do Z because Y wanted to do it
f. Y wouldn't have done it if X had not done this

Consider, for example, the following sentence from the diary of a dying man, referring to his wife (Brodkey, 1996):

I can make her cry by saying: "Don't ask me about the attic fan: do it the way you want it." With the implication, of course, that I won't be here.

The sentence does not make it clear whether the dying man wants his wife to cry or not; but it is clear that he does something (he says something), that because of this, his wife thinks something, that the thought induces in her a feeling, that this feeling leads to some bodily processes, and that these in turn lead to her crying—presumably, involuntary crying. Clearly, a sentence of this kind does not mean the same as its counterpart with *because*, that is, A and B in the following pair do not mean the same:

    A. X made Y cry by saying Z.
    B. X said Z; because of this, Y cried.

Variant A suggests a stronger link between X's words and Y's crying: There is a stronger implication that Y's crying was involuntary and induced by some internal processes (triggered by the feeling), and also that Y would not have cried were it not for X's action. All this is consistent with the proposed explication.

It could be objected that the analysis proposed for by the *make cry* type, which has been posited here as a separate category of *make* causatives, is too specific, because one could also use a *make* causative with reference to nonexpressive bodily behavior, as in the following example: "John made Mary sneeze by putting smelling salts under her nose." Clearly, in this case, neither thinking nor feeling is involved, and yet the sentence is not unacceptable.

But in fact a *make sneeze* sentence fits another type of *make* causative; the *make happen* discussed earlier. Whereas crying or laughing can be seen as "doing" something, sneezing is more likely to be seen (in English) as something that happens to a person rather than something that a person does:

    All she did was cry.
    ?All she did was sneeze.

"Making someone sneeze" can be seen, then, as analogous to "making someone fall." But "making someone cry (or laugh)" cannot be seen in this way, for crying or laughing is something that one does (albeit often involuntarily), not something that happens to one. In any case, this is how the verb *sneeze* is treated by the English lexicon, whereas the verbs *cry* and *laugh* are treated differently.

Once again, if this type were to be collapsed in one formula with one of the previously discussed types, both formulae would loose a great deal of predictive power. First, the counterfactual link holds in the present case between an action of the causer and the action (rather than a thought or a feeling) of the causee; and second, the sentences of the *make cry* type imply that the action of the causee is involuntary, and this information would be lost if component (e) was regarded as optional rather than as part of the invariant of a separate subconstruction (the *make cry* type).

4.7. Making Someone Do Something ("Make of Coercion")

> When we were small Mai used to make us kneel on graters for a thing like that. (Naipaul, 1969, p. 236)

> . . . He . . . made her learn the quotations hanging on the walls, and made her sit still while he unsuccessfully tried to sketch her. She was dispirited and submissive. (Naipaul, 1969, p. 222)

> Granny is making me eat fish. I hate it. (Naipaul, 1969, p. 186)

As these examples suggest, being made to do something implies doing something that one does not want to do under pressure from somebody else. Formulaically, this can be spelled out as follows:

Person X made person Y do Z. =
a. X wanted Y to do Z
b. Y knew this
c. X knew that if X didn't do something to Y, Y wouldn't do it
d. because of this X did (said) something to Y
e. because of this, Y thought "I have to do it"
f. because of this Y did Z
g. Y wouldn't have done Z (at that time) if Y had not thought this

The action that the causee is made to perform does not have to be inherently unpleasant (as in the case of kneeling on graters), and the causer can in fact be solicitous and concerned about the causee's welfare, as in the case of the grandmother making a child eat fish, but even then, the construction itself implies that the action was not performed willingly.

Consider, for example, the following passage:

> He was tired; she made him rest. He was hungry; she gave him food. He had nowhere to go: she welcomed him. (Naipaul, 1969, p. 484)

In this case, rather atypically, the causee appreciates the causer's pressure. Yet here, too, given the situation described in the book, it is quite plausible that he would not have rested had his mother not urged him do so, and that he gave in to his mother's solicitous pressure recognizing that, given her attitude, he had to let her take care of him.

How does one make another person do something that this person is apparently unwilling to do? Presumably, by "doing something to this person" (usually, verbally): by threatening them, pressurizing them, nagging them, or perhaps cajoling them. Typically, the causer's words are directed at the causee and typically, they refer to some possible consequences of the causee's action (or inaction). For example, although one can make a person cry by saying something (e.g., cruel jokes at the causee's expense) to a third person, one cannot make a person apologize, or wash the dishes, by saying something to a third person. Nor can one make a person apologize or wash the dishes by saying something to this person about somebody else or something else:

?She made me apologize by pointing out that Harry had already done so.
?She made me wash the dishes by complaining about her headache.

What does it mean, however, that the action is not performed willingly? Does it mean that the causee doesn't want to do what he or she is doing? At first sight, a component along these lines ("Y didn't want to do it") seems to be fitting, but when one examines a wide range of *make* sentences (with an intentional verb complement), it emerges that not all of them seem entirely consistent with such a component. Sometimes the implication seems to be that the causee had no choice in the matter, rather than that the causee actually didn't want to do it, as in the following sentence:

My wife made me go to the doctor. I was planning to go anyway, but I kept putting it off, so she rang and made an appointment for me.

The component "Y didn't want to do Z" would be too strong to account for such sentences.

The solution that I would like to propose is this: We cannot say that the causee "didn't want to do what he(she) did," but we can say that the causee thought, at some point: "I have to do it," and did it because of this, and further, that the causee would not have done it had he(she) not thought "I have to do it." If we formulated the counterfactual component in terms of the causer's action ("Y wouldn't have done Z if X had not done it"), this would not be sufficient to account for the unwillingness implied by the construction. If, however, we phrase the counterfactual component in terms of the causee's thought ("Y wouldn't have done it if Y had not thought 'I have to do it'"), this does allow us to account for the implied unwillingness, and to do so without saying that the causee "didn't want to do" what he or she intentionally did.

If this analysis is correct, then there is an interesting difference between the counterfactual component in *make* sentences referring to intentional action (as in "X made Y apologize") and those referring to involuntary action (as in "X made Y cry"). A sentence such as "John made Mary cry" implies that Mary wouldn't have cried if John had not done something that upset her. By contrast, a sentence such as "Mary made John apologize" implies that John wouldn't have apologized if he had not thought that he had to do it (rather than that John wouldn't have apologized if Mary had not done something). The latter may hold, too, by implication (John wouldn't have apologized if Mary had not done something), but what we need to spell out to account for the causee's implied unwillingness is the former, i.e. the causee's thought "I have to do it."

4.8. Make of Subjective Necessity

Mutatis mutandis, what applies to *make* sentences describing interpersonal "coercion" applies also to *make* sentences with a nonpersonal causer, such as "The rain made him go inside." In this case, no one is putting pressure on the causee, but the event (the rain) leads the causee to a realization that an action is necessary ("I have to do something"):

Something (X) made person Y do Z. =
a. person Y was in place P
b. something (X) happened in this place (e.g. it started to rain)
c. because of this Y thought: "I have to do something"
d. because of this Y did Z (go inside)
e. Y wouldn't have done Z if X had not happened

Let us test this formula against a further example: "The arrival of the police made me run for my life." To begin with, I was in a place (P). Then the police arrived at that place. Because of this, I thought: "I have to run"; and so I did. I wouldn't have done it had I not thought that I had to do it.

Usually, when an event makes a person do something, it is understood that this event occurred in the place where the person was (e.g., if the rain makes a person go inside, it is understood that it rained in the place where this person was at the time). It is debatable whether or not the identity of place is a necessary condition for this type. Some informants accept sentences such as the following one, where the causing event can take place far away from the action of the causee:

The bush fires in Victoria made them work all night editing the footage.

Other informants, however, are not quite happy with such sentences and prefer versions without *make*, for example:

The bush fires in Victoria kept them working all night.

In the formula proposed earlier, I formulated components (a) and (b) in a way that assumes identity of place, but the matter requires further investigation. On the other hand, some reference to place does seem necessary in the type under discussion, as the following contrasts illustrate:

A. The death of his father made him reassess his plans
   (think—, realize—, reevaluate—, decide—, etc.).
B. ?The death of his father made him resign from his job.

Sentence A is acceptable because the *make think* type discussed earlier (section 3.1) places no conditions on the nature of the event that makes someone think (realize, etc.) something. But sentence B sounds odd, for the *make do* type discussed here is more constrained: Apparently, for the sentence to be fully acceptable, the event that makes a person *do* something has to be presented (or interpretable) as a "local" event (e.g., rain or the arrival of the police on the scene). Consider also the following contrast:

A. He resigned from his job because his father died.
B. ?The death of his father made him resign from his job.

Here again, sentence A is perfectly normal, but sentence B, close in meaning as it may seem to be, is not equally acceptable. The hypothesis that the *make do* type with an inanimate cause requires a reference to a place accounts for such contrasts in acceptability. It should be added, however, that the event that *makes* a person do something may stem from something that this person sees on television, or in a newspaper, or something else of this nature, as in the following example:

> Rupert Murdoch was annoyed. Not with the expansion of. . . . Not with the development of. . . . What made him reach for the phone at around midday Sydney time on September 5 were four paragraphs on page 2 of The Daily Telegraph's business Section. . . . (The Australian Magazine, December 14–15, 1996, p. 11)

What is particularly interesting about this example is that in a sense, there is clearly no external compulsion or coercion here: In a sense, the act of reaching for the phone can be seen as due to a completely free decision. Yet, the formula "Y thought: 'I have to do something'" fits the situation, as described, particularly well: The implication is not that Murdoch "didn't want" to reach for the phone, but rather that he wouldn't have done it at that particular moment had he not thought something along the lines "I have to do something." In essence, the same applies of course to the examples discussed earlier, but perhaps not quite so clearly: The people who are running away because the police have arrived *want* to run away, and the person whom the rain makes go inside *wants* to go inside (because of the rain).

Thus, the construction called here "the *make* of subjective necessity" parallels in one important respect that called "the *make* of coercion": In both cases, the causee does something because he(she) thinks: "I have to do it" (or "I have to do something"). Yet, even here, there is some difference. In the case of the *make* of coercion, the thought attributed to the causee is "I have to do it," whereas in the case of the *make* of necessity, the thought attributed to the causee must take the form of "I have to do something," for it is not always clear what exactly the causee has to do. This last point is highlighted by the following examples from *Alice in Wonderland*, where there was hardly any time for the causee to decide what exactly she had to do:

> . . . [A] sharp hiss made her draw back in a hurry: A large pigeon had flown into her face. (p. 63)

> . . . [A] little sharp bark just over her head made her look up in a great hurry. (p. 50)

It might be objected to that in sentences like these, the action of the causee is thought of as "automatic" rather than as "deliberate." I think, however, that they are not inconsistent with an interpretation that posits a sudden thought flashing through the causee's mind: "I have to do something (now)."

4.9. Make Versus Force

Before we proceed with our survey of various English *make* constructions, it is worth stopping for a moment to compare the *make* of coercion with the lexical verb *force*. What is the difference, for example, between "making someone apologize" and "forcing someone to apologize"?

I believe that comparing "make" and "force" is particularly useful insofar as it throws light on the nature of the unwillingness implied by *make*. For clearly, *forcing* does imply that the causee did not want to do whatever he or she ultimately did, and because *force* is, intuitively, more coercive than *make*, comparing the two helps us to see that it would not be wise to attribute the same component ("Y didn't want to do it") to the *make* of coercion construction as well. I submit that both the differences and the similarities between *force* and *make* of coercion can be accounted for if we propose the following explication for *force*:

Person X forced person Y to do Z (e.g. to apologize). =
a. X wanted Y to do Z
b. X knew that Y didn't want to do this
c. X thought that if X did something to Y
      Y would have to do Z
d. because of this X did something to Y
e. because of this Y had to do Z
f. because of this Y did Z
g. Y wouldn't have done Z if X had not done this to Z
h. when Y was doing Z Y thought: "I don't want to do this"

Finally, let us examine the difference between *make* of subjective necessity and *force* (of real necessity), as in the sentences A and B:

A. The rain made Mary go inside.
B. The rain forced Mary to go inside.

Mutatis mutandis, what applies to coercion applies also to necessity. Sentence A implies that when it started to rain, Mary thought: "I have to go inside," whereas sentence B implies more: that Mary really "had to" go inside. Furthermore, B implies that Mary would not have gone inside had it not started to rain, whereas A suggests, rather, that Mary would not have gone inside if she had not thought "I have to do it." Finally, sentence B clearly implies that Mary did not want to go inside and that as she was doing it, she thought "I don't want to do it," whereas sentence A implies that Mary thought "I have to do it," rather than "I don't want to do it."

4.10. A Mishap Blamed on an Object or Event

Moving now to sentences where an event (rather than a person) makes something happen to someone, we will note, first of all, a type that appears to be parallel to the "making-something-happen-to-someone" type discussed earlier: Just as one can say "He made me fall over," one can also say "It made me fall over," where "it" can refer to an event involving the causee, or to a thing whose presence in a place is linked with an event involving the causee. Typically, what happens to the causee is seen as due either to a local event (as in sentence 1) or to a "bodily" event (as in sentence 2):

1. The box falling off the shelf hit my head and made me fall off the ladder.
2. The sudden drop of the sugar level in her blood made her faint.

In sentences of this kind, the causal link holds between something that happened to a person (usually, to this person's body) and something else that happened to the same person. The second event always appears to be not only unexpected but also undesirable (bad). I propose, then, the following explication for this type of sentence:

Something (X) made Z happen to person Y. =

a. something (X) happened to person Y
b. because of this something bad (Z) happened to Y
c. Z wouldn't have happened to Y
    if X had not happened to Y

As in the case discussed earlier, when the responsibility for a mishap was blamed on a person (e.g., "You made me fall"), the same question also arises here: Was the event really bad (for the person involved) or was it merely unwanted? But the same considerations that point to "bad" rather than "unwanted" in the "personal blame" sentences apply to the type we are discussing now. For example, if the rug made me trip over it, it is hardly necessary to point out that I did NOT want to trip over it (in fact, the very meaning of the verb *trip over* excludes the possibility of the event being "wanted"). The interpretation that says that "something bad" happened to the causee does not run into any such difficulties; and of course something bad does not have to be interpreted as "something tragic": It can refer to a minor mishap, or to a minor misfortune, too.

For the time being at least, then, I stand by the explications sketched earlier. Apparent counterexamples do come to mind, but, as I discuss in the next section, they may be more apparent than real.

4.11. If I Do Something, It Will Make Me VERB ADJ

The claim, or hypothesis, that *make happen* sentences imply some negative consequences for the causee appears to run into difficulties in the case of sentences such as "Spinach will make you grow big and strong," where no negative consequences are envisaged and yet, the same structural pattern appears to be met. Similarly, in Lewis Carroll's *Alice in Wonderland*, Alice often encounters various magical objects that make her grow large or small, by no means always to her disadvantage. Two examples are:

I do hope it'll make me grow large again, for really I'm quite tired of being such a tiny little thing. (pp. 40–41)

. . . [I]f it makes me grow larger, I can reach the key; and if it makes me grow smaller, I can creep under the door; so either way I'll get into the garden, and I don't care which happens! (p. 12)

In these sentences, what happens to Alice is not only not seen as bad but can in fact be seen as good. So how can such sentences be reconciled with the claim that *make happen* sentences with an inanimate causer always imply some negative consequences? The solution would seem to be straightforward: Why not simply abandon the element "bad" in the proposed explication?

For sentences such as those referring to Alice, this would work; but are these sentences really of the same type as sentences such as "It made me fall"? I suggest they are not. The crucial difference is that in Alice's case, what happens to the causee happens because she herself had done something (eaten a magic cake; drunk from a magic bottle), whereas in the case of "It made me fall" sentences, what happens to the causee happens because of something that has happened in the place where the causee was, not because of something that the causee has done.

It would not help, therefore, to simply remove the element "bad" in the explication proposed for *make happen* sentences, along the following lines:

a. something (X) happened (in place P? to person Y?)
b. because of this something (Z) happened to person Y
c. Z wouldn't have happened to Y if X had not happened

As it stands, the formula is unsatisfactory, for if component (a) is formulated simply as "something happened in this place," then the formula doesn't fit sentences referring to Alice, which do not refer to any local event but to something that Alice herself does. If it is formulated as "something happened to person Y," this doesn't fit sentences about Alice either, for the same reason. If, on the other hand, this component were to be formulated as "person Y did something," this would fit the sentences about Alice but would exclude sentences such as "It made me fall."

As far as I can see, the only solution to such difficulties is to treat the two types separately and to phrase the first component as "something happened in this place" for the "it made me fall" type, and as "person Y did something" for the Alice type sentences. Once we have made this move, however, the question of implied negative consequences solves itself too: A reference to bad consequences is appropriate for the first type but not for the second type. For the Alice type sentences, then, we can propose (as a first approximation) the following explication:

person Y did something to thing X (a cake, some drink)

because of this something (Z) happened to this person

Z wouldn't have happened to Y if Y had not done this

Here, too, a thing (X) is presented, so to speak, as a causer of the event involving the causee, but in this case, the causal link includes an action of the causee (an action that also involves the causer).

In support of this distinction between the two types, I would point out that the *do happen* sentences also have a formal characteristic of their own: Almost invariably, they include a predicative adjective, which specifies the result of the caused event. For example, of the following two sentences A and B, A is generally judged to sound better than B:

A. Spinach will make you grow big and strong!

B. ?Spinach will make you grow!

In the sentences about Alice, too, magical objects are said to make her "grow taller" or "grow large" rather than simply "grow."

In fact, there seems to be a close semantic, as well as a formal, relation between the *do happen* sentences under discussion and purely adjectival *make* sentences such as the following ones: "Spinach will make you big and strong!"

Formally, sentences of this type can be represented as follows:

$$NP^1_{Nonhuman} \text{ made } NP^2_{Human} \text{ ADJ}$$

Two more examples (from *Alice in Wonderland*) include:

They looked so good, that it made Alice quite hungry to look at them. (p. 148)

Maybe it's always pepper that makes people hot-tempered . . . , and vinegar that makes them sour—and camomile that makes them bitter—and—barley sugar and such things that make children sweet-tempered. (pp. 119–120)

On the face of it, a verb referring to the causee's action may be either present (as in 1) or absent (as in 2), but semantically it is always there. For example, sentence 2 makes sense on the assumption that people eat and drink the substances mentioned as causers of the resulting states. In fact, in this case, no separate explication appears to be needed and the "make grow big and strong" type can indeed be collapsed with the "make big and strong" type in a single formula:

$NP^1_{Nonhuman}$ made NP^2_{Human} (VERB)ADJ

Whether a verb is present or absent, the same explication (proposed earlier) seems to apply. But because sentences of this kind normally specify a resulting state, one further component (d) appears to be in order:

Something (X) made person Y be like this [ADJ]. =
a. person Y did something to thing X
b. because of this something (Z) happened to this person
c. Z wouldn't have happened to Y if Y had not done this
d. after this Y was like this [ADJ]]

4.12. Local Events With Unexpected Outcomes

Let us also consider briefly sentences referring to various local phenomena such as the following ones (A and B from Chappell, 1978):

A. The storm made all the flowers fall.
B. The wind made the door blow open.
C. The tremor made the tower collapse.

From a formal point of view, the pattern under discussion can be described as follows:

$NP^1_{Nonhuman}$ made NP^2_{Human} $VERB_{Happen}$

The question is what exactly are the semantic implications of this construction.

To start with a cautious explication that would include only more secure components, we could propose the following:

a. something (X) happened in place P
b. because of this something (Z) happened
   to some things (Y) in this place
c. Z wouldn't have happened to Y if X had not happened in this
   place

There are reasons to think, however, that such a broad explication would not be sufficient to account correctly for the construction's range of use. In particular, compare the following two sentences:

A. The wind made the door blow open.
B. The wind made the door blow shut.

All my respondents agree that of the two, sentence A sounds better; and the reason seems to be that for doors, being shut is seen as a normal state, whether the *make* construction implies that something unusual and probably undesirable has happened.

To account for this widely shared intuition, we need to add a component to the explication. The question is: How should this missing component be phrased?

One possibility is to say that what is missing is a reference to "something BAD happening": if a storm makes all the flowers fall, or if a tremor makes a tower collapse, then surely this can be seen as bad; and even if a wind makes a door blow open, this, too, can be seen as bad (for normally, the desired state of a door is to be shut).

But some difficulties remain. In particular, my respondents tend to agree that the following sentence is quite acceptable: "The recent rains have made everything bloom." If we want to accommodate this sentence in the same explication as the earlier ones, we would have to abandon the putative reference to something bad happening, and perhaps try to pursue a different lead: The event in question has to be seen as unexpected. This leads us to the following tentative explication:

Something (X) made something (Z) happen in a place. =
a. something (X) happened in place P
b. because of this something (Z) happened
    to some things (Y) in this place
c. Z wouldn't have happened to Y if X had not happened in this
    place
d. before it happened, people could think that this would not
    happen

Another possibility would be to consider positing two distinct types, one referring to local events causing "bad things to happen to some things in this place," and another, to local events causing the whole place to look different (as in the sentence "The recent rains have made everything bloom"). At the moment, however, I favor the possibility that allows us not to split the type under discussion into two types, and that presents the outcome as simply unusual or unexpected ("before this happened, people could think that this would not happen"). If, after heavy rains, everything blooms and the whole place looks different, this is unusual, unexpected— more so than if, say, a storm "kills" a single rosebush or lemon tree. It is the unexpectedness, then, rather than anything else that seems to be the crucial factor in this type of *make* sentence.

4.13. Making Something Happen to Various Things

One can "break" a dish and one can also "make it break"; and although normally one "opens" a door, in the case of an automatic door one can also "make it open":

A. John opened the door.
B. John made the library door open by standing in front of it and thus activating the photo-mechanism.

What is the difference? Or what are the differences? One difference, I suggest, has to do with the nature of the link between the causer and the causee: Lexical causatives imply that the causer does something TO the causee and that because of this, at the same time something happens to the causee, and that there is a describable outcome:

person X did something to thing Y
because of this at the same time something happened to Y
because of this after this Y was Z

Make causatives (of the type under discussion) imply that the causer does something but not TO the causee. The action may be intentional (as in the case of a person who makes the library door open by deliberately standing in front of it) or accidental (as in the case of a dog who makes an alarm system go off by jumping in front of a sensor). In either case, however, the result can be seen as unexpected—presumably because the agent does not do anything TO the object in question. This leads us to the following explication:

Person X made Z happen to thing Y (e.g., open, go off)
a. X did something
b. because of this something (Z) happened to thing Y
c. Z wouldn't have happened to Y if X had not done this
d. X didn't do anything to Y
e. because of this people could think that Z would not happen to Y

The kind of situation described in the formula is unusual, for normally if something happens to an object because a person has done something (and only for this reason), it can be assumed that the person has done something TO that object. For this reason, sentences like the following one are usually regarded as odd:

?John made the dish break (by placing it on a hotplate)

For if John placed the dish on a hotplate, it can hardly be said that John didn't do anything TO the dish; and if the clause in parentheses is omitted, the sentence is still odd, because it is unclear how John could bear total responsibility for the fact that the dish broke if he has not done anything to it. I say "total responsibility" advisedly, for the *make* construction implies not only a causal link but also a counterfactual link: If John forgets to put a dish away, and then the dish breaks, John could still be held responsible, but one could not say that John made the dish break.

In the case of automatic or semiautomatic devices, however, the formula is applicable: Even if John doesn't do anything to the library door, he can still make it open because his standing in front of it, which activates a photo-mechanism, can be seen as the only reason why the door opens.

5. CAUSATION IN GRAMMAR: TOWARD A SEMANTIC TYPOLOGY OF GRAMMATICAL SYSTEMS

It is generally recognized that languages differ in the amount—and kind—of attention they give to different aspects of reality through their lexical systems: Arabic has numerous words for sand, Southeast Asian languages for rice, and so on. But the idea that languages differ in the amount—and kind—of attention they give to abstract ideas and relations such as causation, time, or human emotions, has seldom been seriously explored. Yet it seems obvious that although cross-linguistic divergences in this latter respect are harder to investigate, their significance is probably far greater than that of more visible differences in the area of concrete lexicon (and in particular, of the vocabulary concerned with environmental features).

In the area of causation, divergencies between different languages are very considerable and very intriguing. At the one extreme, there appear to be languages with hardly any causative constructions at all (apart from purely purposive constructions). Evans (1986) argued that the Australian Aboriginal language Kayardild may be a case in point. At the other extreme, there are languages such as English, with a wide range of causative constructions, especially in the area of human interaction: various *make* causatives, *have* causatives, *get* causatives, *let* causatives, and so on. Between these two poles, there is a wide range of variation—both in the amount of attention given to causal relations and in the kind of qualitative distinctions drawn by different languages.

The observation that among the European languages, English shows the greatest differentiation in the area of causation—more so than French, Italian, or Russian—is entirely in line with Bally's (1920) semantic typology of European languages, advanced in his pioneering early study, "*Impres-sionisme et Grammaire.*" Bally contrasted two "psychological tendencies" manifested in the syntax of different languages: an "impressionistic" one, focusing on phenomena as they present themselves to human beings, and an analytical one, focusing on the presumed relations between causes and effects. He argued that the impressionistic, phenomenological orientation is more in evidence in Russian than it is in German, more in German than it is in French, and more in French than it is in English, and that conversely, the analytical, causal orientation is more in evidence in English than it is in French, more in French than in German, and more in German than in Russian.

In my earlier work (cf. Wierzbicka, 1988, 1992, 1995), I tried to com-plement Bally's observations by showing that Russian syntax pays more attention to accidental, inexplicable causation, to the interplay between human life and the forces of nature, and to the interplay between volition and emotion than does English syntax (with German, Italian, and French occupying intermediate positions in this regard); and that the high degree of attention that the English language gives to causal relations focuses in particular on kinds and shades of human interaction.

But to be able to compare meanings encoded in both the lexicon and the grammar of different languages, we need a suitable methodology, and this includes a coherent semantic theory. Otherwise, the study of syntax degenerates into a domain where people play more or less ingenious games with formalisms and remain oblivious to meanings that motivate formal differences in the first place and that make meaningful comparisons of syntactic constructions in different languages possible.

Let me present one (quite typical) example. A recent study of causatives, included in the prestigious volume *Syntax: An International Handbook of Contemporary Research* (Saebø, 1993, pp. 935–936) discusses the two English sentences:

1. The band caused Max to leave the concert.
2. The guard forced Max to leave the concert.

Having duly assigned to these sentences two different trees and two different logical formulae, the author offers the following astonishing comment:

> In terms of pure meaning, the sole difference between *cause* and *force* is that the latter adds a relation between the two NPs (*the band/guard* and *Max*), i.e., the second (*Max*) enters into the cause proposition as an argument of a predicate not entirely indeterminate. (p. 935)

I agree that the syntactic structure of these two sentences is different, and that the two trees drawn by Saebø are one way of representing this difference. Whether the two added "meaning postulates," that according to Saebø satisfactorily capture the difference between the two sentences are helpful and necessary, is perhaps a matter of opinion. They look as follows (p. 936):

(iii) $\wedge$ x $\wedge$ y $\wedge$ P$\square$[δ(P)(y)(x) $\leftrightarrow$
    α(P(y))(x)]   (a. c. i)

(iv) $\wedge$ x $\wedge$ y $\wedge$ P$\square$[δ(P)(y)(x) $\rightarrow$
    α(P(y))(y)(x) $\wedge$ β(y)]   (control)

But how can anyone claim that the sole difference in meaning between *cause* and *force* is that the latter "adds a relation between the two NPs (*the band/guard* and *Max*)"?

Doesn't sentence 2 imply that Max *didn't want* to leave the concert, that the guard *wanted* Max to leave the concert, that the guard *did something to* Max *because of this*, and that Max *had to* leave the concert *because of this?* Doesn't sentence 1 imply that the band *didn't do* anything *to* Max? And doesn't the fact that there is a syntactic relation between *the guard* and *Max* in sentence 2 have anything to do with the fact that the guard DID SOMETHING TO Max (whereas the band didn't)?

A syntactic analysis that pays as little attention to meaning as Saebø's is not only semantically, but also syntactically weak and has little predictive power. For example, it fails to account for the fact that in the two pairs of sentences that follow, the A sentences are acceptable whereas the B sentences are not:

   3. A. The guard caused Max to die.
      B. ?The guard forced Max to die.
   4. A. The noise caused the crystal chandelier to shatter.
      B. ?The noise forced the crystal chandelier to shatter.

To be able to account for such differences in acceptability, we must pay attention to distinctions like those between "human" and "inanimate" nouns, or "action verbs" and "event verbs." We must also pay attention to the differences in meaning between different causative verbs like *to cause, to force, to make, to get, to let,* and so on—and to the complex interplay between different relevant factors (the category to which the causer belongs, the category to which the causee belongs, the category to which the predicate of the complement clause belongs, the causative verb chosen in a given sentence, and so on).

As the present chapter illustrates, all this can be done, and if it is done the resulting formulae can have full predictive power. To achieve such predictive power, we do not need any formidable technical formalisms.

Nor do we need to endlessly concern ourselves with the "perennially contested issue [of] how (or even if) syntax can be combined with semantics" (Goddard, 1997b, p. 197). Rather, as Goddard argues forcefully, what we need is an analytical framework in which syntax and lexical semantics are integrated from the very beginning.

The overall picture produced by an analysis that pays attention to all the relevant factors is, admittedly, complex and intricate—much more so than one that operates only with tree diagrams and other similar formalisms; but it is, I believe, the only kind of analysis that can achieve descriptive adequacy and explanatory power. It is language itself that is immensely complex. At the same time, if we allow that all languages may have a relatively simple irreducible core, we can use this irreducible core of all languages as a basis for an understanding of the immensely complex and diverse systems that all human languages are.

Syntactic typology that deliberately closes its eyes to the semantic dimensions of formal diversity of languages is, ultimately, sterile and unilluminating. Opening typology to semantics may involve difficulties, but rather than avoiding them, it is surely more fruitful to sharpen our analytical tools and to develop safeguards of various kinds. Above all, we need a semantic metalanguage for a cross-cultural comparison of meanings, whether they are encoded in the lexicon or in grammar. As, I hope, this chapter illustrates, the "Natural Semantic Metalanguage" based on empirically established universal concepts can meet this need.

NOTES

1. This chapter owes a great deal to Cliff Goddard, with whom I have had many discussions on the subject of causatives and who has had a considerable input to the analysis presented here. I am also grateful to Lea Brown and Clare Besemeres who read the first draft of the chapter and offered many valuable criticisms and suggestions for improvement.
2. A spectacular recent example of an analysis which seeks to "explain" something simple and clear with something complex and obscure is provided by Bouchard (1995, p. 123), who analyses the French sentence *Max vient de Paris* (Max comes from Paris) as "Max is oriented towards his being of the deictic center, with the tail end of the orientation being in Paris" (for discussion, see Peeters, 1997).
3. The symbols '*' and '?' preceding examples are linguistic conventions which indicate that the example is either unacceptable ('*') or questionable ('?').

REFERENCES

Bally, C. (1920). Impressionisme et grammaire [Impressionism and grammar]. In *Mélanges d'histoire littéraire et de philologie offerts à Bernard Bouvier, à l'occasion du XXXe anniversaire de sa nomination comme Professeur* (pp. 261–279). Université de Genève. Genève: Société anonyme des éditions Sonor.

Bouchard, D. (1995). *The semantics of syntax: A minimalist approach to grammar.* Chicago: University of Chicago Press.

Brodkey, H. (1996). *This wild darkness: The story of my death.* London: Fourth Estate.

Bugenhagen, R. D. (1994). The exponents of semantic primitives in Mangap-Mbula. In C. Goddard & A. Wierzbicka (Eds.), *Semantic and lexical universals: Theory and empirical findings* (pp. 87–109). Amsterdam: John Benjamins.

Carroll, L. (1929). *Alice's adventures in wonderland.* London: A. & C. Black Ltd.

Chappell, H. M. (1978). *Semantics of some causatives in Chinese and English.* Unpublished undergraduate thesis, Canberra, Australian National University.

Comrie, B. (1974). Causatives and universal grammar. *Transactions of the Philological Society,* 1–32.

Comrie, B. (1985). Causative verb formation and other verb-deriving morphology. In T. Shopen (Ed.), *Language typology and syntactic description* (Vol. 3, pp. 309–348). Cambridge, England: Cambridge University Press.

Evans, N. (1986). The unimportance of CAUSE in Kayardild. *Language in Aboriginal Australia, 2,* 9–17.

Givón, T. (1975). Cause and control: On the semantics of interpersonal manipulation. In J. P. Kimball (Ed.), *Syntax and semantics* (Vol. 4, pp. 59–89). New York: Academic Press.

Goddard, C. (Ed.). (1997a). Studies in the syntax of universal semantic primitives. *Special Issue of Language Sciences, 19*(3).

Goddard, C. (Ed.). (1997b). The universal syntax of semantic primitives.

Goddard, C. (1998). *Semantic analysis: A practical introduction.* Oxford, England: Oxford University Press.

Goddard, C., & Wierzbicka, A. (Eds.). (1994). *Semantic and lexical universals: Theory and empirical findings.* Amsterdam: John Benjamins.

Kachru, Y. (1976). On the semantics of the causative construction in Hindi-Urdu. In M. Shibatani (Ed.), *Syntax and semantics: Vol. 6. The grammar of causative constructions* (pp. 353–369). New York: Academic Press.

Leibniz, G. W. (1961). Table de définitions. In L. Couturat (Ed.), *Opuscules et fragments inédits de Leibniz* (pp. 437–510). Paris: Presses Universitaires de France. (Original work written in 1704)

Naipaul, V. S. (1969). *A house for Mr. Biswas.* Harmondsworth, England: Penguin.

Peeters, B. (1997). Review of Bouchard 1995. *Australian Journal of Linguistics, 16*(2), 242–245.

Rupert Murdoch was annoyed . . . (1996, December 14–15). *The Australian Magazine,* 11.

Ruwet, N. (1976). *Problems in French syntax: Transformational generative studies* (S. Robins, Trans.). London: Longman. (Original work published 1973)

Saebø, K. J. (1993). Causality and finality. In J. Jacobs, A. van Stechow, W. Sternefeld, & T. Vennemann (Eds.), *Syntax: An International Handbook of Contemporary Research* (Vol. 1, pp. 930–939). Berlin: Gruyter.

Shibatani, M. (1973). Semantics of Japanese causativization. *Foundations of Language, 9,* 327–373.

Shibatani, M. (Ed). (1976). *Syntax and semantics: Vol. 6. The grammar of causative constructions.* New York: Academic Press.

Song, J. J. (1996). *Causatives and causation: A universal-typological perspective.* London: Longman.

Speer, A. (1975). *Spandauer Tagebücher* [The Spandau Diaries]. Frankfurt: Propyläen.

Talmy, L. (1976). Semantic causative types. In M. Shibatani (Ed.), *Syntax and semantics: Vol. 6. The grammar of causative constructions* (pp. 43–116). New York: Academic Press.

Wierzbicka, A. (1988). *The semantics of grammar.* Amsterdam: John Benjamins.

Wierzbicka, A. (1991). *Cross-cultural pragmatics: The semantics of human interaction.* Berlin: Mouton de Gruyter.

Wierzbicka, A. (1992). *Semantics, culture and cognition: Universal human concepts in culture-specific configurations.* New York: Oxford University Press.

Wierzbicka, A. (1995). Adjectives vs. verbs: The iconicity of part-of-speech membership. In M. Landsberg (Ed.), *Syntactic iconicity and linguistic freezes* (pp. 223–245). Berlin: Mouton de Gruyter.

Wierzbicka, A. (1996). *Semantics: Primes and universals.* Oxford, England: Oxford University Press.

Wierzbicka, A. (1997). *Understanding cultures through their key words: English, Russian, Polish, German, Japanese.* New York: Oxford University Press.

Wierzbicka, A. (1998). Anchoring linguistic typology in universal concepts. *Linguistic Typology,* 2(1).

Xolodovič, A. A. (Ed.). (1969). *Typologija kauzativnyx konstrukcij* [Typology of Causative Constructions]. Leningrad: Nauka.

Chapter 6

Emergent Grammar

Paul J. Hopper
Carnegie Mellon University

That languages have "grammar," in the sense that they consist of structural units arrayed in patterns determined by grammatical rules, is generally taken for granted within both linguistics and the cognate discipline of psychology. The study of how these grammatical rules are acquired by children on the basis of imperfect and incomplete data is seen by workers in both fields as a major project. A common assumption has been that acquisition is sustained by innate knowledge, which reconstructs and rectifies the missing and defective experiential knowledge, leaving as the child's task, so to speak, the joining of the dots. This kind of explanation, however, requires a strong and very explicit kind of a priori knowledge, of the kind about which many linguists and psychologists are justly skeptical.

Yet, much psycholinguistic research proceeds as if an adult target of a systematic and complete set of grammatical rules was available as the goal of language acquisition, and as if children's abilities developed accordingly. Such projects as "the child's acquisition of the passive," "the child's acquisition of modal verbs," and so on, continue as if the child were filling out the details of an already existent pattern. These teleological implications of innateness are inevitable if the image of a language as an abstract system held together by a system of rules is accepted, and if the common possession of such a system of rules is deemed to be a prerequisite for mutual understanding.

Emergent Grammar is a conception of linguistic structure that proposes to bypass the problem of a fixed, prediscourse adult grammar, with its

attendant problems of necessarily "degenerate" input for both child acquisition and adult maintenance of language, by relocating structure, that is,
"grammar," from the center to the periphery of linguistic communication.
Grammar, in this view, is not the source of understanding and communication but a by-product of it. Grammar is, in other words, epiphenomenal.

The term *emergent* itself I take from an essay by the historian James
Clifford, but I have transferred it from its original context of "culture" to
that of grammar. Clifford (1986, p. 19) remarked that "Culture is temporal,
emergent, and disputed." The same can be said to be true of grammar,
which like speech itself must be viewed as a real-time, social phenomenon,
and therefore is temporal; its structure is always deferred, always in a
process but never arriving, and therefore emergent; and because I can
only choose a tiny fraction of data to describe, any decision I make about
limiting my field of inquiry (for example in regard to the selection of texts,
or the privileging of the usage of a particular ethnic, class, age, or gender
group) is very likely to be a political decision, to be against someone else's
interests, and therefore disputed.

The notion of Emergent Grammar is meant to suggest that structure,
or regularity, comes out of discourse and is shaped by discourse in an
ongoing process. Grammar is, in this view, simply the name for certain
categories of observed repetitions in discourse. It is hence not to be understood as a prerequisite for discourse, a prior possession attributable in
identical form to both speaker and hearer. Its forms are not fixed templates
but emerge out of face-to-face interaction in ways that reflect the individual
speakers' past experience of these forms, and their assessment of the present context, including especially their interlocutors, whose experiences
and assessments may be quite different.

Fundamental to this alternative view of grammar is a changed perspective on the nature of the linguistic sign, defined as a unit that links a
linguistic form with a meaning or function. Standard approaches to linguistic data, both those that call themselves "formal" and those that call
themselves "functional," agree on a fundamentally similar view of the nature of the sign. In this view, signs are equipped at the outset, that is to
say, prior to any act of communication, with all of the information necessary
for their successful communicative use. A language is an inventory of such
signs, together with their combinatorial rules; and discourses are strings
of form–meaning dyads arranged "syntactically" according to these rules.
Both grammar and lexicon exist at an abstract level prior to any use that
is made of them in discourse, and communication depends crucially on
the availability to all parties to a communicative act of an identical system
of signs, rules, and units.

Underlying this view of the linguistic sign, but rarely stated explicitly,
is a particular view of communication and of grammar. It is not the purpose

of this chapter to indulge in an historical and epistemological critique of contemporary linguistic theory, but rather to set out, as objectively as possible, some points of contrast between a linguistics that proceeds from the a priori view of the sign, and an alternative view that makes the sign itself subject to the exigencies of communication and assigns ontological priority to the fact of communication itself. Some of the consequences of making this inversion of the normal assumption are drawn out, with reference to work that either already makes the inversion or can be interpreted without a great deal of effort in terms of the inversion. For some previous statements on the distinction between a priori grammar and emergent grammar, see Hopper (1987, 1988).

Signs whose form and meaning are subject to communicative acts are held to have a structure described as emergent. This means that a sign's form (that is, both its external aspect and the use to which it is put) is provisional, and is dependent, not on an essential inner core of constant meaning, but on previous uses and contexts in which the current speaker has used or heard it. Grammar has the same provisional and context-dependent property as the sign. An approach to grammar that adopts this postulate is referred to as *Emergent Grammar.*

The notion of emergence is a pregnant one. It is not intended to be a standard sense of origins or genealogy, not an historical question of how the grammar came to be the way it is, but instead, it takes the adjective emergent seriously as a continual movement toward structure, a postponement or deferral of structure, a view of structure as always provisional, always negotiable, and in fact, as epiphenomenal, that is, as an effect rather than a cause. The term *emergent* should thus be distinguished from *emerging.* The term emerging might be applied to a subsystem that is becoming part of an already existing grammar, for example, one might speak of an "emerging definite article," one that perhaps still retains some features of a demonstrative but that has attained a degree of obligatoriness with respect to nouns that aligns it typologically with the definite article. The form might then be thought of as an incomplete definite article, or as a definite article in the making. However, this perspective still presupposes that there is a fixed code, and understands a form to be on the way to occupying its rightful place in the synchronic grammatical system. It sees the incompleteness of the category to be in some sense a deficiency that the language is working teleologically to correct. A structure that is emergent, on the other hand, is never fixed, never determined, but is constantly open and in flux. The term emergent refers to the essential incompleteness of a language, and sees lability between form and meaning as a constant and as a natural situation. In the emergence view, there is no natural fixed structure to language. Rather, speakers borrow heavily from their previous experiences of communication in similar circumstances, on similar topics, and with similar interlocutors. Systematicity, in this view, is an illusion produced by the partial settling or *sedimentation* of frequently used forms into temporary subsystems. Grammar is a vast collection of such subsystems. As an unintended outcome of communicative behavior, grammar is a product of "structuration" (Giddens, 1984) rather than a bounded object to be thought of as structure.

Emergent is placed in contrast to the a priori view that understands forms as abstract entities whose existence is presupposed by the possibility of acts of communication, and that views a language as a closed fixed code linking preexistent forms to preexistent meanings. While sedimented forms may appear in some cases to have the same kind of stability as a priori forms, to the point where the small-scale temporary systematicity just referred to can sometimes be summarized by quite similar looking formulae, the ontological and semiotic premises of the two perspectives are in fact quite different. The situation may be compared to that of Einsteinian versus Newtonian physics, where for many experiences of the world, such as driving a car, the differences between the two theories are not visible, whereas for others, such as in calculating the masses and trajectories of high-speed particles, only the Einsteinian perspective is valid; the physicist does not assume two distinct but sometimes intersecting accounts of reality, but understands low velocity phenomena to be interpretable in terms of the single framework required by high-speed phenomena.

Although the primary focus in this chapter is on the possibilities presented by the emergent grammar postulate for the discipline of linguistics, there are more general implications that take the whole question of the communicative basis of language beyond the narrower concerns of linguistics. I therefore briefly present some points of comparison between the two different perspectives to be known as the A-Priori Grammar Perspective (APG) and the Emergent Grammar Perspective (EG).

1. IMPLICATIONS FOR GRAMMAR

Distributed Versus Modular

Grammar in EG is a more scattered and less unified affair than in APG. There is in EG no grammar in the sense of one area (or "module") of language that is set aside as the repository of abstract structure. Instead there are only different kinds of repetition, some of which concern what would more conventionally be called lexical, some idiomatic, and some morphological or grammatical. These repetitions come from various genres and situations of speaking, but come to be recognized as grammatical when enough of them can be identified that they are seen to form a subsystem. The grammar of a language, then, consists not of a single delimited system, but rather, of an open-ended collection of forms that are constantly being restructured and resemanticized during actual use. The mechanism that brings this about is what Haiman (1991) called *routinization,* the fading of existential–situational meaning that occurs when any action is constantly repeated until it becomes routine. The source of the forms that become grammaticized in this way is what Becker called *prior text*: "Prior text is the real a priori of language, not some logical deep structure or anything like that. Prior text is the real source, the real a priori of speaking . . ." (1988, p. 26). We say things that have been said before. Our speech is a vast collection of hand-me-downs that reaches back in time to the beginnings of language. The aggregation of changes and adjustments that are made to this inheritance on each individual occasion of use results in a constant erosion and replacement of the sediment of usage that is called grammar.

Support for such a view of grammar is provided by the fact that *in actual practice,* language is much less grammatical, i.e., less general, than theoretical syntacticians would suggest. For example, the English passive, which is commonly supposed to be a general syntactic rule of English that converts sentences like "A witness contradicted his statement" into "His statement was contradicted by a witness," has been shown to be confined in practice to quite a restricted number of verbs (Gross, 1974). The increasing interest in "corpus linguistics," the study of large-scale patterns of usage that has been made possible by the computer, has also shaken the too ready assumption of large-scale regularity in language. (Stubbs, 1996, is a good recent survey of both methodology and theoretical implications.) A good example is John Sinclair's (1991) observation that the "preposition" *of,* which seems to the grammarian to be a rather normal preposition taking noun phrases as a complement, behaves textually in ways that set it apart from other prepositions and puts into question the classification of this word as a preposition (pp. 81–98). The word frequency lists published by the Lancaster-Oslo-Bergen corpus project show that *of,* with 38% of occurrences of all six prepositions, is almost twice as frequent as the next most frequent preposition *in,* with 22% (Johansson & Hofland, 1987, Vol. 1, p. 19).

Furthermore, prepositions in English characteristically function as the head of a prepositional phrase that itself functions as a sentence adjunct, that is, as an adverbial phrase ("Mrs. Robinson was taken ill *during the performance*"). However, the preposition *of* does not occur in this function. Instead, it appears almost always in a qualifying expression modifying a noun, for example in the possessive construction, as well as appositional constructions like "the city of Atlanta," and so on. Sinclair (1991) concluded that *of* is not really a preposition, but that it forms a category with itself as the sole member. The movement of the preposition *of* away from the other prepositions is illustrative of a situation that has already become sedimented in English.

It must be stressed that this picture of a natural emergence of grammar as a by-product of usage and frequency is complicated by the role of institutional norms of various kinds that may artificially extend or restrict the range of an emergent regularity and fix standardized forms as dictionaries, grammar books, style manuals, and many other institutional artifacts. E. P. Thompson (1991) noted a similar movement from *custom* to *law,* and cited an early source from 1701 that explicitly linked frequency, usage, and institutionalization:

> For a Custom taketh beginning and groweth to perfection in this manner. When a reasonable Act once done is found to be good, and beneficial to the People, and agreeable to their nature and disposition, then do they use it and practise it again and again, and so by often iteration and multiplication of the Act, it becomes a Custom; and being continued without interruption time out of mind, it obtaineth the force of a Law. (pp. 97–98)

The expression "time out of mind" here means "beyond living memory." It strikingly recalls Haiman's routinization. The forgetting of the original semantic motivation for a form during repeated use ("they use and practise it again and again," "by often iteration and multiplication") and its persistence from generation to generation long after the original motivation has ceased ("being continued without interruption") make it increasingly indispensable ("it obtaineth the force of a Law"). "Reasonable acts," of course, do not appear in a cultural or legal vacuum, and so it is also with linguistic expressions: They are anchored in previous expressions, and are repeated because they have been found to be useful, or perhaps prestigious and status conferring. (As with laws, it is not so clear that linguistic expressions are adopted because they are "good, beneficial, and agreeable.") The entry of sets of forms into the canonical grammar of a standard language is comparable in many ways to the passage from custom to written law, from "we do it thus" to "you shall do it thus." There are many reasons for thinking that many of the rules and representations invented by formal linguistics are unconscious appropriations of standardized canonical grammar and stylistics.[1]

Historical-Temporal/Presential-Transcendental

Consistent with this more particularized and fragmentary view of structure is a different attitude toward temporality (Hopper, 1988, 1992; Linell, 1982). Like the acts of communication that engender it, Emergent Grammar exists in time. Its forms are material; they have been used before and they will be used again, on each occasion of use in a different context and with a different sense. They come and go in the speaker's awareness according to whether they are often or rarely heard, and are not totally and simultaneously available to the speaker without regard to context. They are subject to the vagaries of memory, stress, appropriateness, and changes of topic, and to reinforcement or absence of reinforcement from interlocutors. Moreover, because grammar is a question of observed repetitions rather than a preexistent abstract system, it can only be described *in situ*. Emergent regularities are *aggregations*; they are the sediment of frequency. The APG project by contrast must assume the constant availability of the entire language system as it is held to be known to the speaker without regard to time or situation; and structure, lexicon, and meanings exist outside their contexts, and are selected from the inventory of rules and forms during communication for their appropriateness.

Social-Interactive and Dialogic/Psychological-Cognitive

A-Priori Grammar is quintessentially monologic. It postulates "a perfect speaker–hearer in a completely homogeneous speech community" (Chomksy, 1965, p. 3). In this view, explanations for forms do not involve the necessary presence of an interlocutor, or even of a society of speakers. All linguistic knowledge, of all kinds, be it grammatical, semantic, or pragmatic, is stored in the individual speaker's mind, and can be retrieved from there without reference to material acts of communication. Because EG, by contrast, starts out with the assumption of communication, there is always an implicit interlocutor, and forms are constantly being adapted to the needs of the hearer or the audience. This is true for written as well as for spoken texts: Monologic texts, too, presuppose an audience. (Literally talking to oneself may be regarded as bizarre, pathological, or divine, depending on the culture—but it is always abnormal.) The idea that not only meanings but also linguistic forms emerge in contexts of dialogue is important because it by implication denies a basic, stable, core sound–meaning dyad. Speech is performed always in a context of adjustment to others. As Bakhtin (1986) put it:

> Thus all real and integral understanding is actively responsive, and constitutes nothing other than the initial preparatory stage of a response (in whatever form it may be actualized). And the speaker himself is oriented precisely toward such an actively responsive understanding. He does not expect passive understanding that, so to speak, only duplicates his own idea in someone else's mind. Rather, he expects response, agreement, sympathy, objection, execution, and so forth (various speech genres presuppose various integral orientations and speech plans on the part of the speakers or writers). (p. 69)

Grammar, understood as meaningful repetition, is thus distributed among the various participants in a collaborative act of communication (Fox, 1994; Goodwin, 1979). It is also distributed among different genres of speech and among different registers (degrees of formality). Grammar is, in other words, not uniform but relative to context. This is seen in the fact that, typically, speakers' intuitions about sentences deprived of a context are uncertain (see, for example, the many experiments demonstrating this in Greenbaum, 1988). Their uncertainty derives from an absence of grounding in genre, register, audience, and other factors of the material context that give an utterance its meaning. Children do not seem to learn sentences, but rather, they learn to adapt their behavior to increasingly complex surroundings. It is an enterprise that does not stop at the age of 6, but continues throughout a lifetime.

Syntagmatic/Paradigmatic

Because of the belief that the forms and structures of a language form a systematic inventory, A Priori Grammar emphasizes methodologically the collection of paradigmatically arranged forms, typically separating a *lexicon* from a *grammar* and finding principles by which forms such as words can be classified according to their distribution in larger forms such as sentences. Observations about these distributions may moreover lead to the formulation of generalizations about the 'mind' of the speaker. In EG, in which forms are seen as distributed over time, and as being exchanged between speakers, there is an emphasis on the linear, i.e., syntagmatic arrangements of forms, with less inclination to seek all-encompassing generalizations, and even less to attribute these generalizations to an individual 'mind'.

2. IMPLICATIONS FOR LANGUAGE

Communication/Individual Expression

By definition, EG is based on the idea of communication, thought of in the everyday sense of this word. Acts of communication require the presence of multiple speakers, some of whom are sometimes also listeners; language is inconceivable in any other way. In APG, however, communication plays no role. It is rather a postponed agenda, to be accounted for by linguistic encounters among individuals, each of whom is endowed with an identical set of private mentally stored rules for assembling grammatically correct forms. Because the forms of language are thus completely and simultaneously present in the individual, the only basic function for language is individual self-expression set apart from the speech of other individuals.

Partial/Complete-Holistic

The view of language implicit in the APG postulate holds that the forms of language constitute a complete system of units (such as words and morphemes) and rules that is transcendental and atemporal and therefore simultaneously available to each user of the language. Although users may not deploy their rules and units with equal effectiveness, the rules and units are, in principle, identical. In EG, grammar is seen as a more fragmentary entity, indeed not really an entity at all, but rather, the set of sedimented conventions that have been routinized out of the more frequently occurring ways of saying things. Differences among speakers are therefore very real, and communication is typically a question of negotiating areas of common ground (Rommetveit, 1974). The qualitative differences in effectiveness among speakers are not assigned to a special sphere of performance, as they are in APG, but belong to the idea of what language is. Speakers vary in age, education, social class, persona, physical configuration of the vocal tract, gender, recall ability, control of genre, use of other languages, and other parameters, many of which such as fluency (Pawley & Syder, 1983), are not well understood. In APG, these essential differences are suppressed because they are held to ontologically follow rather than precede the global abstract code.

In EG, because the forms of a language do not exist hermetically sealed in the mind of the individual speaker, but are instead distributed during acts of communication among speakers, signs reflect a constant competition among speakers for the control of the meanings of terms and for the definitions of words and expressions, as well as for relative status as determined by such things as accent and choices among alternative forms, priority in turn taking, and recognition of relevance. In APG, by contrast, forms do not require the presence of other speakers. They can—indeed must—therefore be politically and socially neutral until they are deployed in discourse. In discourse, they may eventually play a political role, but by the time they are deployed, their structural status has long been determined (Harris, 1990; Stewart, 1986).

Speakers, as I have noted, are not equal, but differ in their ability to make and exploit this adaptation. They differentially control ranges of vocabulary, phrasing, and phonology, including intonation. They differ also in personality features such as aggressiveness, in opportunities for self-assertion, and in life experiences. Finally, speakers differ in their previous exposure to language varieties having different degrees of prestige and status. All of these different abilities and experiences make for linguistic inequalities among speakers that are inseparable from grammatical differences in any but the narrowest sense of the word. The norms that surround a speaker from birth and all through her life do not merely impinge upon an essentially stable core, but are *constitutive* of language, and determine in both small and large scale what structural regularities are permitted to emerge.

Particular/General

A language, then, from the EG perspective is a less completely available, less circumscribed entity than in the APG perspective. Although some structures may have a high degree of consistency across genres and contexts, the attempt to find a constant invariable code common to all acts of communication is seen as either artificial or futile. A language is seen in EG as a collection of largely prefabricated particulars, available for use in appropriate contexts and language games. These particulars may have some intersecting structure, and indeed, may share material that is relatively stable and common to a wide range of genres and occasions, but this core is much smaller and more restricted than the grammar envisaged in the APG perspective. As more and more genres (including both written and spoken sources) are gathered in, the core grammar common to all of them shrinks vanishingly, until it may be doubted whether there is, ultimately, such a thing as English grammar in any comprehensive sense. (Grammar contracts as texts expand.)

A similar, and closely related, conflict between the particular and the general occurs in the society as a distinction between the individual speaker and the speech community (Johnstone, 1996). APG is forced to assume uniformity and to see individual differences as aberrations. When the fact of communicative need is given ontological priority, however, differences among individual speakers are seen as an expected concomitant of this need. For if the speech community was as underlyingly uniform as some APG theoreticians claim, there would presumably be no need to communicate at all. In EG, language is not a general abstract possession that is uniform across the community, but is an emergent fact having its source in each individual's experience and life history and in the struggle to accomplish successful communication.

Materiality/Abstract Rules and Forms

In EG, the forms of language are seen as material entities that are passed from speaker to speaker in the form of actual utterances that are picked up, remembered, and often changed in direct analogical ways. The way in which this occurs has been described by a number of authors (e.g.,

Bolinger, 1961, 1976; Pawley & Syder, 1983; Tannen, 1987). The forms of language are to be seen as embedded in formulaic constructions that are basically prefabricated but repeated with local variations in a way that Bolinger called "syntactic diffusion," one variation splitting off and founding a new family of constructions. In APG, forms are reproduced in accordance with abstract rules possessed in common by all members of the speech community. APG stresses the uniqueness of each utterance, and claims that a linguistic theory must treat each sentence that is produced as if it were completely novel. In EG, on the other hand, it is held that utterances are closely similar to previous utterances, and that anything that is said has been said in something like that form before. Grammar, in the sense in which the term is generally understood, comes about when certain groups of forms become routinized (Haiman, 1991, 1994). This routinization comes about as the result of a favoring of certain types of expression, which turn out to be useful, or effective, or prestigious. The process is very similar to that of the movement from custom to law mentioned earlier.

3. IMPLICATIONS FOR LINGUISTICS

Textual ("Natural") Data/Constructed Data

The contrasting assumptions of APG and EG extend, of course, also to linguistics. The database upon which linguistic theory has been established over at least the past 30 years was drawn from intuitions about grammatically correct utterances as reconstructed either by the native speaker linguist or by the linguist's native speaker helpers. The adequacy of such a database has been severely questioned in recent years (for a penetrating examination of its premises, see Love, 1990). Structure can only be seen as emergent if forms are examined in their naturally occurring contexts, and this means that linguistics must crucially turn its attention to the problems of textuality; the relationship of writer to text, for example, the theory and practice of transcription, and the development of techniques for studying and displaying the phenomena of emergent structure. EG shifts the emphasis of investigations from what speakers *can* do under laboratory conditions to what they *do* do in the natural environment in which language is at home. It seeks out the frequently occurring patterns and distributions of forms, and shows how in turn frequency affects these forms.

The parallel of biology, with the contrast between physiology and anatomy on one hand and ecology and ethology on the other, which might seem to offer APG the argument that linguists study the forms of language in a prebehavioral, precontextual mode with a view to eventually studying the deployment of these forms in a social setting, is entirely misleading. It is misleading because the form-meaning units are not fixed beforehand.

This apparent fixedness is an illusion brought about precisely because of the reliance on intuitive data that reaches back to remembered snatches of speech whose real context is long lost, and that, in retrospect, appears to be permanently welded to specific meanings.

The assumption of emergent grammar imposes on the linguist a different view of the database for linguistics. Although isolated, made-up clauses and sentences have their uses, and indeed, are often indispensable shortcuts to the study of grammar, the sources of these forms have to be understood in a way that differs from that of the abstract rules and native speaker intuitions that have become part of the dogma of linguistics. The linguist's task is, in fact, to study the whole range of repetition in discourse, and in doing so, to seek out those regularities that promise interest as incipient subsystems. Structure, then, in this view is not an overarching set of abstract principles, but more a question of a spreading of systematicity from individual words, phrases, and small sets. This spreading systematicity is the linguistic counterpart of the sedimentation of frequently used expressions and parts of expressions.

It has often been noted that certain parts of discourse are fixed, and often have been around so long that they have preserved archaic language ("a soft answer turneth away wrath"; "one swallow doth not a summer make"; "birds of a feather flock together"; and so on). But it has less often been noted that proverbial language is only an extreme case of repetition in discourse, at the other end of which are the morphological and syntactic repetitions, some of which are called grammar. In other words, real live discourse abounds in all sorts of repetitions that have nothing to do with grammar as it is usually understood; for instance, idioms, proverbs, clichés, formulas, specialist phrases, transitions, openings, closures, greetings, farewells, favored clause types, and so on (see Hopper, 1987; Johnstone, 1994). There is no consistent level at which these regularities are statable. They are not necessarily sentences or clauses with recurrent internal structure, but they are often used holistically. Their boundaries may or may not coincide with the constituent boundaries of our grammatical descriptions: subject and predicate, noun phrase, prepositional phrase. Moreover, what is a formulaic expression in one context may not be in another (see Lambrecht, 1984).

It has been noted before that to a very considerable extent, everyday language is built up out of combinations of such prefabricated parts. Language is, in other words, to be viewed as a kind of pastiche, pasted together in an improvised way out of ready-made elements. Language is thus to be treated, in Wittgenstein's words, "from outside" (cf. Wittgenstein, 1953/1958)—not as governed by internalized mentally represented rules, but by preexistent material with which discourses can be devised (Smith, 1978, pp. 61–62; Staten, 1984, pp. 85–86). An entirely parallel way of viewing language is to be attributed to Jacques Derrida with his metaphor of language as "graft": New speech acts are "grafted onto" old ones and of course serve in turn as the stock onto which further new speech acts are grafted (Culler, 1982, pp. 134–135). Becker's idea of "prior texts" (e.g., Becker, 1979, pp. 244–245; 1988, p. 69) is also crucial here: Previous actual utterances form the basis of new utterances. Similar observations have been made by Bolinger, Pawley, and others. The psycholinguist Ann Peters also noted in her book *The Units of Language Acquisition* (1983) the advantages that accrue to the study of child language acquisition by considering language to consist not of grammatical rules but of rhythmically and semantically bound "chunks" of verbal material. Stephany (1992) pointed out and illustrated the important role of "grammaticalization"—the emergence of structure out of occasions of use and the child's repetitions of things said. Becker (1984) noted the implication of this view of language as "prior texts" for the teaching of second languages to adults.

It is this prepatterned, prefabricated aspect of speech that accounts best for the characteristic of language for which no dualistic, double-tiered theory can provide an intuitively satisfying explanation: In natural discourse, we compose and speak simultaneously (Smith, 1978, p. 60). There is no room—in fact, no need—for mediation by mental structures. It is in this sense that, as Bolinger pointed out (Bolinger, 1976), speaking is more similar to remembering procedures and things than it is to following rules. It is a question of possessing a repertoire of strategies for building discourses and reaching into memory in order to improvise and assemble them. Now, grammar is not to be seen as the *source* of regularity, but instead as what results when formulas are rearranged, or dismantled and reassembled, in different ways.

Looking at language this way involves a serious adjustment for the linguist, because we have developed the habit of seeing utterances in terms of a fixed framework of rules, and especially because we have been raised on the doctrine of the free generability of sentences, and the privileging of novelty over prior texts. Indeed, novelty is a prized virtue in our society altogether, and we have many ways, some more subtle than others, of censuring perceived repetitions of others' behavior and an enormous vocabulary dealing with repetition whose connotations are mainly negative (copying, imitation, plagiarism). Yet, when one examines actual specimens of speech from the formulaic point of view, the effect is a striking one, perhaps even a memorable one, in that it is then extremely difficult to revert to the old rule-governed syntactic view of discourse. Consider the following example from spoken English, just one of many examples from the Carterette and Jones (1974) corpus:

Well no the problem is and this is what the psychologist has mentioned to me. these kids wont wont show any hope like the see you take a normal uh the average retarded child i mean the one who doesnt have any handicaps like blindness or deafness or something like that. he will improve a little bit. maybe a lot. it depends on how badly disturbed he is. but these people wont because theyre still going to no matter what happens theyre going to be living in a fantasy world. because theyre blind. and they have to imagine and they keep asking one question after the other and then nothing they say makes any sense and nothing is relevant to the situation. and it never will be because they well theres just such a sharp line of differentiation between the normal blind and then the emotionally disturbed blind. (p. 422)

Even a cursory study of such passages reveals several different layers of regularity. The formulas are easily isolated. Note just a few of them:

the problem is
has mentioned to me
these kids
you take
a little bit
maybe a lot
it depends on
no matter what happens
theyre still going to
living in a fantasy world
one question after another
nothing they say makes any sense
relevant to the situation
sharp line of differentiation
emotionally disturbed

—the last with its institutional and authoritarian subtext. It would in fact be difficult or impossible to draw the line between a formulaic and a nonformulaic expression. Moreover, there are single words which could themselves be said to constitute formulas in this context, such as *disturbed, normal.* The stops and starts coincide with the boundaries of formulas, which are presented and modified or withdrawn or capitalized upon in an obvious interactional negotiation. Early in the paragraph, for example, the speaker clearly is about to say "the normal retarded child," but partway into the phrase realizes that for the uninitiated in this context, it clashes with another formula, "the normal child," and launches into a second try, "the average retarded child," which also—once said—appears incongruous (cf. "the average child"), and finally is forced to abandon the search for an appropriate formula and move into a more specific level of discourse in which the properties encapsulated in this context in the adjective "normal" are made explicit:

> these kids wont wont show any hope like the see you take a normal uh the average retarded child i mean the one who doesnt have any handicaps like blindness or deafness or something like that. (Carterette & Jones, 1974, p. 422)

It might be suggested that in this particular passage a sort of secondhand "health care professional" jargon is manifest, in which mannerisms peculiar to a particular set of experts intrude. (Note, for example, the pervasive *will/wont* by which the speaker impresses on the listener her familiarity with general cases of this kind.) Yet, it would be difficult to find a passage of natural discourse about which some analogous remark might not be made. The point is that all discourse is in some sense specialist discourse, molded to the speaker's personality (i.e., personal history), the situation (including the recent history of the interaction and the participants), the register (degree of formality), the genre, and the topic. It is precisely the point about Emergent Grammar that such "heteroglossic" (Bakhtin, 1981, p. 281) aspects of language necessarily become integral parts of the linguistic description, and are not set aside as a separate agenda irrelevant to the linguistic code and its structure.

The systematicity that linguists have come to expect in language exists, of course, but in a more complex way. Now, the linguistic system is not to be seen as something complete and homogeneous, in which "exceptional" phenomena must be set aside as inconvenient irregularities, but as a growing together of disparate forms. This convergence takes place through lateral associations of real utterances. Similarities spread outward from individual formulas, in ways that are motivated by a variety of factors, such as (a) phonological similarity (rhyme, assonance): *He's likely to* → *he's liable to*; and (b) contextual similarity: *I persuaded him to* → *I convinced him to,* and other kinds of resonance (Bolinger, 1961). They do not, however, merge into the kind of uniform grammar which would lead one to posit a uniform mental representation to subtend them.

Rhetoric/Logic

From the time of Aristotle until the Middle Ages and beyond, language was studied in terms of a "three-way path," the trivium, consisting of logic, grammar, and rhetoric. Grammar, of course, originally meant the elementary phase of education in which writing was taught. It consisted of the prerequisites for the study of texts. Grammar came to be associated with the teaching of Latin and exclusively with the syntax and morphology of Latin;

but starting in the 15th century, the word *grammar* came to be applied to other languages (Percival, 1983, p. 303). Especially during the present century, there has been a growing tendency for grammar to be identified with logic, and for the project of linguistics to be one of reducing language to some kind of formal logical skeleton. From time to time, proposals are even made to construct an abstract system that would be common to both fields (logic and grammar). Rhetoric has generally been set aside by modern linguists as a somewhat woolly, unscientific field that presupposes the 'harder' results of grammar and logic. Emergent Grammar is a move toward restoring the centrality of rhetoric by placing communication and its concomitant, routinization, at the head of the implicational chain that leads to structure, and seeing grammar as nothing other than the micro end of rhetoric. Grammar is, in other words, rhetoric seen in small-scale parts of interactions such as phrases, words, and even parts of words as these become sedimented through frequent use in particular contexts.

Conduit and Code Metaphors/Blueprint Metaphor

The controlling metaphors for language and the projects of linguistics in A Priori Grammar can be said to be the *code* and the *conduit*. Language is in this view a code because its forms stand for invisible meanings that exist independently of it. Linguistic forms are often said by linguists to "code" particular meanings; for example, the English word *children* codes the meanings *child* and *plural*. The attendant psycholinguistic metaphors of "encoding" and "decoding" follow easily from the idea of a linguistic code. Moreover, a language is seen as a *conduit* (the metaphor is owed to Reddy, 1979), a kind of pipe through which ideas formulated in the head of one speaker are encoded and transmitted to the head of another speaker, where they are decoded and reconstituted as the same ideas. In this metaphor, language is a form of "telementation" or thought transference (Harris, 1990). The EG metaphor of language is more like the alternative offered by Reddy of a blueprint. Blueprints do not specify every brick and every nail, but with a blueprint, a builder or an engineer is enabled to constitute an artifact by combining a structural outline with a set of conventions and experiences of similar artifacts. Moreover, the meaning of a blueprint is unlikely to be determined without consultations of various kinds involving, perhaps, clients, materials experts, labor union officials, and many others. What the adult has learned when she successfully uses a form is not an intrinsic meaning but a set of contexts in which the form is, or might be, appropriate. Because of this, the meaning changes every time the form is used, just as the meaning of a blueprint changes with each human and material context of construction. If the interlocutor does not perceive, or cannot be persuaded to perceive, an analogy between the current situation of the use of a form and some previous context, communication fails.

This means that the task of "learning a language" must be reconceived. Learning a language is not a question of acquiring grammatical structure but of *expanding a repertoire of communicative contexts.* Consequently, there is no date or age at which the learning of language can be said to be complete. New contexts, and new occasions of negotiation of meaning, occur constantly. A language is not a circumscribed object but a loose confederation of available and overlapping social experiences.

Writing/Speech

In opposition to the 19th century's preoccupation with written texts, and the tendency to identify language with written language, Saussure (1916/1986) and his successors were at pains to point out that it is the essential nature of language to be spoken, and that writing is secondary to speech. Yet, it is only in the past 20 years that the features that differentiate speech from writing have been consciously studied (e.g., Chafe & Danielewicz, 1987; Chafe & Tannen, 1987), and the question of "orality," the phenomenology of speaking in different cultures, has been investigated (e.g., Ong, 1982). In APG, truly oral speech is never explicitly studied; instead, the static grammar of isolated sentences having little connection with normal usage is held to be the best and most typical representative of language. Implausible sentences like "The woman died in 70,000 BC who invented the wheel" and "Seymour sliced the salami with a knife" (both taken from actual papers), which could never occur in natural discourse, were and to a large extent still are the norm in the linguistic literature.

The fact that unnatural discourses of this kind are inconceivable without written language antecedents has been noted by several researchers, and increasingly in the present decade. In a by now classic monograph entitled *The Written Language Bias in Linguistics* (1982), Per Linell showed how the science of linguistics has unconsciously taken as its model of language, in syntax, semantics, and phonology, a standard written form of English. Linell specifically ascribed the preoccupation of APG linguists with the sentence as a basic unit to the ontological foundation of linguistics in written language, even when such a foundation was explicitly denied. That the sentence is an artifact of writing was also noted by the British linguist Roy Harris. In his book *The Language Makers,* Harris (1980) went so far as to say that "the real 'discovery procedure' of modern linguistics is: Assume that standard orthography identifies all the relevant distinctions until you are forced to assume otherwise." He later continued:

> Suppose we strip away this superficial garb of the sentence, what lies beneath it? Something which must have all its words in place, their order determined, their grammatical relationships established, and their meanings assigned—but which simply lacks a phonetic embodiment: a string of words with the sound switched off. In short, a linguistic abstraction for which there is only one conceivable archetype so far in human history: the sentence of writing. (p. 18)

In recent linguistics that is not so indebted to the APG project, there have been three responses to the growing awareness of orality. One has been to focus attention on oral (i.e., nonliterate) cultures. A significant theme of this work was Ong's thesis that "writing restructures consciousness" (Ong, 1982, pp. 78–116), that is, that the historical development of written language resulted in a different kind of mental life, in which the world comes to be interpreted in terms of underlying abstractions and theories. Another has been to study the entire phenomenon of written as distinct from spoken language, in other words the grammar of writing (see Chafe & Tannen, 1987, for a survey). Here, too, radical differences between speaking and writing have come to light, suggesting not so much written and spoken versions of the same language as something more like two grammatically distinct languages. The complex interplay of genres, styles, and registers (degrees of formality) that criss-cross the spoken–written dichotomy has shown the nature of the language-learning enterprise to be far more intricate than is implied in the uniform APG project.

In this chapter, I argued for a rather different view of (a) language than that normally assumed by linguists and psychologists. In it, (a) language is seen as something that is indeterminate, constantly under construction, and structured only by emergent patterns that come and go as the forms that carry them are found useful for their speakers. In this more fluid and temporal picture of (a) language, there are no discretely bounded "modules" of syntax, semantics, morphology, phonology, and pragmatics, but only contextually conditioned ways of saying things. These ways of saying things have been used before. They are handed to us by our personal and institutional biographies, as they were handed to those from whom we heard them. Parts of these things that were said to us are repetitions of other parts, and group themselves through repetition into subsystems that can, provisionally, be called grammatical. Along with our grasp of these formulaic expressions, and learned with them, are the social contexts to which they are appropriate. This is to say that what adults know, and what children learn, is not an abstract system of units with meanings and rules for combining them, but are integrated normative modes of interactive behavior and the accompanying social use of corporeal signs such as words and gestures, to which concepts like language and grammar are almost entirely secondary.

NOTE

1. An interesting example from Green (1973) rests on the following pair of sentences:

    a. John is endeavoring to stop his hiccups, and Bill is acting like he is for the same reason.

    b. John is endeavoring to stop his hiccups, and Bill is acting like he is for the same purpose. (p. 63)

In the discussion of these sentences, one of them is held to be grammatical and the other ungrammatical. The linguist's decision in this case was that (a) was ungrammatical and (b) grammatical because the prepositional phrase introduced by "for" is a *purpose* clause rather than a *reason* clause. Yet, curiously, most informants make the opposite judgment, that "for the same reason" is the natural way to say this in English (see Hopper, 1988, pp. 119–120, fn. 2). Clearly the existence of the ready-made formula "for the same reason" overrides the subtle logic of the grammarian.

REFERENCES

Bakhtin, M. M. (1981). Discourse in the novel (C. Emerson & M. Holquist, Trans.). In M. Holquist (Ed.), *The dialogic imagination: Four essays* (pp. 259–422). Austin: University of Texas Press.

Bakhtin, M. M. (1986). *Speech genres and other essays* (V. W. McGee, Trans.; C. Emerson & M. Holquist, Eds.). Austin: University of Texas Press.

Becker, A. L. (1979). The figure a sentence makes: An interpretation of a classical Malay sentence. In T. Givón (Ed.), *Discourse and syntax* (pp. 243–260). New York: Academic Press.

Becker, A. L. (1984). Toward a post-structuralist view of language learning: A short essay. In A. Guiora (Ed.), *An epistemology for the language sciences* (pp. 217–220). Detroit: Wayne State University Press.

Becker, A. L. (1988). Language in particular: An essay. In D. Tannen (Ed.), *Linguistics in context* (pp. 17–36). Norwood, NJ: Ablex.

Bolinger, D. (1961). Syntactic blends and other matters. *Language, 37*(3), 366–381.

Bolinger, D. (1976). Meaning and memory. *Forum Linguisticum, 1*(1), 1–14.

Carterette, E. C., & Jones, M. H. (1974). *Informal speech: Alphabetic and phonemic texts with statistical analyses and tables.* Berkeley: University of California Press.

Chafe, W., & Danielewicz, J. (1987). Properties of spoken and written language. In R. Horowitz & S. J. Samuels (Eds.), *Comprehending oral and written language* (pp. 83–116). San Diego: Academic Press.

Chafe, W., & Tannen, D. (1987). The relation between written and spoken language. *Annual Review of Anthropology, 16*, 383–407.

Chomsky, A. N. (1965). *Aspects of the theory of syntax.* Cambridge, MA: MIT Press.

Clifford, J. (1986). Introduction: Partial truths. In J. Clifford & G. Marcus (Eds.), *Writing culture: The poetics and politics of ethnography* (pp. 1–26). Berkeley: University of California Press.

Culler, J. (1982). *On deconstruction: Theory and criticism after structuralism.* Ithaca, NY: Cornell University Press.

Fox, B. A. (1994, January). Contextualization, indexicality, and the distributed nature of grammar. *Language Sciences, 16*(1), 1–38.

Giddens, A. (1984). *The constitution of society: Outline of a theory of structuration*. Cambridge, England: Polity Press.

Goodwin, C. (1979). The interactive construction of a sentence in everyday conversation. In G. Psathas (Ed.), *Everyday language: Studies in ethnomethodology* (pp. 97–122). New York: Irvington.

Green, G. (1973). *Semantics and syntactic regularity*. Cambridge, England: Cambridge University Press.

Greenbaum, S. (1988). *Good English and the grammarian*. London: Longman.

Gross, M. (1974). On the failure of generative grammar. *Language, 55*, 859–885.

Haiman, J. (1991). Motivation, repetition and emancipation: The bureaucratisation of language. In H. C. Wolfart (Ed.), *Linguistic studies presented to John L. Finlay* (pp. 45–70). Winnipeg, Manitoba: Algonquian and Iroquoian Linguistics (Algonquian and Iroquoian Linguistics, Memoir 8)

Haiman, J. (1994). Ritualization and the development of language. In W. Pagliuca (Ed.), *Perspectives on grammaticalization* (pp. 3–28). Amsterdam: John Benjamins.

Harris, R. (1980). *The language makers*. London: Duckworth.

Harris, R. (1990). On redefining linguistics. In H. G. Davis & T. J. Taylor (Eds.), *Redefining linguistics* (pp. 18–52). London: Routledge & Kegan Paul.

Hopper, P. J. (1987). *Emergent Grammar. Papers of the 13th Annual Meeting, Berkeley Linguistic Society* (pp. 139–157). Berkeley, CA: Berkeley Linguistic Society.

Hopper, P. J. (1988). Emergent Grammar and the A Priori Grammar postulate. In D. Tannen (Ed.), *Linguistics in context* (pp. 117–134). Norwood, NJ: Ablex.

Hopper, P. J. (1992). Times of the sign: On temporality in recent linguistics. *Time and Society, 1*(2), 223–238.

Johansson, S., & Hofland, K. (1987). *Frequency analysis of English vocabulary and grammar, based on the LOB corpus* (Vols. 1, 2). Oxford, England: Clarendon.

Johnstone, B. (1994). Repetition in discourse: A dialogue. In B. Johnstone (Ed.), *Repetition in discourse: Interdisciplinary perspectives* (Vol. 1, pp. 1–20). Norwood, NJ: Ablex.

Johnstone, B. (1996). *The linguistic individual: Self-expression in language and linguistics*. Oxford, England: Oxford University Press.

Lambrecht, K. (1984). Formulaicity, frame semantics, and pragmatics in German binomial expressions. *Language, 60*(4), 753–796.

Linell, P. (1982). *The written language bias in linguistics*. Linköping, Sweden: University of Linköping.

Love, N. (1990). The locus of languages in a redefined linguistics. In H. G. Davis & T. J. Taylor (Eds.), *Redefining linguistics* (pp. 53–117). London: Routledge & Kegan Paul.

Ong, W. J. (1982). *Orality and literacy: The technologizing of the word*. London: Methuen.

Pawley, A., & Syder, F. (1983). Two puzzles for linguistic theory: Nativelike selection and nativelike fluency. In J. C. Richards & R. W. Schmidt (Eds.), *Language and communication* (pp. 191–227). London: Longman.

Percival, W. K. (1983). Grammar and rhetoric in the Renaissance. In J. J. Murphy (Ed.), *Renaissance eloquence: Studies in the theory and practice of Renaissance rhetoric* (pp. 303–330). Berkeley, CA: University of California Press.

Peters, A. M. (1983). *The units of language acquisition*. Cambridge, England: Cambridge University Press.

Reddy, M. J. (1979). The conduit metaphor: A case of frame conflict in our language about language. In A. Ortony (Ed.), *Metaphor and thought* (pp. 284–324). Cambridge, England: Cambridge University Press.

Rommetveit, R. (1974). *On message structure*. New York: Wiley.

Saussure, F. de. (1986). *Course in general linguistics* (R. Harris, Trans.). La Salle, IL: Open Court. (Original work published 1916)

Sinclair, J. (1991). *Corpus, concordance, collocation.* Oxford, England: Oxford University Press.

Smith, B. H. (1978). *On the margins of discourse.* Chicago: University of Chicago Press.

Staten, H. (1984). *Wittgenstein and Derrida.* Lincoln: University of Nebraska Press.

Stephany, U. (1992). Grammaticalization in first language acquisition. *Zeitschrift für Phonetik, Sprachwissenschaft, und Kommunikationsforschung, 3,* 289–303.

Stewart, S. (1986). Shouts on the street: Bakhtin's anti-linguistics. In G. S. Morson (Ed.), *Bakhtin: Essays and dialogues on his work* (pp. 49–59). Chicago: University of Chicago Press.

Stubbs, M. (1996). *Text and corpus analysis.* Oxford, England: Basil Blackwell.

Tannen, D. (1987). Repetition in conversation as spontaneous formulaicity. *Text, 7*(3), 215–243.

Thompson, E. P. (1991). *Customs in common* (pp. 97–98). New York: New Press.

Wittgenstein, L. (1958). *Philosophical investigations* (3rd ed., G. E. Anscombe, Trans.). New York: Macmillan. (Original work published 1953)

Chapter 7

Syntactic Constructions as Prototype Categories

John R. Taylor
University of Otago, Duneden, New Zealand

Prototype effects are pervasive in human categorization. Nevertheless, the significance of prototype categorization for linguistic theory is still a matter of debate. Many mainstream linguistic theories are predicated on well-defined, clear-cut categories, and thus are incapable in principle of accommodating facts of graded membership in a category and fuzziness of category boundaries. Yet, there is abundant evidence that linguistic categories do exhibit just these kinds of prototype effects. By "linguistic categories," I have in mind not so much the conceptual categories designated by lexical items of a language (i.e., categories such as "bird," "cup," "red") but the categories of linguistic structure that linguists themselves invoke as they go about their business of describing and theorizing about language, that is, notions such as "vowel," "syllable," "noun," "subject (of clause)," "transitive sentence," and countless more.

The topic of this chapter is the prototype structure of syntactic constructions. "Syntactic construction," as used here, is roughly equivalent to "sentence pattern," or, as the case may be, "phrasal pattern." A construction is a schema or template, which captures what is common to a range of expressions, and which, at the same time, sanctions the creation of new expressions of the respective type. Examples of syntactic constructions include the transitive construction (exemplified by *The farmer killed the duckling*), the double object construction (*Joe baked Mary a cake*), the predicate adjective construction (*The house is large*), the prenominal possessive construction (*the man's hat*), and so on.

The constructions within a language do not constitute an unstructured collection of items. Constructions may be related by means of a part–whole relation (one construction functions as part of another construction), or by a relation of instantiation (one construction instantiates a more abstractly characterized construction). For example, the prenominal possessive is an instance of a more abstractly characterized noun phrase construction—a prenominal possessive is a kind of noun phrase. At the same time, a prenominal possessive has, as one of its parts, a noun phrase—*the man*, in *the man's hat*, is itself a noun phrase. Many other constructions, such as the transitive and double object constructions, also have noun phrases among their parts.

A preliminary question is, how to characterize a construction? One aspect consists in a statement of the parts that make up the construction, and their configuration. From this perspective, the double object construction, for example, can be characterized by means of the schema [$NP_1 - V - NP_2 - NP_3$]. As it stands, this schema is obviously inadequate. It implies that we can take any randomly selected verb, and provided that we only combine it as prescribed with any three noun phrases, we will end up with an acceptable double object expression. In order to avoid this result, we need to supplement the syntactic schema with a statement of the kinds of items that are eligible to instantiate its various parts. This requires that we appeal to the semantics of the construction. Indeed, constraints on what can instantiate its parts will largely fall out from a construction's semantics. The general meaning of the double object construction is that one entity (designated by NP_1) intends to benefit NP_2, by acting on NP_3 in such a way that NP_2 comes to have access to NP_3. Only certain kinds of verbs (prototypically, verbs that denote a transfer of possession) are likely to be compatible with the construction's semantics. Equally, not every noun phrase will be eligible to occur in the NP slots of the construction. For example, NP_1 and NP_2 will normally (prototypically) designate human beings rather than inanimate objects, because instigators and recipients are normally (prototypically) human beings.

As with prototypes, the status of constructions in contemporary linguistic theory is controversial. Although central in many older theories (e.g., Bloomfield, 1933) as schemas for the syntagmatic combination of smaller items into larger units, constructions play only a marginal role in many contemporary approaches. Many current linguistic theories seek very general principles of syntactic organization, and propose to derive the properties of individual expressions from these more basic principles. Constructions emerge only as the product of what are presumed to be more basic principles, and are thus, of themselves, of little inherent interest. In recent years, however, largely as a result of work by Fillmore, Lakoff, Langacker, and others, constructions have undergone a rehabilitation, and even find their way into the name of a grammatical model, namely *construction grammar*.[1] A central claim of construction grammar is that knowledge of a language consists, very largely, in knowledge of constructions, and that an expression is acceptable to the extent that it is sanctioned by (can count as an instance of) an established construction. Importantly, this approach entails that not only the syntactic form, but also aspects of the meaning of an expression derive from properties of the sanctioning construction.

Goldberg (1995, p. 4) defined a construction as a "form-meaning pair <F, S> such that some aspect of F or some aspect of S is not strictly predictable from C's component parts or from other previously established constructions." This definition covers more than the narrower understanding of constructions envisaged in this chapter. On Goldberg's definition, single-morpheme lexical items count as constructions, in that the meaning of e.g. *dog* is not predictable from its form, and vice versa. Idiomatic expressions, e.g. *spill the beans*, also have construction status. We can imagine an even more general definition, which would ascribe construction status to any established form-meaning pair, whether or not its properties are fully predictable. For many English speakers, I would imagine, *roast turkey* is an established adjective-noun combination. Although there is nothing idiomatic about either its form or its meaning, the expression could be assigned construction status to the extent that it is an established expression, which (presumably) does not need to be assembled on each occasion on which it is uttered, nor does it need to be interpreted against the sanctioning construction on each occasion on which it is heard.

The chapter has three parts. In part one, I address the relevance of prototype categorization to linguistic inquiry, and substantiate, on the example of the lexical category adjective, my claim that prototype effects pervade even the most basic categories of linguistic description. In part two, I consider some evidence for the status of constructions as objects of speaker knowledge. In part three, I discuss some prototype effects associated with constructions.

1. PROTOTYPE EFFECTS AND LINGUISTIC THEORY

The opposition between "classical" and "prototype" modes of categorization is now commonplace (Lakoff, 1987; Taylor, 1995). Classical categorization assumes an invariant set of core attributes that simultaneously define the category and serve as criteria for membership in it. On the classical view, (a) all members of a category share a common essence, (b) all members of a category are equivalent in their status as category members, and (c) category boundaries are clear-cut.

Since the 1970s, research findings have accumulated that show that the referential possibilities of many ordinary words such as *red*, *cup*, *bird*, are at variance with the classical view (e.g., Berlin & Kay, 1969; Labov, 1973; Rosch, 1978). These findings point to (a) the absence of a set of necessary and sufficient conditions for membership in a category, (b) the privileged status of some entities as "better examples" of the category than others, and (c) the fuzziness of category boundaries. It is also well established that prototype effects are not just a matter of taxonomic classification, but are crucially involved in other kinds of cognitive activity (Rosch, 1978). Statements pertaining to the categorization of "good examples" tend to be processed more quickly and more accurately than statements about marginal members, and reasoning about a category tends to be based on what is known about the good examples, rather than on properties of marginal examples, or on what is taken to be common to all category members.

To be sure, not all "prototype categories" share all of the above properties (Geeraerts, 1989). In some cases, we merely have degrees of representativity of instances within a category whose boundaries can in fact be drawn quite precisely—although penguins might not be representative of the bird category, they are birds nonetheless, not birds to a certain degree. In other cases, we are entitled to speak of degrees of membership in a category, such that the boundaries of the category are indeterminate, and the category might merge at its edges with neighboring categories. It might be difficult to decide conclusively whether a particular color is an instance of *red* or of a neighboring color category, e.g. *orange*, or whether a particular receptacle is to be properly described as a *cup* or as a *bowl*.

Despite the pervasiveness of prototype effects, their significance for linguistic theory is still a matter of debate. Prima facie, one should expect considerable consequences for the theory and practice of lexical semantics. Yet, many have resisted such a move. Wierzbicka (1996) lamented what she claimed is the widespread "abuse" of the prototype notion in linguistics; it is, she claimed, a "thought-saving device," which absolves the linguist-lexicographer from the task of having to search for category-defining invariants. Addressing some of the *loci classici* of the prototype literature, including *game* (Wittgenstein, 1953, pp. 31–32), *bachelor* (Fillmore, 1982), and *lie* (Coleman & Kay, 1981), Wierzbicka proposed definitions that, she maintains, do draw precise boundaries around the concepts. Difficulties in identifying definitional invariants are not a reason to query their existence. However, it has been observed that Wierzbicka is nevertheless obliged to sneak prototype notions into her supposedly clear-cut definitions (Geeraerts, 1993).

Others, although not questioning the reality of prototype effects, have denied that these are located within the linguistic system as such. The claim is that prototype effects pertain only to the referential possibilities (i.e., the denotation or extension) of a linguistic expression, not to the linguistic meaning of the expression (Leech, 1981; Osherson & Smith,

1981). That there might exist central and marginal members of a category does not entail that the meaning of the linguistic expression that designates the category has fuzzy boundaries, or that it is structured around good examples and their attributes. On this view, prototype effects are a function of the world and of a person's conceptualization of it; they do not inhere in the meanings of expressions used to refer to the world.[2]

This view draws on what has been a leading topic in much 20th century linguistics, namely, the postulate of language as an autonomous cognitive system, structured according to its own system-specific categories and principles; while interacting with a speaker's knowledge and conceptualization of the world, the linguistic system is in principle independent of these nonlinguistic skills. In its various elaborations, this view has driven both European structuralism of Saussurian inspiration (e.g., Coseriu & Geckeler, 1981), as well as Chomskyan and Chomsky-inspired approaches (e.g., Fodor, 1983).

In contrast, on an "encyclopaedist" view of semantics, as promoted by Langacker (1987), Lakoff (1987), and Taylor (1995, 1996), the distinction between the purely linguistic meaning of an expression and knowledge pertaining to the entities and states of affairs that the expression may denote, falls away; knowledge about the potential range of application of an expression is part and parcel of knowing its meaning. It is no coincidence that linguists who espouse an encyclopaedist view of meaning (e.g., Geeraerts, Grondelaers, & Bakema, 1994; Hudson, 1995) have been particularly receptive to the prototype notion.

Those who hold to an encyclopaedist view of meaning tend to take a further step, and make the more general claim that there is no distinction in principle between a person's knowledge of a language and other kinds of knowledge. As Goldberg (1995, p. 5) succinctly put it, "Knowledge of language is knowledge." This view entails that linguistic categories "should be of the same type as other categories in our conceptual system" (Lakoff, 1987, p. 58). Because prototype effects are so pervasive in human cognition, it is to be expected that the categories of language itself should exhibit prototype effects.

Consider, for example, the traditional parts of speech, perhaps more appropriately named "word classes," or "word categories." The practice of our dictionaries, which classify each entry under one of the traditional labels of "noun," "adjective," and so forth, could give the impression that there exists a small, finite set of homogeneous word classes, and that each word can be properly and unambiguously categorized with respect to these. (This, certainly, is an assumption that has been taken over, with little modification, by many contemporary linguistic theories.) Yet, the traditional categories typically comprise items that exhibit a range of different, and sometimes mutually exclusive properties, and for many words, in some of their uses at least, a definitive classification is fraught with problems.

I can illustrate some of the issues using the example of adjectives. Although the concept of adjective is a familiar one, it turns out to be well-nigh impossible to come up with a definition that covers all the items that we should like to include within the category, and that excludes everything else. This is true, whether we try to formulate the definition in terms of semantic properties, syntactic properties, or some combination of both. Even so, "core" examples of the category can easily be identified, e.g. *large, young, good*, etc. These are words that designate fairly stable, yet variable, properties of a thing (Croft, 1991). When used predicatively, i.e. in association with the copula (*This house is large*), they ascribe a property to the referent of the subject nominal. When used attributively, i.e. before a noun, they serve to restrict the referential possibilities of the noun, by adding, as it were, an additional feature specification to the noun category; thus *large house* designates a subcategory of house. Because the property that they denote is variable, these adjectives can be modified by degree adverbials such as *rather, (not) very, extremely*. Furthermore, being variable, the adjectival properties can serve as criteria of comparison between two or more entities (*This child is younger than that one*).

Although *large, young, good*, and some others, constitute a fairly homogeneous group, there is considerable variation within the broader category of words that we intuitively want to call adjectives (Taylor, 1992). Many adjectives can only be used attributively; *former colleagues, *colleagues who are former; a corporate decision, *a decision that is corporate*. Many adjectives are incompatible with gradation; **a more corporate decision, *a very former colleague*. Some attributive adjectives do not simply restrict the reference of the associated noun, they effect a more drastic semantic change. *Imaginary events* are not a subcategory of events, neither are *fake Picassos* a kind of Picasso. Some adjectives have a wider range of interpretation when used attributively than when used predicatively: *My very old colleague* could be either a person who has been my colleague for a long time, or a colleague who is advanced in years; *my colleague is very old* invokes only the latter interpretation. A few adjectives can only be used predicatively: *The child is asleep, *the asleep child*.

Given the syntactic and semantic variation within the adjective category, the question of how to demarcate the category from its neighbors is far from trivial. *Falling*, in *falling rain, the rain is falling*, seems to fit the characterization of adjective quite well, as does *cooked* in *cooked food, the food is cooked*. Nevertheless, perhaps because of the transparent relatedness of *falling* and *cooked* to the verbs *(to) fall* and *(to) cook*, and also because of the availability of the categories of present and past participles, we might hesitate to describe these words as adjectives. This, however, begs the question whether participles are a subcategory of adjective, or whether they constitute a different category altogether.

Take as another example the case of expressions like *apple pie*. Probably, the consensus view amongst linguists would be that *apple pie*, along with *noun phrase, university student, computer mouse,* and innumerable others, is a nominal compound, with the structure [$_N$N N]. *Apple*, in other words, is a noun, which functions within the compound as a modifier of the head noun. I have asked several groups of undergraduate linguistics students for their intuitions on these expressions. To my surprise, the majority were of the opinion that *apple*, in *apple pie*, is an adjective for the reason, they said, that it tells you what kind of pie it is. Few, though, were inclined to consider *university*, in *university student*, to be an adjective.

At first sight, these different judgments are puzzling. What kinds of evidence might be relevant to deciding the issue? In connection with the "expert" view of nominal compounds mentioned earlier, which ascribes the structure [$_N$N N] to *apple pie* and *university student*, note that *apple* and *university* actually exhibit very few nounlike properties. As constituents of the compounds, they cannot be pluralized (**an apples pie, *a universities student*); they cannot be modified by an adjective or postnominal phrase (**a home-grown apple pie* in the sense "a pie made from home-grown apples," **a university near here student*, i.e. "a student at a university near here"); and they cannot be replaced by a pronoun (**an it pie, *a one student* are simply bizarre). The main reason for regarding these words as nouns, it would seem, is that they are nouns everywhere else in the language! What, then, about the suggested adjectival status of *apple*? The problem here is that, because there are no defining characteristics of adjectives, i.e. no attributes that are necessarily shared by all members of the category, it is not at all clear what conclusions we should draw from the failure of *apple* to exhibit certain adjectivelike properties. The fact that modification by degree words is ruled out (**a very apple pie*) does not of itself demonstrate the nonmembership of *apple* in the adjective category.

It might nevertheless be felt that *a very apple pie* is not as horribly ungrammatical as some examples given earlier, and some speakers are prepared to tolerate it as marginally acceptable. Interestingly, some other tests, although they fail to deliver unambiguously positive results, do suggest that *apple*, in contrast to *university*, does have a whiff of an adjective to it. Compare the following:

1. a. These so-called ripe bananas are not very ripe.
   b. ??This so-called apple pie is not very apple.
   c. *This so-called university student is not very university.
2. a. I wanted a fresh pie, not a stale one.
   b. ?I wanted a blueberry pie, not an apple one.
   c. *She's a polytechnic student, not a university one.
3. a. I want five pies, two large and three small.

   b. I want five pies, two apple and three blueberry.
   c. ?There were five students, two university and three polytechnic.

Readers may not exactly agree with these grammaticality judgments. This need not threaten the point of the previous examples, which is that acceptability declines as we move from the (a) sentences through to the (c) sentences. The examples suggest that the modifying element in *apple pie*, although it fails to behave like a central member of the adjective class, does betray some weak adjectival properties. In this, it contrasts with *university*, which exhibits hardly any adjectival properties at all. Semantic factors may have something to do with this difference. What something is made of is an "intrinsic" property of a thing, in the sense of Langacker (1987, pp. 160–161).[3] This aspect of substance-denoting words possibly brings them closer to the semantic prototype of the adjective class than is the case with a place specification, as with *university*.

Pursuing the matter further, we find that substance-denoting words vary somewhat in the degree to which they have taken on adjectivelike properties. Consider, as a diagnostic, the ability of the substance-denoting word to be used predicatively. *This ring is gold, This bread is wholemeal, This jacket is wool, This bag is plastic*, are acceptable, suggesting that these substance words are becoming quite firmly entrenched in the adjective class. (It is even possible to coordinate some of these words with more central members of the adjective class: *This ring is gold and very valuable.*) Others are less acceptable in predicative contexts: ?*This wall is brick,* ?*This lake is saltwater,* ??*This salad is fruit,* ??*This cube is ice,* **This ball is snow.* Again, readers might differ in their precise judgments of these sentences; my point is that they are not equally (un)acceptable.[4]

Several aspects of the aforementioned discussion need to be highlighted. First, in trying to determine the word class of *apple* and other items, I appealed to various syntactic "tests." These were based on the behavior of what were intuitively taken to be good examples of the category in question, e.g. that nouns pluralize, that adjectives can be used predicatively. Tests are a standard tool of linguistic argumentation (Croft, 1991). Appeal to tests gives implicit recognition to the prototype notion. Each test diagnoses a feature or attribute of the category in question. Items that "pass" all the tests, i.e. which exhibit the full range of attributes of the target category, *eo ipso* constitute full, central members of the category. Often, an item under investigation passes only some of the tests. Moreover, some tests may fail to give unambiguous results. (It is not at all clear whether [1b] should be dismissed as ungrammatical.) A linguistic category thus turns out to have central members, which pass all the tests; these are surrounded by a periphery of more marginal members, which pass only some of the tests. Focus on the prototypical core of the category generally enables the category to be defined in a clear-cut manner, and to be easily differentiated from neighboring categories. Focus on the more peripheral members invites the conclusion that the boundary between the category and its neighbors is unclear. Not only this, but within the category itself, members may tend to cluster according to their sharing of attributes, and the clusters themselves are likely to have fuzzy boundaries, with their individual members sometimes behaving slightly differently from their associates.

The second point is that the "attributes" that syntactic tests diagnose have to do, in many cases, with the ability of an item to occur in certain kinds of syntactic environment, i.e. to function as part of syntactic constructions of various kinds. The other side of the coin is that a characterization of the containing constructions needs to refer to the kinds of items that are eligible to occur in them. Because words, as a rule, do not cluster in internally homogeneous categories, the instantiations of syntactic constructions also tend to exhibit prototype effects. Such effects are in fact illustrated by the graded acceptability of the predicative sentences in (1) and (3).

It turns out, then, that linguistic categories, whether word classes or constructions, are complex entities, which need to be characterized on a number of semantic and syntactic dimensions. Their properties are not the simple binary features of classical-style definitions, which can be reliably ticked off as in a checklist; they are themselves embedded in a complex network of semantic and syntactic facts. The categorization of words in terms of a small set of word classes inevitably hides considerable variation between individual lexical items, and groups of lexical items. Syntactic analyses, if they are to capture the complexities of actual usage, need to go beyond broadly defined word classes like noun, adjective, etc.

A third point is that a construction schema that includes, as one of its parts, the category *adjective* (or *noun*), tends to inherit the fuzziness associated with the adjective (or noun) category. Prototype effects associated with word categories therefore propagate themselves throughout the grammar. If, for no other reason, syntactic constructions need to be regarded as prototype categories.

A number of linguists have routinely invoked the notion of prototype in their work, and have suggested that the categories of linguistic description should be characterized first and foremost in terms of their core, or best examples (e.g., Huddleston, 1984; McCawley, 1986). But perhaps the most extensive documentation of the fuzziness of categories such as noun, adjective, preposition, is to be found in a series of papers by Ross dating from the 1970s (e.g., Ross, 1972, 1973; see also Ross, 1987). These had little impact at the time. The reason, Harris (1993) surmised, was that syntactic theories that were current in the 1970s presupposed clearly defined lexical categories, and were simply not able to accommodate the kinds of facts that Ross documented. According to a rather uncharitable review of one of Ross's papers (Gazdar & Klein, as cited in Harris, 1993, p. 221), Ross had assembled "little more than a collection of data in search of a theory." Construction grammar may now be the appropriate framework for the incorporation of these kinds of data.

2. CONSTRUCTIONS

Many mainstream theories of syntax, especially those generated over the past few decades by Chomsky's writings, seek very general principles of syntactic well-formedness. Essentially, it is the interaction of these principles that determines the grammaticality of an expression. In this view, constructions are merely "taxonomic epiphenomena" (Chomsky, 1991, p. 417; cf. Lakoff, 1987, p. 467), of little inherent interest in themselves. This approach entails that speakers of a language do not need to learn the constructions in their language; they need only know the general principles that determine their grammaticality.

An alternative view is that constructions have basic status. Expressions are sanctioned by the constructions that they instantiate, rather than by their conformity with general principles. Much of the initial impetus for the development of construction grammar has come from the study of "construction idioms," i.e. constructions whose formal and/or semantic properties manifestly cannot be derived by general principles, and that, like phrasal idioms, need to be individually listed and characterized in the grammar.[5] Take the case of the incredulity response construction, exemplified in (4):

4. a. Him write a novel?!
   b. Me worry?!
   c. John (be) clever?!
   d. Fred (be) going to marry Louise?!
   e. Under the bed a good place to hide it?!

These look like degenerate declarative sentences, lacking tense and subject–verb agreement, and with the peculiar property that the "subject," if a pronoun, appears in oblique form (*him* and *me* rather than *he* and *I*). Phrase-structure rules have been proposed for the generation of this kind of sentence (Akmajian, 1984).[6] Even so, the construction has a number of properties over and above those that the phrase structure rules predict (Fillmore et al., 1990; Lambrecht, 1990). Incredulity response expressions are therefore prime candidates for a constructionist account, whereby the special properties of incredulity responses derive from the construction that they instantiate. These properties concern not only the construction's syntax, but also its semantic-pragmatic value. A speaker, in using the construction, takes up a proposition already introduced into the discourse, only to dismiss it as ridiculous, to challenge its truth, or some such. The construction, in other words, not only expresses a particular speaker attitude, it presupposes a preceding discourse context and even sets up expectations about what is going to follow. (Typical follow-up remarks might be *Ridiculous!*, *You have to be joking!*, and the like.) A further aspect is the construction's distinctive prosody, as well as the possibility of its being associated with "sneering" paralinguistic features. An orthographic representation even requires special punctuation—note the use of the question mark plus exclamation mark in (4).[7]

It may be felt that incredulity response expressions, precisely because of their special qualities, are pretty marginal within the broader grammar of the English language. Indeed, focus on the idiomatic nature of constructions could suggest that alongside construction idioms, which obviously do need to be listed and separately characterized, there exists the nonidiomatic and regular core of the language, which we can continue to characterize in terms of very general syntactic principles.

On the other hand, once we have in place the descriptive apparatus to account for construction idioms, we can easily extend it to the grammatical core of a language. If incredulity responses can be characterized in terms of a pairing of formal and semantic aspects, so too can more standard sentence types, such as transitive sentences (*The farmer killed the duckling*), double object sentences (*Joe baked Sally a cake*), caused motion sentences (*He pushed the box into the room*), middle sentences (*The book sells well*), and so on. The only difference between idiomatic and core constructions is that the former are subject to many more idiosyncratic conditions than are the latter—this, essentially, is what makes them idiomatic. But in terms of their status as constructions, core sentence types do not differ in any fundamental way from "construction idioms."

In point of fact, the distinction between putative core constructions and construction idioms turns out to be ill-founded anyway. Even the most basic sentence types, such as transitive sentences, are subject to a degree of idiomaticity, especially with regard to their more marginal instantiations (Taylor, 1995, pp. 206–220). The transitive prototype involves an agent (encoded by the subject nominal), which intentionally acts on a patient (the direct object nominal), so as to effect a change-of-state in the patient. German has a transitive construction, whose prototype coincides with that of the English construction. Yet, the range of instantiations of the English and the German constructions by no means coincide. The following examples in (5) are unproblematic in English, whereas their German equivalents (6) are unacceptable. English idiomatically permits a much wider range of nonprototypical transitives (e.g., transitives whose subjects are not agents) than German. A full characterization of the transitive constructions in the two languages needs to take account of these differences:

5. a. The hotel forbids dogs.
   b. The tent sleeps six.

6. a. *Das Hotel verbietet Hunde.
   b. *Das Zelt schläft sechs.

Further blurring the distinction is the fact that it is by no means unusual for instantiations of a core construction to achieve idiomatic status. This happens whenever an expression takes on properties over and above, or even at variance, with those that it inherits from the sanctioning construction. Consider the following from Taylor (1995, p. 157):

7. a. Is that a fact?
   b. Would you believe it?

These look like regular instantiations of a more abstractly characterized polar interrogative. Yet, (7a) and (7b) are not normally used to inquire into the polarity of a proposition (the schematic meaning of the polar interrogative), i.e. to inquire whether such and such is a fact or not, or to find out whether an interlocutor would or would not believe something. They are conventionally used to express a degree of speaker surprise, and as such, do not anticipate a response specifying the polarity of the questioned proposition.[8] Because their meaning is at variance with the semantics of the polar interrogative, both expressions in (7) need to be separately listed in a grammar of English; they would, in other words, qualify as constructions in their own right. Note, moreover, that in their idiomatic use, the expressions in (7) are associated with a distinctive prosody, an aspect that needs to be included in the formal specification of the constructions. If (7b) were spoken with sentence accent on *you*, it would lose its idiomatic status as an expression of speaker surprise. It would ask whether or not the addressee, in contrast to other people, believes something, and would thus count as a run-of-the-mill instance of the polar interrogative.

It might be useful at this point to evaluate a constructionist approach against a more mainstream approach, on the example of sentences whose syntax is not patently idiomatic, in the manner of incredulity responses.[9] Consider the two sentences in (8) (cf. Goldberg, 1992, p. 45):

8. a. Joe baked a cake.
   b. Joe baked Sally a cake.

The syntactic phenomenon exemplified in (8b) has been much discussed in recent years. This is the double object phenomenon—the possibility that certain verbs may be followed by two nominals, the first of which designates a "recipient," or "benefactor," whereas the second designates an entity directly affected by the action designated by the verb. On earlier versions of Chomskyan grammar, sentences like (8b) would have been transformationally derived from a "deep" structure corresponding to *Joe baked a cake for Sally.* The more recent view in generativist circles now gives pride of place to lexical items and their properties, and to general principles for the "projection" of lexical items into syntactic structures, whereby the semantic representation of a lexical item determines the syntactic environment(s) in which the item may or must occur. Some workers in the "lexicalist" tradition (e.g., Levin & Rappaport Hovav, 1990) even entertain the idea that syntax might be fully predictable from the semantics of lexical items, in interaction with both general projection principles, and general constraints on syntactic well-formedness.

Because, in (8), the verb *bake* occurs in two distinct syntactic environments, a lexicalist account would need to postulate two distinct lexical entries for the verb, one that sanctions its occurrence with one object, the other that sanctions its occurrence with two objects. The verb, in other words, would be regarded as polysemous. Probably, the transitive polyseme would be regarded as somehow more "basic," in that baking inherently involves the preparation of something edible, but only incidentally an intended recipient. A "lexical rule" would then derive the ditransitive polyseme from the transitive, thereby effecting a slight conceptual shift in its semantics. Roughly, a verb with the semantics in (9a) is the source of a verb with the semantics in (9b).

> 9. a. *x* create *y* (by baking)
>   b. *x* cause *z* to have *y* (as a result of *x* baking *y*)

Linking rules, as discussed by Pinker (1989) and Jackendoff (1990), would then map *x* in (9a) into the syntactic position of subject, and *y* into the object. In the case of (9b), linking rules would map *z* into the first object, and *y* into the second object.

The constructionist account would attribute the contrast in (8), not to a difference between two meanings of the verb, but to two distinct constructions, i.e. the transitive construction and the double object construction. In the transitive construction $[NP_1 - V - NP_2]$, an agent, NP_1, effects a change-in-state in the patient, NP_2. The distinctive feature of double object constructions $[NP_1 - V - NP_2 - NP_3]$ is that the first postverbal nominal designates, prototypically, a benefactor; it is, namely, the intention of the agent, NP_1, that the benefactor, NP_2, should come to have access to the patient, NP_3, as a consequence of the agent's manipulation of the patient.

Thus far, there might appear to be little to choose from between the lexicalist and constructionist accounts. As we delve more deeply, however, the constructionist account begins to be the more attractive option. Consider the fact that the number of distinct syntactic frames in which a verb can occur is usually quite large. Here are some further examples with *bake*:

10. a. Joe is baking (in the kitchen).
    b. The cake is baking (in the oven).
    c. This oven doesn't bake very well.

On a lexicalist account, each of these uses would have to be associated with a distinct lexical representation of the verb, otherwise the linking rules would not work. Consequently, *bake* now turns out to be five-ways polysemous. This, I submit, is highly counterintuitive. Although the five sentences with *bake* perspectivize the activity slightly differently, it is, surely, the *same kind of* activity in each case.

On the constructionist account, the examples in (10) would be sanctioned by the existence of a very broadly characterized intransitive construction [NP – V], which has, as three of its instantiations, the agentive intransitive, where the subject designates an entity that initiates the activity, as in (10a); the inchoative intransitive, where the subject designates an entity that manifests a change-in-state as the activity unfolds, as in (10b); and the middle intransitive, which imputes to the subject a fairly stable property that can crucially affect the successful outcome of the kind of activity designated by the verb (10c).[10] The verb *bake* is eligible to occur in these three constructions to the extent that the kind of activity designated by the verb is compatible with the semantics of the three constructions.

We have seen that a given verb can occur in several different constructions. Moreover, different verbs tend to be compatible with different sets of constructions. A major reason for the recent interest in double object sentences is, precisely, the fact that not every verb that can occur in the transitive construction is eligible to occur in the double object construction, and vice versa. Whereas *give* and *tell* can occur in both constructions, *donate* and *announce* are excluded from the double object construction. The lexicalist approach (e.g., Pinker, 1989) sets up various subcategories of verb, some of which undergo the appropriate lexical rule, some of which do not. The constructionist account (Goldberg, 1995) associates the double object construction with a semantic prototype and various extensions therefrom, each of which is compatible with a cluster of verbs of similar semantics.

The need for such an account becomes even more compelling if we broaden the discussion to include other constructions. Let us change our initial example from "baking a cake" to "boiling an egg," and examine the ability of *boil* to occur in the five constructions exemplified in (8) and (10).

11. a. Joe boiled an egg.
   b. Joe boiled Sally an egg.
   c. *Joe is boiling (i.e., Joe is boiling something, e.g. an egg).
   d. The egg is boiling.
   e. ??This saucepan doesn't boil very well.

Boil, in contrast to *bake,* is inappropriate in both the agentive intransitive and the middle constructions. Why should this be? Consider the constructions' semantics. An agentive intransitive presents the subject referent as the initiator of an activity whose further participants are not specified. The construction will only be appropriate if the initiator makes a substantial input to the activity. Only then is it legitimate to present the activity with respect solely to its initiator. Baking is an activity that requires considerable skill on the part of the initiator, and we even recognize "bakers" as a distinct occupational group. It therefore makes sense (it is potentially quite informative) to say of a person that they "are baking," or to say that one person "can bake" better than another person. But boiling? Not much is required of the initiator here. To boil something does not require a special kind of input from the initiator, such that it might be informative to say of a person that they are engaged in the activity without mention of what is being boiled. With respect to the middle construction, the subject referent has to exhibit properties that substantially affect the outcome of the activity. The outcome of baking is in no small measure dependent on the properties of the oven—how precisely its temperature can be regulated, how well the heat is distributed, and so on. It makes sense to say that some ovens bake well, others do not, in accordance with the schematic characterization of the construction. But the successful boiling of an egg, or of anything else, hardly depends at all on the properties of the receptacle—one saucepan will do as well as another. In brief, (11e) is perceived as unacceptable, not because a lexical or linking rule, or some other general syntactic principle has been violated, but simply because what we know (encyclopaedically) about boiling does not fit the semantics of the construction.[11]

3. CONSTRUCTIONS AS PROTOTYPE CATEGORIES

Constructions are complex entities, which need to be characterized simultaneously from various perspectives—the parts of which they are composed, the configuration of the parts, the contribution of the parts to the overall meaning of the construction, the semantic, pragmatic, and discourse value of the construction, and so on. For some constructions, it is necessary to specify aspects of their prosody, and even aspects of their orthographic representation. Although complex, constructions constitute what Lakoff (1987, p. 538) called a "gestalt"; they are established configurations that are cognitively simpler than a mere ad hoc assembly of their parts (see also Taylor, 1995, p. 206; 1996, pp. 339–340). Precisely because of their complexity, constructions are liable to give rise to prototype effects. An expression may fully match all the specifications of the construction; in this case, it will count as a central, or prototypical instance of the construction. Alternatively, it may match only some of the construction's specifications—in which case, it will turn out to be a more marginal instance of the construction. In the course of the earlier presentation, I have already hinted at some prototype effects associated with syntactic constructions. Here, I highlight three specific issues; (a) centrality and productivity, (b) coercion, and (c) the merging of constructions at their boundaries.

(a) "Centrality" and "Productivity"

It is important to emphasize that a marginal instantiation of a construction is not necessarily lower in acceptability than are more central members. What we do frequently observe, however, as we move away from a construction's prototypical center, is that various kinds of constraint on acceptability come into play. Taylor (1995) discussed this phenomenon in terms of a decline in a construction's *productivity.*

Consider, as an example, the kinds of expression that can occur as the subject of a clause. Clausal subject is a notion that is involved in very many syntactic constructions. One dimension of a clausal subject is that it designates an entity of which something is predicated. Prototypically, a clausal subject will be a referring noun phrase, as in (12).

12. a. [The cat] sat on the mat.
    b. [He] wrote a novel.
    c. [The chickens] were eaten by the fox.

But other kinds of subjects are also possible.

13. a. [Under the bed] is a good place to hide it.
    b. [That the world is flat] should be obvious to everyone.
    c. [There]'s somebody at the door.

The bracketed phrases differ from prototypical subjects in various ways. *Under the bed* has the internal structure of a prepositional phrase, not of a noun phrase. Nevertheless, *under the bed* arguably does constitute a referring expression. It refers, however, not to a thing, but to a place, and (13a) predicates a certain property of this place. Similar remarks apply to *that the world is flat* in (13b). Although this constituent has the internal structure of a clause, it is arguably also a referring expression, its referent being a proposition. With respect to (13c), *there* (if unstressed) does not appear to be referring to anything at all.

There can be no question about the full grammaticality of the sentences in (13), nor can there be any doubt about the status of the bracketed expressions as clausal subjects. For example, the bracketed expressions can participate in "subject-raising" constructions, and can be questioned in a question tag.

14. a. [Under the bed] seems to be a good place to hide it.
    b. [That the world is flat] seems to be obvious to everyone.
    c. [There] seems to be somebody at the door.

15. a. [Under the bed] is a good place to hide it, isn't it?
    b. [That the world is flat] should be obvious to everyone, shouldn't it?
    c. [There]'s somebody at the door, isn't there?

At the same time, the use of nonprototypical subjects is highly con-strained.[12] Take the case of prepositional subjects. On my intuition, the following examples become progressively less acceptable.

16. a. By the fire is a good place to sit.
    b. (?) By the fire is nice and warm.
    c. ?By the fire smells of cat.
    d. ??By the fire is preferred by the cat.
    e. *By the fire filled up with smoke.

A locative prepositional subject seems to be fully acceptable only if the referent is characterized as a certain kind of place, as in (16a) and (13a), and possibly also (16b). Prepositional subjects tend not to be acceptable if some circumstantial property is predicated of a place as in (16c), if the designated location is the subject of a passive sentence (16d), or if some-thing happens in or to the place, as in (16e). Observe that the unaccepta-bility of these examples is not due to the conceptual incoherence of the designated situations. It makes perfectly good sense to say that the region in space designated by *by the fire* gradually filled up with smoke.

If we look at locative prepositional subjects in interrogatives, accept-ability judgments decline even further. Whereas (16b) is only slightly odd, the corresponding interrogative *Is by the fire nice and warm?* is much more questionable. (We should prefer something like *Is it nice and warm by the fire?*) And the use of clausal subjects in interrogatives (*Is that the world is flat obvious to everyone?*) is completely banned. Concerning *there*, restrictions on its use as a clausal subject are quite wide-ranging, and have been extensively discussed (e.g., Lakoff, 1987, pp. 462–585). *There arrived several guests* is acceptable, whereas *There left several guests* is not. *There's a dog barking outside* is fine, whereas *There barked a dog outside* is not.

Such restrictions on acceptability are largely absent with more prototypical subjects, i.e. subjects that are referring noun phrases. For prototypical subjects, it is generally immaterial whether the sentence is affirmative or interrogative, whether the clause is a main or subordinate clause. Provided only that the subject is semantically compatible with the predicate, and with the semantics of the sanctioning construction, practically any noun phrase can be used as the subject of practically any clause. It is in this sense that the use of referring noun phrases as subjects is highly productive. The use of prepositional phrases, clauses, and of *there* as subjects has low productivity in the sense that these marginal instantiations of a clausal subject are acceptable only under special circumstances, in which various kinds of constraints are respected.[13]

(b) Coercion

As pointed out, marginal instantiations of a construction can be just as acceptable as more central instantiations. What happens, in many cases, is that the construction's semantics "coerces" the semantic value of one of its parts, such that the part becomes compatible with the construction's overall meaning.

The term "coercion" is due to Pustejovsky (1991), who used it to refer to the phenomenon whereby the environment in which a word occurs can "force" a specific reading of that word. *Drop a book* coerces the interpretation of *book* as a physical object, whereas *translate a book* coerces the interpretation of *book* as a text in a given language.

Syntactic constructions can also coerce expressions that instantiate them. The possibility of using a prepositional phrase as a clausal subject reflects just this process. A prepositional phrase prototypically designates a spatial relation between entities, as in *a chair [by the fire]*. The use of *by the fire* as a clausal subject forces a nominal reading of the prepositional phrase, i.e. the phrase comes to designate not a spatial relation, but a place.[14]

Consider the following example.

17. Joe sneezed the napkin off the table.

Goldberg (1995, p. 9) cited this sentence in the course of her critique of lexicalism. It would be highly extravagant, she claimed, to postulate, as one of the polysemes of *sneeze*, a reading according to which sneezing involves the displacing of an object by sneezing on it, such that the semantic structure of *sneeze* "projects" into a sentence of the form [NP_1 – V – NP_2 – PP]. *Sneeze* is surely a quintessentially intransitive verb, which designates an involuntary activity on the part of its subject referent.

Nevertheless, (17) is a perfectly acceptable sentence, and one that is easily interpreted. That this is possible at all is due, first and foremost, to the fact that (17) instantiates a very well-established construction in English—what Goldberg (1995) called the caused motion construction. Schematically, a caused motion expression has the structure [NP_1 – V – NP_2 – PP], whereby NP_1 acts on NP_2, thereby causing NP_2 to be propelled along a path designated by PP. The following examples instantiate the construction.

18. a. Ann put the book on the table.
    b. Fred drove the car into the ditch.
    c. Joanne threw the ball over the wall.
    d. Bill mailed the letter to his mother.

The verbs in (18) designate activities that inherently involve the displacement of a direct object nominal. A significant fact about the caused motion construction, however, is that it can also be used with verbs that do not have this characteristic. In these cases, we witness the coercion of a verb's semantics by the construction in which it is used. Writing, drinking, talking, and arguing are not inherently directed at causing the displacement of an entity. Nevertheless, in (19), these activities are construed in such a way that the direct object referent does get displaced (literally or metaphorically) as a consequence of the activity.

19. a. Sam wrote his son out of his will.
    b. Gerald drank us all under the table.
    c. Sue talked us all into a coma.
    d. Henry argued himself into a corner.

Although these uses of *write*, *drink*, etc. represent a departure from the prototypical values of the verbs, the expressions in (19) might still be regarded as "conventionalized," in that *write X out of one's will*, *drink X under the table* almost have the status of established locutions. *Sneeze X off the table* is by no means an established locution. Nevertheless, the expression can still be interpreted with respect to the semantics of the construction. Observe that encyclopaedic knowledge is crucially involved here. We know (encyclopaedically) that sneezing involves a sudden exhalation of breath (and maybe other matter!), whose force may be sufficient to cause a lightweight object such as a napkin to be propelled along a path. Can encyclopaedic knowledge place a limit on what can be achieved by coercion? Indeed it can. It is scarcely possible to "yawn" or to "sigh" a napkin off a table. By virtue of what we know about yawning and sighing, the verbs *yawn* and *sigh* resist coercion by the forced motion construction.

(c) Merging of Constructions at Boundaries

A characteristic of prototype categories that I mentioned at the outset of this chapter concerns the fuzziness of their boundaries. A consequence of this is that one category can merge at its edges with a neighboring category. Thus, red gradually merges into orange, and cups into bowls. If syntactic constructions are prototype categories, we should expect to encounter the same phenomenon in the syntactic domain. If we focus only on the prototypical center of a construction, it will usually be possible to easily distinguish the construction from its neighbors. Marginal instances of a construction may, however, exhibit properties of another construction. These expressions could have ambiguous status vis-à-vis the two constructions.

Many examples of just this situation could be cited. I already hinted at the fuzziness of the boundary between (marginal examples of) adjective and (marginal examples of) noun. A detailed examination of intransitives would reveal a fuzzy boundary between middles and inchoatives. Middles invoke a stable property of the subject referent (*The door opens easily*), whereas inchoatives invite an event reading (*The door suddenly opened*). But consider *The door wouldn't open*. This combines features of both constructions. To the extent that the nonoccurrence of the event at a particular time is a consequence of a stable property of the door, the expression could be difficult to classify with respect to one or the other of the two constructions.

Consider also the case of possessives (Taylor, 1996). The prenominal possessives in (20) can be clearly differentiated, both syntactically and semantically, from the possessive compounds in (21).

20. a. [the boy]'s [shirt]
     b. [the young boy]'s [expensive shirt]

21. a. the [boy's shirt]
     b. the expensive [boy's shirt]

The expressions in (20) designate a shirt, or, as the case may be, an expensive shirt, which is identified as belonging to a specific individual, i.e. the boy. The expressions in (21) designate a specific instance of a kind of shirt, viz. [boy's shirt], which can be characterized as expensive. Observe that in (20) a specific boy is involved, whereas in (21) the shirt is characterized as one suitable for boys in general.

The possessor nominal in the prenominal construction is prototypically human, singular, and definite (Taylor, 1996). This is not to say that the construction is not also compatible with indefinite or plural possessors: *a man's life, people's children*. But with these kinds of possessors, the construction can sometimes be difficult to differentiate from possessive compounds. What, for example, did the archaeologists in (22) discover?

22. The archaeologists discovered fragments of a man's skull.

Did they discover fragments of a skull belonging to an unspecified man, i.e. fragments of [a man]'s [skull] (the prenominal reading)? Or did they discover fragments of a (male) human skull, i.e. fragments of a [man's skull] (the compound reading)? Semantically, there is not much to differentiate these readings. As shown in Taylor (1996), syntactic tests that might throw light on the matter give inconclusive results.

Not only this, but the contrast between a possessive compound and a nonpossessive compound can also become fuzzy. In principle, the two constructions can be clearly distinguished. *A [children's playground]* clearly exemplifies a possessive compound. Equally clearly, *the [city center]* exemplifies a nonpossessive compound. But what about *students union (students' union)*? Uncertainty as to whether the expression merits a possessive apostrophe goes hand in hand with uncertainty as to whether the expression should be construed as a possessive (on the lines of *children's playground*) or as a compound with a plural noun modifier (on the pattern of *accounts clerk, greetings card*).

4. CONCLUDING REMARKS

Prototype effects arise not only with respect to the referential possibilities of lexical items, but also with respect to the very categories of linguistic structure itself.

In the first place, familiar word classes, such as adjective and noun, turn out to be prototypically structured. In many respects, these categories are exactly analogous to real-world categories such as "cup" and "bowl" (Labov, 1973). The lexical categories are most appropriately defined, not by a set of necessary and sufficient conditions for category membership, but in terms of good examples and their properties. As with real-world categories, an item can have marginal status within a word class; such items exhibit only some of the properties that are typical of the category. Moreover, the boundaries of word classes may be fuzzy, such that adjective can merge at its edges with, say, noun. Just as it might be difficult to definitively categorize a receptacle as either a cup or a bowl, so too it can be problematic to decide whether a word, as used in a certain context, is a noun or an adjective.

More complex categories, i.e. syntactic constructions, also turn out to be prototypically structured. A construction may be defined, very generally, as any established pairing of a form with a meaning. In this chapter, I focused on syntactic constructions, i.e. established patterns for the syntagmatic combination of smaller units into larger configurations. Given this definition, syntactic constructions need to be characterized in both their formal and their semantic aspects. Precisely because of their complexity, syntactic constructions are especially likely to give rise to prototype effects, in that examples of a construction may match some, but not all, of the formal and/or semantic aspects. And, just as with word classes and real-world categories, syntactic constructions can merge into each other at their fuzzy boundaries.

Marginality with respect to a construction is not to be equated with a decline in acceptability; marginal instantiations of a construction need not be any less grammatical than more central members. What we often do observe, however, is that more marginal instantiations tend to be subject to various idiomatic constraints that are absent with more central members. Constructions, in other words, tend to be less productive at their periphery than at their center. What we also observe, in some cases, is that a construction coerces its parts, such that a constituent takes on a (for the constituent) nonprototypical value, in accordance with the requirements of the containing construction.

My discussion of constructions raises a more general issue. I take the basic subject matter of linguistic inquiry to be the question, what does it mean to know a language? Or, to slightly rephrase the question, what does a person have to know for it to be possible to say that the person knows a language? Different linguistic theories offer different kinds of answers to these questions. In this chapter, I assumed—and gave some reasons for supporting this assumption—that knowledge of a language consists very largely in knowledge of constructions and their properties. Constructions constitute a vast network of items, which may be linked to one another by relations of instantiation and partonomy. Importantly, a constructionist account need not postulate language-specific cognitive mechanisms. Neither the ability to establish symbolic links between a formal and a semantic characterization, nor the ability to recognize relations of instantiation and partonomy, are specific to language behavior. And, as I argued in this chapter, constructions exhibit prototype effects. In this, too, constructions share affinities with objects of nonlinguistic knowledge.

NOTES

1. "Construction," as used in this chapter, is roughly equivalent to Langacker's (1987) "constructional schema." On construction grammar, see in particular Fillmore, Kay, and O'Connor (1988), Goldberg (1995), Lakoff (1987), and Taylor (1995).

2. A particularly forceful expression of this view is Coseriu (1990).

3. For Langacker (1987), a property is "intrinsic" to a thing if it can be assessed merely by inspection of the thing itself; an "extrinsic" property is one that can be assessed only be reference to something outside of the thing itself. What a pie is made of can be determined by inspection of the pie alone; whether or not a person is a "university student" can only be ascertained by reference to the person's relation to an institution.

4. It might be objected that the predicative construction is compatible with predicate nouns as well as with predicate adjectives (*These men are thieves, What you say is nonsense*); hence examples like those in (1)–(3) say nothing about the noun vs. adjective status of *gold*, etc. Yet, the function of predicates is, precisely, to ascribe a property to the subject referent. Langacker (1991, pp. 65–67) argued that even what look to be clear examples of predicate *nominals* (*Alice is a thief*), acquire, in the construction, a relational profile, comparable to that of an adjective. There are, furthermore, examples where the distinction between predicate noun and predicate adjective genuinely blurs; consider *John is part Swede* (Croft, 1991, p. 103). Although *Swede* is basically a noun, *part Swede* can hardly be analyzed as a nominal.

5. "Construction idioms" that have been examined in recent years include:

   (a) The correlative comparison construction, exemplified by *The more the merrier; The bigger they come the heavier they fall* (Fillmore et al., 1988). Observe that the use of *the* in this construction has no parallels elsewhere in the grammar of English.

   (b) The intrusive *have* construction, common in counterfactuals in informal registers, e.g. *If only you hadn't have told me* (Fillmore, 1985). Although subject to heavy proscription, this construction has been current in spoken English since at least the 15th century.

   (c) A whole set of *there* constructions, closely studied in Lakoff (1987, pp. 462–585).

   (d) Negative polarity questions, e.g. *Didn't Harry leave?* (Lakoff, 1987, pp. 474–477, 533). These are not really polarity questions at all, but hedged assertions, and, as such, can occur in environments in which "genuine" interrogatives are banned. E.g. *Let's call the whole thing off, because didn't Harry leave?* / **because did Harry leave?*

   (e) The double *is* construction, exemplified by the title of Tuggy's (1996) paper: *The thing is is that people speak that way. The question is is why.* This construction is again very frequent in informal, especially unscripted speech.

   (f) The extraposition construction, exemplified by *It's amazing the people you see here* (Michaelis & Lambrecht, 1996). This sentence cannot be regarded as a mere "stylistic" variant of *The people you see here are amazing*; its semantics are quite different.

6. Akmajian's (1984) phrase-structure rules incidentally also generate imperatives of the form, *You write a novel!* This, according to Akmajian, is not a weakness of the rules, but a reason they should be valued, to the extent that incredulity responses and imperatives share a number of formal properties (in both, for example, the expression of the "subject" is optional). On the other hand, there are no imperatives analogous to (4d) and (4e), which argues against even a formal similarity between the two constructions.

   A glance at some other languages confirms the "idiomatic" character of the incredulity response construction in English. The German equivalent of (4a), for example, is as follows (cf. Lambrecht, 1990):

Er und einen Roman schreiben!
He-NOM and a-ACC novel write

Although English and German are historically closely related languages, and many constructions in the one language have close analogues in the other, the incredulity response construction in German differs radically in its formal aspects from its English counterpart. In German, the "subject" is obligatorily in nominative case, and there is a linking *und* "and" between the "subject" and the "predicate."

7. A formal characterization of the incredulity response construction therefore needs to refer, not only to its internal syntax, but also to its prosodic and even orthographic properties. Note that the value of the distinctive punctuation, i.e. *?!*, cannot be computed from the values of its parts. Even the punctuation counts as "idiomatic."

8. The examples in (7), on their idiomatic readings, could be punctuated equally well by a question mark (as befits the syntax of a polar interrogative), or by an exclamation mark (which reflects their pragmatic force).

9. As suggested in the preceding discussion, idiomaticity is a matter of degree. The fact that a verb can take two objects can indeed be regarded as an idiomatic fact about English, to the extent that some languages, e.g. Romance languages, do not have this construction at all, whereas others (e.g. Bantu languages) have double object constructions whose range of instantiations is much broader than in English (Taylor, 1998). These count as idiosyncratic facts about the languages concerned, and have to be learned as such by speakers of the languages.

10. My characterization of the middle construction is unorthodox, in that it does not restrict the subject to a patient entity. In a standard middle, e.g. *The book sells well*, the book is the thing that is sold, whereas in *The oven doesn't bake very well*, the oven is an instrument used in baking. There are, however, good syntactic and semantic reasons for bringing patient-subject intransitives and instrumental-subject intransitives together in a single construction (Dixon, 1991, chap. 10).

11. This is not to say, of course, that an exceptional situation may not arise in which it might indeed be appropriate to characterize a receptacle as one that "boils well," or to characterize a person as the one who "boils." Such a possibility only serves to confirm the validity of a prototype account of the respective constructions.

12. As a further symptom of this, consider the possibility of embedding the sentences in (13) under a main clause predicate. Whereas (a) and (c) fare quite well in this environment, sentences with clausal subjects do not:

   a.   I doubt whether [under the bed] is a good place to hide it.
   b.   *I doubt whether [that the world is flat] should be obvious to everyone.
   c.   I doubt whether [there]'s somebody at the door.

13. The marginality of (5b)—*The tent sleeps six*—within the transitive construction is confirmed by the fact that transitives with locative NP subjects are subject to idiosyncratic constraints. If *The tent sleeps six* is acceptable on the reading "The tent is big enough for six people to sleep in it," we might expect *The house lives six* to be acceptable, with the reading "The house is big enough for six people to live in it." The latter sentence is, of course, totally unacceptable. Locative transitives on the pattern of *The tent sleeps six*, it would appear, are acceptable only with very few verbs, notably *sleep* and *seat* (*The plane seats 400*); in my terms, they exhibit a very low degree of productivity.

14. For Pustejovsky (1991), "coercion" consisted in the selection of a reading that is already contained in the semantic specification of an item. Consistent with my commitment to an encyclopaedist semantics, I use the term in a broader sense, to include the "forcing," by the construction in which an expression occurs, of a nonprototypical reading of the expression.

REFERENCES

Akmajian, A. (1984). Sentence types and the form-function fit. *Natural Language and Linguistic Theory, 2,* 1–23.

Berlin, B., & Kay, P. (1969). *Basic color terms.* Berkeley: University of California Press.

Bloomfield, L. (1933). *Language.* London: Allen & Unwin.

Chomsky, N. (1991). Some notes on economy of derivation and representation. In R. Freidin (Ed.), *Principles and parameters in comparative grammar* (pp. 417–454). Cambridge, MA: MIT Press.

Coleman, L., & Kay, P. (1981). Prototype semantics: The English verb lie. *Language, 57,* 26–45.

Coseriu, E. (1990). Semántica estructural y semántica "cognitiva" [Structural semantics and "cognitive" semantics]. In M. Alvar (Ed.), *Profesor Francisco Marsá: Jornadas de filología* (Collecció Homenatges 4, pp. 239–282). Spain: University of Barcelona.

Coseriu, E., & Geckeler, H. (1981). *Trends in structural semantics.* Tübingen, Germany: Gunter Narr.

Croft, W. (1991). *Syntactic categories and grammatical relations.* Chicago: University of Chicago Press.

Dixon, R. M. W. (1991). *A new approach to English grammar, on semantic principles.* Oxford, England: Clarendon.

Fillmore, C. J. (1982). Towards a descriptive framework for spatial deixis. In R. J. Jarvella & W. Klein (Eds.), *Speech, place, and action* (pp. 31–59). London: Wiley.

Fillmore, C. J. (1985). Syntactic intrusions and the notion of grammatical construction. *Proceedings of the eleventh annual meeting of the Berkeley Linguistics Society,* 73–86.

Fillmore, C. J., Kay, P., & O'Connor, C. (1988). Regularity and idiomaticity in grammatical constructions: The case of *Let alone. Language, 64,* 501–538.

Fodor, J. A. (1983). *The modularity of mind.* Cambridge, MA: MIT Press.

Geeraerts, D. (1989). Prospects and problems of prototype theory. *Linguistics, 27,* 587–612.

Geeraerts, D. (1993). Vagueness's puzzles, polysemy's vagaries. *Cognitive Linguistics, 4,* 223–272.

Geeraerts, D., Grondelaers, S., & Bakema, P. (1994). *The structure of lexical variation: Meaning, naming, and context.* Berlin: Mouton de Gruyter.

Goldberg, A. (1992). The inherent semantics of argument structure: The case of the English ditransitive construction. *Cognitive Linguistics, 3,* 37–74.

Goldberg, A. (1995). *Constructions: A construction grammar approach to argument structure.* Chicago: University of Chicago Press.

Harris, R. A. (1993). *The linguistics wars.* New York: Oxford University Press.

Huddleston, R. (1984). *Introduction to the grammar of English.* Cambridge, England: Cambridge University Press.

Hudson, R. (1995). *Word meaning.* London: Routledge & Kegan Paul.

Jackendoff, R. (1990). *Semantic structures.* Cambridge, MA: MIT Press.

Labov, W. (1973). The boundaries of words and their meanings. In C. J. Bailey & R. Shuy (Eds.), *New ways of analyzing variation in English* (pp. 340–373). Washington, DC: Georgetown University Press.

Lakoff, G. (1987). *Women, fire, and dangerous things: What categories reveal about the mind.* Chicago: University of Chicago Press.

Lambrecht, K. (1990). "What, me worry?"—'Mad Magazine sentences' revisited. *Proceedings of the sixteenth annual meeting of the Berkeley Linguistics Society,* 215–228.

Langacker, R. W. (1987). *Foundations of cognitive grammar* (Vol. 1). Stanford: Stanford University Press.

Langacker, R. W. (1991). *Foundations of cognitive grammar* (Vol. 2). Stanford: Stanford University Press.

Leech, G. (1981). *Semantics* (2nd ed.). Harmondsworth, England: Penguin.

Levin, B., & Rappaport Hovav, M. (1990). Wiping the slate clean: A lexical semantic exploration. *Cognition, 41,* 123–155.

McCawley, J. D. (1986). What linguists might contribute to dictionary making if they could get their act together. In P. C. Bjarkman & V. Raskin (Eds.), *The real-world linguist: Linguistic applications in the 1980s* (pp. 1–18). Norwood, NJ: Ablex.

Michaelis, L. A., & Lambrecht, K. (1996). Toward a construction-based theory of language function: The case of nominal extraposition. *Language, 72,* 215–247.

Osherson, D. N., & Smith, E. E. (1981). On the adequacy of prototype theory as a theory of concepts. *Cognition, 9,* 35–58.

Pinker, S. (1989). *Learnability and cognition.* Cambridge, MA: MIT Press.

Pustejovsky, J. (1991). The generative lexicon. *Computational Linguistics, 17,* 409–441.

Rosch, E. (1978). Principles of categorization. In E. Rosch & B. B. Lloyd (Eds.), *Cognition and categorization* (pp. 27–48). Hillsdale, NJ: Lawrence Erlbaum Associates.

Ross, J. R. (1972). The category squish: Endstation Hauptwort. *CLS, 8,* 316–328.

Ross, J. R. (1973). Nouniness. In O. Fujimura (Ed.), *Three dimensions of linguistic theory* (pp. 137–258). Tokyo: Tokyo Institute for Advanced Studies of Language.

Ross, J. R. (1987). Islands and syntactic prototypes. *CLS, 23,* 309–320.

Taylor, J. R. (1992). Old problems: Adjectives in cognitive grammar. *Cognitive Linguistics, 3,* 1–36.

Taylor, J. R. (1995). *Linguistic categorization: Prototypes in linguistic theory* (2nd ed.). Oxford, England: Clarendon.

Taylor, J. R. (1996). *Possessives in English: An exploration in cognitive grammar.* Oxford, England: Clarendon.

Taylor, J. R. (1998). Double object constructions in Zulu. In J. Newman (Ed.), *The semantics of giving* (pp. 67–96). Amsterdam: John Benjamins.

Tuggy, D. (1996). The thing is is that people talk that way. The question is is why? In E. Casad (Ed.), *Cognitive linguistics in the Redwoods* (pp. 713–752). Berlin: Mouton.

Wierzbicka, A. (1996). *Semantics: Primes and universals.* Oxford, England: Oxford University Press.

Wittgenstein, L. (1953). *Philosophical investigations* (G. E. M. Anscombe, Trans.). Oxford, England: Basil Blackwell.

Chapter 8

Patterns of Experience in Patterns of Language[1]

Adele E. Goldberg
University of Illinois, Urbana-Champaign

1. INTRODUCTION

It is often assumed that the general overall form and meaning of a sentence is determined by the main verb, because in simple cases, this does seem to be the case. For example in a sentence like (1), it is *give* that seems to be responsible for the fact that there are three arguments involved and it is *give* that seems to give the sentence its meaning of transfer from one animate being to another.

1. Pat gave Chris a book.

However, a careful look at other sentences with this double object form reveals that the form and the associated meaning are not naturally attributed to the main verb in all cases.

Notice that (2) entails that Pat intended to give Chris the cake. The sentence cannot be used if Pat baked the cake simply as a favor to Chris because Chris was too busy to do it.

2. Pat baked Chris a cake.

On the other hand, this latter interpretation is available for the paraphrase of (2) in (3):

3. Pat baked a cake for Chris (because Chris was out of the country).

The question arises, where does the semantics of intended transfer associated with (2) come from? It is not a necessary part of the meaning of *bake* (witness 3), and it is not associated with any of the noun phrases. One possibility is to allow the additional meaning component, the semantics of "someone (intending to) cause someone to receive something" to be attributed directly to the formal pattern, Subj V Obj Obj2 (see Goldberg, 1992, 1995).[2]

Recognizing that the formal pattern is itself imbued with meaning allows us to account for the following contrast in a straightforward way:

5. a. Pat sent a package to the boarder/the border.
   b. Pat sent the boarder/*the border a package. (Partee, 1965/1979, p. 60)

We can see from (5a) that *send* itself does not entail that the goal must be an animate, although such a constraint does hold of (5b). Instead of positing a special sense of *send* to account for (5b), we can assign the constraint that the goal be animate (a recipient) directly to the double object construction. There is no such constraint on the construction in (5a), so the paraphrased sentence allows the goal to be a nonanimate location in space.

To take one more example, *sneeze* is a textbook example of an intransitive verb (see 6a) and yet, it can appear transitively in (6b):

6. a. Pat sneezed.
   b. Pat sneezed the foam off the cappuccino. (Ahrens, 1995)

It is unnatural to assume that it is *sneeze* that is responsible for the fact that there are three syntactic complements involved in (6b) or for the fact that the sentence entails that someone caused something to move somewhere. In fact, *sneeze* can occur in several other patterns as well:

7. a. She sneezed a terrible sneeze. (cognate object construction)
   b. She sneezed her nose red. (the resultative construction)
   c. She sneezed her way to the emergency room. (the *way* construction)

If we wanted to retain the assumption that the main verb is responsible for the overall form and meaning of the sentence, we would need to posit special senses of *sneeze* to account for each of (7a–c) as well as for (6b).

Instead of positing a new verb sense whenever a new syntactic frame is available, it makes sense to associate some aspects of meaning directly to the formal pattern itself. This allows us to account for the full semantic interpretation without positing implausible and ad hoc verb senses (for additional arguments, see Goldberg, 1995).

In this view, each of these formal patterns and its associated meaning(s)[3] forms a *construction* of the language. The definition of a CONSTRUCTION is given below:

> C is a CONSTRUCTION iff$_{defn}$ C is a form–function pair, such that some aspect of the form or some aspect of the function is not strictly predictable from C's component parts.

Within the theory of construction grammar (also cognitive grammar, see Langacker, this volume), grammar consists of a network of interrelated constructions (see Fillmore & Kay, in press; Fillmore, Kay, & O'Connor, 1988). Both words and larger phrasal patterns are constructions in this technical sense: Both pair form with meaning or conditions of use. In this view, the syntax or grammar of a language is represented in the same general way as the words of the language, although there are clearly differences in internal complexity, degree of phonological specificity, and so on. The entire language is captured by an extended lexicon, or "constructicon."

2. PATTERNS OF EXPERIENCE IN PATTERNS OF LANGUAGE

Argument structure constructions are a special subclass of constructions that provide the basic means of clausal expression in a language. Examples of argument structure constructions in English are presented in Table 8.1.

Each of these argument structure constructions designates a basic pattern of experience, for example, someone causing someone to receive something (the double object construction), something causing something to move (the caused-motion construction), or an instigator causing something to change state (the resultative construction). We can form the following hypothesis:

> **Scene-encoding hypothesis:** Constructions that correspond to basic simple sentence types encode as their central senses, event types that are basic to human experience.

Languages are expected to draw on a finite set of possible event types, such as that of something causing a change of state or location, something

TABLE 8.1
English Argument Structure Constructions

Construction/Example	Meaning	Form
1. Double Object Pat faxed Bill the letter.	X causes Y to receive Z	Subj V Obj Obj2
2. Caused-Motion Pat sneezed the foam off the cappuccino.	X causes Y to move Z	Subj V Obj Obl
3. Resultative She kissed him unconscious.	X causes Y to become Z	Subj V Obj XCOMP
4. Intr. motion The fly buzzed into the room.	X moves Y	Subj V Obl
5. Transitive Pat cubed the meat.	X acts on Y	Subj V Obj
6. Possessive Sam landed/secured a good job.	X acquires/possesses Y	Subj V Obj

undergoing a change of state or location, someone experiencing something, something moving, something being in a state, someone possessing something, and so forth. These event types are quite abstract. We do not expect to find distinct basic sentence types that have semantics such as something turning blue, someone becoming upset, something turning over. For recent related views of argument structure, see Pinker (1994), Jackendoff (1995, in press), and Hovav and Levin (1996).

The constructions serve to carve up the world into discretely classified event types. Langacker (1991) argued that language in general is structured around certain *conceptual archetypes*:

> . . . certain recurrent and sharply differentiated aspects of our experience emerge as archetypes, which we normally use to structure our conceptions insofar as possible. Since language is a means by which we describe our experience, it is natural that such archetypes should be seized upon as the prototypical values of basic linguistic constructs. (pp. 294–295)

The scene-encoding hypothesis can be viewed as a special case of this claim.

Support for the hypothesis that the central senses of argument structure constructions designate scenes that are semantically privileged in being basic to human experience comes from certain language acquisition facts. In particular, verbs that lexically designate the semantics associated with argument structure constructions are learned early and used most frequently (Clark, 1978, 1993); also, certain grammatical markers are applied earliest to "prototypical" scenes (Slobin, 1985), i.e., scenes that are claimed to be associated with the central senses of constructions.

Clark (1978) observed that "general purpose" or "light" verbs such as *put, make, go, do,* and *get* are often among the first verbs to be used. These verbs designate meanings that are remarkably similar to the meanings associated with argument structure constructions. For example, *go* has the meaning associated with the intransitive motion construction; *put* has semantics very close to that of the caused-motion construction; *make* has the semantics associated with the resultative construction. *Do* corresponds to the meaning associated with the basic sense of the simple intransitive and/or simple transitive construction. *Get* may well code the semantics of yet another construction, that instantiated by verbs such as *receive, have, take.*

Clark cited other studies that showed that words corresponding to these concepts are among the first to be used cross-linguistically as well (e.g., Bowerman, 1973, for Finnish; Grégoire, 1937, for French; Park, 1977, for Korean; and Sanches, 1978, for Japanese). Children use these verbs with a general meaning close to that of adults.[4]

In addition to being learned early cross-linguistically, these verbs are also the most commonly used verbs in children's speech. Clark (1978) cited the raw tabulations of verbs used by four children whose mean length of utterance was 2.5, collected by Bloom, Miller, and Hood (1975), and Bloom and Lahey (1978). Table 8.3 gives the relative frequencies of the most commonly used verbs.

Notice that *go, put, get, do,* and *make* (and *sit*) are far more frequent than any other verbs. The meanings of these verbs correspond closely to the meanings of the argument structure constructions described earlier (cf. Table 8.2). The fact that these "light" verbs, which are drawn from a small set of semantic meanings cross-linguistically, are learned earliest and used most frequently is evidence that this small class of meanings is cognitively privileged.

Slobin (1985) observed that children's first use of certain grammatical marking is applied to "prototypical scenes":

> In Basic Child Grammar, the first Scenes to receive grammatical marking are "prototypical," in that they regularly occur as part of frequent and salient activities and perceptions, and thereby become organizing points for later elaboration . . . (p. 1175)

TABLE 8.2
Light Verbs and the Constructional Meanings They Correspond To

Verb	Constructional Meaning	Construction
put	X causes Y to move Z	Caused Motion
make	X causes Y to become Z	Resultative
go	X moves Y	Intr. motion
do	X acts on Y	Transitive
get	X acquires/possesses Y	Possessive

TABLE 8.3
Relative Frequencies of Early Verbs

Verb	F	Verb	F	Verb	F
go	417	read	86	draw	52
put	287	play	85	take	48
get	252	find	69	fall	30
do	169	fit	65	come	25
make	132	eat	60		
sit	129	fix	59		

Note. Adapted from Bloom, Miller, and Hood (1975). Reprinted by permission of the University of Minnesota Press.

He illustrated this claim by arguing that the grammatical marking of transitivity is first used to describe what he terms the "Manipulative Activity Scene." This scene corresponds to the experiential gestalt of a basic causal event in which an agent carries out a physical and perceptible change-of-state in a patient by means of direct manipulation.

That is, markers of transitivity, both object markers in accusative languages and subject markers in ergative languages, are first applied to the arguments of verbs involving direct physical action, e.g. *give, grab, take, hit,* and not on verbs such as *say, see, call out.* In Kaluli (Schieffelin, 1985), children do not overextend ergative inflection to the subjects of intransitive verbs, even when they have an active meaning, e.g. *run, jump.* Slobin thus concluded that children are not grammaticizing the notion of actor in general, but are grammatically marking manipulative activity scenes.

Whereas the transitive construction and others are later abstracted or extended to cover a wider range of meanings (see section 4), the initial meaning of the construction is a basic experiential gestalt. Thus, a basic pattern of experience is encoded in a basic pattern of the language.[5]

Verbs, on this view, are associated with richer encyclopedic meanings, and are not necessarily decomposable into abstract semantic structures of the same sort as are argument structure constructions (cf. Bolinger, 1965; Fillmore, 1975, 1976; Goldberg, 1995; Higginbotham, 1989; Lakoff, 1987; Langacker, 1987, for arguments that a richer semantics is required for lexical meaning).

3. THE ACQUISITION OF CONSTRUCTIONS

If it is correct that the basic syntactic frames of a language (its "subcategorization" frames) are associated directly with meanings, then what children learn when they learn the syntactic patterns of simple sentences is the particular way certain basic scenarios of human experience are paired with forms in their language.

More specifically, we might view the constructional semantics as emerging from an abstraction over the particular semantics of learned instances with particular verbs. That is, initial acquisition of syntactic patterns seems to be on a verb-by-verb basis (Akhtar, in press; Akhtar & Tomasello, in press; Bates & MacWhinney, 1987; Bowerman, 1982; MacWhinney, 1982; Schlesinger, 1977; Tomasello, 1992; Tomasello & Brooks, in press; see also Gropen, Epstein, & Schumacher, in press, for discussion of the somewhat more productive use of nouns). Children tend to conservatively produce the patterns they have heard.

At the same time, it is clear that children cannot continue to learn syntactic patterns on a verb-by-verb basis indefinitely or we might expect to find a language in which argument structures varied on a verb-by-verb basis in an unrestrained way. Because languages are in fact much more regular, having a few systematically related argument structure constructions, with semantically similar verbs showing a strong tendency to appear in the same argument structure constructions, it seems that learners must be attempting to categorize the instances they hear into patterns (Allen, 1997; Morris, 1998; Tomasello & Brooks, in press).

It is likely that this categorization is driven by an increase in vocabulary size. That is, in order to learn an ever-increasing vocabulary and associated syntactic patterns, it may be necessary to categorize individual instances into classes. This idea was supported by Bates and Goodman (1996) who argued that syntactic proficiency is strongly correlated with vocabulary size. In particular, they argued that the single best estimate of grammatical status at 28 months, which is when syntactic encoding becomes produced more regularly as measured by the MacArthur Communicative Development Inventory (CDI), is the total vocabulary size at 20 months, which is the heart of the vocabulary burst. In fact, Bates and Goodman showed that grammar and vocabulary stay tightly coupled across the 16–30 month range. This correlation would be expected if the increasing vocabulary size is in fact directly forcing certain syntactic generalizations.

On this view, the fact that children learn the light verbs so early (as discussed in the previous section) may play a direct role in the acquisition of argument structure constructions. In particular, if the child is categorizing learned instances into more abstract patterns, and is associating a semantic category with a particular formal pattern, it would be natural for the meaning of the most frequent and early verbs occurring in a particular pattern to form the prototype of the category. For example, if *put* is the most frequent verb associated with the syntactic pattern, Subj V Obj Obl, and is also learned very early, expressions with *put* could act as a center of gravity for other expressions having the same form. The end result of this categorization would be the direct association of the general meaning of *put*, "someone causes something to be moved somewhere" with the formal pattern, giving rise to the "caused-motion" construction. The strong effect of early acquisition and frequency has been documented in connectionist net simulations (Elman, 1993; see also Allen, 1997, for connectionist modeling of argument structure constructions).[6]

3.1. A Look at "Syntactic Bootstrapping"

Gleitman and her colleagues proposed that formal patterns aid in the acquisition of verb meaning (Fisher, Hall, Rakowitz, & Gleitman, 1994; Gleitman, 1994; Landau & Gleitman, 1985; Naigles, 1990). They have termed this "syntactic bootstrapping." A question arises, if we assume that instances are required for acquisition of the construction, is it still possible that the construction is used as an aid to the interpretation of new verbs? Clearly it is possible. Once the constructional meaning has begun to emerge, it can in turn facilitate the acquisition of new verbs.

There is in fact experimental evidence that demonstrates that children pay attention to the grammatical elements of their language in order to figure out the meanings of expressions (Brown, 1957; Katz, Baker, & McNamara, 1974). Syntactic bootstrapping can be seen as an instance of this syntactic cueing, and it, too, has experimental support (Fisher et al., 1994; Naigles, 1990; Naigles, Gleitman, & Gleitman, 1993).

The strongest interpretation of the syntactic bootstrapping hypothesis would be that every syntactic frame in which a verb occurs directly reflects a particular component of the verb's meaning.[7] This would imply that verb meaning can be gleaned from the set of syntactic frames alone without additional context. Pinker (1989, 1994) argued against this position on theoretical grounds. He noted that an error would result if the child presumed that *float* had a motion component of meaning upon hearing (8), because *float* does not necessarily imply motion (see 9).

8. The bottle floated into the cave.

9. The bottle floated in the sink.

Taking our earlier example, *sneeze*, the learner would be misled if (s)he assumed upon hearing (6b) that this verb had a causal or a motion component to its meaning. In constructional terms, the verb need not directly encode or elaborate the meaning associated with the construction. Instead, a common option in English is for the verb to code the *means* of affecting the event associated with the construction. For example, floating is the means of motion in (8), and sneezing is the means of causing motion in (6b; see Goldberg, 1995, in press, for discussion). Thus, although the verb and constructional meaning are systematically related, the former is not necessarily merely an elaboration of the latter. Sethuraman, Goldberg, and Goodman (1997) also provided experimental evidence against the strong interpretation of syntactic bootstrapping. We demonstrated that without the aid of context, children do not attempt to formulate a consistent meaning for a nonsense verb across syntactic frames.

A somewhat weaker interpretation of the claim that syntactic frames aid in the acquisition of verb meaning is that the formal patterns act as a sort of "zoom lens" in directing the listener's attention to certain aspects of the nonlinguistic context (Fisher et al., 1994; Gleitman, 1994). This implies that a single syntactic frame can provide important cues as to what aspect of the scene a verb refers to.

The notion of constructional meaning can make the nature of the zoom lens more precise. The formal patterns are associated with fairly specific meanings such as those given in Table 8.1. Given a nonlinguistic context, the construction can indicate what aspect of the context is being discussed. For example, using the double object pattern would indicate that a scene of transfer is being conveyed. Once the learner's attention is drawn to the relevant scene, the verb can be assumed to code the most salient action in that scene, for example, "kick." Note, then, that the action denoted by the verb does not itself necessarily correspond directly to the scene designated by the construction (e.g., "kicking" does not entail giving), but is only some action that is saliently and centrally involved in that scene. In fact, because the novel verb has a distinct form from the verbs the learner already knows, the learner is highly likely to associate a distinct meaning with it. This could actually bias the learner away from the meaning "give" simpliciter, because by hypothesis, the verb *give* has already been acquired by the time the child could use the construction as a zoom lens.

4. EXTENSIONS FROM THE BASIC PATTERNS

It is clear that we talk about many more abstract and complex things than the simple scenes mentioned in Table 8.1. This raises the question of how the meaning of basic sentence patterns of a language get extended so as to allow the full range of expressive power that we witness.

4.1. Constructional Polysemy

One dimension along which the construction's meaning can vary is that of its causal interpretation. Two examples are given below.

Caused-Motion Construction: Subj V Obj Obl

The Subj V Obj Obl pattern is used to imply a variety of meanings related to caused-motion. Each of the senses is listed below with an example illustrating that sense:

A. "X causes Y to move Z" (central sense).
   Pat pushed the piano into the room.
B. Satisfaction conditions imply: "X causes Y to move Z."
   Pat ordered him into the room.
C. "X enables Y to move Z."
   Pat allowed Chris into the room.
D. "X causes Y not to move from Z."
   Pat blocked Chris out of the room.
E. "X helps Y to move Z."
   Pat assisted Chris into the room.

A strikingly similar range of meaning extensions appears with the double object pattern:

Double Object Construction: Subj V Obj Obj2

A'. "X causes Y to receive Z" (central sense).
    Joe gave Sally the ball.
B'. Satisfaction conditions imply: "X causes Y to receive Z."
    Joe promised Bob a car.
C'. "X enables Y to receive Z."
    Joe permitted Chris an apple.
D'. "X causes Y not to receive Z."
    Joe refused Bob a cookie.
E'. "X acts to cause Y to receive Z at some future point in time."
    Joe bequeathed Bob a fortune.
F'. "X intends to cause Y to receive Z."
    Joe baked Bob a cake.

Senses A and A', B and B', C and C', and D and D' are remarkably parallel, indicating that the range of extensions from the basic sense is not random. But notice the range of extensions is not exactly the same in both cases, because only the caused-motion construction has an extension based on assistance (E) and only the double object construction has an extension based on future consequences or intention (E' & F').

It is clear from these examples that the full interpretation of the sentence depends on both the construction's central sense and the meaning of the verb it combines with. There is a question as to whether the best way to describe these extensions involves *constructional polysemy* (Goldberg, 1995), whereby each construction is notated with the particular extensions it allows, or rather whether the final interpretation is a result of an on-the-fly combination of the verb's lexical meaning and the construction's meaning (van der Leek, 1996). I prefer the former view, that it is a conventional fact about the construction that it allows the range of verb classes it does, for the following reason. Although the range of extensions is not random and is typically natural or "motivated," which extensions are conventional it is not strictly predictable, and must be recorded as part of our knowledge of the language. Consider, for example, sense F' of the double object construction. Although the same extension of the ditransitive exists in some other languages, it does not exist in all. And in certain languages, the ditransitive form has a wider range of meaning than it does in English, including general benefaction (see Comrie, 1982; Polinsky, in press). It is also the case that although one can typically predict the resultant meaning of combining a particular verb class with the construction, it is not predictable that the verb class should be allowed to combine with the construction in the first place (see Goldberg, 1995; Pinker, 1989).

Novel expressions are normally only natural to the extent that they can be construed as falling into existing patterns. For example, consider the following novel attested uses of verbs in the double object construction:

10. a. "We will *overnight* you that package as soon as it comes in" (reported by Mark Turner, personal communication, December 4, 1994).
    b. "Her ex-husband pleaded guilty and *bargained* himself a reduced prison term" (*Los Angeles Times*, February 2, 1994).

Although the particular uses of these verbs are novel, the uses can be seen to fall into more general, well-established patterns. *Overnight* is used to stand metonymically for "sending mail that arrives the next day." This interpretation of *overnight* allows it to fall into the class of verbs of sending, a class that is frequently attested in the double object construction by *send, ship, mail, fax,* and *E-mail. Bargain* in (10b) is used as a verb of future having, a well-attested class including other verbs such as *bequeath, leave, will, guarantee.* What is novel in these cases, then, is not a new interpretation for the construction, but rather novel construals of particular words. The novel construal of these verbs allows the verbs to fall into well-attested conventionalized classes.

Notice that examples like the following sound distinctly more marked than those in (10):

11. ??? Pat helped/assisted Chris a job
    intended to mean, Pat helped Chris to get a job.

The oddness of (11) stems from the fact that verbs of assistance are not conventionally found in the double object construction. If verbs and constructions were able to freely combine without constraint, we would expect (11) to sound acceptable.

This being said, it is also clear that language is constantly in flux, and today's novel construal of a verb may be reanalyzed as an altogether new type of relationship between verb and construction tomorrow. In this way, new clusters of cases that were not conventional may come to be conventional. That is, if novel extensions with similar semantics gain in frequency, the resulting clusters would take on the conventional character of those described earlier.

4.2. Metaphorical Extensions

Another way in which constructional meaning can be extended is through the use of systematic general metaphors of the type discussed by Lakoff and Johnson (1980; see also Clark, 1973). For example, English and many other languages have a metaphor that involves talking about changes-of-state in terms of changes of location. Examples of this metaphor include:

12. a. He *dragged* himself *out of* the depression.
    b. The cereal *went from* crunchy *to* soggy in a matter of minutes.

It is quite a familiar and uncontroversial idea that words in a language can be used metaphorically. Several of the words in (12) refer literally to motion including *drag, out of, go, from, to*, but are being used to designate aspects of changes of state: becoming depressed or soggy. If we adopt the idea that the construction's basic meanings are concrete and physical as suggested in Table 8.1, then it is clear that the constructions, just like the words of a language, can be used with metaphorical interpretations. Although the literal sense of the construction used in (12) designates motion, it is used here to convey changes of state. Because words and phrasal constructions are of the same general type of entity, pairings of form, and meaning, this metaphorical use of constructions is expected.

Another systematic metaphor, causal events as transfers, is exemplified by the following expressions:

13. a. The situation presented us with a dilemma.
    b. The circumstances laid a new opportunity at our feet.
    c. The document supplied us with some entertainment.

Each of these examples describes a causal event: The situation caused a dilemma; the circumstances caused us to find a new opportunity; the document caused us to enjoy some entertainment. Notice that there is no literal transfer: Nothing moves from one place to another, and yet, we use verbs like *present, lay (at someone's feet), supply.* That is because we can understand the causing of an effect in terms of the transfer of that effect. This metaphor licenses the following expressions:

14. a. The medicine brought him relief.
    b. The rain bought us some time.
    c. The music lent the party a festive air.

Again, the verbs *bring, buy,* and *lend* are verbs of transfer. They are licensed by the metaphor. Moreover, the double object construction itself, because it literally designates transfer, not causation, is licensed to be used by the metaphor that allows us to understand causation in terms of transfer. More specifically, the syntax is based on the source domain of the metaphor.

5. CONCLUSION

This chapter attempts to give a brief introduction to the idea that the basic clausal patterns of a language represent pairings of form and function, or *constructions.* In this view of grammar, there is no strict division between the lexicon and grammar: Both words and phrasal patterns are pairings of form and function. In fact, knowledge of language is claimed to consist only of knowledge of interrelated pairings of form and function.

The semantics of the clausal patterns has been argued to be based on fundamental patterns of experience, acquired through a process of categorizing over learned instances. Once constructions emerge from the input, they can be used in a top-down fashion to facilitate the acquisition of new verbs.

The semantics of particular constructions has been argued to be extended via constructional polysemy and metaphorical projection, yielding the fuller expressive power that is evident in the data.

NOTES

1. I would like to thank Mike Tomasello for detailed editorial comments on this paper.
2. Here and in the following, the form of constructions is characterized in terms of grammatical relations: Subject, object, secondary object, oblique, and so forth, in order to abstract over the linear order of constituents. For example, the same double object construction is assumed to be involved in the following expressions:

    4. a. What did Pat fax Bill? (double object + question construction)
       b. It was Pat who faxed Bill the letter. (double object + cleft construction)

3. It is not necessary that every syntactic form be uniquely associated with a particular semantics; there are cases of constructional polysemy (see section 4.1) and constructional ambiguity, where the same form is paired with distinct meanings.

4. Clark (1978) provided the following interpretations for the children's early uses in her data:

> *Put:*   "cause to be or go in some place."
>
> *Make:*   "construct," "produce," or "cause some state to come into being or be produced."
>
> *Go:*   "move," often accompanied by a locative phrase or particle.
>
> *Do:*   "perform an action," generally occurring with an agent noun phrase and sometimes with an additional patient argument. (p. 43)

5. At the same time, it is not being claimed that *all* clause-level constructions encode scenes basic to human experience. Nonbasic clause-level constructions such as cleft constructions (e.g., *It was Pat who left early*), question constructions, and topicalization constructions (e.g., *Pat, she can't stand*), and passives combine with argument structure constructions to provide an alternative information structure of the clause by allowing various arguments to be topicalized or focused.

   That is, children must also be sensitive to the *pragmatic information structure* of the clause (Halliday, 1967; Lambrecht, 1994), and must learn additional constructions that can encode the pragmatic information structure in accord with the message to be conveyed.

6. The idea that constructional meaning emerges from generalization over lexical instances allows for the fact that the prototypical meanings of constructions vary somewhat cross-linguistically (see P. Brown, in press, for a discussion of early verbs in Tzeltal).

7. This is one reading of Landau and Gleitman (1985).

REFERENCES

Ahrens, K. (1995). *The mental representation of verbs.* Unpublished doctoral dissertation, University of California, San Diego.

Akhtar, N. (in press). Learning basic word order. In E. Clark (Ed.), *Proceedings of the Stanford Child Language Research Forum.* Stanford, CA: Center for the Study of Language and Information Publications.

Akhtar, N., & Tomasello, M. (in press). Young children's productivity with word order and verb morphology. *Developmental Psychology.*

Allen, J. (1997). *Argument structures without lexical entries.* Unpublished doctoral dissertation, University of Southern California.

Bates, E., & Goodman, J. (in press). On the emergence of grammar from the lexicon. In B. MacWhinney (Ed.), *The emergence of language.* Mahwah, NJ: Lawrence Erlbaum Associates.

Bates, E., & MacWhinney, B. (1987). Competition, variation and language learning. In B. MacWhinney (Ed.), *Mechanisms of language acquisition* (pp. 157–193). Hillsdale, NJ: Lawrence Erlbaum Associates.

Bloom, L., & Lahey, M. (1978). *Language development and language disorders.* New York: Wiley.

Bloom, L., Miller, P., & Hood, L. (1975). Variation and reduction as aspects of competence in language development. In A. Pick (Ed.), *Minnesota Symposia on Child Development* (Vol. 9, pp 3–55). Minneapolis: University of Minnesota Press.

Bolinger, D. (1965). The atomization of meaning. *Language, 39,* 170–210.

Bowerman, M. (1973). *Early syntactic development: A cross-linguistic study with special reference to Finnish.* Cambridge, England: Cambridge University Press.

Bowerman, M. (1982). Reorganizational processes in lexical and syntactic development. In E. Wanner & L. R. Gleitman (Eds.), *Language acquisition: The state of the art* (pp. 319–346). New York: Cambridge University Press.

Brown, P. (in press). Early Tzeltal verbs: Evidence for the acquisition of verb argument structure. In E. Clark (Ed.), *Proceedings of the Stanford Child Language Research Forum.* Stanford, CA: Center for the Study of Language and Information Publications.

Brown, R. (1957). Linguistic determinism and parts of speech. *Journal of Abnormal and Social Psychology, 55,* 1–5.

Clark, E. V. (1978). Discovering what words can do. *Papers from the Parasession on the Lexicon, Chicago Linguistic Society* (pp. 34–57).

Clark, E. V. (1993). *The lexicon in acquisition.* Cambridge, England: Cambridge University Press.

Clark, H. H. (1973). Space, time, semantics and the child. In T. Moore (Ed.), *Cognitive development and the acquisition of language* (pp. 27–63). New York: Academic Press.

Comrie, B. (1982). Grammatical relations in Huichol. In S. Thompson & P. Hopper (Eds.), *Syntax and semantics: Vol. 15. Studies in transitivity* (pp. 95–115). New York: Academic Press.

Elman, J. (1993). Learning and development in neural networks: The importance of starting small. *Cognition, 48,* 71–99.

Fillmore, C. J. (1975). An alternative to checklist theories of meaning. *Berkeley Linguistics Society, 1,* 123–131.

Fillmore, C. J. (1976). Frame semantics and the nature of language. In S. Harnad, H. Steklis, & J. Lancaster (Eds.), *Origins and evolutions of language and speech.* New York: New York Academy of Sciences.

Fillmore, C., & Kay, P. (1996). *Construction grammar.* Unpublished manuscript, University of California, Berkeley.

Fillmore, C., Kay, P., & O'Connor, M. C. (1988). Regularity and idiomaticity in grammatical constructions: The case of *Let Alone. Language, 64,* 501–538.

Fisher, C., Hall, D. G., Rakowitz, S., & Gleitman, L. (1994). When it is better to receive than to give: Syntactic and conceptual constraints on vocabulary growth. In L. Gleitman & B. Landau (Eds.), *The acquisition of the lexicon* (pp. 333–376). Cambridge, MA: MIT Press.

Gleitman, L. (1994). The structural sources of verb meanings. In P. Bloom (Ed.), *Language acquisition: Core readings* (pp. 174–221). Cambridge, MA: MIT Press.

Goldberg, A. E. (1992). The inherent semantics of argument structure: The case of the English ditransitive construction. *Cognitive Linguistics, 3*(1), 37–74.

Goldberg, A. E. (1995). *Constructions: A construction grammar approach to argument structure.* Chicago: University of Chicago Press.

Goldberg, A. E. (in press). Relationships between verb and construction. In M. Verspoor & E. Sweetser (Eds.), *Lexicon and grammar in cognitive linguistics.* Philadelphia: John Benjamins.

Grégoire, A. (1937). *L'apprentissage du langage* [The acquisition of language] (Vol. 1). Paris: Droz.

Gropen, J., Epstein, T., & Schumacher, L. (in press). Context sensitive verb learning: Children's ability to associate conceptual and semantic information with the argument of the verb. *Cognitive Linguistics.*

Halliday, M. A. K. (1967). Notes on transitivity and theme in English. *Journal of Linguistics, 3,* 199–244.

Higginbotham, J. (1989). Elucidations of meaning. *Linguistics and Philosophy, 12,* 465–517.

Hovav, M. R., & Levin, B. (1996). Building verb meanings. *Proceedings of the Tenth Annual Conference of the Israel Association for Theoretical Linguistics and the Workshop on the Syntax-Semantics Interface.* Bar Illan University and Northwestern University.

Jackendoff, R. (1995). Boundaries of the lexicon. In Evereart et al. (Eds.), *Idioms: Structural and psychological perspectives.* Hillsdale, NJ: Lawrence Erlbaum Associates.

Katz, N., Baker, E., & MacNamara, J. (1974). What's in a name? A study of how children learn common and proper names. *Child Development, 45,* 469–473.

Lakoff, G. (1987). *Women, fire and dangerous things.* Chicago: University of Chicago Press.

Lakoff, G., & Johnson, M. (1980). *Metaphors we live by.* Chicago: University of Chicago Press.

Lambrecht, K. (1994). *Information structure and sentence form: A theory of topic, focus, and the mental representation of discourse referents.* Cambridge, MA: Harvard University Press.

Langacker, R. (1987). *Foundations of cognitive grammar* (Vol. 1). Stanford: Stanford University Press.

Langacker, R. (1991). *Foundations of cognitive grammar 2.* Stanford: Stanford University Press.

Landau, B., & Gleitman, L. R. (1985). *Language and experience: Evidence from the blind child.* Cambridge, MA: Harvard University Press.

MacWhinney, B. (1982). Basic syntactic processes. In S. A. Kuczaj II (Ed.), *Language development: Syntax and semantics* (Vol. 1, pp. 73–137). Hillsdale, NJ: Lawrence Erlbaum Associates.

Morris, W. (1998). *Emergent grammatical relations.* Unpublished doctoral dissertation, University of California, San Diego.

Naigles, L. (1990). Children use syntax to learn verb meanings. *Journal of Child Language, 17,* 357–374.

Naigles, L., Gleitman, H., & Gleitman, L. (1993). Children acquire word meaning components from syntactic evidence. In E. Dromi (Ed.), *Language and cognition: A developmental perspective* (pp. 104–140). Norwood, NJ: Ablex.

Park, T.-Z. (1977). *Emerging language in Korean children.* Unpublished master's thesis, Institute of Psychology, Bern.

Partee, B. H. (1979). Subject and object in modern English. In J. Hankamer (Ed.), *Outstanding dissertations in linguistics series.* New York: Garland. (Original work published 1965)

Pinker, S. (1989). *Learnability and cognition: The acquisition of argument structure.* Cambridge, MA: MIT Press.

Pinker, S. (1994). How could a child use verb syntax to learn verb semantics? In L. Gleitman & B. Landau (Eds.), *The acquisition of the lexicon* (pp. 377–410). Cambridge, MA: MIT Press.

Polinsky, M. (in press). *Double object constructions.* Oxford, England: Oxford University Press.

Sanches, M. (1978). *On the emergence of multi-element utterances in the child's Japanese.* Unpublished manuscript, University of Texas at Austin.

Schieffelin, B. B. (1985). The acquisition of Kaluli. In D. I. Slobin (Ed.), *The cross linguistic study of language acquisition* (Vol. 1). Hillsdale, NJ: Lawrence Erlbaum Associates.

Schlesinger, I. M. (1977). *Production and comprehension of utterances.* Hillsdale, NJ: Lawrence Erlbaum Associates.

Sethuraman, N., Goldberg, A. E., & Goodman, J. (1997). Using the semantics associated with syntactic frames for interpretation without the aid of context. In E. V. Clark (Ed.), *Proceedings of the Twenty Eighth Annual Child Language Research Forum* (pp. 283–294). Stanford: Center for the Study of Language and Information Publications.

Slobin, D. (1985). Crosslinguistic evidence for the language-making capacity. In D. Slobin (Ed.), *A crosslinguistic study of language acquisition* (Vol. 2). Hillsdale, NJ: Lawrence Erlbaum Associates.

Tomasello, M. (1992). *First verbs: A case study of early grammatical development.* Cambridge, England: Cambridge University Press.

Tomasello, M., & Brooks, P. J. (in press). Early syntactic development: A construction grammar approach. In M. Barrett (Ed.), *The development of language.* London: University College Press.

van der Leek, F. (1996). Rigid syntax and flexible meaning: The case of the English ditransitive. In A. E. Goldberg (Ed.), *Conceptual structure, discourse and language.* Stanford: Center for the Study of Language and Information Publications.

Chapter 9

The Acquisition of WH-Questions and the Mechanisms of Language Acquisition

Robert D. Van Valin, Jr.
State University of New York at Buffalo

1. INTRODUCTION[1]

It is no understatement to say that the central issue in the theory of language acquisition is whether children actually learn language and construct a grammar based on the data to which they are exposed, or whether they set the parameters of an autonomous language acquisition device (LAD), which is itself a theory of universal grammar (UG). Some of the arguments which have been taken to be the most compelling for the parameter-setting approach come from two types of cases; 1. the existence of a universal grammatical principle for which there seems to be no evidence available to children in the input, and 2. the production of forms during language development which have no direct model in the adult speech to which children are exposed but which are a possibility sanctioned by UG and which occur in other languages. WH-questions and their acquisition provide important examples of both types and have been cited in the literature as strong evidence in favor of the parameter-setting model (e.g., Chomsky, 1986; Crain, 1991; de Villiers & Roeper, 1991).

The first type of argument involves the principle of subjacency, which is proposed as a universal constraint on the formation of WH-questions and related constructions; it is illustrated in example 1.

1. a.   Mulder believes that Scully hid the files.
    a′. What does Mulder believe that Scully hid?

    b.   Mulder believes the rumor that Scully hid the files.

    b'. *What does Mulder believe the rumor that Scully hid?

    c.   Scully interviewed the witness who saw the alien spacecraft.

    c'. *What did Scully interview the witness who saw?

Subjacency precludes the possibility of moving a WH-word out of an embedded clause which is part of a complex noun phrase (NP) (*the rumor* + clause), as in (1b'), or a restrictive relative clause (*the witness* [head noun] + clause), as in (1c'). It has long been argued that subjacency is a prime example of the argument from the poverty of the stimulus, because, it is claimed, there is no evidence available to the child regarding it in the input (Chomsky, 1986). The second type of argument involves the production by children learning English of long-distance WH-questions containing a medial WH-expression, as reported in Thornton (1990, 1995), and illustrated in example 2.

    2. a. Who do you think who is in the box?

        b. Who do you think who the cat chased?

        c. What do you think what Cookie Monster likes?

        d. How do you think how Superman fixed the car?

English-speaking adults do not produce WH-questions like those in (2), but such constructions are grammatical in languages like German and Romani (McDaniel, Chiu, & Maxfield, 1995). The production of forms like those in (2) is interpreted as the child making use of an available option in UG which is, however, inappropriate for English. This is construed as evidence in favor of the parameter-setting model, since it seems to provide a ready account of why a child would produce forms found not in the language being acquired but in other languages.

    In this chapter, these arguments are reexamined in light of a conception of syntax and acquisition rather different from the Chomskyan Principles and Parameters (P and P) model assumed in them. It is argued that the usual conclusions in favor of the parameter-setting approach do not necessarily follow and that there are alternative explanatory accounts which do not make the same assumptions about cognitive organization and about the mechanisms of language acquisition. The theoretical framework assumed is Role and Reference Grammar (RRG; Van Valin, 1993; Van Valin and LaPolla, 1997), a theory which posits a direct mapping between syntax and semantics in which discourse pragmatics plays an important role, but which does not postulate any covert syntactic representations or transformational-type rules. This chapter shows that a unified, motivated account of the phenomena in (1) and (2) can be given which does not involve an autonomous LAD/UG. This chapter does not argue against the correctness or plausibility of models positing an autonomous, parameterized LAD/UG; no evidence or arguments are given to this effect. Rather, the point is that these phenomena can be accounted for without recourse to such models.

The discussion proceeds as follows. In section 2, the arguments for the parameter-setting model based on (1) and (2) are summarized. In section 3, the relevant features of RRG are presented. In section 4, the RRG account of subjacency presented in Van Valin (1991, 1993, 1995) is summarized and its implications for acquisition discussed. In section 5, the acquisition of WH-questions in both simple and complex sentences is investigated, with special attention paid to the structures in (2) in English as well as in other languages. Conclusions are presented in section 6.

2. THE PARAMETER-SETTING APPROACH

Within the P and P framework, language acquisition is a logical problem, in that the content of the LAD is deduced by means of the following formula:

3. Final knowledge state (= Adult grammatical competence)
   <u>– Input from experience</u>
   = Initial knowledge state (= LAD/UG)

Given a characterization of the final state of linguistic knowledge, i.e. adult grammatical competence, it is possible, it is argued, to determine the content of the initial knowledge state, i.e. the LAD/UG, by factoring out what is available to the child from experience. If there is some feature of adult grammatical competence which is not derivable from experience, then it must be a property of the LAD/UG. This is the well-known "argument from the poverty of the stimulus," and a paradigm case of it concerns the principle of subjacency, which was illustrated in (1). Subjacency restricts movement across so-called "bounding nodes," i.e. the nodes dominating certain important types of phrasal units: sentence (SN), clause (CL) and noun phrase (NP).[2] Only one bounding node can be crossed in a single movement. For English, the bounding nodes are NP and CL. The sentences in (1a′) and (1b′) are repeated below with bounding nodes and traces indicated.[3]

4. a. $[_{SN_1}$ What$_i$ does $[_{CL_1}$ Mulder believe $[_{SN_2}$ t_i that $[_{CL_2}$ Scully hid t_i]]]]
   b. *$[_{SN_1}$ What$_i$ does $[_{CL_1}$ Mulder believe $[_{NP}$ the rumor $[_{SN_2}$ t_i that $[_{CL_2}$ Scully hid t_i]]]]]

In (4a) *what* moves from its D-structure position as the internal argument (direct object) of *hide* to the special position for WH-words, which is outside the clause but inside the sentence,[4] leaving a trace (t_i). This move crosses only one bounding node, CL_2. The second move to the matrix-sentence WH-position also crosses only one bounding node, in this case CL_1; SN is not a bounding node in English. Hence (4a) does not violate subjacency and is grammatical. The first step in the derivation of (4b) is the same as for (4a); the problem arises with the second step. The move from the embedded-sentence WH-position to the matrix-sentence WH-position necessarily crosses two bounding nodes, NP and CL_1, and consequently, the derivation violates subjacency, yielding an ungrammatical sentence. This constraint, as formulated in P and P theory, is purely structural and arbitrary; it is not motivated by any larger cognitive, communicative, or other considerations.

The standard argument regarding the acquisition of subjacency is that there is no conceivable evidence available to children regarding it. Children never hear sentences like (1a'), (1b') or (1c') and therefore, have no empirical basis for inducing the constraint. Moreover, it is argued, there is no semantic or other explanation for it. Hence, in terms of (3) it must be part of the initial knowledge state of the language acquirer; in other words, it must be part of the LAD/UG. This conclusion is apparently reinforced by the fact that in other languages, e.g. Chinese, Japanese, Lakhota, in which WH-words appear in situ,[5] subjacency still seems to be operative. Given that subjacency constrains the movement of elements across bounding nodes and there is no displacement of WH-words in these languages, Huang (1981) proposed that in these languages, subjacency applies not in the overt syntax, but at the abstract covert level of logical form. In these languages, subjacency constrains movement which is not overtly manifested, and it is difficult to imagine how children could learn a constraint on movement in a language which provides no overt evidence of movement in the first place. Thus, subjacency is argued to be a principle of the LAD/UG, based on the argument from the poverty of the stimulus. In terms of acquisition, the default settings of the parameters are "no overt movement" with respect to whether WH-movement is overt or covert and (NP, CL, SN) with respect to the choice of bounding nodes; this precludes movement out of embedded clauses completely. Encountering a sentence with a nonsubject WH-word at the beginning of the sentence, like *What do you want?*, tells the child that overt movement is a feature of the language, and upon hearing a sentence like, *What did Mommy say that Daddy brought?*, leads to the conclusion that either CL or SN is not a bounding node, since this sentence shows that movement out of embedded clauses is possible. The choice of (CL, NP; English) or (SN, NP; Italian) depends on further contrasts for which there is positive evidence in the input.

The second argument for the parameter-setting approach comes from cases in which children produce structures which are not found in the language to which they are exposed but which are sanctioned by UG as a different setting of a parameter. In German, long-distance WH-movement of the kind exemplified in (1a′) is generally disfavored, whereas the following construction involving local WH-movement is grammatical;

5. a. Was glaubst Du, mit wem   Daniel spricht?
      what believe you with who.DAT   speaks
      "With whom do you believe Daniel is talking?"
      (McDaniel et al., 1995)
   b. Was hat er gesagt, wie er den Kuchen backen will?
      what has he said   how he the cake   bake   will
      "How did he say he will bake the cake?"
      (Weissenborn, Roeper, & de Villiers, 1991)
   c. Wie denkst Du, wie er das getan hat?
      how think   you how he that done   has
      "How do you think he did that?"
      (de Villiers, Roeper, & Vainikka, 1990)

In the construction in (5a) and (5b), the first WH-word, *was* 'what' is analyzed as indicating simply that the sentence is a WH-question, and the second WH-word, *wem* 'whom' in (5a) and *wie* 'how' in (5b), actually expresses the content of the question; it will be referred to as the "defining WH-expression" in the construction. In the (c) construction, a copy of the defining WH-word from the second clause occurs in sentence-initial position as well. These patterns are also found in Romani (McDaniel et al., 1995), Hungarian (Horvath, 1997), Croatian and Serbian.[6] What is of interest here is that despite the fact that English-speaking adults do not produce structures like those in (5), some children acquiring English do. Examples similar to (5c) were given in (2); examples similar to (5a,b) are given in (6), from Thornton (1995).

6. a. Which Smurf do you think who has roller skates on?
   a′. What do you think which Smurf really has roller skates?
   b. Which animal do you think what really says "woof woof"?
   b′. What do you think which animal says "woof woof"?

In (6a,b) the defining WH-expression occurs sentence initially with a non-referential WH-word appearing medially, whereas the (a′, b′) sentences are the analogs of the German structures in (5a,b) with the defining WH-expression medially and *what* occurring in the matrix clause to mark the sentence as a question. The constructions in (6a,b) are not found in German or Romani, but they do have a possible analog in languages such as Irish (McCloskey, 1979) in which all of the complementizers in a sentence with WH-movement show 'agreement' with the WH-element, as exemplified in (7).[7]

7. a. [$_{CL}$ Mheas mé [$_{SN}$ gurL   [$_{CL}$ dhúirt sé [$_{SN}$ gurL
            thought I   COMP[-WH]   said   he
        [$_{CL}$ thuig   sé an t-úrscéal.
            understood he the novel
        'I thought that he said that he understood the novel.'
    b. [$_{SN}$ Cén t-úrscéal$_i$ aL   [$_{CL}$ mheas mé [$_{SN}$ t_i aL
            novel which COMP[+WH]   thought I
        [$_{CL}$ dúirt sé [$_{SN}$ t_i aL [$_{CL}$ thuig sé t_i]]]]]]
            said he   understood he
        'Which novel did I think he said he understood?'

In the declarative sentence in (7a), the complementizer is *gurL,* which corresponds roughly to English *that,* whereas in (7b) the complementizer is *aL,* which is argued to be in agreement with the WH-expression or its trace. Note that even the matrix clause has a complementizer in (7b). Thornton (1995) argued that the medial WH-words in (6a,b) are complementizers that agree overtly with the WH-trace in their specifier position. Hence, these sentences are examples of complementizer WH-agreement analogous to that found in Irish.

Why would children learning English produce such structures, in the complete absence of any models for them in the speech to which they are exposed? Put another way, why would children learning English produce German-, Romani- or Irish-style WH-questions? The answer given by Thornton (1995), McDaniel et al. (1995), and others is that they are realizing one of the options made available by the LAD/UG, albeit an incorrect one for English. It is assumed that the only way that children would hit upon structures found in other languages in the absence of any empirical input is for the possibilities to be given in advance in the LAD/UG. Hence, sentences like those in (2) and (6), together with those concerning subjacency, are interpreted as strongly favoring the P and P concept of an autonomous parameterized LAD/UG and as showing that children do not simply generalize from the data to which they are exposed. As de Villiers and Roeper (1991) put it, "the evidence received by the child is small, sometimes contradictory, and clearly insufficient to account for the grammar unless a parametric system is assumed" (p. 1).

It is incumbent upon anyone proposing a model of language development which does not posit an autonomous LAD/UG to provide an explanation for these phenomena. In the RRG conception of language acquisition presented in Van Valin (1991), children construct the grammar of their language based on (a) their initial cognitive endowment, which does not include an autonomous LAD/UG but which is nevertheless richly structured as suggested by Bruner (1983), Slobin (1973, 1985) or Braine (1992, 1994), and (b) the evidence to which they are exposed. In the remainder of this chapter, an RRG account of these phenomena is sketched, and the first step is a brief presentation of the essential features of the theory that are relevant to this discussion.

3. ESSENTIAL FEATURES OF ROLE AND REFERENCE GRAMMAR

The organization of RRG is given in Fig. 9.1. In this chapter, I concentrate on aspects of the syntactic representations and the role of discourse-pragmatics in the mapping between syntax and semantics, ignoring other facets of the theory not directly relevant to this discussion. The most comprehensive presentation of the theory is in Van Valin and LaPolla (1997).

Clause structure is not represented in RRG in terms of X-bar syntax or even traditional immediate constituency structure; rather, it is captured in a semantically based theory known as the "layered structure of the clause." The essential components of this model of the clause are (a) the *nucleus,* which contains the predicate, (b) the *core,* which contains the nucleus plus the arguments of the predicate in the nucleus, and (c) the *periphery,* which contains the adjunct modifiers of the core. The structure of a simple English clause is given in Fig. 9.2, and in Table 9.1 the semantic units underlying the layered structure of the clause are summarized.[8] In WH-questions in languages like English, the WH-expression occurs in a position called the precore slot, illustrated in Fig. 9.3. Note the lack of any empty syntactic positions or traces in the representation; in the linking from semantics to syntax, the WH-expression is mapped directly from its position in the semantic representation into the precore slot, and in the linking

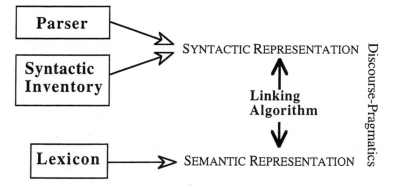

FIG. 9.1. Organization of RRG.

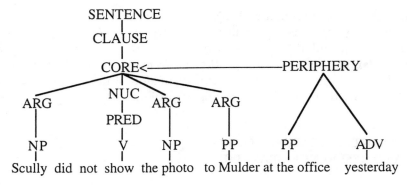

FIG. 9.2. Structure of a simple English clause according to RRG.

TABLE 9.1
Semantic Units Underlying the Syntactic
Units of the Layered Structure of the Clause

Semantic Element(s)	Syntactic Unit
Predicate	Nucleus
Argument in semantic representation of predicate	Core argument
Nonarguments	Periphery
Predicate + Arguments	Core
Predicate + Arguments + Nonarguments	Clause (= Core + Periphery)

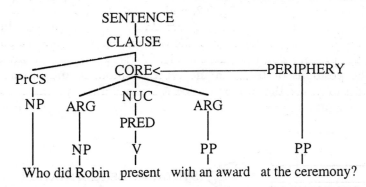

FIG. 9.3. Diagram of English WH-question with WH-expression in precore slot.

from syntax to semantics, it is mapped directly from the precore slot to its position in the semantic representation. The details of the RRG semantic representations are not given here, except to note that terms used for the semantic roles of the two primary arguments of a transitive verb are *actor* and *undergoer*, e.g. *Mary* [actor] *wrote the article* [undergoer], *The article* [undergoer] *was written by Mary* [actor].

The structure of the complex sentences such as (1a) is given in Fig. 9.4; (see Van Valin and LaPolla, 1997, section 8.4.1, and Foley and Van Valin, 1984, section 6.2.2, for justification for this structure). A complex NP like (1b), on the other hand, has roughly the structure given in Fig. 9.5; the internal structure of NPs is not represented in any of these figures.

The second aspect of RRG pertinent to this discussion is the theory of information structure, which is based on Lambrecht (1994). Two notions are especially relevant to the issue of WH-question formation, namely, narrow focus and focus domain. WH-questions are typically narrow focus,

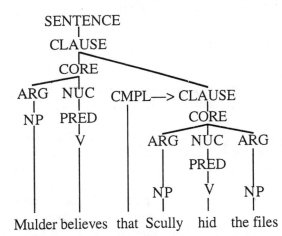

FIG. 9.4. Structure of complex sentence in RRG terms.

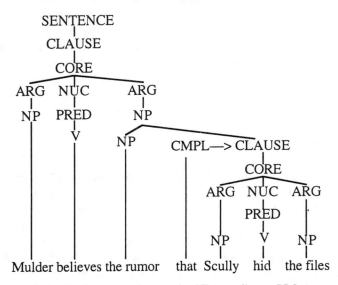

FIG. 9.5. Structure of a complex NP according to RRG.

in that the focus of the question is a single constituent represented by the WH-expression, e.g. *WHAT did Mary buy?*, and the answers to such WH-questions are also narrow focus constructions, e.g. *She bought A NEW CAR* (the focus element is in small caps). Yes–no questions may also be narrow focus, e.g. *Did Mary buy A NEW CAR?—No, she bought A NEW BOAT.* There is an important distinction between unmarked and marked narrow focus. All languages have an unmarked focus position in the clause; in English, it is the last constituent of the core, whereas in verb-final languages, it is the position immediately before the verb. Consider the following English sentence with different focal stress options.

8. a. Dana sent the package to LESLIE yesterday.
   b. Dana sent the package to Leslie YESTERDAY.
   c. Dana sent THE PACKAGE to Leslie yesterday.
   d. Dana SENT the package to Leslie yesterday.
   e. DANA sent the package to Leslie yesterday.

Focal stress on *Leslie* in (8a) is a case of unmarked narrow focus, whereas focal stress on any other constituent of the clause, as in (8b), yields marked narrow focus. The most marked narrow focus is on the subject, as in (8e).[9]

The other important notion is that of focus domain, which actually subsumes two distinct concepts, the potential focus domain and the actual focus domain. The potential focus domain is the part of the sentence in which a focal element may occur, whereas the actual focus domain is the element(s) actually in focus in a particular utterance. In English, simple sentences such as in (8), the entire clause is the potential focus domain, but the actual focus domain (indicated by small caps) is different in each example. The potential focus domain in complex sentences is constrained by the following principle, taken from Van Valin (1993).

9. The potential focus domain in complex sentences: A subordinate clause may be within the potential focus domain if it is a direct daughter of (a direct daughter of . . .) the clause node which is modified by the illocutionary force operator. (p. 121)

The matrix clause node is the one modified by the illocutionary force operator over the clause, and therefore according to the principle in 9, only an embedded clause which is a direct daughter (of a clause which is a direct daughter, etc.) of this clause node can be within the potential focus domain in a complex sentence. Comparing the diagrams in Figs. 9.4 and 9.5, we see that the embedded clause is a direct daughter of the matrix clause node in Fig. 9.4 but not in Fig. 9.5, and consequently, the embedded clause is in the potential focus domain in Fig. 9.4 but not in Fig. 9.5. This distinction has important implications for the phenomena discussed in sections 1 and 2, as we see in the next two sections.

4. THE RRG ACCOUNT OF SUBJACENCY PHENOMENA

Because RRG does not posit the same type of clause structures as P and P or any kind of movement rules, movement across bounding nodes cannot be the explanation for subjacency phenomena in this theory. Rather, the explanation involves the interaction of information structure and syntactic structure. The detailed technical account is given in Van Valin (1993, 1995) and in Van Valin and LaPolla (1997); what is presented here is an informal summary.[10]

In the discussion in the previous section, it was noted that both yes–no and WH-questions are a kind of focus construction, often narrow focus, and accordingly, the focus of the yes–no question or the WH-expression must be interpreted as being within the actual focus domain. Since the actual focus domain must always be within the potential focus domain, it follows that the focus of the yes–no question or of the WH-expression must be interpreted as being within the potential focus domain. This leads to the following constraint on question formation, adapted from Van Valin (1994).

10. General restriction on question formation: The element questioned (the focus NP in a simple, direct yes–no question, or the WH-expression or the argument position with which a displaced WH-word is associated in a simple, direct WH-question) must be in a clause within the potential focus domain.

The application of the constraint to yes–no questions can be seen in (11) and (12).

11. a. After you left the party, did you take Mary to the movies?
    b. Yes.
       No. (= didn't take Mary, ≠ didn't leave the party).
       No, Bill did. (= Bill took Mary, ≠ Bill left the party).
       No, Susan.
       ?No, before. (Better: No, it was before we went to the party.)
       No, the park. (= went to the park, ≠ after you left the park).

12. a. Did Max return the papers which the secretary photocopied to the lawyer?

b. Yes.
   No. (= Max didn't return the papers, ≠ the secretary didn't pho-
   tocopy)
   No, Bill did. (= returned the papers, ≠ photocopied the papers)
   No, the envelopes.
   No, the IRS agent. (= to the IRS agent, ≠ that the IRS agent
   photocopied)

Neither the adverbial subordinate clause in (11) nor the relative clause in
(12) is within the potential focus domain, and according to (10) the focus
of the question cannot be interpreted as falling on an element within
either of them. This accounts for the possible interpretations of the answers
in (11) and (12); all of the impossible answers require the actual focus
domain to be within the embedded clause, whereas all of the possible
answers have the actual focus domain in the matrix clause. Contrast these
examples with (13).

13. a. Does Mulder believe that Scully hid the files?
    b. No, the photographs.

As we saw in Fig. 9.4, the structure in (13a) meets the condition in (9),
and therefore (10) predicts that it should be possible for the actual focus
domain to be in the embedded clause. The felicity of the possible answer
in (13b) shows that this is the case. One way of thinking about the motivation for the constraint in (10) is as follows: Questions are requests for
information, and the focus of the question signals the information desired
by the speaker. It makes no sense, then, for the speaker to place the focus
of the question in a part of a sentence which is presupposed, i.e. which
contains information which the speaker knows and assumes that the hearer
knows or can deduce easily. The content of adverbial clauses and restrictive
relative clauses is normally presupposed, and consequently, constructing
questions with the focus in one of these structures generates a pragmatic
contradiction.

The interpretation of (10) with respect to WH-questions depends on
whether the WH-expression appears in situ or in the precore slot in simple,
direct WH-questions (i.e., not echo, rhetorical, or other types of questions).
In languages with WH in situ, the WH-expression must occur in the potential focus domain. In languages with displaced WH-expressions, such
as English, it is obviously not the position of the WH-expression in the
matrix precore slot that is relevant; rather, it is the position it is interpreted
as filling in the semantic representation that is relevant. In (1a′) and (1b′),
what is interpreted as the undergoer of *hide* in the embedded clause,
whereas in (1c′) it is interpreted as the undergoer of *see* in the embedded

clause. According to (10), the questions should only be grammatical if the clause in which the WH-word functions as (in these cases) the undergoer is in the potential focus domain. How do we determine whether it is within the potential focus domain? The principle in (9) constrains the potential focus domain in complex sentences. Applying it to (1a), whose structure is given in Fig. 9.4, we see that the embedded clause is a direct daughter of the matrix clause node, and therefore the embedded clause is in the potential focus domain. Accordingly, we would predict that a question like (1a′) should be grammatical, because it meets the condition in (10), and this is correct. In (1b), on the other hand, the embedded clause is not a direct daughter of the matrix clause node, as Fig. 9.5 clearly shows. Hence, the embedded clause is not within the potential focus domain, and consequently we would predict that a question like (1b′) should be ungrammatical, because it fails to meet the principle in (10). This is correct. The structural representation for a relative clause was not given in section 3, but it is very similar to Fig. 9.5 in its essential features, i.e. the embedded clause is part of an NP with a head noun. Hence, the result of applying the principles in (9) and (10) to the sentence in (1c) is the conclusion that a question like that in (1c′) should be ungrammatical, which it is.

It should be clear even from this brief, informal sketch that RRG provides an account of subjacency phenomena which does not require movement rules or multiple levels of syntactic representation for languages like English and which does not require postulating covert movement for WH-in-situ languages like Chinese and Lakhota. Van Valin (1995) took the basic analysis proposed for WH-question formation and extended it to account for the same restrictions on other extraction phenomena such as topicalization and relative clause formation.

This account has important implications for acquisition. As noted in section 2, it is commonly asserted that the speech to which children are exposed provides no evidence concerning constraints on WH-question formation and related constructions, but there is in fact abundant evidence with respect to the range of possible interpretations of yes–no questions from their own interactions with caretakers and peers and from observing the verbal interactions of others. It was discussed earlier that the focus of yes–no questions must be within the potential focus domain, and thus, these questions are subject to the same constraints as WH-questions and related constructions (see Van Valin, 1994, for detailed exemplification). It has never been argued that the source of a child's knowledge of the principles governing the interpretation of yes–no questions is anything other than the verbal interactions in which the child is involved, and this suggests the following hypothesis regarding the acquisition of constraints on WH-questions. Children learn the basic notions of topic and focus (e.g., Bates, 1976; Clancy, 1993; Greenfield & Smith, 1976; Ninio & Snow, 1996), and on the basis of their verbal interactions with caregivers and others, together with some general principles of rational human behavior to be discussed later, they formulate the restriction in (10) with respect to yes–no questions. The constraint on yes–no questions is extended to other types of questions, in particular, WH-questions. Thus, the child's knowledge of restrictions on WH-question formation has its source in the acquired constraints on yes–no questions. Is there any empirical evidence that such an extension of syntacticopragmatic constraints could take place? A telling example of this transfer of restrictions can be found in Wilson and Peters' (1988) study of a 3-year-old blind child's production of WH-questions, which apparently violated extraction constraints; some of his deviant WH-questions are given in (14).

14. a. What are you cookin' on a hot __? [Answer: 'stove']
    b. What are we gonna go at (to) Auntie and __?
    c. What are we gonna look for some __ with Johnnie?

Wilson and Peters showed that the constructions had their origin in a question and answer game that the child engaged in with his primary caregiver. Examples are given in sentences 15(a) and (b).

15. a. Caregiver: What did you eat? Eggs and . . .
       Child: Mbacon.
    b. Caregiver: Oh, that's a . . .
       Child: Aleph.
       Caregiver: That's a aleph.

In this routine, the caregiver left a gap in his utterance which the child was expected to fill in. The child learned the game, and then the constraints on question formation derived from it were incorrectly taken to apply to movement WH-questions as well; when the child learned to make WH-questions in which the WH-word occurred in the precore slot, he applied these constraints to them, leading to the questions in (14). The account that Wilson and Peters gave of these questions provides evidence that children can in fact extend the constraint learned for one type of question to other types.

Does the RRG account of subjacency require a parameterized, autonomous LAD/UG? The answer is no. Van Valin (1986, 1993) argued that the principle in (10) is ultimately derivable from Grice's (1975) cooperative principle and the maxim of quantity. Kempson (1975) derived it from the maxim of quantity as follows:

The speaker believes the hearer knows (and knows that the speaker knows) a certain body of propositions (i.e., that there is a pragmatic universe of discourse) and in making a certain utterance . . . he believes that the hearer, knowing the conventions of the language and hence the conditions for the truth of the proposition in question, will recognize a subset of those conditions as being part of that pragmatic universe of discourse and hence neither assertible, deniable or queriable (without violating the quantity maxim), and a second mutually exclusive subset of the conditions as being outside the pragmatic universe of discourse. This latter set, he will interpret as being asserted, denied, commanded or queried. (p. 190)

The syntactic expression of "this latter set" is what we have been calling the actual focus domain.

This Gricean foundation is very important: *These principles are considered to be general principles of rational behavior and are not strictly linguistic in nature.* In terms of the phenomena under discussion, it has never been claimed that constraints on the interpretation of yes–no questions are innate or even part of grammatical competence; they could be part of what Chomsky called "pragmatic competence," which he characterized as follows:

[Pragmatic competence] may include what Paul Grice has called a "logic of conversation." We might say that pragmatic competence places language in the institutional setting of its use, relating intentions and purposes to the linguistic means at hand. (Chomsky, 1980, pp. 224–225)

The Gricean nature of an important syntactic constraint like (10) has significant implications for the question of modularity (see Van Valin, 1986, 1991, for detailed discussion).

There are two major parts to the account we have sketched here, pragmatic constraints and syntactic structure, and both have their origins in general principles of cognition. We have just outlined the derivation of the principle in (10) from Gricean general principles of rational behavior. Braine (1992) showed how something like the theory of clause structure sketched in section 3 could be acquired on the basis of what he called the "natural logic" of cognition and the evidence to which the child is exposed; this natural logic is a general feature of human cognition and is not restricted to language. Thus, this account of subjacency phenomena does not presuppose an autonomous LAD/UG. In terms of the logical problem of language acquisition summarized in (3), one would conclude that knowledge of the principle in (10) is not part of the initial knowledge state of the child, if an account such as this one is correct.

5. THE ACQUISITION OF WH-QUESTIONS

We now turn to issues in the acquisition of WH-questions themselves. Although much attention has been paid to the order of acquisition of WH-expressions, little attention has been devoted to the order of acquisition of different question types, i.e. subject vs. object questions. The first question to be investigated, then, is the order of acquisition of different question types; in particular, do children learning English produce subject questions first, object questions first, or both types roughly simultaneously? This question is asked with respect to both simple and complex sentences. The second issue concerns the WH-questions in (2) and (6) which do not appear to be modeled on any structures that the children have been exposed to. These constructions are found in other languages, e.g. German, Romani, and Irish, and an account of them can shed light on the hypotheses made by children learning English.

The first issue, whether children produce subject or object questions first in simple sentences, might appear to have an obvious answer: Because subject questions do not involve subject-auxiliary inversion and look just like declarative sentences with the subject replaced by a WH-expression, they are syntactically simpler and should be produced first by children. Moreover, Gazdar (1981) claims that they are also the first type comprehended by children. Hence, if complexity were the primary factor in this aspect of acquisition, then one would expect that subject questions be produced and comprehended first. Interestingly enough, this is not what happens. Stromswold (1995) reported the results of an analysis of the early production of WH-questions by 12 children in the CHILDES database, and she also reviewed studies of comprehension. She found that with respect to *who*-questions, the overall pattern was that subject and object questions appear at roughly the same time; of the 11 children for which she had data, 6 produced object questions first, 4 produced subject questions first, and 1 produced them initially at the same age.[11] With respect to *what*- and *which*-questions, e.g. *What bit you?* (subject) vs. *What did you see?* (object) and *Which girl ran away?* (subject) vs. *Which girl did you see?* (object), on the other hand, the pattern strongly favored object questions first. Of 12 children, 7 produced object *what*-questions first, 4 produced the two types at the same time, and only 1 produced subject *what*-questions first. With respect to *which*-questions, there were complete data for only 6 children, of which 5 produced object questions first and 1 began to produce the two types at the same age. Despite the individual variation, the general pattern is that object WH-questions appear earlier in children's speech than subject WH-questions.[12] With respect to comprehension, Stromswold (1995) concluded that "contrary to Gazdar's (1981) claim, previous acquisition studies do not uniformly suggest that children acquire matrix subject questions before object questions" (p. 16).

This seems rather remarkable, especially in light of the fact that object WH-questions are more syntactically complex than subject questions. Why should this be the case?[13] Instead of looking at these questions from a strictly syntactic point of view, let's look at them from a pragmatic perspective, i.e. in terms of information structure. In section 3, it was noted that WH-questions are normally narrow focus, i.e. *WHO brought the big dog?* or *WHAT did Dana give Kim?*, and moreover, it was pointed out that languages have an unmarked focus position in the clause. In English, this is the last position in the core, as illustrated in (8). Assuming that children's first questions involving multiple-argument verbs contain simple transitive rather than ditransitive verbs, object position correlates with the least marked narrow focus position and subject position with the most marked narrow focus position. Hence, object questions involve unmarked narrow focus, whereas subject questions involve marked narrow focus. The pattern observed by Stromswold correlates with the *pragmatic* markedness of the question type, not with syntactic markedness. Pragmatic and syntactic considerations lead to opposite conclusions with respect to the complexity of early WH-questions, and it is the pragmatic analysis that provides a natural account of why object WH-questions should emerge first. Moreover, since animacy is known to have discourse-pragmatic consequences, the possible effects of animacy on the emergence of *who*-questions discussed in note 12 make sense in this account.

Stromswold also investigated the emergence of long-distance questions in complex sentences, e.g. (1a′), and, as one would expect on both syntactic and pragmatic grounds, object questions emerge first. This is not surprising on syntactic grounds, because subject long-distance questions are more constrained that object questions because of the *that*-trace effect.[14] From a pragmatic perspective, in a sentence like (1a) the unmarked focus position is the final position in the core of the embedded clause, if it is in the potential focus domain following (9). Hence, long-distance object questions would be expected to appear before subject questions. We return to this issue below.

The second issue to be addressed is the medial-WH questions in (2) and (6). It will be useful to divide these sentences into three types; (a) those with the defining WH-expression medially, as in (6a′, b′); (b) those in which the defining WH-expression is sentence-initial, as in (6a,b); and (c) those that are ambiguous between the first two possibilities, as in (2). The questions in (6a′, b′) resemble the German questions in (5a,b); they are repeated below.

16. a. What do you think which Smurf really has roller
      skates? (=(6a′))
    b. What do you think which animal really says
      'woof woof'? (=(6b′))

17. a. Was glaubst Du, mit wem   Daniel spricht?   (=(5a))
      what believe you with who.DAT   speaks
      'With whom do you believe Daniel is talking?'

b. Was hat er gesagt, wie er den Kuchen backen will?   (=(5b))
what has he said   how he the cake   bake   will
'How did he say he will bake the cake?'

Let's look at the German examples first. The initial WH-expression serves
to mark the sentence as a WH-question; if it were missing, the sentence
would be interpreted as a declarative utterance with an indirect question
complement, e.g. *Er hat gesagt, wie er den Kuchen backen will* 'He said how
he will bake the cake'. What is interesting about these German sentences
is that although the whole sentence is in the potential focus domain, each
clause is marked *separately and explicitly* as being within it. This can be seen
most clearly in the following contrast between English and German.

18. a. When did he say that he will be leaving?
    b. Wann hat er gesagt, daß er abfahren wird?
       when has he said   that he leave   will
    b′. Was hat er gesagt, wann er abfahren wird?
        what has he said   when he leave   will

The English question in (18a) is ambiguous, as it could be answered *yesterday* meaning "he said it yesterday" or *next week* meaning "he will leave
next week." The German questions could be given (18a) as a gloss, but
they are not both ambiguous; (18b′) has only one of the readings of the
English example in (a): in (b′) the actual focus domain is in the embedded
clause and the question concerns when someone will leave, not when
something is said. The sentence in (b) is ambiguous, like its English counterpart, but there is a preference for interpreting the question as being
about the matrix clause. The choice of complementizer, *daß* 'that' vs. *wann*
'when', indicates whether the actual focus domain must be within the embedded clause or not. English has no morphosyntactic means of signaling
this contrast; there are presumably prosodic contrasts to indicate it.

Learning the focus domains for the language being acquired is an
important part of language learning from an RRG perspective, and an
important question that arises for the child when a new distinction is
mastered is, how is the relevant contrast signaled? Having figured out that
the actual focus domain is sometimes in the matrix clause and sometimes
in the embedded clause, the child must determine whether this contrast
is indicated morphosyntactically, prosodically, or both.[15] German and Romani children come to the conclusion that it is morphosyntactically coded
in their languages, and some English children apparently hypothesize this
as well, even though adult English speakers do not mark it morphosyntactically. Because the actual focus domain can always be in the matrix clause,
the crucial thing to be signaled is whether it is in the embedded clause.

This can be done by replacing *that* in the embedded clause with a WH-expression, as in all of the examples in (2) and (6). If the children follow what we may call the "German model," the defining WH-expression occurs in the embedded clause, with a nonspecific WH-word occurring in the matrix precore slot to indicate that the sentence is a WH-question. Given Grice's (1975) maxim of relevance, the occurrence of the defining WH-expression in the embedded clause is to be expected, because it is the possibility of the actual focus domain being in the embedded clause which is at issue.

There is, however, another strategy that some English children adopt; it is exemplified in (6a,b), repeated below.

19. a. Which Smurf do you think who has roller skates on? (=(6a))
    b. Which animal do you think what really says "woof woof"? (=(6b))

In these constructions, the defining WH-expression occurs in the matrix precore slot, and the medial WH-expression again serves to indicate that the actual focus domain is in the embedded clause. This is a more "English-like" structure than those in (16), since the defining WH-expression is sentence-initial, but it also serves to signal the location of the actual focus domain. This pattern could be construed as analogous to the Irish phenomena in (7b). In this construction, each clause following the WH-word is marked by a complementizer which indicates that the clause is in the potential focus domain, and the actual focus domain is in the last clause so marked.[16] In (7b), there are two embedded clauses, and the actual focus domain is in the most deeply embedded one. This system, like the one in German, yields unambiguous sentences where English would have ambiguous ones. The Irish sentences corresponding to the two readings of a sentence like (18a) are given in (20) (J. McCloskey, personal communication, March 28, 1997).

20. a. Cén fáth   aL   dhúirt Ciarán goN
       what reason COMP(+WH) said   COMP(–WH)
       mbeadh sé i láthair?
       would.be he present
       "Why did Ciarán say that he'd be present?"
    b. Cén fáth   aL   dhúirt Ciarán aL
       what reason COMP(+WH) said   COMP(+WH)
       mbeadh sé i láthair?
       would.be he present
       "Why did Ciarán say that he'd be present?"

The sentence in (20a) with the complementizer *goN* marking the embedded clause is preferentially interpreted with the actual focus domain being the matrix clause, just like (18b) in German. In (20b), on the other hand, the complementizer *aL* on the embedded clause indicates that it is part of the potential focus domain, and because it is the most deeply embedded clause in the sentence, it is also the actual focus domain. Hence, this question must be interpreted as asking why Ciarán would be present, not why he said something.

The third group of questions, those in (2), involve identical WH-expressions in initial and medial positions in the sentence. Here again, the medial WH-expression explicitly indicates that the actual focus domain is in the embedded clause. Thornton (1995) noted a striking pattern with respect to these questions:

> [T]he medial-*wh* in children's questions initially appeared across the board, in subject, object and adjunct questions. . . . Longitudinal data from several children showed that before long, the medial-*wh* disappeared from the object and adjunct questions of these children. remaining only in their subject-extraction questions. At a given time, then, there will be children who always produce a medial-*wh*, irrespective of extraction site, and others, who only produce a medial-*wh* when extracting from subject position. (p. 147)

The disappearance of the medial WH-expressions begins with the recognition by the child that the language being acquired does not in fact indicate morphosyntactically that the actual focus domain is in an embedded clause, and the pattern described by Thornton follows the markedness of narrow focus in the different syntactic positions. In terms of the analysis of the sentences in (8), the medial WH-expression should first disappear from object questions, then adjunct questions, and finally subject questions. Subject extraction out of an embedded clause is doubly marked, in markedness terms, for the following reason. The default situation with respect to focus domains is for the actual focus domain to be in matrix clauses; hence, for it to be in embedded clauses is marked. Second, as we have noted several times, the unmarked position for narrow focus is the final core argument position, i.e. object position with a transitive verb, and the most marked position for it is subject position. Hence, subject extraction out of an embedded clause is marked narrow focus in a marked location for the actual focus domain. This is summarized in Table 9.2. Thus, if any "extraction site" were to be overtly signaled, it would be in a subject question out of an embedded clause. As noted earlier, subject questions out of an embedded clause appear much later than the corresponding object questions, and this too is a reflection of the markedness expressed in Table 9.2.

There is one additional observation in Thornton (1995) to be considered. She noted that for some children, when the defining WH-expression is referential, e.g. *which Smurf* or *which animal* as in (6a,b), the medial

TABLE 9.2
Markedness of WH-Question Formation

Type of Question	Position of Narrow Focus	Location of Actual Focus Domain
Object from main clause	–	–
Subject from main clause	+	–
Object from emb. clause	–	+
Subject from emb. clause	+	+

WH-expression is optional, whereas when the defining WH-expression is nonspecific or nonreferential, e.g. *who* or *what* as in (2a–c), then the medial WH-expression always seems to be present. Given that the function of the medial WH-expression is to signal that the actual focus domain is in the embedded clause, why should the referential specificity of the defining WH-expression reduce the need for the medial WH-expression? To see the answer to this question, we need to first step back and examine the usefulness of overtly indicating that the actual focus domain is in an embedded clause. As noted in section 3, WH-expressions are mapped directly from the matrix precore slot to an argument position in the semantic representation of the sentence in the RRG analysis, and in a complex sentence, it is necessary to determine, first of all, which clause's semantic representation is the one to which the WH-expression is to be linked. Overtly signaling the clause in which the actual focus domain occurs morphosyntactically, as German, Romani, and Irish do, is obviously extremely helpful. In terms of the principle in (9), each clause that is a direct daughter of (a direct daughter of) the clause node modified by the illocutionary force operator is overtly marked as to whether it is in the potential focus domain; the most deeply embedded clause in that sequence of clauses marked as being within the potential focus domain is the clause containing the actual focus domain. Following the principle in (10), the WH-expression must be linked to the semantic representation of the clause containing the actual focus domain. Hence, the utility of the medial WH-marking relates to the demands of linking in questions in complex sentences.

Another type of information that would facilitate the linking is the semantic content of the WH-expression itself. The basic idea is the more information about the referent of the WH-expression that is available, the easier it is to determine how it is to be linked in the sentence. *Who,* for example, must have an animate, normally human, interpretation, and, as pointed out in note 12, this makes it a very good candidate for interpretation as an actor. *What,* on the other hand, is compatible with virtually any verb in almost any function, but the fact that it is often used for inanimates means that it is more likely to be interpreted as undergoer than as actor. In contrast, the range of possible interpretations for *which tire on your new car* is much, much smaller, and accordingly, the task of interpreting *which tire on your new car* is much easier than with *what*. The idea that the referential or descriptive content of WH-expressions aids the interpretive process in "extraction constructions" has been discussed by Comorovski (1989), Kroch (1989), Rizzi (1990), Cinque (1990), and Chung (1994), among others. With respect to WH-expressions, they may be ranked in terms of increasing specificity or referentiality; *what* < *who* < *which N*. *Who* is rated higher in referentiality than *what* because its referent must be animate and an individuated entity, whereas the referent of *what* is unmarked for animacy and need not be individuated; in grammatical terms, *who* must be replaced in the answer by a count noun, whereas *what* may be replaced by either a count or a mass noun. We now have two types of information which facilitate the linking in WH-questions in complex sentences, the referential content of the defining WH-expression and the occurrence of a medial WH-expression, and there appears to be an inverse correlation between the two: The greater the referential content of the defining WH-expression, the smaller the need for a medial WH-expression. When the referential content of the defining WH-expression is minimal, as with *what*, then the medial WH-expression is present. When the referential content of the defining WH-expression is substantial, as with *which Smurf*, then the medial WH-expression need not be present. This predicts that when children begin to abandon medial WH-expressions, they will drop them out of *who* questions before *what* questions, *ceteris paribus*.[17] Of the two types of information, the overt morphosyntactic marking of the clause containing the actual focus domain is more directly useful for the linking system, and consequently the need for it is not completely obviated by the increase in referential content of the defining WH-expression.

It has been argued that the motivation for the medial WH-elements in these long-distance questions is to indicate morphosyntactically that the actual focus domain is within an embedded clause, and that this facilitates the task of linking the WH-expression to the semantic representation of the appropriate clause. This syntax-to-semantics linking is part of the comprehension process, and accordingly, it would be useful to look briefly to see whether there are any parallels between children's early production and comprehension of long-distance WH-questions. de Villiers et al. (1990) reported on a series of comprehension experiments with children ages 3 to 6 years old, and the results are quite interesting within the context of this discussion. Their subjects fell generally into two groups: The 3- and 4-year-old subjects produced a greater number of long-distance interpretations of the test stimuli and fewer adultlike responses, whereas the 5- and 6-year-old subjects produced strikingly fewer long-distance interpretations of the test stimuli but more adultlike responses overall. That is, the younger subjects were more likely to interpret the WH-expression as being related to the embedded clause than were the older subjects; in RRG terms, they were more likely to interpret the actual focus domain as being within the embedded clause. Moreover, the younger subjects often answered "the wrong questions," i.e. they responded to the medial WH-expression rather than to the one in the matrix precore slot; this is what was meant earlier by "fewer adultlike responses." For example, in answer to the test question *How did the boy say how he hurt himself?*, the younger subjects were just as likely to say "he fell off a chair" (embedded *how*-question) as "in a loud voice" (matrix *how*-question). This result is not so surprising, however, if, as argued earlier, some of the children are adopting a German- or Irish-like strategy of marking overtly the fact that the actual focus domain is within the embedded clause. As noted earlier, given Grice's maxim of relevance, the occurrence of the defining WH-expression in the embedded clause is to be expected, because it is the possibility of the actual focus domain being within the embedded clause which is at issue. de Villiers et al. (1990) did a follow-up experiment in which they gave children sentences like *How did the boy choose to eat what?* and found that children 4 years old and below were prone to answer just the final *what.* Does this correlate in any way with the production data reported in Thornton (1990, 1995)? All of the examples of medial-WH long-distance WH-questions cited in Thornton (1990, pp. 240–247) were from children in the 3–4-year-old age range; in Thornton (1995), she gave additional constructions of this type from a child 5 years, 4 months old. It thus appears that the ages at which children are most likely to answer the nonmatrix WH-word and to give embedded-clause answers to long-distance WH-questions are also the ages at which they are most likely to produce long-distance WH-questions containing a medial WH-expression.

de Villiers et al. (1990) noted the similarity to the German phenomena and made the following comment with respect to the behavior of the younger subjects:

> We argue then that the children treat the two wh-words as linked as if it were German. Now we can see why simply answering the *how* question [in *How did the boy choose to eat what?*–RVV] is inadequate: It leaves one question unaddressed. From the child's perspective then, the downstairs answer, with an upstairs copy, is a better answer. (p. 281)

But why is it a better answer? de Villiers et al. offer no explanation for this. The RRG account, on the other hand, does supply a reason for why the downstairs answer is the better answer. I have argued that the motivation for the medial WH-expression is to mark explicitly that the actual focus domain is within the embedded clause, and it appears that the

3–4-year-old children are very concerned with the location of the actual focus domain. They are, in effect, working out the principle in (9) and marking the important contrast morphosyntactically. Following Grice's maxim of relevance, they take the occurrence of an embedded WH-expression as a signal that the actual focus domain is within the embedded clause. At the same time, they are also working on the principle in (10) and the structure of complex sentences. Two things appear to happen at around age 5. First, the ones who marked the actual focus domain in embedded clauses overtly realize that this is not, in fact, a property of English and cease doing it, and second, children develop more sophisticated analyses of the structure of complex sentences. In particular, it is reasonable to assume that children start out by analyzing all clausal complements as if they have the structure given in Fig. 9.4, and that by the ages of 5 and 6, they have discovered that complements with a WH-complementizer have a rather different structure which interacts with the principle in (9) to preclude the possibility of the actual focus domain being within them.[18] If they overgeneralize this conclusion, it will lead to the comprehension behavior reported in de Villiers et al. (1990) for the older children. Thus, it appears that the results from comprehension studies complement nicely the production data, and the RRG analysis provides an account of why they should in fact complement each other the way they do; it also ties in with the account of subjacency given in the previous section.

6. CONCLUSION

This chapter has focused on issues relating to WH-questions and their acquisition, with the goal of showing that phenomena that have been cited as necessitating the positing of an autonomous, parameterized LAD/UG can in fact be accounted for without recourse to such a construct. Three phenomena were examined; restrictions on the formation of WH-questions and related constructions (subjacency phenomena), the order of emergence of subject and object WH-questions in the speech of children learning English, and long-distance WH-questions containing medial WH-expressions produced by children learning English. In each case, a Role and Reference Grammar account was proposed, and at no time was it necessary to postulate an autonomous LAD/UG with parameters as part of the account. The crucial explanatory construct in the RRG analyses is information structure, which, it was argued in Van Valin (1986, 1993), derives ultimately from the set of very general principles of rational human behavior, both linguistic and nonlinguistic, proposed in Grice (1975). Moreover, RRG assumes that children are born with a rich cognitive endowment of the type sketched by Braine, Bruner, Slobin, and others, which makes language learning and other types of learning possible (see Van Valin & LaPolla, 1997, epilog). What is most striking about two of the three cases discussed is that they involve either learning a constraint or producing forms not directly modeled in the speech to which the child is exposed. Such cases have typically been cited as evidence for an autonomous, parameterized LAD/UG, but it has been shown in this chapter that alternative explanatory accounts are possible which do not postulate such a mechanism as underlying language acquisition.

Many language acquisition researchers who reject the parameter-setting approach also reject the idea of working within a well-defined theoretical framework, preferring to employ general linguistic concepts and cognitive notions and avoiding the analytic constraints imposed by a theory. The alternative account presented herein is not based on general linguistic notions like *topic* or *focus* and general cognitive notions like *complexity*; rather, it has been built on a theoretical foundation that not only defines and ties the relevant concepts together, but also provides the necessary conceptual edifice in which explanation is possible. Explanation is only achievable within a well-defined theoretical framework, and therefore, progress toward understanding complex acquisition phenomena such as those discussed in this chapter can only be made when researchers operate within a theory, such as Role and Reference Grammar.

NOTES

1. I would like to thank Jeri Jaeger, Jean-Pierre Koenig, and Lynn Santelmann for comments on an earlier draft, James McCloskey for providing insights and data regarding Irish, and Holger Dießel for sharing his intuitions about the German data. Abbreviations; ACC "accusative," ARG "argument," CMPL, COMP "complementizer," CP "complementizer phrase," DAT "dative," IP "inflection phrase" (= clause), NOM "nominative," NP "noun phrase," NUC "nucleus," PrCS "precore slot," PRED "predicate," PRES "present tense," PSTP "past participle."
2. The technical P and P terms for the first two units are "complementizer phrase" (CP) (= sentence) and "inflection phrase" (IP) (= clause).
3. In P and P and earlier versions of Chomskyan theory, when a constituent like a noun phrase is moved by a rule, its structural position in the phrase-structure tree remains, and the moved element and its original structural position are coindexed, so that the original position of the moved element can be recovered for semantic interpretation. These empty, coindexed structural positions are called "traces."
4. The technical term for this in P and P is "specifier of complementizer phrase" (SPEC, CP).
5. That is, the WH-words occur in the same place in the clause as the corresponding non-WH-words in statements and do not appear in the special initial WH-position, as in English *you want what?* This is the most common way of forming WH-questions in human language; the English-style "movement" WH-question is not the norm universally.

6. Romani, the language of the Gypsies, is a member of the Indo-Aryan branch of Indo-European.
7. The "L" segment in the complementizers indicates that these morphemes induce lenition in the initial consonant of the following word; it is not part of the phonemic or phonetic representation of the word.
8. It should be noted that the terms "sentence" and "clause" do not mean exactly the same thing in RRG that they do in P and P, i.e. RRG sentence ≠ P and P CP and RRG clause ≠ P and P IP. These differences do not, however, substantially affect the discussion in this chapter.
9. The default interpretation of the subject in English is as a topic, rather than as a focal element, hence the marked status of focal subjects in English. See Lambrecht (1984) and references cited therein for more discussion.
10. Other accounts which treat subjacency as involving syntactic and pragmatic factors include Erteschik-Shir (1973), Erteschik-Shir and Lappin (1979), Kluender (1992), and Kuno and Takami (1993).
11. When the relative frequency of the production of subject vs. object *who*-questions is taken into account, the results bolster the conclusion that object questions appear first. Stromswold (1995) noted

> even though the results of the initial analysis . . . indicated that the earlier acquisition of *who* object questions than *who* subject questions was likely to be the result of chance, once the greater frequency of *who* subject questions is taken into account, with some degree of confidence, we can reject the null hypothesis that chance alone accounted for the earlier acquisition of object questions than subject questions. (p. 32)

12. A possibly important factor involved in these differences is animacy: The referent of *who* is always animate, normally human, whereas the referents of *what* or *which* may or may not be animate. There is a tendency for subjects to be animate, as has often been noted, and this might influence the early appearance of *who* subject questions in contrast to *what* and *which* subject questions. However, it should be noted that the noun in *which* expressions could equally easily be animate (*which boy, which doggie*) as inanimate (*which block*), and yet the pattern with these expressions is strongly object questions first.
13. Stromswold offered an explanation in terms of the different ways subject and object traces are governed. Object traces are head-governed by the verb, whereas subject traces are antecedent-governed by the WH-word in specifier of COMP. She suggested that antecedent government may be more problematic for the child and therefore object traces (and therefore object questions) would appear first. In Chomsky (1992), however, this distinction is abandoned, and he claimed that all traces are antecedent governed; head-government is eliminated from the theory. In this version of P and P theory, this explanation would not be valid.
14. The *that*-trace effect, i.e. the grammaticality of *Who_i do you think t_i is leaving?* vs. the ungrammaticality of **Who_i do you think that t_i is leaving?*, is accounted for by the empty category principle in P and P theory. In Van Valin (1993) and Van Valin and LaPolla (1997), it was argued that these effects are related to the impossibility of marked narrow focus on the subject in certain syntactic environments (see also Table 9.2).
15. Whether the actual focus domain can occur within embedded clauses must be learned, because not all languages allow it. Hearing a question–answer pair like the one in (13) would be enough to tell the child that the actual focus domain can be within embedded clauses.
16. McCloskey (1979) argued that *aL* marks the binding domain of the "extracted" element, be it a WH-expression, the relative pronoun (or equivalent) of a relative clause, or a

topicalized phrase, and in Van Valin (1995), it was shown that this "binding domain" corresponds to the potential focus domain in RRG terms.

17. Thornton (1995) cited both the Irish examples in (7) and so-called "WH-agreement" in Chamorro (Chung, 1994) as analogs of medial WH-expressions in children's English. Chung argued that WH-agreement in Chamorro is obligatory if the extracted element is nonreferential but optional if it is referential, a striking parallel to the English facts which Thornton points out. Chung counted both *hafa* "what" and *hayi* "who" as nonreferential and therefore as requiring WH-agreement, but she noted that this was absolutely true only for *hafa* and not for *hayi*, as there are speakers who permit long-distance questions with *hayi* without WH-agreement (1994, pp. 17–18). This differential behavior is not surprising, given the differences in referential content between them.

18. For the structure of WH-complements, see Van Valin and LaPolla (1997, Section 8.6.3, Figure 8.33, p. 504).

REFERENCES

Bates, E. (1976). *Language and context: The acquisition of pragmatics.* New York: Academic Press.

Braine, M. D. S. (1992). What sort of innate structure is needed to 'bootstrap' into syntax? *Cognition, 45,* 77–100.

Braine, M. D. S. (1994). Is nativism sufficient? *Journal of Child Language, 21,* 9–31.

Bruner, J. (1983). *Child's talk: Learning to use language.* New York: Norton.

Chomsky, N. (1980). *Rules and representations.* New York: Columbia University Press.

Chomsky, N. (1986). *Knowledge of language.* New York: Praeger.

Chomsky, N. (1992). A minimalist program for linguistic theory. *MIT Occasional Papers in Linguistics* (No. 1). Cambridge, MA: MIT.

Chung, S. (1994). WH-agreement and 'referentiality' in Chamorro. *Linguistic Inquiry, 25,* 1–44.

Cinque, G. (1990). *Types of A-bar dependencies.* Cambridge, MA: MIT Press.

Clancy, P. (1993). Preferred argument structure in Korean acquisition. In E. V. Clark (Ed.), *Proceedings of the Twenty-Fifth Annual Child Language Acquisition Research Forum* (pp. 307–314). Stanford: Center for the Study of Language and Information (CSLI).

Comorovski, I. (1989). Discourse-linking and the WH-island constraint. In J. Carter & R.-M. Déchaine (Eds.), *Proceedings of the Nineteenth Annual Meeting of NELS.* Amherst, MA: GLSA (Graduate Linguistics Students Association) Publications.

Crain, S. (1991). Language acquisition in the absence of experience. *Behavioral and Brain Sciences, 14,* 597–612.

de Villiers, J. G., & Roeper, T. (1991). Introduction: Acquisition of WH-movement. In T. L. Maxfield & B. Plunkett (Eds.), *Papers in the acquisition of WH. Proceedings of the UMass roundtable* (pp. 1–18). Amherst, MA: GLSA Publications.

de Villiers, J. G., Roeper, T., & Vainikka, A. (1990). The acquisition of long-distance rules. In L. Frazier & J. de Villiers (Eds.), *Language processing and language acquisition* (pp. 257–297). Dordrecht: Kluwer.

Erteschik-Shir, N. (1973). *On the nature of island constraints.* Unpublished doctoral dissertation, MIT, Cambridge.

Erteschik-Shir, N., & Lappin, S. (1979). Dominance and the functional explanation of island phenomena. *Theoretical Linguistics, 6,* 41–85.

Foley, W. A., & Van Valin, R. D., Jr. (1984). *Functional syntax and universal grammar.* Cambridge, England: Cambridge University Press.

Gazdar, G. (1981). Unbounded dependencies and coordinate structure. *Linguistic Inquiry, 12*, 155–184.

Greenfield, P. M., & Smith, J. H. (1976). *The structure of communication in early language development.* New York: Academic Press.

Grice, H. P. (1975). Logic and conversation. In P. Cole & J. Morgan (Eds.), *Syntax & semantics: Vol. 3. Speech acts* (pp. 41–58). New York: Academic Press.

Horvath, J. (1997). The status of 'Wh-expletives' and the partial Wh-movement construction in Hungarian. *Natural Language & Linguistic Theory, 15*, 509–572.

Huang, C.-T. J. (1981). Move WH in a language without WH movement. *The Linguistic Review, 1*, 369–416.

Kempson, R. (1975). *Presupposition and the delimitation of semantics.* Cambridge, England: Cambridge University Press.

Kluender, R. (1992). Deriving island constraints from principles of predication. In H. Goodluck & M. Rochmont (Eds.), *Island constraints* (pp. 223–258). Dordrecht: Kluwer.

Kroch, A. (1989). *Amount quantification, referentiality, and long WH-movement.* Unpublished manuscript, University of Pennsylvania.

Kuno, S., & Takami, K. (1993). *Grammar and discourse principles: Functional syntax and GB theory.* Chicago: University of Chicago Press.

Lambrecht, K. (1994). *Information structure and sentence form.* Cambridge, England: Cambridge University Press.

McCloskey, J. (1979). *Transformational syntax and model theoretic semantics: A case study in Modern Irish.* Dordrecht: Reidel.

Ninio, A., & Snow, C. E. (1996). *Pragmatic development.* Boulder, CO: Westview Press.

McDaniel, D., Chiu, B., & Maxfield, T. (1995). Parameters for WH-movement types: Evidence from child language. *Natural Language & Linguistic Theory, 13*, 709–753.

Rizzi, L. (1990). *Relativized minimality.* Cambridge, MA: MIT Press.

Slobin, D. I. (1973). Cognitive prerequisites for the development of grammar. In C. Ferguson & D. Slobin (Eds.), *Studies of child language development* (pp. 175–208) New York: Holt, Rinehart & Winston.

Slobin, D. I. (1985). Crosslinguistic evidence for the language-making capacity. In D. Slobin (Ed.), *The crosslinguistic study of language acquisition* (Vol. 2, pp. 157–256). Hillsdale, NJ: Lawrence Erlbaum Associates.

Stromswold, K. (1995). The acquisition of subject and object WH-questions. *Language Acquisition, 4*, 5–48.

Thornton, R. (1990). *Adventures in long distance moving: The acquisition of complex WH-questions.* Unpublished doctoral dissertation, University of Connecticut.

Thornton, R. (1995). Referentiality and WH-movement in child English: Juvenile D-linkuency. *Language Acquisition, 4*, 139–175.

Van Valin, R. D., Jr. (1986). Pragmatics, island phenomena, and linguistic competence. *CLS 22(2): Papers from the Parasession on Pragmatics and Grammatical Theory*, 223–233.

Van Valin, R. D., Jr. (1991). Functionalist linguistic theory and language acquisition. *First Language, 11*, 7–40.

Van Valin, R. D., Jr. (1993). A synopsis of Role and Reference Grammar. In R. D. Van Valin, Jr., (Ed.), *Advances in Role and Reference Grammar* (pp. 1–164). Amsterdam/Philadelphia: John Benjamins.

Van Valin, R. D., Jr. (1994). Extraction restrictions, competing theories and the argument from the poverty of the stimulus. In S. Lima, R. Corrigan, & G. Iverson (Eds.), *The reality of linguistic rules* (pp. 243–259). Amsterdam & Philadelphia: John Benjamins.

Van Valin, R. D., Jr. (1995). Toward a functionalist account of so-called extraction constraints. In B. Devriendt, L. Goossens, & J. van der Auwera (Eds.), *Complex structures: A functionalist perspective* (pp. 29–60). Berlin: Mouton de Gruyter.

Van Valin, R. D., Jr., & LaPolla, R. J. (1997). *Syntax: Structure, meaning and function*. Cambridge, England: Cambridge University Press.

Weissenborn, J., Roeper, T., & de Villiers J. G. (1991). The acquisition of WH-movement in German and French. In T. L. Maxfield & B. Plunkett (Eds.), *Papers in the acquisition of WH: Proceedings of the UMass roundtable* (pp. 43–78). Amherst, MA: GLSA Publications.

Wilson, B., & Peters, A. (1988). What are you cookin' on a hot?: A three-year-old blind child's violation of universal constraints on constituent movement. *Language, 64,* 249–273.

Chapter 10

Mental Spaces, Language Modalities, and Conceptual Integration

Gilles Fauconnier
University of California San Diego

In working on matters related to language over the years, my greatest surprise has been to find out how little of the rich meanings we construct is explicitly contained in the forms of language itself. I had taken it for granted, at first, that languages were essentially coding systems for semantic relations, and that sentences, when appropriately associated with "natural" pragmatic specifications, would yield full meanings. Quite interestingly, this is not the way language works, nor is it the way that meaning is constructed. Rather, language, along with other aspects of expression and contextual framing, serves as a powerful means of prompting dynamic on-line constructions of meaning that go far beyond anything explicitly provided by the lexical and grammatical forms. This is not a matter of vagueness or ambiguity; it is in the very nature of our systems of thought. But grammar, in this scheme, is not to be disdained, for although it does not provide the landscape or the means of moving through it, it does show us the way. It guides our elaborate conceptual work with an admirable economy of overt indications, and an impressive reliability in moving us along conceptual paths.

Mental spaces are part of this story. They organize the processes that take place behind the scenes as we think and talk. They proliferate in the unfolding of discourse, map onto each other in intricate ways, and provide abstract mental structure for shifting of anchoring, viewpoint, and focus, allowing us to direct our attention at any time onto very partial and simple structures, while maintaining an elaborate web of connections in working memory, and in long-term memory. We are not conscious of these processes. What we are conscious of, to a high degree, is language form on one hand, and experiencing "meaning" on the other. The effect is magical; as soon as we have form, we also have meaning, with no awareness of the intervening cognition. Introspectively, our experience in this regard is analogous to perception—we see an object because it is there, we understand a sentence instantly because it "has" that meaning. This remarkable and invisible efficiency of our meaning-assigning capacities drives our folk theories about language, which conflate form and meaning, just as folk theories about the world conflate existence and perception.

The technical description of mental space phenomena is developed in a number of publications.[1] I would like to attempt, in this chapter, to give a more informal view of the phenomena, their complexity, and their importance for psychologists interested in language and thought.

AN EXAMPLE—CONNECTORS AND ACCESS PATHS

Consider the simple statement *Max thought the winner received $100*. Perhaps the most obvious way to understand this is to assume that there was a contest, that prizes were given out, that one person won the contest and received a prize, and that Max, who was aware of all this, believed that prize to have been $100. But the statement by itself contains none of this. It just fits a plausible scenario, which our background knowledge makes available. We shall see that it also fits many other scenarios, some of which might be more appropriate in some contexts, and some of which are extremely implausible. What exactly then is the sentence telling us?

An important part of what the language form is doing is prompting us to set up mental spaces, elements, and connections between them. The form provides key indications about the mental process in which we need to engage, but it is also deeply underspecified, which accounts for the multiplicity of scenarios that it may successfully fit. An interesting challenge for cognitive science at large is to understand how this underspecification can be resolved, how and why in certain situations certain mental space configurations are unconsciously chosen over others, and how the understander converges on specific appropriate scenarios and connection patterns.

Mental spaces are small conceptual packets constructed as we think and talk, for purposes of local understanding and action. They are very partial assemblies containing elements, and structured by frames and cognitive models. They are interconnected and can be modified as thought and discourse unfold.

In our example, two mental spaces are set up.[2] One is the base space, B, the initial space with partial structure corresponding to what has already been introduced at that point in the discourse, or what may be introduced freely because it is pragmatically available in the situation. Another mental space, M, subordinate to this one will contain partial structure corresponding to 'what Max thinks'. It is structured by the form '_received $100' (the subordinate complement clause of *thought*). That form evokes a general frame <x receive y>, of which we may know a great number of more specific instances (receive money, a shock, a letter, guests, etc.). The expression *Max thought* is called a space builder, because it explicitly sets up the second mental space. *Max* and *the winner* are noun phrases and will provide access to elements in the spaces. This happens as follows: The noun phrase is a name or description that either fits some already established element in some space, or introduces a new element in some space. That element in turn may provide access to another element, through a cognitive connection (called a connector), as we shall illustrate and explain. Elements are conceived of as high-order mental entities (like nodes in Shastri's models[3]). They may or may not themselves refer to objects in the world. In our example, the name *Max* accesses an element **a** in B, the base space (which intuitively might correspond to a real or fictive person called Max). The description *the winner* accesses an element **w** that we call a role, and is assumed to belong to a general frame of winning (**w** wins), and also to a more specific instance of that frame appropriate for the given context (winning a particular race, lottery, game, etc.). Roles can have values, and a role element can always access another element that is the value of that role. So we can say *The winner will get $10*, without pointing to any particular individual. This is the role interpretation. Or we can say *The winner is bald*, where being bald is a property of the individual who happened to win, not a condition for getting the prize. This is the value interpretation. Roles, then, are linked cognitively to their values by a role-value connector.

The two mental spaces B and M are connected. There can be counterparts of elements of B in M. For example, if we said *Max thinks he will win*, intending the pronoun *he* to refer back to Max, then space B would contain **a** (for Max) and space M ('*Max thinks _*') would contain a counterpart **a'** of **a**. In space M, a relation equivalent to '**a'** wins' would be satisfied, whereas the same relation would not necessarily be satisfied in the base B for **a** (the counterpart of **a'**). It is convenient to use mental space diagrams such as that shown in Fig. 10.1 to represent this evolving structure.

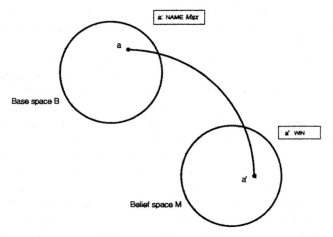

FIG. 10.1.   Mental space diagram.

An important principle defines a general procedure for accessing elements:

Access Principle

If two elements **a** and **a′** are linked by a connector **F** [**a′** = F(**a**)] then element **a′** can be identified by naming, describing, or pointing to, its counterpart **a**.

This very general principle applies to all types of connectors across and within mental spaces (identity, analogy, metaphor, metonymy, role/value). A simple example of its application would be *Max thinks Harry's name is Joe.* An element **e** associated with the name *Harry* is set up in the base. Its counterpart **e′** in M satisfies <**e′** named *Joe*>. And **e′** is accessed by means of its counterpart **e** in the base, using the name *Harry* associated with **e**. In other words, even though *Harry* is the appropriate name in one space, it can be used to access the corresponding element in another space, where another name is appropriate.

Returning now to the original example, let's see what the accessing possibilities might be. Suppose first that the access principle does not apply at all. Then the description *the winner* must identify a role **w** directly in space M. The structure added to M by the sentence is <**w** receive $100>. This is a pure role interpretation within space M. It does not access any corresponding value for that role. Therefore, the interpretation is that Max thought there was a contest, and that he thought it was a feature of that contest to award $100 to whoever wins. This accessing strategy is noncommittal as to whether the speaker also assumes there was such a contest, and as to whether an actual winner was ever selected, or as to whether Max thinks that a winner was selected. The sentence under this strategy would be appropriate in a variety of contexts. For example, mini-discourses like the following could include the above strategy:

The Boston marathon will take place next week. Max thought the winner received $100, but it turns out there won't be any prize money.

My friends were under the impression that I was running a lottery in my garage. Max thought the winner received $100. But they were all wrong, there was no lottery.

Suppose now that the accessing principle operates, but only within the subordinate space M, linking the role "winner" to a value of that role, **b**. As before, Max believes that there was a contest, and moreover that some-body won and he has additional beliefs about the person whom he assumes won. The structure in M is now <**b** receive $100>. Although a likely default is that the $100 was prize money, this is no longer imposed. Max may believe that something else happened, causing the person who won to receive $100 independently. In plain English, this is illustrated most dis-tinctly by a situation in which (according to the speaker) Max believes (perhaps incorrectly) that Susan won a race, and that she also inde-pendently got $100 for the used car that she was selling.

In the two accessing possibilities just considered, a word (*winner*) simply evokes a script within a single space. But the access principle may also operate across spaces. The speaker may have a particular contest in mind, for which there is a role *winner*, set up as an element **w** in the base B. That role can have a value **a** (for example, Harry) with a counterpart **a′** in M. The access principle allows *the winner* to access **w**, and then its value **a**, and finally the counterpart of **a**, element **a′** in the subordinate space M. The structure set up in M is <**a′** receive $100>. The interpretation is that the speaker presents Harry as the winner, and says that Max thought Harry received $100. This is compatible with Max knowing nothing about the contest, or believing that someone other than Harry won, and that Harry got the $100 for selling the used car, or as a consolation prize in the contest.

Other accessing paths are available for this simple sentence, if counter-part roles are considered, or if the extra space introduced by the past tense is taken into account, or if other spaces are accessible at that point in the discourse to provide counterparts. Typically, an understander does not have to consider all possibilities. The intended path will be favored by the space configuration in the discourse at the point when the statement is made. We might already have the role *winner* in space B, or in space M but not B. We might already have different values in M and B for the "same" role (**w** and its counterpart **w′**), and so on. In other cases, of course, the understander will lack sufficient information, and may have to revise a space configuration, or may simply misunderstand a speaker's intent.

Our example had a subordinate space corresponding to "belief." There are many other kinds of spaces, but they all share these complex accessing possibilities. For instance, time expressions are space builders and set up new spaces in discourse. Consider (as part of a larger discourse) *In 1968, the winner received $100.* As before, we have a base B and a subordinate space M, corresponding to 1968, set up by the space builder *In 1968.* And as before, the noun phrase *the winner* can access a role in M, or the counterpart role in M of a role in B, or the counterpart in M of a value in B, or a value of a role in M. Situations that fit these respective strategies might be:

- There was a certain type of game in 1968 (no longer played today) in which you got $100 for winning;
- There is a certain sports competition, say the Boston marathon, which exists today (role **w** in space B) and also existed in 1968 (counterpart role **w′** in space M). In 1968 (as opposed to today), whoever won got $100;
- The winner of the chess championship held today is Susan; back in 1968, in unrelated circumstances (e.g., selling her used car), Susan received $100;
- The winner back in 1968 of the contest we are talking about was Harry, and that year, Harry received $100 (perhaps for selling his used car).

The access paths available in this example involving time (1968) are exactly the same as the access paths in the previous example involving belief. Even though time and belief are conceptually quite different, they give rise, at the level of discourse management considered here, to the same mental space configurations. More generally, we find that mental spaces are set up for a wide variety of conceptual domains that include time, belief, wishes, plays, movies, pictures, possibility, necessity, hypotheticals and counterfactuals, locatives, and reality. The connectors, the access principle, the role/value distinctions work uniformly across this broad range of cases.

The choice of an access path and of particular connectors is underspecified (or sometimes not specified at all) by the language forms. This is not vagueness, however. A speaker has a particular path in mind, and it must be recovered by the understander. Paths can be forced by elaboration. For instance, in our previous example case, one might have said:

In 1968, the winner received $100, but Harry, although he won, only got $50, because he was fined for yelling at the umpire.

This will force the role reading inside space M: The rules of the game at the time were that the winner got $100. The rest of the statement is about the particular individual who won, and the fact that *he* only got $50. This could also have been expressed using a role/value link: *That year, the winner only got $50, because he was fined for yelling at the umpire.*

Such examples illustrate (very partially) the kinds of accessing strategies that may be available, and that may have to be reconstructed in understanding what is meant. An important feature of such constructions from a psychological and processing point of view is that in many cases, the access paths will collapse, because counterparts in the relevant spaces do not differ from each other. This is in fact the default assumption that we typically make in the absence of explicit information to the contrary. We call this default principle "optimization" of spaces. So, for example, using our *winner* example once more, *Max thought the winner received $100*, if spaces B and M are identically structured in terms of background assumptions and connections (existence and nature of the contest, identity of the winner, focus on the nature of the prize), there will no longer be any difference between the interpretations provided by the connecting paths. The role *winner* and its value (say Harry) will be the same in both spaces, and the import of the statement, with any connecting path, will be the same. It will be about the prize amount that Harry, qua winner, received in the contest. Notice that this is in fact the interpretation that first came to mind when we saw the sentence presented as a statement in isolation. Because there had been no prior discourse structure set up, we directly made the most simple (i.e., optimized) default assumptions, and obtained a sensible interpretation. The hidden assumption we made was that the two spaces (base and belief) had matching structure. In addition, we completed the resulting configuration by means of the most obvious available background scenario (contest with prize money) that would fit <winner> and <_ receive $100>.

However, as soon as a sentence is part of extended discourse, it will be prompting strategies *within* the mental space configuration already set up at the time when that sentence comes into the discourse. Explicit links and structures present *at that time* in the meaning-building process will constrain the construction of accessing paths and the imposition of scenarios. In particular, such existing discourse connections may prevent optimization, default strategies, or the adoption of default scenarios.

Crucially, then, the apparently simple or prototypical cases are only special (default) instances of the general space-building operations. The drawback of studying sentences in isolation (as a linguist or as a psycholinguist) is that only the defaults will emerge. Those defaults, far from helping us understand the general strategies, actually occlude them from the observer by effectively conflating them.

MODALITY—THE CASE OF ASL

Spoken languages offer considerable evidence for mental space organization. But interestingly, independent evidence is also available from sign languages such as ASL, which operate in a different modality, visual-gestural rather than oral-auditory. Van Hoek (1996), Liddell (1995, 1996), Poulin (1996) are among those who very successfully pursued an approach initiated by Richard Lacy in unpublished work in the late 1970s. Their research provided extensive evidence for mental space constructions in ASL. As Liddell demonstrated, sign languages additionally make use of grounded mental spaces in their grammars by taking advantage of the spatial modality.

The clearest example of this is the signing space set up by signers in order to perform various referential and conceptual operations. As Scott Liddell (1996) wrote:

> Sign languages are well known for their ability to create, as part of the most ordinary discourse, elaborate conceptual representations in the space in front of the signer. Because of the importance of space in ordinary signed discourse, signed languages have come to be structured in ways which take advantage of those spatial representations. Pronouns and some types of verbs can be produced at specific locations in space or directed toward specific areas of space to produce distinctive meanings. Signs of this type can also be directed toward things that are physically present, including the signer, the addressee, other participants, and other entities. . . . The linguistic uniqueness of the ability to make semantic distinctions by producing signs toward an apparently unlimited number of locations is beyond question. (p. 145)

The physical signing space with referential loci that one can point to serves to ground a corresponding mental space in which elements are being introduced and structured. Subspaces can then be set up with overt counterpart structure analogous to the mental space connections described earlier for our English example. Strikingly, the access principle operates transparently in such cases. As Karen Van Hoek showed, one can point to loci in order to access the counterparts in some space of the elements corresponding to those loci. The choice of accessing strategies is particularly interesting, because it depends on subtle distinctions having to do with focus, viewpoint, and the ultimate goals of the conversational exchange. Figure 10.2 is an example from Van Hoek's work. The notation is explained below the transcription.

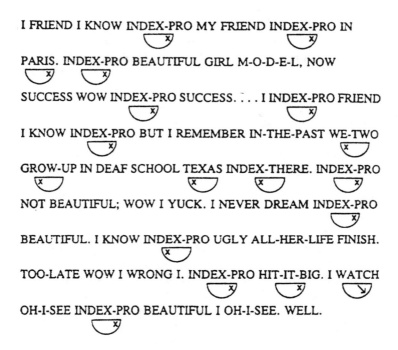

I FRIEND I KNOW INDEX-PRO MY FRIEND INDEX-PRO IN
PARIS. INDEX-PRO BEAUTIFUL GIRL M-O-D-E-L, NOW
SUCCESS WOW INDEX-PRO SUCCESS. . . . I INDEX-PRO FRIEND
I KNOW INDEX-PRO BUT I REMEMBER IN-THE-PAST WE-TWO
GROW-UP IN DEAF SCHOOL TEXAS INDEX-THERE. INDEX-PRO
NOT BEAUTIFUL; WOW I YUCK. I NEVER DREAM INDEX-PRO
BEAUTIFUL. I KNOW INDEX-PRO UGLY ALL-HER-LIFE FINISH.
TOO-LATE WOW I WRONG I. INDEX-PRO HIT-IT-BIG. I WATCH
OH-I-SEE INDEX-PRO BEAUTIFUL I OH-I-SEE. WELL.

'My friend, I know her—my friend, she's in Paris. She's a beautiful girl, a model now, and wow is she successful. . . . I—she's a friend, I know her, but I remember in the past, we grew up together in the deaf school in Texas. She wasn't beautiful; I would think, "Yuck." I never dreamed she would become beautiful. I knew she would be ugly all her

life. Too late I realized I was wrong. She hit it big. I look at her and I think, "Oh, I see, she's beautiful, I see. . . . Well . . ."'

The notation used for ASL examples is as follows: ASL signs are represented by English glosses; where more than one word is needed to gloss a single sign, the glosses are joined by hyphens. Some of the glosses have small semicircles under them, representing the space in front of the signer. Arrows represent the direction of movement for a sign which is articulated with a path movement; Xs represent the space in which a stationary sign is articulated. The third-person pronoun and the sign meaning 'there' are articulated almost identically, as both consist of a pointing gesture. They are frequently distinguished by differences in palm orientation, but in some contexts they are phonologically identical.

FIG. 10.2. ASL discourse.

In this short piece of discourse, two different loci are set up in the signing space for the same individual (the beautiful friend). One locus is to the left of the signer—

and corresponds to present time and to the Paris location. The other locus, to the right of the speaker—

corresponds to past time, with location in Texas. In almost all of the discourse, the present/Paris locus is used to access "the friend," except in the part corresponding to "I knew that she would be ugly all her life," where the point of view shifts to the past, and the other locus (past/Texas) is used. Then it shifts back to present time, and the present locus ("I see, she's beautiful, . . .). Immediately after this passage, the signer was asked more about his memories and went on with the discourse shown in Fig. 10.3, which shifted viewpoint and focus back to the past, and now accessed the same individual (the beautiful friend) from the past locus (to the right of the signer).

With examples like these and many others, Van Hoek showed that, just like in our 1968 example, the elements in one mental space may be accessed from the referential locus in the signing space appropriate for that particular mental space (e.g., past), or from a locus for its counterpart in some higher space (e.g., present/Base). The spatial modality allows the spaces to be grounded: One can actually point or direct other signs toward one or the other referential locus, as one would in pointing deictically at relevant objects, physically present in the context. Liddell (1995a, 1995b) showed how the manipulation of such grounded spaces (token space, surrogate space, and real space) is incorporated into the grammar of ASL to yield intricate reference mechanisms. Poulin (1996) showed how such spaces can be shifted to reflect changes in viewpoint or epistemic stance. This is typically accomplished physically by body shifts, and repositioning, as shown in Fig. 10.4. In A, the two referents i and j are set up as loci in the signing space in front of the signer. In B, there is a body shift to the right, and the signer identifies with referent i (taking the viewpoint of i so to speak). In C, there is a body shift to the left, and the signer now identifies with the other referent, j.

Liddell (1995b) showed in great detail the link between such referential processes incorporated into ASL grammar, and general linguistic and non-linguistic mental space building and grounding.

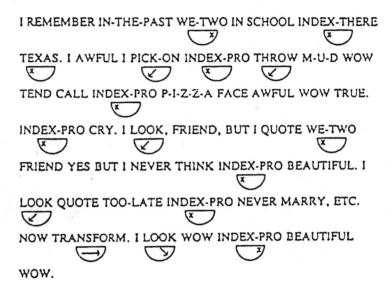

'I remember in the past, we were in school in Texas. I was awful, I picked on her, I threw mud at her, wow, I used to call her pizza-face, really awful. She would cry. I would look at her—we were kind of friends, but I never thought she would be beautiful. I would always look at her like "It's too late for her, she'll never marry," and so on. Now she's transformed. I look at her and wow, she's beautiful.'

FIG. 10.3. ASL discourse.

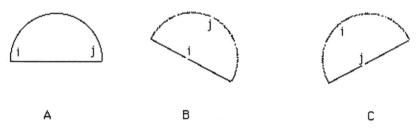

FIG. 10.4. Use of space and referential shift.

The relevant language universals here are the modality-independent principles of connections and access across mental spaces. The modality-specific universals are the ways in which these mental configurations can be indicated through language (spoken or signed). In both spoken and signed languages, we find grammatical devices for building spaces (adverbials, subject–verb combinations, conjunctions, etc.); in spoken language, pronominal systems and other anaphoric devices code linearly the construction or reactivation of mental space elements. In sign language, the same effect is achieved by constructing grounded spaces, which take advantage of the spatial modality.

TENSE AND MOOD

The spaces we have been talking about are set up dynamically throughout an ongoing discourse, on the basis of linguistic and nonlinguistic clues and information. The general scheme is one of new spaces built relative to existing ones, as shown in Fig. 10.5.

A piece of discourse will start with a base B. Space M_1 is then set up subordinate to B, then space M_{11}, subordinate to M_1, and so on. Returning to the base B, one can open space M_2, then M_{21}, and so forth, then return to B a number of times, opening spaces M_i, and daughter spaces M_{ij}, M_{ijk}, and so on.

At any given stage of the discourse, one of the spaces is a *base* for the system, and one of the spaces (possibly the same one) is in *focus*. Con-

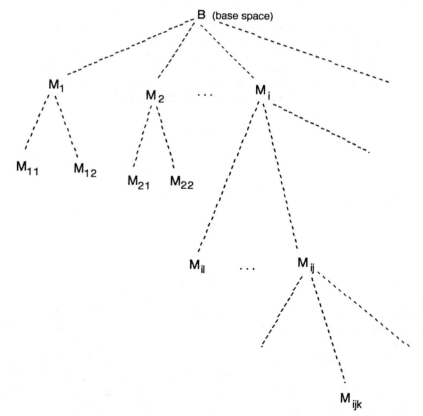

FIG. 10.5. Relationship of new spaces to existing ones.

struction at the next stage will be relative either to the base space or to the focus space.[4] The discourse moves through the lattice of spaces; viewpoint and focus shift as we go from one space to the next. But at any point, the base space remains accessible as a possible starting point for another construction.

Dinsmore (1991) and Cutrer (1994) showed that a major function of tense in language is to establish local time-ordering relations between neighboring mental spaces, and to keep track of viewpoint and focus shifts. Cutrer (1994) developed a sophisticated set of principles for mental space connections guided by tense, and explained thereby many mysterious features of the ways in which we construct time and viewpoint organization with language. We cannot, here, go into the mechanics of tense and time, but the following example, borrowed from Fauconnier (1997) helps to give an informal idea of what is going on.

The example is a very short piece of discourse:

Max is 23. He has lived abroad. In 1990, he lived in Rome. In 1991 he would move to Venice. He would then have lived a year in Rome. (p. 73)

The space-building dynamics associated with the production and/or understanding of this ministory run as follows:

1. We start with a single space, which is the base, and also the initial viewpoint and focus. We structure that space with the information that Max is 23 years old.
2. Keeping that space in focus, we add the (present) information that Max has lived abroad. This information is presented via a past event space ("Max live abroad").
3. In the next sentence, *in 1990* is a space builder. It sets up a new focus space, in which we build the content "Max live in Rome." This is also the new event space, because we are considering the event/state of Max living in Rome.
4. This focus space now becomes a viewpoint from which to consider Max's next move. Intuitively, when we say *In 1991, he would move . . .* , we are presenting 1991 as a future with respect to 1990. The 1990 space ("Max in Rome") becomes a viewpoint from which to set up the next focus (and event) space, 1991, with the content "Max move to Venice." We could have said the same thing differently by using the base (present time) as a viewpoint: *In 1991, Max moved to Venice.*
5. The last sentence, *He would then have lived a year in Rome*, keeps 1990 as the viewpoint, and 1991 as the focus, while using an event space ("live a year in Rome') that is past time relative to the focus 1991.

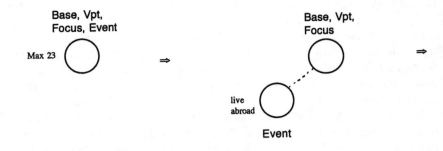

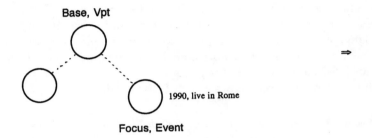

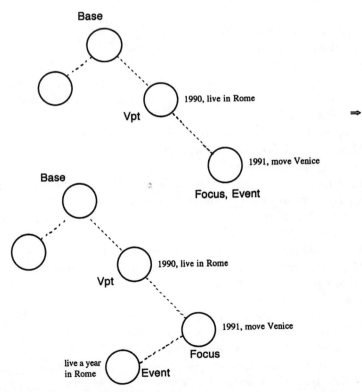

FIG. 10.6. Space configuration showing shift of viewpoint, event, and focus.

Schematically, the space configuration develops with successive shifts of event, focus, and viewpoint, as shown in Fig. 10.6.

The virtue of this type of cognitive organization is to allow local manipulation of the spaces with losing sight of the entire configuration. Because time is the relevant dimension here, we need some indication of the time relationship between spaces. Typically, tense will provide us with indications of *relative* time relationship. Cutrer (1994) proposed putatively universal semantic tense-aspect categories, with language-specific means of expressing some of their combinations. She also introduced a crucial distinction: New structure introduced into spaces may be marked as FACT or as PREDICTION, depending on the semantic tense aspect. Much of Cutrer's work is devoted to establishing the constraints on the space configurations that are set up in this way. The (putatively universal) categories constrain the configuration in specific ways. For instance, in the case of PAST, we have:

PAST applied to space N indicates that:
i)   N is in FOCUS.
ii) N's parent is VIEWPOINT.
iii) N's time is prior to VIEWPOINT (i.e., prior to N's parent).
iv) events or properties represented in N are FACT (in relation to the parent VIEWPOINT space).

These general constraints are coded grammatically by languages in different ways. So what we call the grammatical "simple past," "past participle," and so on, are distinguished from the semantic PAST, which specifies mental space relationships. English has the following coding system:

PAST is coded by the simple past (*lived, went, brought*) or by *have + past participle* if the verb is in infinitival position ("*will have forgotten*," "*may have left*," "*claims to have forgotten*"). Code: Verb+past or *have* + (Verb + *past participle*).

FUTURE is coded by *will* + Verb.

The construction of connected spaces, with viewpoint and focus shifts is reflected in the language code by retracing the path from the base to the focus space, using grammatical tenses.

In our example, when the sentence *In 1991, he would move to Venice* comes into the discourse, K is the FOCUS/EVENT space, N (1990) is the VIEWPOINT space, and M is the BASE. The grammatical coding reflects the path followed from the BASE to the FOCUS:

Base Space M —PAST→ Viewpoint Space N —FUTURE→ Focus Space K

The coding will appear on the verb *move*, because the verb is introducing new structure into the current focus space. The FUTURE connection of K to N will be coded in English by (*will* + Verb *move*). The PAST connection of N to M will be coded by the simple past. The full coding from base to focus is compositional:

$$simple\ past + (will + Verb\ move)$$
$$\Rightarrow \quad (past + will) + move$$
$$\Rightarrow \quad would\ move$$

Languages have different ways of coding the time path, and grammar may highlight some aspects of the path, while underspecifying others. What seems to be universally available is the construction of paths, and the shifts of focus and viewpoint within the dynamic evolving mental space configuration.

General principles govern the ways in which focus and viewpoint (and even base) are allowed to shift. Cutrer (1994) proposed detailed principles of discourse organization, which include constraints like the following:

- only one FOCUS, one BASE at any given moment of the discourse interpretation;
- new spaces are built from BASE or FOCUS;
- FOCUS can shift to EVENT, BASE, or previous FOCUS;
- VIEWPOINT can shift to FOCUS or BASE.

The account of tense developed by Dinsmore and Cutrer explains why tense does not directly reflect conceptual time as one might think (and as many semantic accounts suggest). Instead, the grammar of tense specifies partial constraints on time and fact/prediction status that hold locally between mental spaces within a discourse configuration. We may obtain actual information about time by combining this with other pragmatic information made available. Accordingly, the same tense may end up indicating very different objective time relations relative to the speech event:

*The boat **leaves** next week.*

*When he **comes** tomorrow, I'll tell him about the party.*

*If I **see** him next week, I'll ask him to call you.*

[the "present" tense in this example corresponds to a "future" time]

*I'm **walking** down the street one day when suddenly this guy **walks** up to me . . .*

*He **catches** the ball. He **runs**. He **makes** a touchdown.* (morning-after sports report)

[the "present" tense in this example corresponds to a "past" event]

*Do you have a minute? I **wanted** to ask you a question.*
*I wish I **lived** closer to my family, now.*
*If I **had** time now, I would help you.*

[the "past" tense corresponds to a "present" time]

*If I **had** the time next week, I would go to your party.*
*I can't go to the concert tonight. You'll have to tell me how it **was**.*

["past" tense corresponds to a "future" time]

*That **will be** all for now.*
*He's not on the train. He **will have** missed it.*

["future" tense corresponds to a "present" time]

More generally, tenses are used not just to reflect local time relations between neighboring spaces, but are also used to reflect epistemic distance, that is, whether a space is hypothetical or counterfactual with respect to its parent space. The coding system remains the same, and a particular tense sequence may reflect both time and epistemic distance. Here are some examples offered by Sweetser (1996):

If you have Triple-A, then if you go to a telephone, you can solve your problem.
If you had Triple-A, then if you went to a telephone, you could solve your problem.
If you had had Triple-A, then if you'd gone to a telephone, you could have solved your problem. (p. 323)

We can interpret all three as referring to present time, but with different epistemic stances. The first is neutral as to the chances that you have Triple-A. The second suggests that maybe you don't have it. And the third is counterfactual—"you don't have Triple-A, but if you did . . .". Alternatively, one could interpret the second sentence as referring to a past event and being neutral as to what happened, and as to whether you had Triple-A, and the third sentence as referring to a past event, and being counterfactual. The embedded tenses (*go, went, had gone,* and *can solve, could solve, could have solved*) reflect the full epistemic and time path from the base, regardless of the corresponding objective time.

Mood (subjunctive vs. indicative) can serve to indicate distinctions in space accessibility. So, for example, a sentence like *Diogenes is looking for a man who is honest* opens a space in which "Diogenes finds an honest man." Because of the access principle that was discussed earlier, the description *a man who is honest* can either access a new element directly in that space, or can identify a new element in the base, and access its counterpart in the "look for" space. The first accessing path corresponds to a nonspecific interpretation; any honest man will do. The second accessing path corresponds to a specific reading: There is a particular honest man that Diogenes is looking for. In French, the equivalent of the verb copula *is* can be marked as either indicative or subjunctive:

> *Diogène cherche un homme qui **est** honnête.* [Indicative]
>
> *Diogène cherche un homme qui **soit** honnête.* [Subjunctive]

The first sentence with the indicative allows both accessing paths, as in English, with perhaps a preference for access from the base (the specific interpretation). The second sentence on the other hand allows only direct access to an element in the *look for* space, that is, the nonspecific reading. This is because the subjunctive forces the description to be satisfied in the embedded *look for* space.

A range of intricate space accessibility phenomena linked to grammatical mood was studied by Mejías-Bikandi (1993, 1996). Rich aspectual phenomena, involving spaces and viewpoint are discussed in Doiz-Bienzobas (1995).

MAPPINGS AND CONCEPTUAL INTEGRATION

Language, on the surface, seems to have its own very special principles, structures, and formal constraints. It has been studied extensively as an autonomous product of the human mind, and claims have even been made that this autonomy is reflected at the biological level in the form of specialized, innately based, genetically transmitted, neurobiological structures. In contrast, cognitive linguistics has repeatedly uncovered, behind the idiosyncrasies of language, evidence for the operation of more general cognitive processes. Mappings between mental spaces are part of this general organization of thought. Although language provides considerable data for studying such mappings, they are not in themselves specifically linguistic. They show up generally in conceptualization, and there is no reason to think that they are limited to humans. A striking case of a general cognitive operation on mental spaces, that is reflected in many language phenomena, but not restricted to such phenomena, is conceptual integration. There has been a good deal of recent research on conceptual integration and blending.[5] In this section, I give a quick overview of some of the results Mark Turner and I have obtained in our joint work on this topic.

Conceptual integration consists in setting up networks of mental spaces that map onto each other and blend into new spaces in various ways. In everyday thinking and talking, we use conceptual integration networks systematically in the on-line construction of meaning. Some of the integrations are novel, others are more entrenched, and we rarely pay conscious attention to the process because it is so pervasive.

A basic conceptual integration network contains four mental spaces. Two of these are called the input spaces, and a cross-space mapping is established between them. The cross-space mapping creates, or reflects, more schematic structure common to the inputs. This structure is constructed in a third space, called the generic. A fourth space, called the blend, arises by selective projection from the inputs. It develops emergent structure in various ways, and can project structure back to the rest of the network.

There are simple everyday nonlinguistic examples of this around us all the time. For instance, we can create new activities by blending known activities with new environments. Coulson (1997) considered the case of children in a dormitory inventing a game, based on basketball, in which you must throw a crumpled-up sheet of paper into a wastepaper basket. This new game is a blend. One input is partial knowledge of basketball, the other input is the trash disposal situation with crumpled paper, a wastepaper basket, and so on. The partial mental mapping relates a ball to crumpled paper, a basketball basket to a wastepaper basket, players to children. In the new game, as defined by the blend, some properties are projected from the "basketball" input (scoring points when the ball falls into the basket, opponents in a game, winning and losing, etc.), some properties are projected from the "trash disposal" input (the basket is on the floor, not high up in the air, the ball has specific properties of crumpled paper, etc.), and some properties are shared by the two inputs (throwing a projectile into a receptacle). Many other properties of the game will emerge from affordances of the context (particular ways of throwing, conventions for scoring, fouls, etc.). The generic space linked to the cross-space mapping in this case is the more schematic situation of throwing some object into a container. This very simple example illustrates central properties of integration, in particular the fact that it is creative (a new activity, different from basketball, and different from throwing away paper, is produced) and underspecified (there is more than one way to project from the inputs, and more than one possible emergent structure).

The overall result of this dynamic process is a network of the type shown in Fig. 10.7.

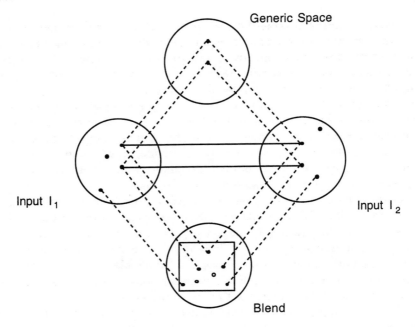

- Cross-space mapping (solid lines)

- Selective projection from Inputs (dotted lines)

- Composition, Completion, Elaboration

- Emergent structure and Integration (evoked by a square in the blend)

FIG. 10.7. Diagram of basic conceptual integration network.

In the example, input I_1 is partial structure from basketball, input I_2 is partial structure from trash disposal, the generic space is the highly schematic throwing of an object into a container, and the blend is the emergent game of trashcan basketball.

Cognitive work on such a network consists in aligning the input spaces and developing a corresponding generic space, projecting selectively into the novel blended space, and structuring the blended space through pattern completion and elaboration (by mental simulation or actual action). Integration of this type occurs in many cases of action and design, such as computer interfaces or automatic bank tellers. The Macintosh desktop interface integrates two previously known inputs (computer commands and office work) by mapping them onto each other metaphorically, and by integrating them into a novel integrated conceptual and physical space (the interface, with its specific properties). Fauconnier and Turner (in press) showed in some detail how blending operates here, and how it conforms to a general set of optimality principles. In the same vein, Barbara Holder (1997) discussed the nice example of ATMs, where a cross-space mapping connects the inputs of computer manipulation and banking activity, and the ATM itself integrates aspects of both inputs in a physically and conceptually novel design.

Many linguistic constructions originate in conceptual blends, and reflect them formally in systematic ways. The most transparent case is perhaps noun compounding, where an integration is reflected by a compound consisting of two nouns linked respectively to an element in each of the inputs. For example, Coulson's game with the crumpled paper in the dorm could be called *trashcan basketball.* One noun is the name of the game in one input, the other noun is linked to a salient element in the other input. By picking other elements, the same game might get called, more or less felicitously, *dorm basketball, basketball paperthrowing, wastepaper ball,* and so on. Almost all cases of noun-noun or adjective-noun compounding involve some degree of conceptual integration. It is only in the simplest possible default cases (and perhaps not even in those cases) that such compounds reduce to Boolean union of properties. So, for example (Turner & Fauconnier, 1995), if we call a big American car a *land yacht,* we will be mapping two inputs (travel on land, travel on sea) with counterparts such as 'vehicle/boat', 'driver/skipper', 'road/ocean', and selectively projecting into a blend, where some features of yachts now apply to certain automobiles (see Fig. 10.8).

We can see the access principle at work here, because the term *yacht* is being used to access its counterparts in the other spaces. We also see that the compound is formed by using names of elements that are not counterparts in the cross-space mapping (land and yacht).

Adjectives typically trigger integration processes. When we are concerned with a child playing at the beach with a shovel, and say things like *The child is safe, The beach is safe, The shovel is safe,* there is no fixed property that "safe" assigns to *child, beach,* and *shovel.* The first means that the child will not be harmed, but so do the second and the third—they do not mean that the beach will not be harmed or that the shovel will not be harmed. *Safe* does not assign a property; it prompts us to evoke scenarios of danger appropriate for the noun and the context. We worry about whether the child will be harmed by being on the beach or by using the shovel. Technically, the word *safe* evokes an abstract frame of *danger* with roles like victim, location, and instrument. Modifying the noun with the adjective prompts us to integrate that abstract frame of *danger* and the specific situation of the child on the beach into a counterfactual event of *harm* to the child. We build a specific counterfactual scenario of *harm* in which *child, beach,* and *shovel* are assigned to roles in the *danger* frame. Instead

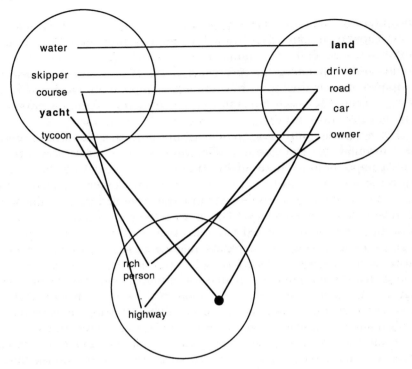

FIG. 10.8. Diagram for the conceptual blend *land yacht*.

of assigning a simple property, the adjective is prompting us to set up a conceptual integration network where the inputs are, on the one hand, a frame of danger, and on the other, the specific situation of the child on the beach with a shovel. The output of the integration (the blend) is the counterfactual scenario in which the child is harmed. The word *safe* implies a disanalogy between the counterfactual blend and the specific input, with respect to the entity designated by the noun. If the shovel is safe, it is because in the counterfactual blend, it is too sharp, but in the specific situation, it is too dull to cut.

This process is general, and underspecified, as we see by assigning the same values to different frame roles in the relevant scenario. In *The shovel is safe*, the child is the victim in the blend if we are concerned about the shovel's injuring the child, but the shovel is the victim in the blend if we are concerned about the child's breaking the shovel. Furthermore, any number of roles can be recruited for the *danger* frame. In the counterfactual blend for "the jewels are safe," the jewels are neither victim nor instrument; they have the role *possession* and the *owner* is the victim. If we ship the jewels in packaging, then the counterfactual blend for "the packaging is safe" has *jewels* as victim, external forces as *cause of harm,* and *packaging* as *barrier to external forces.* Other examples showing the variety of possible roles would be "Drive at a safe speed," "Have a safe trip," and "This is a safe bet."

Even more elaborate blends, involving several roles, are constructed for other syntactically simple expressions, like "The beach is shark-safe" versus "The beach is child-safe." In the context of buying fish at a supermarket, the label on the tuna can read, "This tuna is dolphin-safe" to mean that the tuna was caught using methods that prevent accidents from happening to the dolphins. This blend looks more spectacular, but is constructed using the same integration principles as in the unremarkable "safe beach" or "safe trip."

Safe is not an exceptional adjective with special semantic properties. The principles of integration are needed quite generally. Color adjectives, for instance, require noncompositional conceptual integration. *Red pencil* can be taken to mean a pencil whose wood has been painted red on the outside, a pencil that leaves a red mark (the lead is red, or the chemical in the pencil reacts with the paper to produce red, etc.), a pencil used to record the activities of the team dressed in red, a pencil smeared with lipstick, not to mention pencils used only for recording deficits. Theories of semantics typically prefer to work with examples like "black bird" or "brown cow" because these examples are supposed to be the prototypes of compositionality of meaning, but in fact, even these examples illustrate complicated processes of conceptual integration. From a psychological perspective, the key point in all this is the uniformity and availability of the cognitive operation (conceptual integration) in the full array of cases— those that look unexceptional and those that are more evidently noncompositional, such as:

> "*The political war over the future of Medicare, a cannonade of oratory and <u>statistical rotten tomatoes</u> that has already thoroughly spattered both parties, is about to resume.*"[6]

The example of *safe* shows how an apparently simple expression can covertly introduce counterfactual scenarios and mappings. In fact, counterfactuals, which play a key role in our reasoning capacities, are themselves very good examples of conceptual integration. The meaning of expressions like *If I were you, I would hire me* involve a mapping from a reality space, where *you* is doing the hiring, to a counterfactual space in which the speaker's dispositions, but not her or his situation have been transferred to the addressee *you.* The space connection between speaker in reality, and the addressee in the counterfactual, allows the counterfactual employer to be identified as *I* by virtue of the access principle. Such counterfactuals are also clearly analogical. They invite an analogical interpretation in an intuitively obvious way: Compare the present situation in which *you* are doing the hiring to one in which *I* am in your place, confronted with the same decisions to make, and the same candidates. Then export some features (like "who I would hire") from one situation to the other. However, what we find in the linguistic expression, "*I would hire me*," cannot be a reflection of either one of these situations. It is not being suggested that the employer should hire herself, or that the employee should take power and hire himself. The linguistic expression signals a blend, which has been set up by the cross-space analogical mapping between the two situations. In the blend, we find partial projection of input 1, the employer and the employee (*me*) being hired, and partial projection of input 2, the speaker's dispositions and decisions. The projections, underspecifications, and optimality constraints that govern them, are studied in some detail in Fauconnier (1997), and in Turner and Fauconnier (1998). It turns out that all counterfactuals are analogical and require some degree of blending. Just like the cases of the compounds, some cases of counterfactuals are more visible than others. Eve Sweetser came across the following comment on Dostoievski:

"*If Dostoevsky had lived in America, and had had a sunnier disposition, he might have been Emerson.*"

And the following appeared in the *Los Angeles Times*:

[A woman who had already been in a coma for 10 years was raped by a hospital employee, and gave birth to a child. A debate ensued concerning whether the pregnancy should have been terminated. The article reporting the case ended with a comment by law professor Goldberg.]

"*Even if everyone agrees she [the comatose woman] was pro-life at 19, she is now 29 and has lived in PVS [persistent vegetative state] for 10 years. Do we ask: 'Was she pro-life?' Or do we ask more appropriately: 'Would she be pro-life as a rape victim in a persistent vegetative state at 29 years of life?' *"

The inputs are respectively the one in which the young woman falls into a coma at 19, is raped and becomes pregnant at 29, and the one in which she leads a normal life, her opinions may change, and she is now 29 years old. This second input space is of course fictive (counterfactual). Selective projection operates from these two inputs into the blend. From the first, we project recent events—the rape, the pregnancy, and also the coma without its consequences. From the second, we project the typical evolution of a young woman in command of her faculties, capable of understanding the situation, including the aspects of the situation that pertain to a person in a coma. In the blend, the young woman is a rape victim, is in a coma, and has all the faculties and judgment of an ordinary person—namely herself if things had gone otherwise. Clearly, the blend is not constructing a "possible world." Its function is to allow the operation of certain analogies and lines of reasoning, because it remains linked within the integration network to the other spaces and to the applicable cultural models.

Metaphor is another area where integration networks are routinely constructed. Take the stock example *This surgeon is a butcher.* The statement underscores the clumsiness of the surgeon and its undesirable effects. But such inferences are not simply transferred from the domain of butchers to the domain of surgery. Butchers are in fact typically quite deft in their own domain of meat cutting, and their actions in that domain (producing roasts, steaks, and so on) are considered desirable. In an integration network, two input spaces with very partial structures from meat carving and surgery are mapped onto each other, on the basis of shared generic properties (cutting flesh, sharp instruments, white coat, professional activity, etc.). But neither the clumsiness nor its catastrophic consequences, appear in those input spaces. They emerge in the blend. In the blend, there is projection on one hand of the operating room, the patient, and the surgeon, and on the other of the butcher's tools, the butcher's methods and manner of carving, and so forth. Emergent structure ensues from simulation of this unusual situation, and we are able to grasp instantly the nefarious effects of the procedure. The resulting failings of the surgeon, represented with considerable hyperbole in the blend, are projected back to the input space of surgery, where they yield an inference of gross incompetence.

Mark Turner (personal communication) offered the following simple example to illustrate this very general process. The reference is to the stock market, a bull market until recently. Investors in such a market are commonly called bulls. When the market showed signs of weakness, a financier, Arnie Owen, was quoted in the *Wall Street Journal* as saying *"Everybody has their horns pulled in."* In the input space of cattle behavior, bulls can't pull in their horns. In the input space of finance, investors don't have horns, but they can pull back on their investing. In the blend, the investors end up as bulls with retractable horns. This emergent and inferentially efficient structure in the blend is not available through direct source/target metaphorical mapping.

In Fauconnier and Turner (in press, in preparation), we showed how integration allows basic metaphors and metonymies to operate very generally in conceptual integration networks to produce complex, and often multiple, blends. This is the case for instance in the well-known ANGER as HEAT and FAILING as DYING metaphors. Interestingly, blending allows mapping between inputs that may clash in certain relevant respects such as intentional, causal, or temporal structure.

When we examine the full range of conceptual integration networks, we find that there is no sharp distinction of kind between simple framing, nontypical framing, analogy, source-target metaphor, and multiple metaphor. Rather, we have a continuum within the range of networks, with simple Fregean semantics at one end, and elaborate metaphor at the other, with the same integration principles in all cases applying to a variety of topological configurations. On this continuum, we find points that are prototypical in certain respects, and it is those prototypical points that we associate with the notions, familiar and superficially different in appearance, of predicate-calculus, framing, analogy, simple metaphor, abstract metaphor. We have been able to show (Fauconnier & Turner, in preparation) that the mapping schemes in all these cases were the same, and that they were compositional in an interesting cognitive, but not truth-conditional, sense. One may get an intuitive sense of this continuum by looking at a set of examples like the following, ordered along a dimension of complexity of integration networks: *Paul is the father of Sally. He is my genetic father but not my real father. Zeus is the father of Athena. I am your father for today* (friend of the family taking care of a child for a short time). *George Washington is the father of our country. Newton is the father of modern physics. Fear, father of cruelty* (Ezra Pound). *The child is the father of the man* (Wordsworth).

CONCLUSION

I have tried to give an idea of the elaborate backstage cognition that operates behind everyday utterances through spoken or signed modalities. This brief and informal overview does not do justice to other extensive work in this area. In particular, the construction of richer discourse and narrative has not been described here. Sanders and Redeker (1996), Cutrer (1994), and Mushin (1998) provided fascinating case studies and elaborations of the mental space model to deal with them. Rubba (1996) showed how multiple spaces are constructed on the basis of sparse linguistic information and elaborate, but covert, cultural and cognitive models. Fridman-Mintz and Liddell (1998) also found that multiple and successive connected spaces are constructed in short narratives in ASL. Work by Hutchins (1995) showed how conceptual blending can use material anchors to produce situated behavior, such as navigation of ships and planes. Coulson (1997) developed integration accounts of rhetorical strategies, noun and adjective compounding, and argumentative counterfactuals.

Turner (1996), Oakley (1995), and Freeman (1997) developed elaborate analyses of mental space construction and integration in literary narratives, poetry, and general rhetoric. Zbikowski (1997) showed how similar processes operate in music. Lakoff and Nunez (in preparation) found many cases of conceptual blends in mathematics in addition to the ones pointed out in Fauconnier and Turner (in press).

The role of conceptual blending in grammar was demonstrated in Mandelblit (1997) and Fauconnier and Turner (1996). Mandelblit and Zachar (in press) explore some consequences of these findings for the epistemology of cognitive science.

Two central points stand out in all of this work, and are particularly relevant for cognitive psychology:

1. Backstage cognition: Language works in concert with "behind the scenes" understandings and cognitive processes. Language is neither a representation of such processes, nor a representation of meaning. Rather, it serves as a powerful and directed, but vastly underspecified, set of prompts for triggering the dynamic processing itself, and the corresponding construction of meaning. Backstage cognition has not received the attention it deserves from linguists because it is largely unconscious, immediate, and structurally invisible.

2. An especially important set of such processes (that are especially well-hidden from conscious view) concerns mental spaces and their associated cognitive operations.

There is little doubt that mental space constructions permeate much of our thought, our use of language, and other forms of expression. The study of such general cognitive operations should be a fertile ground for experimental psychology. The findings in this area converge nicely with those of Bloom (1974, 1991), Barsalou (1996), and Mandler (1997).

NOTES

1. Fauconnier (1994, 1997), Cutrer (1994), Fauconnier and Sweetser (1996), Fauconnier and Turner (in press), Huumo (1996).
2. I simplify the account here for expository purposes, by leaving out additional spaces set up by the past tense operators.
3. Shastri and Grannes (1996).
4. This is the scheme developed in Dinsmore (1991).
5. Fauconnier and Turner (1994, 1996, in preparation), Coulson (1995, 1997), Oakley (1995), Robert (in press), Mandelblit (1997), Mandelblit and Zachar (in press), Turner (1996).
6. Michael Wines, "Political Stakes Increase in Fight to Save Medicare," *New York Times*, Monday, 3 June 1996.

REFERENCES

Barsalou, L. (1996). *Perceptual symbol systems*. Unpublished manuscript, University of Chicago.

Bloom, L. (1974). Talking, understanding, and thinking. In R. L. Schiefelbusch & L. L. Lloyd (Eds.), *Language perspectives—Acquisition, retardation, and intervention*. Baltimore, MD: University Park Press.

Bloom, L. (1991). Representation and expression. In N. Krasnegor, D. Rumbaugh, R. Schiefelbusch, & M. Studdert-Kennedy (Eds.), *Biological and behavioral foundations for language development*. Hillsdale, NJ: Lawrence Erlbaum Associates.

Coulson, S. (1995). Analogic and metaphoric mapping in blended spaces. *Center for Research in Language Newsletter, 9*(1), 2–12.

Coulson, S. (1997). *Semantic leaps: Frame-shifting and conceptual blending*. Unpublished doctoral dissertation, University of California, San Diego.

Cutrer, M. (1994). *Time and tense in narratives and everyday language*. Unpublished doctoral dissertation, University of California, San Diego.

Dinsmore, J. (1991). *Partitioned representations*. Dordrecht: Kluwer.

Doiz-Bienzobas, A. (1995). *The preterite and the imperfect in Spanish: Past situation vs. past viewpoint*. Unpublished doctoral dissertation, University of California, San Diego.

Fauconnier, G. (1994). *Mental spaces*. New York: Cambridge University Press.

Fauconnier, G. (1997). *Mappings in thought and language*. Cambridge, England: Cambridge University Press.

Fauconnier, G., & Sweetser, E. (1996). *Spaces, worlds, and grammar*. Chicago: University of Chicago Press.

Fauconnier, G., & Turner, M. (1994). *Conceptual projection and middle spaces* (Tech. Rep. No. 9401). San Diego: University of California, Department of Cognitive Science.

Fauconnier, G., & Turner, M. (1996). Blending as a central process of grammar. In A. Goldberg (Ed.), *Conceptual structure, discourse, and language* (pp. 113–130). Stanford: Center for the Study of Language and Information. Stanford: CSLI Publications.

Fauconnier, G., & Turner, M. (in press). Conceptual integration networks. *Cognitive Science*.

Fauconnier, G., & Turner, M. (in preparation). *Making sense*. Manuscript in preparation.

Freeman, M. (1997). Grounded spaces: Deictic -self anaphors in the poetry of Emily Dickinson. *Language and Literature, 6*(1), 7–28.

Fridman-Mintz, B., & Liddell, S. (1998). Sequencing mental spaces in an ASL narrative. In J.-P. Koenig (Ed.), *Discourse and cognition: Bridging the gap*. Stanford: Center for the Study of Language and Information.

Holder, B. (1997). *Blending and your ATM*. Unpublished manuscript, University of California, San Diego.

Hutchins, E. (1995). *Cognition in the wild*. Cambridge, MA: MIT Press.

Huumo, T. (1996). A scoping hierarchy of locatives. *Cognitive Linguistics, 7*(3), 265–299.

Lakoff, G., & Nunez, R. (1998). The metaphorical structure of mathematics: Sketching out cognitive foundations for a mind-based mathematics. In L. English (Ed.), *Mathematical reasoning: Analogies, metaphors, and images*. Mahwah, NJ: Lawrence Erlbaum Associates.

Liddell, S. K. (1995). Real, surrogate and token space: Grammatical consequences in ASL. In K. Emmorey & J. Reilly (Eds.), *Language, gesture, and space* (pp. 19–41). Hillsdale, NJ: Lawrence Erlbaum Associates.

Liddell, S. K. (1996). Spatial representations in discourse: Comparing spoken and signed language. *Lingua, 98*, 145–167.

Mandelblit, N. (1997). *Creativity and schematicity in grammar and translation: The cognitive mechanisms of blending*. Unpublished doctoral dissertation, University of California, San Diego.

Mandelblit, N., & Zachar, O. (in press). The notion of unit and its development in cognitive science. *Cognitive Science.*

Mandler, J. (1997). Representation. In D. Kuhn & R. Siegler (Vol. Eds.), *Handbook of child psychology: Vol. 2. Cognition, perception, and language.* New York: Wiley.

Mejías-Bikandi, E. (1993). *Syntax, discourse, and acts of mind: A study of the indicative/subjunctive in Spanish.* Unpublished doctoral dissertation, University of California, San Diego.

Mejías-Bikandi, E. (1996). Space accessibility and mood in Spanish. In G. Fauconnier & E. Sweetser (Eds.), *Spaces, worlds, and grammar* (pp. 157–178). Chicago: University of Chicago Press.

Mushin, I. (1998). Viewpoint shifts in narrative. In J.-P. Koenig (Ed.), *Discourse and cognition: Bridging the gap.* Stanford: Center for the Study of Language and Information.

Oakley, T. (1995). *Presence: The conceptual basis of rhetorical effect.* Unpublished doctoral dissertation, University of Maryland.

Poulin, C. (1996). Manipulation of discourse spaces in ASL. In A. Goldberg (Ed.), *Conceptual structure, discourse and language* (pp. 421–433). Stanford: CSLI Publications.

Robert, A. (in press). Blending in mathematical proofs. In J.-P. Koenig (Ed.), *Conceptual discourse, structure, and language* (Vol. 2). Stanford: Center for the Study of Language and Information.

Rubba, J. (1996). Alternate grounds in the interpretation of deictic expressions. In G. Fauconnier & E. Sweetser (Eds.), *Spaces, worlds, and grammar* (pp. 227–261). Chicago: University of Chicago Press.

Sanders, J., & Redeker, G. (1996). Perspective and the representation of speech and thought in narrative discourse. In G. Fauconnier & E. Sweetser (Eds.), *Spaces, worlds, and grammar* (pp. 290–317). Chicago: University of Chicago Press.

Shastri, L., & Grannes, D. (1996). A connectionist treatment of negation and inconsistency. In G. Cottrell (Ed.), *Proceedings of the 18th Annual Conference of the Cognitive Science Society* (pp. 142–147). Mahwah, NJ: Lawrence Erlbaum Associates.

Sweetser, E. (1996). Mental spaces and the grammar of conditional constructions. In G. Fauconnier & E. Sweetser (Eds.), *Spaces, worlds, and grammar* (pp. 318–333). Chicago: University of Chicago Press.

Turner, M. (1996). *The literary mind.* New York: Oxford University Press.

Turner, M., & Fauconnier, G. (1995). Conceptual integration and formal expression. *Journal of Metaphor and Symbolic Activity, 10*(3), 183–204.

Turner, M., & Fauconnier, G. (1998). Conceptual integration in counterfactuals. In J.-P. Koenig (Ed.), *Discourse and cognition: Bridging the gap.* Stanford: Center for the Study of Language and Information.

Van Hoek, K. (1996). Conceptual locations for reference in American Sign Language. In G. Fauconnier & E. Sweetser (Eds.), *Spaces, worlds, and grammar* (pp. 334–350). Chicago: University of Chicago Press.

Zbikowski, L. (1997). *Conceptual blending and song.* Unpublished manuscript, University of Chicago.

Author Index

Y

Yeh, W., 36, *36*
Yekovich, F. R., 59, *66*

Z

Zachar, O., 277, *279*
Zbikowski, L., 277, *279*
Zola-Morgan, S., 45, *66*

Subject Index

A

Adjective(s), 20, 130, 157, 169
  basic grammatical class, 1, 49, 182, 185, 197
  definition, 1, 182
  integration processes, 271–273, 276
  predicative, 144, 177, 199
  prototype categorization, 179
  with/as nouns, 183–184, 196, 198–199, 271
Adverb(s), 182, 261
  adverbial phrase, 1, 159
  adverbial subordinate clause, 232
  container/durative adverbial phrase, 75–77, 90
  lexical concept, 44
  punctual, 78
  syntactic structure, 57
  temporal features of, 70, 75, 77–78
American Sign Language (ASL), 47, 258–262
A-priori grammar perspective (APG), *see* Chapter 6
Aspect, 68–79

B

Brain imaging, 95

C

Categorization, 6, 67, 95
  prototypes, *see* Chapter 7
Causation/causatives, 83–84
  in cross-linguistic perspective, 116–120, 148
  in English, 120–126
  in grammar, 148–151
  manipulation, 125–148
Children
  acquisition of language, 90, 167, 172, *see also* Introduction and Chapter 9
  clauses, 216
  cross lingual verbs, 207–208, 211
  grammar code, 48, 50
  obliques, 87
  rules, 155–156, 162
  syntactic patterns in sentences, 208–210, 216
  spoken, 168
  and mental spaces, 269
Clause(s), *see also* Sentence
  active subject, 29
  adverbial, 57
  as basic pattern of a language, *see* Chapters 8 and 9
  basic syntactic structures, 67
  canonical, 31
  in communication, 63–64
  complement, 133, 150, 253
  conception evoked by, 31
  conceptualization of events, 68
  in emergent grammar, 166, 173
  favored types, 166
  full, 26–27
  grammatical subject as starting point, 108
  internal topic, 26
  linkage, 33
  meaningful units, 57
  multiple, 80
  paradox of clausal grammar, 53–55
  parenthetical, 148
  participants in events, 80–89
  passive, 29
  predicate, 200

DATE DUE

DATE DUE	
JAN 11 2000	

UPI